An Introduction to
Computer Simulation

An Introduction to Computer Simulation

M. M. Woolfson
and
G. J. Pert

Department of Physics,
University of York

OXFORD

UNIVERSITY PRESS

OXFORD
UNIVERSITY PRESS

Great Clarendon Street, Oxford OX2 6DP

Oxford University Press is a department of the University of Oxford
and furthers the University's aim of excellence in research, scholarship,
and education by publishing worldwide in

Oxford New York

Athens Auckland Bangkok Bogotá Buenos Aires Calcutta
Cape Town Chennai Dar es Salaam Delhi Florence Hong Kong Istanbul
Karachi Kuala Lumpur Madrid Melbourne Mexico City Mumbai
Nairobi Paris São Paulo Singapore Taipei Tokyo Toronto Warsaw

and associated companies in Berlin Ibadan

Oxford is a registered trade mark of Oxford University Press

Published in the United States
by Oxford University Press Inc., New York

British Library Cataloguing in Publication Data
Data available

Library of Congress Cataloging in Publication Data
(Data applied for)

ISBN 0 19 850423 3 (Hbk)
ISBN 0 19 850425 X (Pbk)

Typeset by Newgen Imaging Systems (P) Ltd., Chennai, India

Printed in Great Britain
on acid-free paper by Biddles Ltd., Guildford, Surrey

Preface

Dramatic growth in computer power has markedly changed our way of life and we now take for granted machines that were inconceivable twenty years ago and that routinely carry out tasks that were once unimaginable. It is inevitable that this revolution has also had a considerable impact on the way that we perform scientific tasks. Experiments are controlled by computer, the data logged and analysed by computer, so allowing a continuously increasing range of accuracy and sophistication in what can be done. Theory relies on extensive numerical calculation to evaluate the complex formulae derived by analytical means. An important new methodology has been developed using simulation, intermediate between theory and experiment, in which synthetic experiments are devised using basic theoretical concepts.

At its fundamental level physics is a simple subject investigating the forces between a limited set of bodies – often only two. This theory may lead to very complex mathematical relations, even for a very simple system, which need large-scale computer calculations to yield values to be compared with experiment. Theory such as this can be extended to more complex systems, but still comprising relatively few particles (for example, nuclei or atoms). In all these cases, although extensive computational effort is needed to generate representative values, all that is being done is still, essentially, the calculation of complex equations generated by the underlying theory.

There exists, however, another class of problems, more closely related to those in the everyday world, in which we investigate complex systems comprising a large number of particles with a correspondingly large number of interactions. Since these are usually the problems of the macroscopic (real) world – though not always – we generally use the methods of classical physics to investigate them. These problems are generally handled by simulation. This involves the construction of a *model* that is a simplified representation of the prototype system. Only those elements of the system are retained which will enable the model accurately to predict the behaviour of the prototype system within the range of interest; only the prototype itself will be accurate over its entire range. The model may be experimental (for example, tested in a wind-tunnel) or, more commonly these days, computational.

Computer simulation models usually work at a very basic level. The simulation is performed using the underlying equations defining the problem. For example, a many-body dynamical problem may involve a large number of bodies ($\sim 10^6$) interacting by a known mutual force (e.g. electrostatic). Problems may be broken down into two groups – simulation using particles and simulation using continua. In the latter case averaging over very large numbers of real particles, which describe the system, defines macroscopic quantities (such as density, pressure, temperature) from the microscopic values (such as particle position, velocity). Clearly there are methods intermediate between these extremes based on particle distribution functions. Generally continuum methods consider that particles are in local thermal equilibrium, that is, locally having some form of Boltzmann distribution, so that the methods of classical thermodynamics are appropriate.

The prototype is usually a complex system with several separate interacting sub-systems. The model must represent this, although some sub-systems may not be active under the conditions of investigation. The translation of the model into a computer program should reflect this structure. Thus the program will consist of several sub-units which may be either called upon during the calculation, or pre-processed to generate data, which are subsequently accessed during the run. In either case the program should be constructed from sub-programs (subroutines or procedures) which reflect the structure of the model through its sub-systems. These sub-programs should be flexible and appended to the main program. This allows separate, independent testing of them and also their use in other models.

The simulation will yield large quantities of output data. Such data must be either handled on-line or post-processed. By far the most convenient type of visual representation is in the form of graphs. A major development in computing over the past decade has been in the area of computer graphics, and this is a very valuable tool combined with the simulation, usually used as a post-processor on stored output data. Key output values will be calculated on-line and output to a file during the program run.

Clearly if a model is to have predictive value we must be sure that it accurately represents the experiment. To do this we *validate* the model. There are several steps in this process. The first and most obvious step is error checking at the program level. This ensures that the program is performing in the way intended. It is usually achieved by running the code for a set of cases in which output values are already known, either from analytical calculation or from earlier simulations. This is usually a long and painstaking task, but one that must not be skimped. The second is to check the model itself, verifying that it can reproduce experimental results, which is achieved by running the code against an extensive experimental data set, and identifying and *interpreting* the discrepancies. This is always a very instructive task and may give important insights into the experiment.

Computer simulation models of this type have a very wide range of application in both physics and engineering. The aim of this book is to give a general introduction to the general methods used in simulation. It does not describe computational methods used as a theoretical tool – for example, atomic physics calculations. It is an introductory text and is therefore not exhaustive. The intended readership is at the undergraduate level, from the second year onwards, and those of postgraduate status and beyond for whom this is a first introduction to the subject. For less advanced readers appendices are provided which are intended to fill in possible gaps in their knowledge of some basic material.

In line with the overall purpose of this text, some advanced material is not included. Thus multi-dimensional computational fluid dynamics does not receive the attention its practical importance deserves. The other main omission is the treatment of particle transport phenomena associated with neutron or radiative transfer. We hope that what we do provide is a starting point from which the interested reader may access the more detailed literature in any particular field of interest.

A suite of FORTRAN computer programs is provided (see p. xv) which cover most of the methods described and will enable the reader to tackle problems provided at the end of each chapter. These programs are written in transparent form, with many COMMENT statements, and are designed to be user-friendly rather than over-elaborate. Some subroutines are derived from those in *Numerical Recipes* (Press, Flannery, Teukolsky and Vetterling, 1986), which is recommended as a useful source of subroutines to those wishing to write their own programs. Some of the provided programs can, if required, give output files suitable as input to standard graphics packages. Several of the figures throughout the text have been produced by GNUPLOT,[1] a flexible and easy-to-use general-purpose package.

An important message we wish to pass on is that, in computational terms, one should not be constantly reinventing the wheel. Where there is existing well-tested and well-proven software – be it subroutines, graphics packages or special-purpose packages – then one should be ready to call upon it. Sometimes it will need to be modified and, where this is done, our exhortation about validation must be followed. The ease with which programs produced

---

[1] GNUPLOT – an interactive plotting program. © 1986–1993 Thomas Williams and Colin Kelley. Further information is available from info-gnuplot@dartmouth.edu.

by others can be used will depend on their clarity; for this reason each individual should write any major program with the thought that someone else may wish to use it and understand it. Another, and more selfish, reason to write clear programs is that, otherwise, even the author will not understand her or his own program after the passage of a few weeks or months.

York   G. J. P.
May 1998   M. M. W.

Contents

Appendices

Problems – solutions and comments

References

Index

Programs available

Many of the programs mentioned in this book are available for downloading from the Internet at the Oxford University Press web site:

http://www.oup.co.uk/Pert

The programs available are listed below.

OSCILLAT	TROJANS	SATELLIT	DRUNKARD
POLYWALK	SHOOTEMP	TRIDIAG	HEATRI
HEATEX	HEATCRNI	RADBAR	LEAPDF
GAUSSOR	HOTPLATE	MAGELEC	CLUSTER
FLUIDYN	PIC	METROPOL	MCPLATE
REACTOR	WAVE	TWODWAVE	HEATELEM
FINELEM2	FINDATA	ADVDIF	MAC
BLAST	BLAST.DAT	MARKOV3	CONJUG
CHOLESKY	ICCG		

1 *Models and simulation*

1.1 What is a model?

According to one of his biographers, Einstein, at the age of five, was very fond of constructing models; his favourite toy was a set of building bricks and he also constructed card houses. Not a very scientific activity, it might be thought, yet the making of models is at the very heart of physics and other sciences as well. The essence of a model is that it should be a simplified representation of some real object or physical situation which serves a particular, and perhaps limited, purpose. For example, a child may use modelling clay to make a model of a car. The body will be crudely shaped with score marks on the surface to represent doors, windscreen etc., and four discs will be stuck on the sides to represent wheels. Augmented with the imagination of a child the model achieves its purpose as a toy although it lacks most of the attributes of a real car. More complex models of cars are possible – the wheels can be made to revolve, some form of power can be added, either a spring-driven or an electric motor, a steering mechanism can be incorporated with radio control – but at the end of the day the only 'perfect' model of a car, including the factor of scale, is the prototype, a car itself.

In the example we have given, the car being modelled is a macroscopic object consisting of a relatively small number of components, and its behaviour is well understood and predictable. The physical systems we wish to study are often very complex, containing entities we cannot see and whose existence and properties we can only infer. An atom consists of a nucleus containing protons and neutrons surrounded by a system of electrons, the number of which equals the number of protons for a neutral atom. The first model consistent with this picture was given by Niels Bohr in 1913. Electrons were then pictured as tiny particles possessing mass and charge and considered to be orbiting around the nucleus, much as planets orbit the sun except that the centrally-directed forces were electrical rather than gravitational. The difficulty with this model was that classical theory predicted that the electrons, which are accelerating charged particles, should radiate energy and so spiral inwards towards the nucleus. Bohr postulated that the electrons could only exist in stationary states for which the angular momentum had to be some multiple of a small basic quantity, $h/2\pi$, where h is the Planck constant which came from an earlier theory for black-body radiation. In stationary states the electrons do not radiate but they can jump spontaneously from a state of higher energy to another at lower energy, and when they do so they emit a photon with energy equal to the difference in energy of the two states. The Bohr model worked quite well for the hydrogen atom, for which it was able to explain the Lyman and Balmer series of spectral lines, but it failed for more complex atoms. It required the introduction of quantum mechanics by Schrödinger and Heisenberg in 1926 before there was a satisfactory model for many-electron atoms.

In describing the Bohr atom we have introduced the concept of a mathematical rather than a physical model. While some mechanical system of spheres and wires could be constructed to represent the Bohr model it would not serve any useful purpose, whereas the mathematical model can be subjected to analysis to explore its strengths and weaknesses.

Another area in which modelling is useful is that of the structure of solids. Figure 1.1 shows a representation of a simple crystal structure where atoms, all of the same kind, form a simple cubic lattice. For such a crystal at absolute zero temperature, in a classical model, all the atoms are at rest, although in the quantum-mechanical model there is motion corresponding to zero-point energy. The equilibrium of the crystal comes about because of the balance of forces on each atom, or equivalently because the whole crystal is in a state of minimum energy. Displacement of an atom in any direction results in a restoring force towards the equilibrium position. For very small displacements the magnitude of the restoring force is approximately proportional to the displacement and so the vibrations of individual atoms are of simple harmonic form – the so-called harmonic approximation. For larger amplitudes, which occur at higher temperatures, the proportionality between the magnitude of the restoring force and the displacement breaks down and anharmonic vibrations occur, so that the period depends on the vibrational amplitudes. It would be possible, although difficult and not very useful (except, perhaps, as

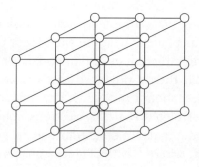

Fig. 1.1   A simple cubic structure.

a lecture demonstration), to construct a physical model with spheres and springs to represent such a system, but to explore its properties in depth requires analysis by a mathematical model.

1.2   Why we use models and how

Many physical systems of interest are extremely complex, with many inter-acting elements governing their behaviour. An obvious way to explore the way that a complete system behaves is to construct it and to do a series of controlled experiments on it. In this way empirical understanding is achieved of the way that behaviour is affected by the parameters of the system, and that is the basis of experimental method. However, if it is a nonlinear system the effect of two changes made together is very different from the sum of the changes made separately so that it may be impossible to derive enough information to enable reliable predictions of behaviour to be made over the complete possible range of parameters. Alternatively, building or running the experiment may be expensive or dangerous. For example, the nuclear powers of the world have, in the past, carried out tests of nuclear weapons as a result of which they have a good understanding of the factors which govern the nature of the resultant explosion. Many of them wish to retain some develop-ment of weapons, although it is now generally accepted that tests of such weapons are damaging to the environment and a danger to life on earth. Thus the alternative of constructing a mathematical model may be an attractive, or even an essential, alternative. Complex computer programs have been written incorporating all the knowledge gained from previous tests so that new weapons can be tested by computer simulation without the need actually to explode them.

1.2.1   *A simple harmonic oscillator*

We can get an idea of the principles behind modelling by looking at a simple harmonic oscillator. A mechanical model for this would be a pendulum with a small mass on the end of a cord, as in Fig. 1.2. The force on a small particle of mass m is proportional to the displacement in the x direction, and directed towards the equilibrium point which we shall take as the origin. With no other forces acting, the differential equation describing the motion is just Newton's second law of motion:

$$m \frac{d^2 x}{dt^2} = -kx. \tag{1.1}$$

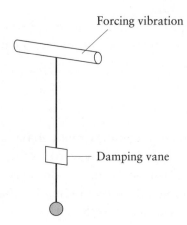

Forcing vibration

Damping vane

Fig. 1.2 A pendulum with damping and a forcing vibration.

The solution of this simple differential equation is

$$x = A\cos(\omega t + \varepsilon),\tag{1.2}$$

where A and ε are arbitrary constants depending on the initial boundary conditions and $\omega = (k/m)^{1/2}$.

The system can be made more realistic by adding two extra forces. The first is an imposed periodic driving force with an angular frequency, ω_c, of the form $F\cos(\omega_c t)$, and the second a resisting force proportional to the velocity of the form $-f(dx/dt)$. This latter force is of the usual form for the resistance on a body moving through a medium and subjected to a Stokes' law drag. In the mechanical model, displayed in Fig. 1.2, the viscous drag is produced by air resistance on the small vane shown and the driving force is a periodic displacement of the frame on which the pendulum is suspended. From an analytical point of view the form of the differential equation describing the resultant motion is

$$m\frac{d^2x}{dt^2} + f\frac{dx}{dt} + kx = F\cos(\omega_c t),\tag{1.3}$$

for which the standard solution is, for $f < 4km$,

$$x = A\exp\left(-\frac{f}{2m}t\right)\sin\left(\sqrt{\frac{k}{m} - \frac{f^2}{4m^2}}\,t + \eta\right) + R\cos(\omega_c t + \varepsilon),\tag{1.4a}$$

and for $f \gtrsim 4km$,

$$x = \exp\left(-\frac{f}{2m}t\right)\left\{C\exp\left(\sqrt{\frac{f^2}{4m^2} - \frac{k}{m}}\,t\right) + D\exp\left(-\sqrt{\frac{f^2}{4m^2} - \frac{k}{m}}\,t\right)\right\}$$

$$+ R\cos(\omega_c t + \varepsilon),\tag{1.4b}$$

where

$$R = \frac{F}{[(k - \omega_c^2 m)^2 + f^2 \omega_c^2]^{1/2}} \tag{1.4c}$$

and

$$\tan(\varepsilon) = \frac{-f\omega_c}{k - \omega_c^2 m}. \tag{1.4d}$$

The possible ambiguity in the value of ε is resolved by the condition that $\sin(\varepsilon)$ has the sign of the numerator of (1.4d) and, since f and ω_c are both positive, $-\pi \leqslant \varepsilon \leqslant 0$.

The values of A, η, C and D in (1.4a) are arbitrary and depend on the boundary conditions but, because of the exponential factors, the first term is a transient one which eventually dies away, leaving the second-term steady-state solution. This has the same frequency as the driving force and an amplitude, R, which depends on all the constants in (1.3). It is clear that for fixed values of m, f and k the amplitude will be a maximum when

$$\omega_c = (k/m)^{1/2}, \quad \text{when } k - \omega_c^2 m = 0 \tag{1.5}$$

In(1.4c) denominator is minimum

and the driving frequency is the same as the natural frequency of the undriven system. For this resonance condition the divisor in (1.4d) is zero, corresponding to $\varepsilon = -\pi/2$, which means that the driven motion lags $\pi/2$ behind the driving force.

Another situation of interest is when a free and undamped mass is subjected to a driving force – which is what happens if electromagnetic radiation falls on a free electron – where

$$k = 0, \quad f = 0 \quad \text{and} \quad F = eE, \tag{1.6}$$

with E the amplitude of the electric field. From (1.4c) and (1.4d) it can be found that the amplitude and phase of the induced vibration of the free electron are

$$R = \frac{F}{\omega_c^2 m} \quad \text{and} \quad \varepsilon = \pi. \tag{1.7}$$

This shows that the vibration of the free electron is exactly π out of phase with the forcing vibration; when the force is in the negative x direction the motion is in the positive x direction, and vice versa.

Once the solution, (1.4a) or (1.4b), is available then the behaviour of the pendulum can be found for any circumstance by inserting the appropriate values of m, k, f, ω_c and F. However, let us suppose that the *magnitude* of the damping force is no longer proportional to the velocity of the mass but is proportional to some arbitrary power of the speed – that is, $|dx/dt|^\alpha$. The direction of the force is still opposed to the direction of motion, so the differential equation will appear in the form

$$m\frac{d^2x}{dt^2} + f\left|\frac{dx}{dt}\right|^{\alpha-1}\frac{dx}{dt} + kx = F\cos(\omega_c t). \tag{1.8}$$

It is not possible to find an analytical solution for this equation for all values of α, so to study the behaviour of such a system it is necessary to resort to numerical methods. There are many available techniques for the numerical solution of differential equations, of varying degrees of complexity and efficiency, and in the following section some basic ones will be described.

1.3 Techniques for solving first-order ordinary differential equations

1.3.1 *Euler methods*

A first-order ordinary differential equation can be written in the form

$$\frac{dy}{dx} = f(x, y), \tag{1.9}$$

with the boundary condition $y = y_0$ when $x = x_0$. Figure 1.3a shows a typical curve together with the point (x_0, y_0). The simplest method of solving the differential equation, the *Euler method*, is to assume that going a small distance along the curve from (x_0, y_0) is approximately the same as going a short distance along the tangent to the curve at (x_0, y_0). If the integration step length, that is, the step in the independent variable x, is h, then from Fig. 1.3a it will be seen that the estimated coordinates of the next point on the curve are

$$x_1 = x_0 + h,$$

$$y_1 \approx y_0 + h\tan(\psi) = y_0 + h\left(\frac{dy}{dx}\right)_{x=x_0} = y_0 + hf(x_0, y_0),$$

$$\approx y_0 + \delta_1 \quad \text{ref. } p\,8$$

and, in general,

$$x_{n+1} = x_n + h,$$

$$y_{n+1} = y_n + hf(x_n, y_n). \tag{1.10}$$

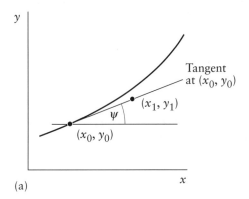

(a)

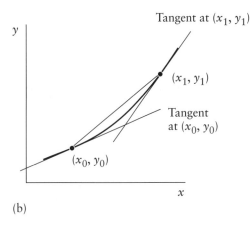

(b)

Fig. 1.3 (a) The Euler method. (b) The Euler predictor-corrector method. The slope of the chord is approximately the average of the slopes at (x_0, y_0) and (x_1, y_1).

It should be clear from the figure that unless h is very small the solution will quickly deviate from the true curve.

A great improvement on the Euler method, at the expense of a modest increase in computational complexity, is the *Euler predictor-corrector* (EPC) *method*, the principle of which is illustrated in Fig. 1.3b. To take one step in the integration without error it is required to go along the chord from (x_0, y_0) to (x_1, y_1). It can be shown that the slope of this chord is approximately the average of the slopes of the curves at the two ends. A Taylor series, centred on the point (x_0, y_0) and truncated after two terms, gives

$$y_1 \approx y_0 + h\left(\frac{dy}{dx}\right)_0 = y_0 + hf(x_0, y_0). \tag{1.11a}$$

SAME $\longrightarrow$

$\therefore y_1 - y_0 = hf(x_0, y_0)$

Similarly, with centring on (x_1, y_1),

$$y_0 \approx y_1 - h\left(\frac{dy}{dx}\right)_1 = y_1 - hf(x_1, y_1). \tag{1.11b}$$

$y_1 - y_0 = hf(x_1, y_1)$

$\therefore 2(y_1 - y_0) = h\{f(x_0, y_0) + f(x_1, y_1)\}$

≠ and, more generally, $\dfrac{y_{n+1}-y_n}{h}=\frac{1}{2}\{f(x_n,y_n)+f(x_{n+1},y_{n+1})\}$

∴ $y_{n+1}=y_n+\dfrac{h}{2}\{f(x_n,y_n)+f(x_{n+1},y_n)\}$ On rhs we now use Y_{n+1} from Euler eqn 1.13a as estimate of y_{n+1} to get y_{n+1} rqd in lhs.

From these two equations the slope of the chord is found as

$$\neq \frac{y_1-y_0}{h}=\frac{1}{2}\{f(x_0,y_0)+f(x_1,y_1)\}.=\frac{1}{2}\{f(x_0 \tag{1.12}$$

Since y_1 appears on both sides it cannot directly be derived from (1.12) but an estimated, or predicted, value of y_1 can be found from the simple Euler approach. A general form of the EPC method is

Euler

$$\begin{cases} Y_{n+1}=y_n+hf(x_n,y_n), & \text{same as 1.13a p.6} \tag{1.13a}\\[2mm] x_{n+1}=x_n+h, \end{cases}$$

followed by a corrected estimate

Euler PC

$$y_{n+1}=y_n+\tfrac{1}{2}h\{f(x_n,y_n)+f(x_{n+1},Y_{n+1})\}. \tag{1.13b}$$

We shall be describing other predictor-corrector methods, all of which have the same general pattern. Firstly, a predicted value of y_{n+1}, Y_{n+1}, is obtained by an *open equation* which extrapolates from already known values of y. Secondly, the prediction is improved, or 'corrected', by a *closed equation* which contains Y_{n+1} as well as previously known values.

The simple Euler method requires one function evaluation per step and the EPC method requires two. However, an analysis based on the use of the Taylor series shows that the error in integrating over a fixed interval in the simple Euler method is $O(h)$ while that of the EPC method is $O(h^2)$. This means that halving the integration step length halves the error in the simple Euler method but reduces the error in EPC by a factor of 4 (see Table 1.1).

1.3.2 *The Runge–Kutta method*

Next we describe the four-step *Runge–Kutta* (RK) process which requires four function evaluations per step and is a very good all-purpose method in terms of combining simplicity and accuracy. The operation of the RK method is summarized in the following set of equations:

$$\delta_1=hf(x_0,y_0) \qquad \text{ref. p.6}$$

$$\delta_2=hf(x_0+\tfrac{1}{2}h,y_0+\tfrac{1}{2}\delta_1)$$

$$\delta_3=hf(x_0+\tfrac{1}{2}h,y_0+\tfrac{1}{2}\delta_2)$$

$$\delta_4=hf(x_0+h,y_0+\delta_3)$$

Table 1.1 The performance of the Euler, Euler predictor-corrector (EPC) and four-step Runge–Kutta methods in solving $dy/dx = y$ for the range $x = 0.0$ to 1.0 with $y = 1$ when $x = 0$. The results are obtained with integration steps $h = 0.1$ and $h = 0.2$.

x	y (Euler)		y (EPC)		y (Runge–Kutta)		e^x
	$h = 0.2$	$h = 0.1$	$h = 0.2$	$h = 0.1$	$h = 0.2$	$h = 0.1$	
0.0	1.000000	1.000000	1.000000	1.000000	1.000000	1.000000	1.000000
0.1		1.100000		1.105000		1.105171	1.105171
0.2	1.200000	1.210000	1.220000	1.221025	1.221400	1.221403	1.221403
0.3		1.331000		1.349233		1.349859	1.349859
0.4	1.440000	1.464100	1.488400	1.490902	1.491818	1.491824	1.491825
0.5		1.610510		1.647447		1.648721	1.648721
0.6	1.728000	1.771561	1.815848	1.820429	1.822106	1.822118	1.822119
0.7		1.948717		2.011574		2.013752	2.013753
0.8	2.073600	2.143589	2.215335	2.222789	2.225521	2.225539	2.225541
0.9		2.357948		2.456182		2.459601	2.459603
1.0	2.488320	2.593743	2.702708	2.714081	2.718251	2.718280	2.718282

and finally

$$y_1 = y_0 + \tfrac{1}{6}(\delta_1 + 2\delta_2 + 2\delta_3 + \delta_4). \tag{1.14}$$

The value of δ_1 is the Euler estimate of the increment in y, based on the slope at the initial point, while δ_2 and δ_3 are both estimates of the increment based on the estimated slope at $x = x_0 + \tfrac{1}{2}h$. Finally, δ_4 is an Euler-type estimate of the increment based on the estimated slope at the end-point of the integration step. These four estimates are then combined with weights proportional to $1 : 2 : 2 : 1$ to give the final estimated increment.

The error in the RK method is $O(h^4)$, which means that the error is reduced by factor of 16 when the step length is halved. The performance of the Euler, EPC and RK methods is shown in Table 1.1 for solution of

$$\frac{dy}{dx} = y$$

with $y = 1$ when $x = 0$ for the range $x = 0$ to 1. The analytical solution is $y = e^x$, so it is possible to compare the performance of the three methods. While halving the step length does not exactly reduce the error by factors of 2, 4 and 16 for the three methods, the ratios of errors are similar to those expected theoretically. Note also the progressive improvement of these techniques as the power of h in the error term increases.

1.3.3 *The Adams–Moulton method*

The predictor-corrector methodology which has been demonstrated for the Euler method is one of a family of more accurate and sophisticated integration techniques. To illustrate this we shall consider the *Adams–Moulton method* applied to a differential equation of the form (1.9). This method requires that values from four previous steps of integration are available, and we shall refer to these as (x_0, y_0), (x_1, y_1), (x_2, y_2) and (x_3, y_3). The objective is to find y_4 corresponding to x_4; since all the steps in x are equal – say, h – we can, without loss of generality, take the value $x_n = nh$.

As a first predictor stage we fit a cubic function in x to the four known values of $f(x, y)$, which we shall indicate as f_0, f_1, f_2 and f_3. This can be done by fitting a Lagrange polynomial which is of the form

$$\phi(x) = \frac{(x - x_1)(x - x_2)(x - x_3)}{(x_0 - x_1)(x_0 - x_2)(x_0 - x_3)} f_0 + \frac{(x - x_0)(x - x_2)(x - x_3)}{(x_1 - x_0)(x_1 - x_2)(x_1 - x_3)} f_1$$

$$+ \frac{(x - x_0)(x - x_1)(x - x_3)}{(x_2 - x_0)(x_2 - x_1)(x_2 - x_3)} f_2 + \frac{(x - x_0)(x - x_1)(x - x_2)}{(x_3 - x_0)(x_3 - x_1)(x_3 - x_2)} f_3. \qquad (1.15)$$

By setting x successively equal to x_0, x_1, x_2 and x_3 it may be confirmed that the right-hand side of (1.15) gives f_0, f_1, f_2 and f_3 respectively, thus showing that $\phi(x)$ is the correct cubic function going through the four points. An estimated value for y_4 may be obtained from

$$y_4 = y_3 + \int_{3h}^{4h} \phi(x)\mathrm{d}x. \qquad (1.16)$$

Taking the first term on the right-hand side of (1.15) and inserting the known values of x gives the contribution to the integral on the right-hand side of (1.16) as

$$-\frac{f_0}{6h^3} \int_{3h}^{4h} (x^3 - 6hx^2 + 11h^2 x - 6h^3) \, \mathrm{d}x = -\frac{9}{24} hf_0.$$

The contributions of the other terms can be found in similar fashion and the open equation (1.16) gives the predicted value

$$Y_4 = y_3 + \frac{h}{24} (-9f_0 + 37f_1 - 59f_2 + 55f_3). \qquad (1.17)$$

With this predicted value, Y_4, a good estimate can be made of f_4, which we indicate as $_ef_4$. Now a cubic is fitted to the values of f_1, f_2, f_3 and $_ef_4$. This polynomial is inserted in (1.16) to get a better estimate of y_4, which will be better because the equation is of closed form and is not being extrapolated. The final accepted value of y_4 is found as

$$y_4 = y_3 + \frac{h}{24} (f_1 - 5f_2 + 19f_3 + 9_ef_4). \qquad (1.18)$$

The application of (1.17) to get a predicted value of y_4 followed by (1.18) to get a better value constitutes the Adams–Moulton method. It has similar error characteristics to the Runge–Kutta method and is more efficient in only requiring two evaluations per step, but it is not self-starting and requires some other method (such as the Runge–Kutta) to generate y_1, y_2 and y_3 before it can be used.

1.3.4 *The Numerov method*

A final predictor-corrector method, which can be very useful at times, is the *Numerov method*, which applies to second-order ordinary differential equations when there is no first-order term present, that is, of the form

$$\frac{d^2y}{dx^2} = f(x, y). \tag{1.19}$$

This method is best explained by application of the Taylor series to the points (x_0, y_0), (x_1, y_1), (x_2, y_2) with equal spacing, h, in x, from which we obtain

$$y_2 = y_1 + h(y_1') + \frac{h^2}{2}(y_1'') + \frac{h^3}{6}(y_1''') + \frac{h^4}{24}(y_1^{(4)}) + \frac{h^5}{120}(y_1^{(5)}) + \cdots \tag{1.20a}$$

and

$$y_0 = y_1 - h(y_1') + \frac{h^2}{2}(y_1'') - \frac{h^3}{6}(y_1''') + \frac{h^4}{24}(y_1^{(4)}) - \frac{h^5}{120}(y_1^{(5)}) + \cdots, \tag{1.20b}$$

where the superscripts on the *y*s indicate the order of differentiation. Truncating the right-hand sides of both these equations after four terms and then adding gives the open equation for the estimate of y_2:

$$Y_2 = 2y_1 - y_0 + h^2(y_1'') = 2y_1 - y_0 + h^2 f(x_1, y_1). \tag{1.21}$$

The closed equation is derived from (1.20a) and (1.20b) by retaining six terms on the right-hand sides and then adding the two equations to give

$$y_2 = 2y_1 - y_0 + h^2(y_1'') + \frac{h^4}{12}(y_1^{(4)}). \tag{1.22}$$

The final term on the right-hand side of (1.22) can be expressed in terms of second derivatives by another application of the Taylor series in the form

$$(y_2'') = (y_1'') + h(y_1''') + \frac{h^2}{2}(y_1^{(4)}) + \cdots \tag{1.23a}$$

and

$$(y_0'') = (y_1'') - h(y_1''') + \frac{h^2}{2}(y_1^{(4)}) - \cdots. \tag{1.23b}$$

Adding these two equations, rearranging and then expressing the second derivatives in functional form leads to

$$\frac{h^4}{12}(y_1^{(4)}) = \frac{h^2}{12}\{f(x_2, y_2) - 2f(x_1, y_1) + f(x_0, y_0)\}. \tag{1.24}$$

Now the result (1.24) is inserted into (1.22) and the predicted value of y_2 from (1.21) is used on the right-hand side to give the closed equation

$$y_2 = 2y_1 - y_0 + \frac{h^2}{12}\{f(x_2, Y_2) + 10f(x_1, y_1) + f(x_0, y_0)\}. \tag{1.25}$$

Like the Adams–Moulton method, the Numerov method is not self-starting, although it only requires the values at two previous steps. There are two new function evaluations per time step, $f(x_1, y_1)$ in (1.21) and $f(x_2, Y_2)$ in (1.25), which makes it very economical, but the very good characteristic it has is that the error is $O(h^5)$.

The methods given here for the numerical solution of ordinary differential equations are a small selection of the methods available, but they form a very useful set for solving the kinds of problem that usually arise in physics. A useful general reference is Press *et al.* (1986).

1.4 Solution of the forced, damped oscillator

We now return to the problem of solving equation (1.8), which is a second-order differential equation with a first-order term of the general form

$$\frac{d^2y}{dx^2} = f\left(x, y, \frac{dy}{dx}\right). \tag{1.26}$$

This can be solved by the Runge–Kutta method or by the Adams–Moulton method by breaking it up into two coupled first-order equations:

$$\frac{dy}{dx} = u \tag{1.27a}$$

and

$$\frac{du}{dx} = f(x, y, u). \tag{1.27b}$$

This type of problem is a special case of the situation where there are two general dependent variables and the differential equations are of the form

$$\frac{dy}{dx} = Y(x, y, u) \tag{1.28a}$$

and

$$\frac{du}{dx} = U(x, y, u). \tag{1.28b}$$

Starting with the boundary conditions $y = y_0$ and $u = u_0$ when $x = x_0$, the solution proceeds as follows:

$$\delta_{1,y} = hY(x_0, y_0, u_0)$$

$$\delta_{1,u} = hU(x_0, y_0, u_0)$$

$$\delta_{2,y} = hY(x_0 + \tfrac{1}{2}h, y_0 + \tfrac{1}{2}\delta_{1,y}, u_0 + \tfrac{1}{2}\delta_{1,u})$$

$$\delta_{2,u} = hU(x_0 + \tfrac{1}{2}h, y_0 + \tfrac{1}{2}\delta_{1,y}, u_0 + \tfrac{1}{2}\delta_{1,u})$$

$$\delta_{3,y} = hY(x_0 + \tfrac{1}{2}h, y_0 + \tfrac{1}{2}\delta_{2,y}, u_0 + \tfrac{1}{2}\delta_{2,u})$$

$$\delta_{3,u} = hU(x_0 + \tfrac{1}{2}h, y_0 + \tfrac{1}{2}\delta_{2,y}, u_0 + \tfrac{1}{2}\delta_{2,u}) \tag{1.29}$$

$$\delta_{4,y} = hY(x_0 + h, y_0 + \delta_{3,y}, u_0 + \delta_{3,u})$$

$$\delta_{4,u} = hU(x_0 + h, y_0 + \delta_{3,y}, u_0 + \delta_{3,u})$$

$$y_1 = y_0 + \tfrac{1}{6}(\delta_{1,y} + 2\delta_{2,y} + 2\delta_{3,y} + \delta_{4,y})$$

$$u_1 = u_0 + \tfrac{1}{6}(\delta_{1,u} + 2\delta_{2,u} + 2\delta_{3,u} + \delta_{4,u}).$$

The pattern of these equations is similar to that of (1.14) and can be extended to deal with any number of dependent variables. A FORTRAN program OSCILLAT, which solves equation (1.8) for different initial boundary conditions and values of α by the Runge–Kutta procedure, is provided (see p. xv). It is written in a transparent form and well provided with comment statements, and it is recommended that it should be studied before use.

Table 1.2 The steady-state amplitudes for frequencies around resonance for the standard OSCILLAT problem with $\alpha = 1.5$.

ω_c (rad s^{-1})	Amplitude $(10^{-3}\,\text{m})$	ω_c (rad s^{-1})	Amplitude $(10^{-3}\,\text{m})$
300	1.0	317	7.2
305	1.5	318	6.0
310	2.6	320	3.9
312	3.6	322	2.6
314	5.6	325	1.8
315	6.7	330	1.1
316	7.5		

The program is fairly robust and can handle a wide range of situations. The standard parameters provided with the program are:

$$m = 0.001\,\text{kg}, \quad f = 0.003\,\text{N s m}^{-1}, \quad k = 100\,\text{N m}^{-1},$$

$$F = 0.01\,\text{N}, \quad \omega_c = 300\,\text{rad s}^{-1}, \quad x(0) = 0, \quad u(0) = 0.$$

The program has been run with $\alpha = 1.5$ and a range of forcing angular frequencies, ω_c, around the resonance frequency $316.2\,\text{rad s}^{-1}$. The resulting steady-state amplitudes, after the initial transients have died down, are given in Table 1.2. The values are not too precise as they have been estimated from graphical output, an example of which is shown in Fig. 1.4, but they indicate clearly the nature of the resonance curve.

1.5 General ideas about simulation

In building computational models the skill required is to simulate *as well as possible* a physical system with a view to investigating its behaviour. The term 'as well as possible' is subject to a whole range of conditions. If the system under investigation is a system of planets orbiting the Sun, then the number of bodies is small, the force law governing their motions is well known and the only limitation in the accuracy of the simulation is the amount of computational effort that is brought to bear. On the other hand, the physics of the system we are examining might be quite well known but the system may be so large and complex – a galaxy of 10^{11} stars, for example – that we cannot hope to simulate it perfectly. Yet another kind of situation is where the physics is not so well defined and all we know is the general form of the behaviour – for

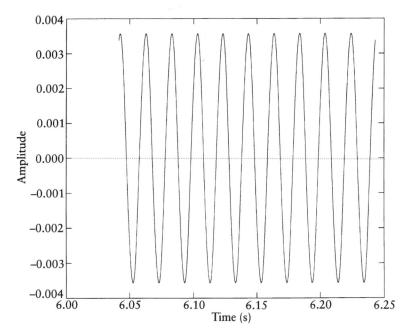

Fig. 1.4 An OSCILLAT graph for one of the runs giving Table 1.2, with $\omega_c = 312\,\text{rad}\,\text{s}^{-1}$.

example, where oil extraction is being modelled and the nature of the sub-surface rocks is imperfectly known.

1.5.1 *The Trojan asteroids*

We shall illustrate aspects of simulation by considering two different N-body problems. The first problem is a well-known one – that of the Trojan aster-oids. The planet Jupiter is accompanied in its orbit by two groups of asteroids which precede it and follow it at an angular distance of $\pi/3$. It can be shown analytically that these are positions of stable equilibrium but, using the program TROJANS (see p. xv), we shall be able to confirm this by computa-tion. This program has several components. The main program, NBODY, includes the Runge–Kutta procedure with automatic step control. The input of the basic parameters and the definition of the initial state of the system are controlled by the subroutine START which, for the present application, enables the starting positions and velocities of the bodies to be entered manually. For other applications START can be rewritten to compute the initial boundary condition if that is appropriate. The subroutine ACC gives the acceleration of each body in terms of the positions and velocities of all

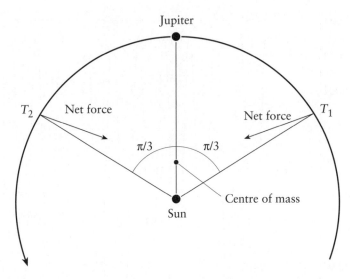

Fig. 1.5   The positions of Trojan asteroids $\pi/3$ ahead of and behind Jupiter in its motion around the Sun.

the bodies. In the Trojan asteroid case there is no dependence on velocities, but there will be such a dependence in our second example. The subroutine STORE stores intermediate values of the time and corresponding positions of the bodies; for this example this is done every 50 time steps of the computation. Finally there is a routine, OUT, which produces data files suitable for input to a graphics package. For different N-body problems the main program NBODY may be used with different specially written subroutines for the particular problem under investigation.

Ignoring the other planets of the solar system, Jupiter and the Sun move around their common centre of mass, as illustrated in Fig. 1.5. The stable position of a Trojan asteroid is $\pi/3$ ahead of or behind Jupiter with respect to motion relative to the Sun. The combination of the gravitational attraction of the Sun and of Jupiter gives a resultant force on a Trojan asteroid towards the centre of mass. This gives a centripetal acceleration of the correct magnitude for the asteroid to move around the centre of mass with the same period as Jupiter. With the Sun as origin it can be shown that, for a circular orbit, the speed of Jupiter is given by

$$V_{\mathrm{J}}=\left\{\frac{G(M_{\odot}+M_{\mathrm{J}})}{R_{\mathrm{SJ}}}\right\}^{1/2}, \tag{1.30}$$

where $M_{\odot}$ and M_{J} are the masses of the Sun and Jupiter respectively, and R_{SJ} is the distance between them. Relative to the Sun, V_{J} is also the speed of the

Table 1.3 The initial parameters for the Trojan asteroids problem.

	Sun	Jupiter	Trojan 1	Trojan 2
Mass	1	0.001	0	0
x	0	0	-4.50333	4.50333
y	0	5.2	2.6	2.6
z	0	0	0	0
V_x	0	-2.75674	-1.37837	-1.37837
V_y	0	0	-2.38741	2.38741
V_z	0	0	0	0

asteroids, and their components of velocity in the x and y directions are therefore easily found. For calculations involving the solar system it is convenient to use solar system units, where unit mass is the mass of the Sun, unit distance is the astronomical unit (AU) and unit time is one year. For such a system the gravitational constant, G, is $4\pi^2$. With this system the numerical values for the initial conditions of the Trojan problem, where all positions and speeds are relative to a stationary Sun, are given in Table 1.3.

The program TROJANS can be run with any specified body as origin. If the parameters in Table 1.3 are used with the sun specified as origin then the asteroids stay rigidly in their original positions. However, with some modification of the parameters from their ideal values the asteroids do not stay in their initial positions but oscillate about them – which illustrates the stability of their equilibrium positions. The graphical output for a run of 1000 years (more than 80 orbits of Jupiter), reproduced in Fig. 1.6, shows the motion of the asteroids with respect to Jupiter, rotated so as to be on the y-axis. The initial asteroid positions and velocities are those in Table 1.3, rounded off to three significant figures so that some movement of the asteroids is apparent.

1.5.2 *An orbiting satellite under tidal stress*

The second example is one where an exact representation of the physical situation is not possible but where a simulation gives the expected form of behaviour. A satellite in orbit around a planet is subjected to a tidal stress which stretches it along the direction of the radius vector. If the orbit is non-circular then the stress is variable and the satellite expands and contracts along the radius vector in a periodic fashion. Since the satellite will not be perfectly elastic there will be hysteresis effects and some of the mechanical energy will be converted into heat which is radiated away. The overall effect is that while the system as a whole is losing mechanical energy it must conserve

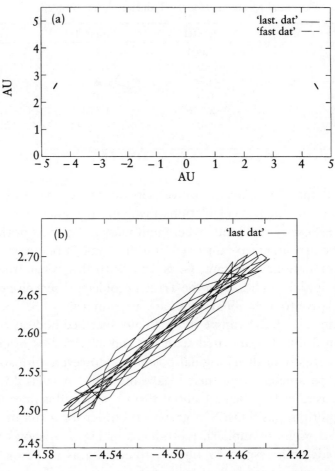

Fig. 1.6 (a) Movement of Trojan asteroids in 1000 years: relative to Jupiter with coordinates (0, 5.2); (b) an enlarged view of the motion of the leading asteroid.

angular momentum. For a planet of mass M and a satellite of mass m ($\ll M$), in an orbit of semi-major axis a and eccentricity e, the total energy is

$$E = -\frac{GMm}{2a},\qquad(1.31\text{a})$$

and the angular momentum is

$$H = \{GMa(1-e^2)\}m.\qquad(1.31\text{b})$$

If E is to decrease then a must become smaller, but if H is then to be constant then e must become smaller – that is to say, that the orbit must round off.

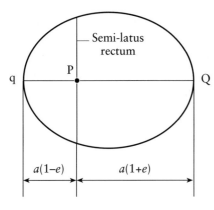

Fig. 1.7 The elliptical orbit of a satellite relative to the planet at one focus. Points q and Q are the nearest and furthest points from the planet, respectively.

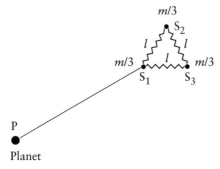

Fig. 1.8 The satellite is represented by three masses, each $m/3$, connected by springs each of the same unstrained length, l.

The quantity which remains constant is $a(1-e^2)$, the *semi-latus rectum*, which is indicated in Fig. 1.7. The model we shall use to simulate this situation is shown in Fig. 1.8. The planet is represented by a point mass, P, and the satellite by a distribution of three masses, each $m/3$, at positions S_1, S_2 and S_3, forming an equilateral triangle when free of stress. The masses are connected, as shown, by springs, each of unstressed length l and the same spring constant, k. Thus a spring constantly stretched to a length l' will exert an inward force

$$F = k(l' - l).$$

However, we introduce a dissipative element in our system by making the force dependent on the rate of expansion or contraction of the spring, giving a force law

$$F = k(l' - l) - c \frac{dl'}{dt}, \tag{1.32}$$

where the force acts inwards at the two ends. It is the second term in (1.32) which gives the simulation of the hysteresis losses in the satellite.

The program to examine this model, SATELLIT (see p. xv), has as its main routine NBODY, which is identical to that used in TROJANS. The input to the program, controlled by START, is as follows:

number of bodies $= 4$
mass of first body (planet) $= 2 \times 10^{27}\,\mathrm{kg}$
mass of remaining bodies $= 3 \times 10^{22}\,\mathrm{kg}$
initial time step $= 10\,\mathrm{s}$
total simulation time $= 125\,000\,\mathrm{s}$
body chosen as origin $= 1$
tolerance $= 100\,\mathrm{m}$
initial distance of satellite $= 1 \times 10^{8}\,\mathrm{m}$
unstretched length of spring $= 1 \times 10^{6}\,\mathrm{m}$
initial eccentricity $= 0.6$.

The simulation is somewhat unrealistic in that the satellite is very close to the planet; the planet mass equals that of Jupiter and if the planet *were* Jupiter the satellite would hit it! However, the parameters are chosen to give a reasonable computational time and the principles of the orbital round-off process will still be illustrated. The graphical output of the program is given in Fig. 1.9 and

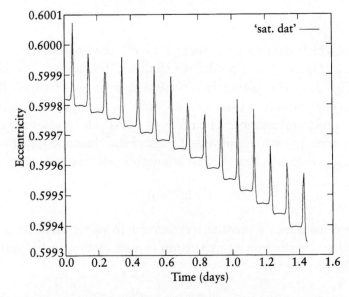

Fig. 1.9 The orbital eccentricity as a function of time. The spikes are due to an exchange between spin and orbital angular momentum around closest approach.

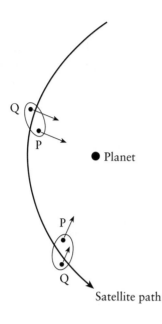

Fig. 1.10 The lag and lead in the tidal bulge of the satellite give spin angular momentum on approach and subtract it on recession.

needs explanation. There are two types of angular momentum in the simulation, one being that of the centre of mass of the satellite in its orbit around the planet and the other being that of the spin of the satellite around its centre of mass. The orbital period is 0.1 day, and this will be seen to be the period of the spikes in the eccentricity values. The initial position of the satellite is at its furthest distance from the planet so the first spike, and hence all the others, occur when the satellite is closest to the planet. The reason for the spikes can be understood by reference to Fig. 1.10, where the satellite is shown approaching the near point. It is stretched by the tidal force, but due to inertia the satellite tidal bulge lags behind the radius vector. The departure of the satellite from a spherical form can be thought of as a sphere plus two bobs of matter at the points P and Q and the gravitational forces on these are shown. Since the force at P will be greater than that at Q there will be a net torque imparting angular momentum to the satellite, causing it to spin faster. This angular momentum is provided at the expense of the orbital angular momentum and it will be seen in (1.31b) that if H falls in value for constant a then e must increase. When receding from the near point the tidal bulge is ahead of the radius vector and the effect is reversed. With the spikes explained in this way the trend in eccentricity is steadily downwards, which is the predicted rounding-off process. It should be pointed out that the spikes and the rounding off are not directly connected. If the dissipation term is removed then the spikes will remain on the background of an otherwise constant eccentricity.

This particular simulation illustrates another feature of computational modelling. Although the explanation of the spikes is quite straightforward and easily understood, it may not have been obvious *ab initio* that such spikes would occur. A good simulation may well bring out new, unexpected and important features of the system under investigation.

1.6   Types of simulation and their applications

To tackle the many types of problem which are solved in computational physics it will not be surprising that several different kinds of method are available. Here we shall just describe the most common methods in a general way and indicate the kinds of problem that they can solve. This general background is intended to do no more than convey the essence of the variety of techniques available to the computational physicist and the range of problems to which they can be applied. The subject will here be painted in broad brush strokes to give the general pattern of the subject; the filling in of detail will come in the following chapters.

1.6.1   *The Monte Carlo method*

During the Second World War scientists in the USA were working on the design of an atomic bomb and they were meeting problems which they needed to solve quickly and for the solution of which they had little previous direct experience to guide them. One such problem involved the way that neutrons would penetrate a barrier, a problem with features which made it different from, say, the absorption of light or X-rays in a medium. A neutron could react with matter in different ways – it could be unaffected, be scattered either elastically or inelastically, or be absorbed – and the probabilities of these events would be dependent on the energy of the neutron. Although the dependence on energy of each of the individual probabilities was known, there was no way of solving this problem by conventional mathematical analysis. Eventually it was solved by Ulam and von Neumann in a novel numerical way. They followed the progress of a single neutron passing into the barrier. The distance it would travel before it approached a nucleus could be estimated but when it was close to the nucleus several things could happen with various probabilities. To decide on what would happen, Ulam and von Neumann did the numerical equivalent of throwing a die, or spinning a roulette wheel – hence the name of the method. By following the path of the neutron, making a Monte Carlo decision for each interaction, it could be found whether or not it penetrated the barrier. By repeating this process for a large number of individual neutrons the proportion that would penetrate the barrier could be found with reasonable precision.

We can illustrate the general characteristic of the Monte Carlo method by a simple example – the *random-walk* problem, sometimes known as the drunkard's walk. The problem can be expressed as follows: given that a body makes n steps each of length d but in random directions, how does the expected final distance from the starting-point depend upon n? This can be solved by analysis, and indeed it was solved by Einstein in 1905 in relation to Brownian motion, the movement of light particles bombarded by the molecules of a liquid in which they are suspended. We shall set up a simplified form of the problem which we shall then solve by a numerical simulation. In the simplified form the body starts at the origin of a square grid of unit side and in each step the body can move only $+1$ or -1 in the x or y directions, with an equal probability for each of the four directions. The way that the choice of direction will be made is to generate a random number, r, with a uniform probability density in the range 0 to 1. The direction of motion is then chosen by

$$+x \qquad \text{for } 0 \leqslant r \leqslant 0.25$$

$$-x \qquad \text{for } 0.25 < r \leqslant 0.5$$

$$+y \qquad \text{for } 0.5 < r \leqslant 0.75$$

$$-y \qquad \text{for } 0.75 < r \leqslant 1,$$

or something equivalent, giving the required equal probability to each of the four directions. The program DRUNKARD (see p. xv) for carrying out this calculation incorporates a simple random number generator which is good enough for the present purpose but which would not be adequate for a more sophisticated application. The properties and qualities of random number generators will be discussed further in Chapter 4.

The analysis used by Einstein for Brownian motion showed that the root-mean-square distance for n steps of unit length in random directions is $n^{1/2}$. It can also be shown that the same result is obtained with our simplified random walk where the steps are confined to one of four principal directions. This is illustrated in Table 1.4, the third column of which gives the results of running DRUNKARD for the standard random-walk problem. It can be seen that the numerical results in the third column agree quite well with the mathematical analysis.

Another kind of random walk problem is to find the root-mean-square (rms) path length for n steps under the condition that the walk is not allowed to cross itself. This could be a model of a polymer molecule in two dimensions

Table 1.4 The results from the program DRUNKARD. Column 3 shows the results from the standard random-walk problem. Column 4 gives the result where the condition is imposed that the walk may not cross itself.

n	Standard random walk		Non-crossing random walk	
	$n^{1/2}$	Program	Program	$n^{0.63}$
2	1.41	1.40	1.50	1.55
4	2.00	1.97	2.32	2.39
8	2.83	2.87	3.63	3.71
16	4.00	3.93	5.97	5.74
32	5.66	5.77	9.17	8.88
64	8.00	8.23		
128	11.31	11.24		
256	16.00	15.83		
512	22.63	22.79		
1024	32.00	30.85		

(say, on the surface of a liquid), where each of the n polymer units is regarded as a step and the molecule cannot go through itself. The length of the 'walk' is then the distance between the two ends of a molecule. This is a problem that Einstein could not have solved but it is one that can be tackled by numerical methods. There are two possible numerical strategies which give different results. In the first one the normal random-walk procedure is followed, as in DRUNKARD, but whenever a crossing occurs that trial is abandoned. In the other strategy if a step produces a crossing then the step is repeated to see whether a non-crossing path is available. The latter of these is the strategy used in the program POLYWALK (see p. xv) where up to four attempts are made to avoid a crossing, after which the trial is abandoned. The results are shown in the fourth column of Table 1.4 up to $n = 32$. Looking for the possibility that the rms distance may depend on some power of the number of steps, Fig. 1.11 shows the logarithm of the rms distance, as found by the program, plotted against $\log(n)$. The points lie on a fairly good straight line with slope 0.63, and the value of $n^{0.63}$ is shown in the final column. Although this relationship breaks down for larger values of n, we have found by numerical means a useful relationship as long as it is restricted to its range of validity.

These simple examples illustrate the general principles of the Monte Carlo method which will be treated in more detail in Chapter 4.

1.6.2 *Particle methods*

The techniques used to solve the astronomical problems described earlier in this chapter are examples of particle methods of a very simple kind, where the number of bodies (particles) is very small. In these simple problems the

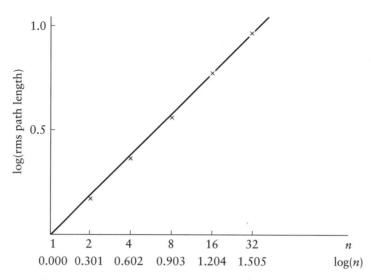

Fig. 1.11   Results from a non-crossing random walk from POLYWALK.

interactions of all pairs of particles were considered. In general, where there are N bodies then the number of pair interactions is $\frac{1}{2}N(N-1)$ and for the $N=4$ SATELLIT problem the six interactions could easily be handled. However, scientists are often interested in systems containing large numbers of particles – for example, galaxies containing 10^{11} stars or plasma systems or liquids containing 10^{24} or so charged or uncharged particles. It is clear that for such problems all pair interactions cannot be considered, so that some other approaches are necessary. However, nowadays molecular–dynamic simulations can be carried out with 10^7–10^8 particles if there are only short-range forces to consider or if long-range forces are handled by the PIC method (Section 3.7).

One basic approach which greatly reduces the number of particles to be considered is the use of *superparticles*, each of which represents large numbers of the real particles. If one is interested in the spiral structure of galaxies, which depend on gravitational instabilities in a rotating system, then a distribuon of 10^5 particles (stars) is quite capable of representing this to the required degree of definition. However, in order that the gravitational forces are properly represented, each 'superstar' must have the mass of 10^6 normal stars.

Since it is impossible to treat all pair interactions, even with superparticles, then instead of calculating the force on each particle due to all the other particles taken individually a statistical approach is used where the overall field on each particle due to all the other particles taken together is estimated. One way of doing this is to consider that particles exist in *cells*, parallelepiped-shaped regions, usually but not always cubes. The force on a particular particle due to material in a distant cube may be approximated as that which there would be if all the particles were at the centre of the cube. For some of the closer particles smaller cubes may be used or the pair interactions may be calculated.

Another, but quite different, use of cells is to represent an extensive volume of material (say, a liquid) as a periodic structure so that all the cells have the same contents and the cells pack together to fill the whole of space. If the forces between particles are of short range then only close-neighbour interactions need be considered; a particle which moves out of a cell through one wall is replaced by the corresponding particle moving into the cell through the opposite wall. This kind of cell model has been very successful in modelling liquid structure where short-range Lennard-Jones type forces are involved.

The representation of a continuous medium by particles can be quite useful even when the particles cannot be individually identified as real particles, which are atoms or molecules in the case of a liquid. Instead the particles can be considered as the carriers of quantities associated with the medium – mass, heat content, entropy, charge, etc. – and the way in which density, temperature, pressure and other properties vary with time is represented by the variation in the distribution of the particles. The particles are assigned to cells and the aggregated properties of the particles in a cell are associated with the centre of the cell. Two kinds of cell structure are possible. The first is the Eulerian mesh system, which is fixed in space and through which the particles move; the other, the Lagrangian mesh system, is attached to the particles so as the particles move so does the mesh. The latter system is difficult to use where large distortions of the mesh would occur.

Sometimes the material can be uniform in properties (such as a volume of water of constant density and temperature), and the particles can then just represent the presence or absence of material. The study of the formation of waves on a beach or splashes when an object falls into a liquid are examples of where such a model could be useful.

The above just gives the flavour of the range of particle methods and their applications. A full treatment, with detailed descriptions of the methods and examples of their use, will be given in Chapters 3 and 7.

1.6.3 *Continuum physics – the finite-difference method*

There are many problems in physics where some property of a material – temperature, density or solvent concentration, for example – varies continuously in space and time and where the rates of change from point to point are described by partial differential equations. Such systems can sometimes be handled by particle methods, but if the problem has some symmetry then finite-difference methods are usually preferred. In these methods the property under investigation – say, concentration, n – is defined at the points of a mesh which cover the region of interest. The partial differentials, quantities such as $\partial n/\partial t$ and $\partial^2 n/\partial x^2$ which occur in the differential equations, are approximately represented by linear combinations of grid-point values at the current time, which are known, and of grid-point values after some increment of time, which are to be determined. If some boundary values are known, a linear system of equations is found which can be solved for the new grid-point values.

Various kinds of differential equation require different approaches, and the kinds of problem that can be solved are those involving diffusion processes, which include heat flow, wave motions of various kinds and systems involving Poisson's equation. A range of finite-difference methods and applications will be fully described in Chapter 2.

1.6.4 *Continuum physics – the finite-element method*

The finite-element method can be an alternative to finite-difference methods in some applications, but there are types of problem for which it is most suitable and for which finite-difference methods would be difficult to apply. Where it comes into its own is in linear steady-state problems in two or three dimensions involving configurations with little symmetry and complex boundaries and where there is some global relation which the system must satisfy, such as minimum energy. The region of the problem is defined by a set of points, called *nodes*, connections between which define *elements*, shapes in one, two or three dimensions which together either exactly or approximately define the region of interest including the boundary. An example of a set of nodes and elements defining a two-dimensional irregular region is shown in Fig. 1.12. The objective of the finite-element method is to find the values of the quantity of interest, say ϕ, at the nodal points in an equilibrium situation.

The condition for the solution of the global relation plus the boundary conditions of the problem can be transformed to the condition of minimizing some integral, I, over the region, the integrand of which includes ϕ and partial differentials of ϕ. This integral can be evaluated on the assumption that within each element the potential at each point is given by linear interpolation from the defining nodal points and that the components of the gradient, $\partial\phi/\partial x$ etc., are uniform within the element and also given by the associated nodal ϕ values. The integral is thus evaluated as a function of the nodal values and the condition that I should be a minimum is that $\partial I/\partial\phi_i = 0$ for all i, where

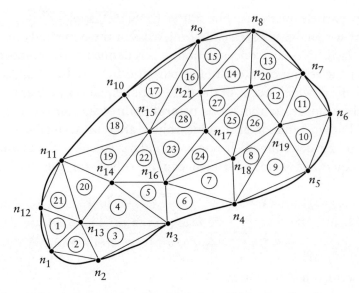

Fig. 1.12   A complex shape represented by 21 nodes and 28 triangular elements.

ϕ_i is the value of ϕ at the ith nodal point. This leads to a set of linear equations in the values of ϕ which can be solved. The finite-element method is described fully in Chapter 6.

1.7   Complex models – a systems approach

Thus far we have discussed methods for treating simple systems where a few interactions dominate the behaviour. However, the real power of simulation lies in its power to model complex systems with a very large number of interactions in which many dissimilar physical processes are occurring simultaneously. A typical example is the interior of a star. At its core the density and temperature are sufficiently high that nuclear reactions transform the hydrogen to helium, releasing substantial amounts of energy in the process. The temperature is maintained by the balance of the energy release against the heat loss which is principally by radiation. The radiative heat loss is controlled by the ability of the radiation to escape through a partially absorbing medium, the opacity of which is a function of its thermodynamic state. The density throughout the star is determined by the balance between the inward gravitational force and the pressure, which will be a combination of normal gas pressure and radiation pressure.

Each of the principal processes – force balance and energy balance – can be represented by an appropriate equation with the characteristic macroscopic quantities – pressure, density, temperature, etc. – as variables. However, they also involve quantities such as the rate of nuclear reactions, opacity, etc., which depend on the behaviour of the medium at the microscopic level. Calculation at this detail is not appropriate within the overall model and we therefore consider *sub-systems* in which these quantities are calculated as *parameters* for use in the calculation of the *complete system*. These quantities are evaluated by *pre-processing* in terms of analytic functions or data tables for later use.

In a similar fashion the general state of the system may be subsequently analysed – *post-processed* – to yield specific data for another application or to compare with experiment, for example, to compare the luminosity from the simulation with that of real stars.

This idea of breaking down the complex system into a set of simpler interacting sub-systems is a powerful one. In many problems, particularly those involving time development, many physical processes occur simultaneously. Each one can be described by a relatively simple set of equations, but taken together they present a problem of great complexity in the way that they influence the same quantities. However, if we advance time in small steps we may imagine each process occurring independently of the others in time, the increments in any variable being very small. We develop the history of the system through the stepwise sequential advance of each sub-system, an approach known as *time-splitting*.

Since a stationary state is obtained as a limit of its time development, the same ideas can be employed in steady systems. In this case the time-splitting appears as a form of iteration and care is then necessary to ensure that the sequencing of the sub-systems is not important.

Complex simulation involving several distinct interacting processes is subject to the same constraints as those for experimental models (Langhaar, 1980). A complete practical system will involve a very large number of interacting processes, many of which will be relatively weak and can be ignored. It is, however, crucial to identify *all* those which make a significant contribution and include them within the model. In principle, this can be achieved by examination of the appropriate dimensionless products representing the effect, but often experience and understanding indicate their importance. A particular problem with general-purpose models is *scale effects*, whereby the interactions change their roles as the scale (size) of the problem changes. This can be a particular difficulty when the user and constructor are separate (for example, for a commercial package) where the former requires different configurations from those envisaged by the latter. A good example concerns problems involving fluid surfaces: at small scales surface tension dominates and gravity is negligible, but at large scales the relative importance of the two effects is reversed.

Computer simulation always involves a compromise between the number of sub-systems required to enable an accurate description to be made of the essential physics, and the size and speed of the available computer on which the resulting program is to be run.

1.8 Validation and testing

Our model is at some stage intended to be a representation of a real system – the prototype. The output values calculated by the model should agree with the same quantities measured on the prototype within an acceptable accuracy limit. How can we be sure this is the case when experimental data are not available for comparison? Indeed, a major objective of our model may be to predict the behaviour of the prototype *without* performing the experiments. To this end, testing and validation are essential.

There are three sources of error in constructing a computer simulation model: programming errors, numerical errors and modelling errors. *Programming errors* are errors which cause the program not to perform in the intended way. The simpler ones will be identified by the compiler or as run-time errors. More subtle errors produce unexpected behaviour and, if this is recognized, careful testing will usually reveal the fault. The most troublesome errors are those which give reasonable-looking, but incorrect, results. If possible, it is always sensible to test the program in special cases for which either the results are known or where some features of the result can be predicted.

Numerical errors are errors introduced by the need to use numerical calculations rather than exact analytical forms. They are caused by *round-off error*, due to the finite word size of the computer, resulting in the limited accuracy of real numbers, which can be minimized by careful programming; and by *truncation errors*, due to the limited expansions of analytic expressions in numerical forms, which are avoided by judicious algorithm selection.

Finally, *modelling errors* result from the incomplete representation of the model compared to that of the complete physical reality if any of the missing terms gives rise to significant effects.

It is essential to ensure that the final simulation code is free of these errors if it is to be used to give reliable predictions of the experimental behaviour of a prototype. To this end, there must be extensive testing to validate the code. This should take several forms. Output inspection and comparison with expected behaviour reveal many programming errors. Checks of limited sections of the code against analytic solutions and earlier codes enable tests to be made for programming and numerical errors. Modelling errors can be identified by extensive testing against experimental results. The validation process is perhaps the most important aspect of modelling. It must not be skimped and every opportunity should be taken to check against new analytic and experimental results, and the model improved when found to be deficient.

Problems

1.1   For a body of very small mass starting from rest at a distance x_0 from another body with mass M, and accelerating under their mutual gravitational attraction, it can be shown that the relationship between time, t, and distance from the body, x, is

$$t = \sqrt{\frac{x_0^3}{2GM}} \left\{ \cos^{-1}\left(\sqrt{\frac{x}{x_0}}\right) + \sqrt{\frac{x}{x_0}\left(1 - \frac{x}{x_0}\right)} \right\}.$$

With $G = 6.67 \times 10^{-11}\,\text{N}\,\text{m}^2\,\text{kg}^{-2}$, $M = 2 \times 10^{30}\,\text{kg}$ and $x_0 = 2 \times 10^{11}\,\text{m}$, it is found that, for $x = 1.6 \times 10^{11}\,\text{m}$, $t = 4.729\,214\,6 \times 10^6\,\text{s}$.

Write a simple program for the Numerov method, with one initial Runge–Kutta step to get it started, to calculate the motion to time t with 10, 12, 14, 16, 18 and 20 steps. Check that the error varies approximately as the fifth power of the step length.

1.2   Run the program OSCILLAT with $\alpha = 1.5$ for

$$m = 0.001\,\text{kg}, \qquad k = 100\,\text{N}\,\text{m}^{-1}, \qquad F = 0.01\,\text{N},$$

$$\omega = 316.2\,\text{rad}\,\text{s}^{-1}, \qquad x(0) = 0, \qquad u(0) = 0,$$

and with damping factors $f = 1$, 10^{-1}, 10^{-2}, 10^{-3}, 10^{-4}, 10^{-5} and $10^{-6}\,\text{N}\,\text{m}^{-1}\,\text{s}$. Find the steady-state amplitude, A, in each case and plot $\log A$ against $\log f$. Find an approximate relationship linking A and f in the range $f = 1$ to $10^{-3}\,\text{N}\,\text{m}^{-1}\,\text{s}$.

1.3   Run the program TROJANS with planets in the orbit of Jupiter but with masses 2.5×10^{-4}, 5×10^{-4}, 10^{-3}, 2×10^{-3} and $4 \times 10^{-3}\,\text{M}_\odot$, the other input data as in Table 1.3 rounded off to three significant figures. For each planetary mass find the total range of the asteroid wandering, taking the average from the leading and trailing asteroids. Find a relationship linking the range of wandering and the planetary mass.

1.4   Equation (1.31) gives the angular momentum of a satellite in orbit about a planet. In terms of the greatest planet–satellite distance, D, and eccentricity, e, this can be written as $H = \{GM \odot D(1-e)\}^{1/2} m$. Hence the following combinations of D and e give the same angular momentum:

D (m)	6.6667×10^7	8.0×10^7	1.0×10^8	1.3333×10^8	2.0×10^8
e	0.4	0.5	0.6	0.7	0.8

Run SATELLIT with these parameters, the others being those that gave Fig. 1.9. Estimate de/dt for each value of e and show that there is an approximate linear relationship between these two quantities.

1.5   Modify program DRUNKARD so that the probability of a step being: in the *same direction* as the last step is 0.5; in the *opposite direction* to the last step is 0.1; and at *right angles* to the last step, for each possible way, is 0.2. For $n = 2^r$ steps, with $r = 1$ to 10, find the average distance, d, travelled. Show that no simple law of the form $d = n^\alpha$ is valid over the whole range.

1.6   Modify the program POLYWALK so that the probability of a step: in the positive x direction is 1/3; in the negative x direction is 0; in the positive y direction is 1/3; and in the negative y direction is 1/3. For $n = 2^r$ steps, with $r = 1$ to 8, find the average distance, d, travelled. Show that no simple law of the form $d = n^\alpha$ is valid over the whole range.

2 *Finite-difference methods*

2.1 Finite differences for ordinary derivatives

Many problems in physics can be expressed as the solution of either ordinary or partial differential equations. In this chapter, we shall be dealing with a class of problem where some quantity which is continuous in nature, such as charge, density or concentration, varies both in space and in time. These are the problems of continuum physics and there are a number of powerful and convenient ways of solving such problems using the concept of *finite differences*.

Consider the continuous function $y=f(x)$ shown in Fig. 2.1 and assume that the value at $x=X$, $f(X)$, is known together with the values of all the derivatives at that point. To estimate the value at some other point, $x=X+h$, we can use the Taylor series

$$f(X+h)=f(X)+hf'(X)+\frac{h^2}{2!}f''(X)+\frac{h^3}{3!}f'''(X)+\cdots$$

$$+\frac{h^n}{n!}f^{(n)}(X)+R_{n+1}. \tag{2.1}$$

The remainder, R_{n+1}, represents the error when the series is truncated after $n+1$ terms and, as long as the function is differentiable up to $f^{(n+1)}$, it can

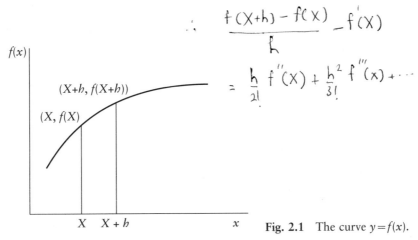

$$\therefore\ \frac{f(X+h)-f(X)}{h}-f'(X)$$

$$=\frac{h}{2!}f''(X)+\frac{h^2}{3!}f'''(X)+\cdots$$

Fig. 2.1 The curve $y=f(x)$.

always be expressed in the form

$$R_{n+1} = \frac{h^{n+1}}{(n+1)!} f^{(n+1)}(\xi), \qquad (2.2)$$

where ξ is in the range X to $X+h$.

If, for example, $f(x)=\sin(x)$, then $f'(x)=\cos(x)$, $f''(x)=-\sin(x)$ and $f'''(x)=-\cos(x)$. From $\sin(\pi/4)=\cos(\pi/4)=2^{-1/2}$ we can estimate the values of $\sin(0)$, $\sin(\pi/3)$ and $\sin(\pi/2)$ from the Taylor series centred on $\pi/4$, taking the first four terms of the series

$$\sin\left(\frac{\pi}{4}+h\right) \approx \sin\left(\frac{\pi}{4}\right)+h\cos\left(\frac{\pi}{4}\right)-\frac{1}{2}h^2\sin\left(\frac{\pi}{4}\right)-\frac{1}{6}h^3\cos\left(\frac{\pi}{4}\right), \qquad (2.3)$$

where $h=-\pi/4$, $\pi/12$ and $\pi/4$, respectively. The estimates are given in Table 2.1, together with the true values, the error and the range of possible errors as calculated from (2.2). It will be seen that the errors increase with increasing h and are all within the ranges indicated by (2.2).

The above application of Taylor's theorem was to estimate the function for general values of the independent variable given the values of the function and its derivatives at one particular value of the independent variable. We now look at the inverse problem – given $f(x)$ for a number of equally-spaced values of x, is it possible to deduce the values of the derivatives? If we rewrite (2.1) as

$$f'(X) = \frac{f(X+h)-f(X)}{h} - \frac{h}{2!}f''(X) - \frac{h^2}{3!}f'''(X)-\cdots, \qquad (2.4)$$

then it is clear that, as long as h is small, the first term on the right-hand side gives an estimate of $f'(X)$. The estimate is based on the gradient of a chord connecting the two values $f(X)$ and $f(X+h)$, as shown in Fig. 2.2. This estimate is a *forward-difference estimate* since it gives the slope at $x=X$ from the value of $f(X)$ and the value at one increment of x in the forward direction, that is, $f(X+h)$. Similarly, a *backward-difference estimate* can also be made

Table 2.1 Taylor series estimates with four terms included.

h	$\pi/4+h$	$\sin(\pi/4+h)$ (estimated)	$\sin(\pi/4+h)$ (true)	Error	Estimated range of $|error|$ from (2.2)
$-\pi/4$	0	$-0.009\,274$	$0.000\,000$	$-0.009\,274$	$0.000\,000$–$0.011\,211$
$\pi/12$	$\pi/3$	$0.865\,880$	$0.866\,025$	$-0.000\,145$	$0.000\,138$–$0.000\,170$
$\pi/4$	$\pi/2$	$0.987\,282$	$1.000\,000$	$-0.012\,718$	$0.011\,211$–$0.015\,854$

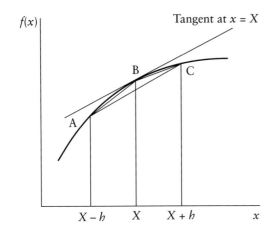

Fig. 2.2 Estimates of $f'(x)$ from: forward difference (slope of chord BC); backward difference (slope of chord AB); and central difference (slope of chord AC).

from

$$f'(X) \approx \frac{f(X) - f(X-h)}{h}. \tag{2.5}$$

The errors in both the forward-difference and the backward-difference estimates of slope are roughly proportional to h, assuming that the first term neglected in (2.4) is the dominant one. This can be written as

$$f'(X) = \frac{f(X+h) - f(X)}{h} + O(h). \tag{2.6}$$

The error is indicated as $+O(h)$, but that is not to say that the error is necessarily positive.

A much better estimate of $f(X)$ can be made from the chord connecting the points at $X-h$ and $X+h$, as shown in Fig. 2.2. From

$$f(X+h) = f(X) + hf'(X) + \frac{h^2}{2!} f''(X) + \frac{h^3}{3!} f'''(X) + \frac{h^4}{4!} f^{(4)}(X) + \cdots$$

$$f(X-h) = f(X) - hf'(X) + \frac{h^2}{2!} f''(X) - \frac{h^3}{3!} f'''(X) + \frac{h^4}{4!} f^{(4)}(X) - \cdots \tag{2.7}$$

we obtain by subtraction and rearrangement

2·7 → Subtraction 2·8

2·7 → Addition 2·9.

$$f'(X) = \frac{f(X+h) - f(X-h)}{2h} + O(h^2). \tag{2.8}$$

The fact that the estimate from (2.8), the *central-difference estimate*, has an error dependent on h^2, rather than on h, makes it a better estimate than is given by either (2.5) or (2.6).

Table 2.2   Values of x and $\sin(x)$ for obtaining finite-difference estimates of derivatives.

x	$\sin(x)$
$\pi/8$	0.382 683
$3\pi/16$	0.555 570
$\pi/4$	0.707 107
$5\pi/16$	0.831 470
$3\pi/8$	0.923 880

We can illustrate the above analysis by finding estimates of $d\sin(x)/dx$ at $x=\pi/4$ (for which the true value is 0.707 107) using the data given in Table 2.2. We find the following: $\cos\frac{\pi}{4} = \sqrt{\frac{1}{2}} = \sqrt{.50} = .7$

Difference	h	Estimate	Error
Forward	$\pi/16$	0.633 376	-0.073731
Forward	$\pi/8$	0.552 008	-0.155099
Central	$\pi/16$	0.702 574	-0.004533
Central	$\pi/8$	0.689 073	-0.018034

The interval in x, $h=\pi/16$, is a fairly large one, but the example illustrates the much higher precision of the central-difference estimate. We can also see that when h is doubled the error in the forward estimate approximately doubles but the error in the central-difference estimate increases by a factor of 4, that is, it is proportional to h^2. These estimates are referred to as *finite-difference estimates* of the first derivative.

We now turn our attention to the second derivative. This can also be expressed in a finite-difference form by manipulation of equations (2.7). Adding the equations and rearranging,

$$f''(X) = \frac{f(X+h)+f(X-h)-2f(X)}{h^2} + O(h^2). \tag{2.9}$$

Applying equation (2.9), and again using Table 2.2, we find the following estimates for $d^2\sin(x)/dx^2$, for which the true value for $x=\pi/4$ is -0.707107:

h	Estimate	Error
$\pi/16$	-0.704845	0.002 262
$\pi/8$	-0.698069	0.009 038

Again, the dependence of the error on h^2 is evident.

2.2 The use of finite differences

Consider the following problem, illustrated in Fig. 2.3. A bar of length 1 m has a circular cross-section, the radius of which varies linearly from 2 cm at one end to 1 cm at the other. The curved sides of the bar are heavily lagged and the wide end and narrow end are constrained to be at temperatures 500 K and 300 K respectively. The thermal conductivity of the material of the bar is $200\,\mathrm{W\,m^{-1}K^{-1}}$. Find the rate of heat flow along the bar and also determine the temperature at intervals of 10 cm along its length.

The lagging ensures that the heat flow is along the length of the bar to a good approximation, despite its truncated conical form, so we may treat it as a one-dimensional problem. The usual equation for one-dimensional heat flow is

$$Q = -\kappa A \frac{\mathrm{d}\theta}{\mathrm{d}x}, \qquad (2.10)$$

where Q is the rate of heat flow, κ the thermal conductivity, A the cross-sectional area and θ the temperature. In this case we have a variable cross-section and can express A as a function of distance along the bar as

$$A = \pi \left\{ \frac{2-x}{100} \right\}^2 \mathrm{m}^2. \qquad (2.11)$$

Inserting the numerical value of κ and rearranging, the problem comes to that of solving

$$\frac{\mathrm{d}\theta}{\mathrm{d}x} = -\frac{50Q}{\pi(2-x)^2}, \qquad (2.12)$$

with boundary conditions $\theta = 500\,\mathrm{K}$ when $x = 0$ and $\theta = 300\,\mathrm{K}$ when $x = 1\,\mathrm{m}$. Although this is a first-order ordinary differential equation, which normally

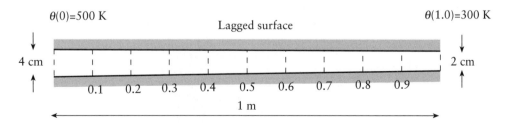

Fig. 2.3 A bar of truncated conical form. Temperatures are required at the cross-sections marked, which are 10 cm apart.

requires just one boundary condition, in this case two boundary conditions are imposed and the equation contains an a priori unknown quantity, Q.

2.2.1 *The shooting method*

One way of solving this kind of *boundary-value problem* is by the *shooting method*. A first estimate for Q is made, for example, by assuming that the bar has a uniform cross-section equal to the average cross-section and then using (2.10) with a uniform temperature gradient. Starting with the boundary condition at $x=0$ the equation is then solved by, say, the Runge–Kutta method to $x=1\,\mathrm{m}$. The temperature will usually not match the imposed boundary condition. If the temperature found is lower than $300\,\mathrm{K}$ it shows that the assumed value of Q is too high. A lower estimate is made of Q and from the solution of the differential equation another value for the temperature at $x=1\,\mathrm{m}$ is found. In this way it is possible systematically to find the correct value of Q by successive approximations.

The program SHOOTEMP (see p. xv) carries out this type of process. Variation of a statement function at the beginning of the programme adapts it to solve other problems. The average area of cross-section of the bar is, approximately, $\bar{A}=\pi(0.02^2+0.01^2)/2\,\mathrm{m}^2$ and the corresponding uniform temperature gradient is $(300-500)/1\,\mathrm{K\,m^{-1}}$. Inserting these values in (2.10) gives an approximate value of $30\,\mathrm{W}$ for Q. The steps in the successive approximations using SHOOTEMP, with $h=0.01\,\mathrm{m}$, are as given in Table 2.3. For the final value of Q, which gave the correct second boundary condition, the temperatures at intermediate points of the bar are given in Table 2.4.

The approach to the correct solution in Table 2.3 was by an approximate process of linear interpolation. Thus the target value for $\theta(1.0)$ was $300\,\mathrm{K}$; for $Q=25.14\,\mathrm{W}$, $\theta(1.0)$ was $0.06\,\mathrm{K}$ below while for $25.13\,\mathrm{W}$ it was $0.02\,\mathrm{K}$ above.

Table 2.3 Successive estimations of Q and the corresponding temperature at the end of the bar. An analytical solution gives $Q=8\pi(25.1327)$.

Estimated Q (W)	$\theta(1.0)$ (K)
30.0	261.27
25.0	301.06
25.1	300.26
25.2	299.46
25.14	299.94
25.13	300.02
25.1325	300.00

Table 2.4 Temperatures at intervals of 10 cm along the bar for the result in the final row of Table 2.3.

x (m)	θ(x) (K)	x (m)	θ(x) (K)
0.0	500.0	0.6	414.3
0.1	489.5	0.7	392.3
0.2	477.8	0.8	366.6
0.3	464.7	0.9	336.3
0.4	450.0	1.0	300.0
0.5	433.3		

This suggested that Q should be one-quarter of the way from 25.13 W to 25.14 W. Clearly such a process of linear interpolation could be incorporated in the program so that the answer was found automatically.

2.2.2 Solution by linear equations

There is another type of computational process, using finite differences, which can solve this type of boundary-value problem without going through successive approximations. In the steady state the value of Q must be the same for all cross-sections of the bar. If the values of θ at $N+1$ equally-spaced points $x_0, x_1, \ldots, x_N$ are $\theta_0, \theta_1, \ldots, \theta_N$ then, from (2.10), for points i and $i+1$ we can write

$$\left(\frac{d\theta}{dx}\right)_i A_i = \left(\frac{d\theta}{dx}\right)_{i+1} A_{i+1}, \qquad (2.13)$$

where A_i is the cross-sectional area at the point i. If we represent $(d\theta/dx)_{i-1/2}$, the gradient at the point mid-way between points $i-1$ and i, by the central-difference estimate, $(\theta_i - \theta_{i-1})/h$, where h is the spacing of the points, then we are able to write for $i=1$ to $N-1$ a set of central-difference-based equations

$$\left(2 - \frac{i-1/2}{N}\right)^2 (\theta_i - \theta_{i-1}) = \left(2 - \frac{i+1/2}{N}\right)^2 (\theta_{i+1} - \theta_i)$$

or

$$\left(2 - \frac{i-1/2}{N}\right)^2 \theta_{i-1} - \left(8 + \frac{1}{2N^2}[1+4i^2] - \frac{8i}{N}\right)\theta_i + \left(2 - \frac{i+1/2}{N}\right)^2 \theta_{i+1} = 0.$$

$$(2.14)$$

The squared quantities are proportional to the areas at the points $i-1/2$ and $i+1/2$, respectively. If the bar is divided into five segments, so $N=5$, then for points $i=1,2,3,4$ this gives a set of equations

$$
\begin{aligned}
-6.50\theta_1+2.89\theta_2 &= -3.61\theta_0 & \text{(2.15a)} \\
2.89\theta_1-5.14\theta_2+2.25\theta_3 &=0 & \text{(2.15b)} \\
2.25\theta_2-3.94\theta_3+1.69\theta_4 &=0 & \text{(2.15c)} \\
1.69\theta_3-2.90\theta_4 &= -1.21\theta_5 & \text{(2.15d)}
\end{aligned}
$$

Since the boundary conditions, θ_0 and θ_5, are fixed, this set of equations is easily solved. Equation (2.15a) gives θ_1 in terms of θ_2; substitution for θ_1 in terms of θ_2 in (2.15b) gives θ_2 in terms of θ_3 and substitution for θ_2 in terms of θ_3 in (2.15c) gives θ_3 in terms of θ_4. Finally, substitution for θ_3 in terms of θ_4 in (2.15d) gives an explicit solution for θ_4. Then, by working backwards through the steps the other values of θ can also be found.

This systematic approach to the solution of equations (2.15) arises because of their particular form. The matrix of non-zero coefficients on the left-hand side of the equations has the pattern

$$
\begin{bmatrix}
x & x & & & & & & & & \\
x & x & x & & & & & & & \\
 & x & x & x & & & & & & \\
 & & x & x & x & & & & & \\
 & & & x & x & x & & & & \\
 & & & & x & x & x & & & \\
 & & & & & x & x & x & & \\
 & & & & & & x & x & x & \\
 & & & & & & & x & x & x \\
 & & & & & & & & x & x
\end{bmatrix}. \qquad \text{(2.16)}
$$

This pattern of coefficients gives what is called a *tridiagonal matrix*. The subroutine TRIDIAG (see p. xv) follows the procedure described above, with first forward and then backward substitution, to solve a set of equations with coefficients of the appropriate form. This subroutine is used with the main program HEATRI (see p. xv) to solve the temperature profile problem. The value of N is taken as 100, corresponding to the integration step length $h=0.01$ for the shooting method, and the results for temperature are exactly as given in Table 2.4. The value of Q is deduced from (2.10) by estimating the temperature gradient from the temperatures at $i=0$ and $i=1$ with the cross-sectional area at $i=1/2$. This value of Q, 25.131 W, is slightly different from that found from the shooting method.

The problem we have dealt with here is a one-dimensional steady-state problem with only one independent variable which entailed the solution of a first-order ordinary differential equation. However, many problems of physical interest are not steady-state, so that time is introduced as another independent variable, and/or may be in more than one dimension, which also increases the number of independent variables. Such problems are often expressed in the form of partial differential equations and we shall now see how to generalize the finite-difference concept into these areas by application to the simple diffusion equation.

2.3   The diffusion equation

In Fig. 2.4 we show a section of a column of solution, of uniform unit cross-section, with a varying concentration along its length. We may describe the concentration, n, as the number of particles of solute (the dissolved substance) per unit volume. Unless the concentration is uniform there will be a constant net passage of solute from more concentrated to less concentrated regions so the concentration will be continuously changing in both space and time.

If there is a gradient of concentration, $(\partial n/\partial x)_x$, at the cross-section A, at height x, then in a short time δt there will be a net transfer of particles in the positive x direction across A of

$$\delta N_x = -D\left(\frac{\partial n}{\partial x}\right)_x \delta t. \tag{2.17}$$

This relationship is known as Fick's law, and D is the coefficient of diffusion.

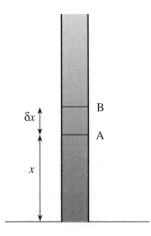

Fig. 2.4   A column of solution with a concentration gradient.

At cross-section B, a further distance of δx along the column, the corresponding transfer of particles in the positive x direction is

$$\delta N_{x+\delta x} = -D\left(\frac{\partial n}{\partial x}\right)_{x+\delta x} \delta t. \tag{2.18}$$

We now use

$$\left(\frac{\partial n}{\partial x}\right)_{x+\delta x} = \left(\frac{\partial n}{\partial x}\right)_x + \left(\frac{\partial^2 n}{\partial x^2}\right)_x \delta x, \tag{2.19}$$

which is a two-term Taylor series representation of the left-hand side. In (2.19), $(\partial n/\partial x)_x$ is playing the role of $f(x)$ in (2.1).

The net flow of particles into the region between A and B, which has volume δx, gives a change of concentration

$$\lim_{\delta x \to 0} (\delta n) = \lim_{\delta x \to 0} \left(\frac{\delta N_x - \delta N_{x+\delta x}}{\delta x}\right) = D\frac{\partial^2 n}{\partial x^2}\delta t$$

and hence

$$\lim_{\delta t \to 0}\left(\frac{\delta n}{\delta t}\right) = \frac{\partial n}{\partial t} = D\frac{\partial^2 n}{\partial x^2}.$$

The partial differential equation

$$\frac{\partial n}{\partial t} = D\frac{\partial^2 n}{\partial x^2} \tag{2.20}$$

is known as the *diffusion equation*, and its general form describes a range of physical situations. For example, if the problem involved heat flow in the x direction in a bar of uniform cross-section, well lagged except at its ends, then the corresponding equation for temperature, θ, along the bar would be

$$\frac{\partial \theta}{\partial t} = \frac{\kappa}{c\rho}\frac{\partial^2 \theta}{\partial x^2}, \tag{2.21}$$

where κ is the thermal conductivity of the material of the bar, c its specific heat capacity and ρ its density.

The nature of diffusion expresses physical behaviour in terms of time development. Thus we know the physical state, that is, the value of the state variable (n or θ) as a function of space at a specified initial time. Physically the system develops in time as the state changes in space subject to known conditions at the boundaries. Problems which develop in this way are known as *initial-value problems*. The reversal of time in such problems – that is to say, running the problem backwards – always leads to chaotic behaviour.

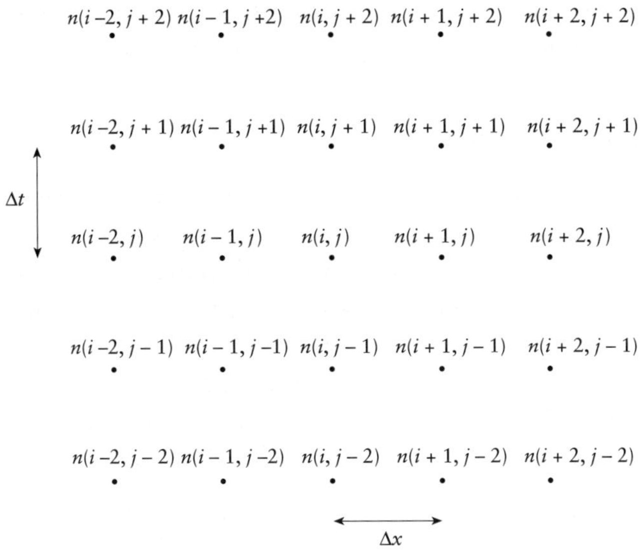

$n(i-2, j+2)$ $n(i-1, j+2)$ $n(i, j+2)$ $n(i+1, j+2)$ $n(i+2, j+2)$

$n(i-2, j+1)$ $n(i-1, j+1)$ $n(i, j+1)$ $n(i+1, j+1)$ $n(i+2, j+1)$

Δt $n(i-2, j)$ $n(i-1, j)$ $n(i, j)$ $n(i+1, j)$ $n(i+2, j)$

$n(i-2, j-1)$ $n(i-1, j-1)$ $n(i, j-1)$ $n(i+1, j-1)$ $n(i+2, j-1)$

$n(i-2, j-2)$ $n(i-1, j-2)$ $n(i, j-2)$ $n(i+1, j-2)$ $n(i+2, j-2)$

Δx

Fig. 2.5 Concentrations at points separated by Δx and times separated by Δt.

2.4 Finite-difference representation of partial derivatives

In Fig. 2.5 we show a grid, at the points of which are given the concentrations at different positions and times for the column of solution in Fig. 2.4. The separation of the grid points in the horizontal direction, Δx, gives equispaced positions along the bar which are labelled $i-2$, $i-1$, i, $i+1$,..., while in the vertical direction the separations Δt correspond to equal time intervals and the different time points are labelled $j-2$, $j-1$, j, $j+1$,.... By analogy with (2.8) and (2.9), we write the following finite-difference approximations:

$$\left(\frac{\partial n}{\partial t}\right)_{i,j} = \frac{n(i,j+1)-n(i,j-1)}{2\Delta t}, \tag{2.22}$$

$$\left(\frac{\partial^2 n}{\partial t^2}\right)_{i,j} = \frac{n(i,j+1)+n(i,j-1)-2n(i,j)}{(\Delta t)^2} \tag{2.23}$$

$$\left(\frac{\partial n}{\partial x}\right)_{i,j} = \frac{n(i+1,j)-n(i-1,j)}{2\Delta x} \tag{2.24}$$

$$\left(\frac{\partial^2 n}{\partial x^2}\right)_{i,j} = \frac{n(i+1,j)+n(i-1,j)-2n(i,j)}{(\Delta x)^2} \tag{2.25}$$

We shall now see how to apply these finite-difference representations in a variety of ways to the solution of the diffusion equation.

2.5   The explicit method

The aim in solving a diffusion problem is to determine the time evolution of the concentration (or other quantity such as temperature) at a number of representative points of the system. Thus if all the concentrations are known at time t_j then one step of the process is to determine them at time $t_{j+1} = t_j + \Delta t$. If this can be done, then, given the initial state, the pattern of concentrations can be found at all future times. The easiest form of finite-difference equation corresponding to (2.20) is found by using a forward-difference form for $\partial n / \partial t$ rather than the central-difference form (2.22). This gives

$$\frac{n(i,j+1) - n(i,j)}{\Delta t} = D \frac{n(i+1,j) + n(i-1,j) - 2n(i,j)}{(\Delta x)^2}$$

or

$$n(i,j+1) = r\{n(i+1,j) + n(i-1,j)\} + (1-2r)n(i,j), \qquad (2.26)$$

where

$$r = \frac{D\Delta t}{(\Delta x)^2}. \qquad (2.27)$$

If boundary conditions are known – for example, as fixed concentrations at the two ends of the column (or temperatures at the ends of a bar) – then (2.26) enables concentrations at all points at time t_{j+1} to be found explicitly from the concentrations at time t_j. We can illustrate this by considering the heat flow in a bar of length 1 m, well lagged except for the two ends, with a uniform cross-section, thermal conductivity $200\,\mathrm{W\,m^{-1}K^{-1}}$, specific heat capacity $1000\,\mathrm{J\,kg^{-1}K^{-1}}$ and density $2700\,\mathrm{kg\,m^{-3}}$. Initially the bar is at a uniform temperature of $300\,\mathrm{K}$ but the two ends are maintained at temperatures of $300\,\mathrm{K}$ and $500\,\mathrm{K}$ respectively. The problem is to follow the sequence of temperature profiles in the bar to some steady-state condition. For this problem the value of r, corresponding to that given in (2.27), is

$$r = \frac{\kappa \Delta t}{\rho c (\Delta x)^2}. \qquad (2.28)$$

With $\Delta x = 0.1\,\mathrm{m}$, r can be made a convenient value by the right choice of Δt. Thus with $\Delta t = 33.75\,\mathrm{s}$, $r = 0.25$ and θ representing temperature, equation (2.26) takes the form

$$\theta(i,j+1) = 0.25\{\theta(i+1,j) + \theta(i-1,j)\} + 0.5\theta(i,j). \qquad (2.29)$$

The progression of temperatures for the first two time steps is as follows:

```
300 300 300 300 300 300 300 300  300   300  500
300 300 300 300 300 300 300 300  300   350  500
300 300 300 300 300 300 300 300  312.5 375  500
```

The calculation is easily programmed and graphical results from the program HEATEX (see p. xv) are shown in Fig. 2.6 with $r = 0.25$. It will be seen that as time progresses so the temperature profile goes towards a straight line, corresponding to a uniform value of $\partial\theta/\partial x$. From (2.21) it is seen that this will make the right-hand side, and hence the left-hand side, equal to zero – which is the steady-state equilibrium position.

To see the effect of changing the value of r, Table 2.5 shows the results for a run of total time 1200 s but with various values of Δt, and hence of r. It is possible to find an analytical solution of (2.21) with the required boundary conditions for all x and t in the form of an infinite sum of Fourier terms. However, an examination of Table 2.5 shows that as the time interval becomes smaller so the solution tends towards a particular temperature profile which we may take to be close to the analytical solution.

What we see is that as Δt, and thus the value of r, increases so the error increases but in a steady and monotonic way. However, for the very last value of Δt, 75 s, where $r = 0.556$, the solution is drastically different; it oscillates as x increases, has internal values lower than 300 K, the lower boundary condition, and is clearly an unphysical solution. It will not seem surprising that there is a breakdown in the solution as Δt increases since the finite-difference approximations become less valid.

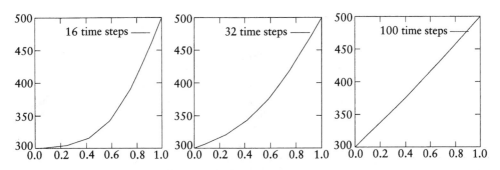

Fig. 2.6   Output from HEATEX.

Just by considering the validity of the finite-difference approximations then, as Δx and Δt are made increasingly smaller, so we might expect the numerical solution to approach ever closer to the analytical one. To test this assumption in Table 2.6, we give the values from HEATEX at $x = 0.2$, 0.4, 0.6 and 0.8 m for a run with a total simulated time of 100 s with a constant $\Delta t = 1$ s, which should give a good finite-difference approximation to $\partial n/\partial t$, albeit a forward-difference one, and values of Δx which steadily decrease. What we find is that when Δx is reduced below a certain limit the solution becomes wildly unstable. An examination of Tables 2.5 and 2.6 would lead us to the conclusion that for stable behaviour r should be less than about 0.5 but that, within that constraint, Δx and Δt should be as small as possible. Later, by an analytical approach, we shall show that these conclusions are indeed valid.

Table 2.5 Runs of HEATEX for a total simulated time of 1200 s for various values of Δt (and r) with $\Delta x = 0.1$. Values are given at internal points only since the boundary conditions are fixed.

Δt (s)	r	x								
		0.1	0.2	0.3	0.4	0.5	0.6	0.7	0.8	0.9
1	0.007	304.8	310.8	319.2	330.9	347.1	368.5	395.3	426.9	462.4
2	0.015	304.8	310.8	319.2	330.9	347.2	368.5	395.3	427.0	462.4
5	0.037	304.8	310.9	319.2	331.0	347.2	368.6	395.3	427.0	462.5
10	0.074	304.8	310.9	319.2	331.0	347.3	368.7	395.5	427.1	462.5
20	0.148	304.8	310.9	319.2	331.1	347.5	368.9	395.7	427.3	462.6
30	0.222	304.8	310.9	319.3	331.2	347.6	369.1	395.9	427.5	462.8
40	0.296	304.8	310.9	319.3	331.3	347.8	369.4	396.2	427.7	462.9
50	0.370	304.8	310.9	319.4	331.4	348.0	369.6	396.4	427.9	463.0
60	0.444	304.8	310.9	319.4	331.5	348.1	369.8	396.6	428.1	463.1
75	0.556	297.5	326.1	296.1	363.2	310.6	410.6	359.0	458.0	446.9

Table 2.6 Results from HEATEX for a run of simulated time 100 s with $\Delta t = 1$ s and $\Delta x = (1/N)$m. The temperatures are given at four internal points.

N	r	x (m)			
		0.2	0.4	0.6	0.8
5	0.0019	300.01	300.16	302.69	331.16
10	0.0074	300.00	300.01	300.82	323.47
20	0.0296	300.00	300.00	300.34	320.93
40	0.1185	300.00	300.00	300.22	320.30
80	0.4741	300.00	300.00	300.19	320.15
85	0.5352	300.00	299.31	1876.6	-8.380×10^4
90	0.6000	304.79	2.136×10^7	3.544×10^{11}	5.638×10^{13}
95	0.6685	2.021×10^5	-3.649×10^{13}	5.215×10^{18}	-2.658×10^{21}
100	0.7407	5.457×10^8	6.553×10^{18}	9.609×10^{24}	1.689×10^{28}

2.6 The Crank–Nicholson implicit method

In the explicit method the finite-difference representation of $\partial\theta/\partial t$ was in the forward-difference form

$$\frac{\partial\theta}{\partial t} = \frac{\theta(i,j+1)-\theta(i,j)}{\Delta t}. \tag{2.30}$$

It would be equally valid to consider the right-hand side of (2.30) as a central-difference representation of $\partial\theta/\partial t$ centred on the space–time point $(i,j+\frac{1}{2})$. Now from (2.25) we have

$$\left(\frac{\partial^2\theta}{\partial x^2}\right)_{i,j} = \frac{\theta(i+1,j)+\theta(i-1,j)-2\theta(i,j)}{(\Delta x)^2}, \tag{2.31}$$

and similarly,

$$\left(\frac{\partial^2\theta}{\partial x^2}\right)_{i,j+1} = \frac{\theta(i+1,j+1)+\theta(i-1,j+1)-2\theta(i,j+1)}{(\Delta x)^2}. \tag{2.32}$$

In the Crank–Nicholson method the second partial derivative $(\partial^2\theta/\partial x^2)_{i,j+(1/2)}$ is expressed as an average of (2.31) and (2.32), so that the heat-transfer finite-difference equation, centred on the point $(i,j+\frac{1}{2})$, becomes

$$\frac{\theta(i,j+1)-\theta(i,j)}{\Delta t} = \frac{\kappa}{2\rho c}\left\{\frac{\theta(i+1,j)+\theta(i-1,j)-2\theta(i,j)}{(\Delta x)^2}\right.$$

$$\left. + \frac{\theta(i+1,j+1)+\theta(i-1,j+1)-2\theta(i,j+1)}{(\Delta x)^2}\right\},$$

or, with rearrangement,

$$-r\theta(i-1,j+1)+2(1+r)\theta(i,j+1)-r\theta(i+1,j+1)$$

$$= r\theta(i-1,j)+2(1-r)\theta(i,j)+r\theta(i+1,j), \tag{2.33}$$

where r is defined in (2.28). In Fig. 2.7, which is similar to Fig. 2.5, we show the terms which occur in the Crank–Nicholson equation. It is an *implicit* equation in that knowledge of the solution at time t_j gives functional (linear) relationships between the values at different points at time t_{j+1} and does not give each of the t_{j+1} values explicitly, as happens with the use of (2.26). Given that the right-hand side is known, then, with known boundary conditions, the coefficients of the terms on the left-hand side form a tridiagonal matrix which we previously met in Section 2.2.

A program HEATCRNI is available (see p. xv) for solving one-dimensional heat-flow problems by the Crank–Nicholson method; the program differs from HEATEX only in the subroutine CYCLE. It also needs to be linked with the subroutine TRIDIAG. We now apply HEATCRNI to the problem described in Section 2.5 for various values of Δt and corresponding r. Table 2.7 gives the results for a total simulated time of 1200 s with values of r ranging up to 8.8889. It is clear in this case that values of r much larger than 0.5, the value at which the explicit method became unstable, still give stable, although not necessarily accurate, results for the implicit method. The values of temperature gradually drift with increasing r but no physically unrealistic results occur until r becomes

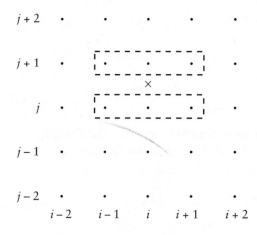

Fig. 2.7 The Crank–Nicholson equations are centred on the point $(i, j+\frac{1}{2})$ marked by a cross. The finite-difference representations involve the six terms contained in the dashed boxes.

Table 2.7 Runs of HEATCRNI for a total simulated time of 1200 s for various values of Δt (and r) with $\Delta x = 0.1$. Values are given at internal points only since the boundary conditions are fixed.

Δt (s)	r	x								
		0.1	0.2	0.3	0.4	0.5	0.6	0.7	0.8	0.9
10	0.074	304.8	310.8	319.2	330.9	347.1	368.5	395.2	426.9	462.4
20	0.148	304.8	310.8	319.2	330.9	347.1	368.5	395.2	426.9	462.4
30	0.222	304.8	310.8	319.2	330.9	347.1	368.5	395.2	426.9	462.4
40	0.296	304.8	310.8	319.2	330.9	347.1	368.5	395.2	426.9	462.4
50	0.370	304.8	310.8	319.2	330.9	347.1	368.5	395.2	426.9	462.4
60	0.444	304.8	310.8	319.2	330.9	347.1	368.5	395.3	426.9	462.4
80	0.593	304.8	310.8	319.1	330.9	347.1	368.5	395.3	427.0	462.4
100	0.741	304.8	310.8	319.1	330.9	347.1	368.5	395.3	427.0	462.5
120	0.889	304.8	310.8	319.1	330.9	347.1	368.6	395.3	427.0	462.5
150	1.111	304.8	310.8	319.1	330.9	347.2	368.6	395.4	427.1	462.5
200	1.482	304.8	310.7	319.1	330.9	347.2	368.7	395.4	427.3	462.5
300	2.222	304.6	310.5	318.9	330.9	347.4	368.5	395.2	429.9	460.0
400	2.963	304.5	310.2	318.5	330.8	348.1	370.3	395.1	421.5	473.2
600	4.444	304.1	309.3	317.1	328.9	347.0	372.8	405.7	436.2	431.6
1200	8.889	303.5	307.9	314.0	323.3	337.8	360.8	397.5	456.2	550.0

greater than about 3, as is seen in the last two rows of the table when the change of temperature along the bar is no longer monotonic. In terms of computational effort the extra work per cycle in the implicit method is compensated by it being possible to take larger time steps and hence to reduce the number of cycles.

In Table 2.7 the interval Δx has been kept fixed and Δt and r have varied. We expect that as Δt becomes smaller so the calculated temperatures at the internal points of the bar will tend towards values which are better estimates – as long as the numerical algorithm is stable. The reason for this is that the finite-difference formula for $\partial \theta / \partial t$ given by (2.30) is more accurate the smaller is the value of Δt. As previously mentioned, we might also expect to obtain better estimates if we use smaller values of Δx, and it is clear from (2.28) that we can make both Δx and Δt smaller while retaining constant the value of r. Table 2.8 shows the temperature estimates at four internal points of the bar, at $x = 0.2$, 0.4, 0.6 and 0.8, where the calculations have been done with various values of Δx and Δt but always with $r = 0.8889$.

It can be seen that as both Δx and Δt become smaller so the results tend to converge towards a particular solution. In Table 2.8 the value for $x = 0.8$ m in the final row shows a rise of 0.1, but this is due to a combination of round-off error in the computer and rounding off the printed output to one place of decimals. To reach a total simulated time of 480 s there were 1024 cycles of the Crank–Nicholson process in each of which a tridiagonal matrix of 159 rows was processed, and there is bound to be some error due to the limited precision of the representation of numbers in the computer. Actually when all the calculations giving Table 2.8 are repeated with double-precision real numbers it is found that the indicated temperature for $x = 0.8$ m does slightly rise between $\Delta t = 1.875$ and $\Delta t = 0.46\,875$ from 390.647 464 to 390.650 045. For $r > \frac{1}{2}$ the Crank–Nicholson method can produce 'oscillatory' solutions. In this case it appears as an oscillation superimposed on the exact solution.

Table 2.8 Temperature estimates at four internal points of the bar. Values of Δx and Δt are reduced together such that $r = 0.8889$. The total simulated time is 480 s.

Δx (m)	Δt (s)	x (m)			
		0.2	0.4	0.6	0.8
0.20 000	480	301.5	306.2	325.0	400.0
0.10 000	120	300.8	305.4	327.2	391.0
0.05 000	30	300.6	305.0	326.9	390.6
0.02 500	7.5	300.6	304.9	326.8	390.6
0.01 250	1.875	300.5	304.9	326.7	390.6
0.00 625	0.46 875	300.5	304.9	326.7	390.7

2.7 Differential boundary conditions

The heat-flow problems which have been considered so far have involved
boundary conditions where the temperatures at the boundaries have been
either constant or a known function of time. In Fig. 2.8 we illustrate a problem
in which other kinds of boundary conditions can occur. The bar of uniform
cross-section and length L is buried in insulated material except for one
end-face which is in an enclosure maintained at a fixed temperature. The heat
flow through the bar must be parallel to the axis of the bar and this will be
zero through the left-hand insulated face. The equation corresponding to
(2.17) for heat flow is

$$\delta Q_x = -\frac{\kappa}{\rho c}\left(\frac{\partial\theta}{\partial x}\right)_x \delta t, \qquad (2.34)$$

and since δQ_x is zero at the insulated face then so must be the gradient of
temperature at that face.

The right-hand face will, in general, be at a temperature which is different
from that of the enclosure and will exchange heat with it by radiation. If the
end of the bar absorbs and radiates as a black body then the net rate of heat
loss through the exposed end will be

$$H = A\sigma(\theta_4^4 - \theta_{\text{ext}}^4) \qquad (2.35)$$

where A is the cross-sectional area of the bar, σ is the Stefan constant, θ_4 the
temperature of the exposed end of the bar and θ_{ext} is the temperature of the
enclosure. If the quantities are in SI units then H will be in watts.

Both these boundary conditions can be accommodated by the use of what
are known as *false points*. The bar is divided into four sections delineated by
the equidistant points labelled $0, 1, 2, 3, 4$. Two extra points, with the same
spacing, are added outside the bar as shown and labelled -1 and 5. For the

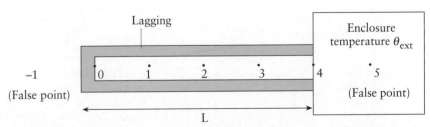

Fig. 2.8 A uniform bar, lagged except for one end in a temperature enclosure.

interior points the explicit equations are used:

$$\theta(1,j+1)=r\theta(0,j)+(1-2r)\theta(1,j)+r\theta(2,j) \tag{2.36a}$$

$$\theta(2,j+1)=r\theta(1,j)+(1-2r)\theta(2,j)+r\theta(3,j) \tag{2.36b}$$

$$\theta(3,j+1)=r\theta(2,j)+(1-2r)\theta(3,j)+r\theta(4,j). \tag{2.36c}$$

For the end-points we use the false positions, so that

$$\theta(0,j+1)=r\theta(-1,j)+(1-2r)\theta(0,j)+r\theta(1,j) \tag{2.37a}$$

$$\theta(4,j+1)=r\theta(3,j)+(1-2r)\theta(4,j)+r\theta(5,j). \tag{2.37b}$$

Since there is no heat flow across the insulated end, the slope of the temperature must be zero and if this is represented by the central-difference formula then it is clear that $\theta(-1,j)=\theta(1,j)$, so that we may rewrite (2.37a) as

$$\theta(0,j+1)=2r\theta(1,j)+(1-2r)\theta(0,j). \tag{2.38a}$$

At the exposed end of the bar, where $x=L$, the slope must be such as to give the heat flow $Q=H$, that is,

$$-\kappa A \frac{\partial \theta}{\partial x} = A\sigma(\theta_4^4-\theta_{\text{ext}}^4). \tag{2.39}$$

Using the central-difference representation of the partial derivative on the left-hand side and rearranging, we find

$$\theta(5,j)=\theta(3,j)-\frac{2\sigma\Delta x}{\kappa}\{\theta(4,j)^4-\theta_{\text{ext}}^4\}. \tag{2.40}$$

Substituting this value of $\theta(5,j)$, equation (2.37b) becomes

$$\theta(4,j+1)=2r\theta(3,j)+(1-2r)\theta(4,j)-\frac{2r\sigma\Delta x}{\kappa}r\{\theta(4,j)^4-\theta_{\text{ext}}^4\}. \tag{2.38b}$$

Equations (2.36) plus the modified equations (2.38) enable θ to be advanced in time.

The program RADBAR (see p. xv) solves these equations. There is a standard problem provided with the program, for which $\kappa=401\,\text{W}\,\text{m}^{-1}\text{K}^{-1}$, $c=386\,\text{J}\,\text{kg}^{-1}\text{K}^{-1}$, $\rho=8920\,\text{kg}\,\text{m}^{-3}$, $\theta_{\text{ext}}=290\,\text{K}$ and the bar, of length $1.0\,\text{m}$, has a uniform initial temperature of $500\,\text{K}$. Table 2.9 shows the results of running the program with eight intervals in the bar and with values of

Finite-difference methods

Table 2.9 Temperatures given by RADBAR for different values of r and different elapsed times.

r	Time (s)	Distance from exposed end of bar (m)								
		0.000	0.125	0.250	0.375	0.500	0.625	0.750	0.875	1.000
0.10	40.2	393.2	484.0	499.2	500.0	500.0	500.0	500.0	500.0	500.0
	80.4	380.0	463.7	493.6	499.4	500.0	500.0	500.0	500.0	500.0
	120.6	372.6	449.1	486.1	497.4	499.7	500.0	500.0	500.0	500.0
	160.8	367.2	438.2	478.5	494.2	498.9	499.8	500.0	500.0	500.0
	402.5	350.0	403.3	444.5	471.8	487.4	495.0	498.3	499.4	499.7
0.15	40.2	387.2	482.3	500.0	500.0	500.0	500.0	500.0	500.0	500.0
	80.4	378.6	461.5	493.8	499.6	500.0	500.0	500.0	500.0	500.0
	120.6	371.6	447.5	485.8	497.6	499.8	500.0	500.0	500.0	500.0
	160.8	366.4	436.9	478.0	494.5	499.1	499.9	500.0	500.0	500.0
	402.5	349.7	402.7	443.9	471.5	487.3	495.1	498.4	499.5	499.8
0.20	26.8	342.9	500.0	500.0	500.0	500.0	500.0	500.0	500.0	500.0
	53.6	386.9	468.6	500.0	500.0	500.0	500.0	500.0	500.0	500.0
	80.4	376.1	458.5	493.7	500.0	500.0	500.0	500.0	500.0	500.0
	107.2	372.4	449.0	487.9	498.7	500.0	500.0	500.0	500.0	500.0
	402.5	349.4	402.0	443.2	471.1	487.2	495.1	498.4	499.6	499.8
0.25	33.5	303.6	500.0	500.0	500.0	500.0	500.0	500.0	500.0	500.0
	67.0	396.8	450.9	500.0	500.0	500.0	500.0	500.0	500.0	500.0
	100.5	361.1	449.6	487.2	500.0	500.0	500.0	500.0	500.0	500.0
	134.0	370.2	437.0	481.3	496.9	500.0	500.0	500.0	500.0	500.0
	402.5	348.9	401.0	442.2	470.3	486.8	495.0	498.4	499.6	499.8
0.30	40.2	264.3	500.0	500.0	500.0	500.0	500.0	500.0	500.0	500.0
	80.4	415.1	429.3	500.0	500.0	500.0	500.0	500.0	500.0	500.0
	120.6	327.5	446.2	478.8	500.0	500.0	500.0	500.0	500.0	500.0
	160.8	379.9	420.4	475.4	493.6	500.0	500.0	500.0	500.0	500.0
	402.5	348.6	399.1	440.5	469.0	486.2	494.9	498.5	499.6	499.9
0.40	53.7	185.7	500.0	500.0	500.0	500.0	500.0	500.0	500.0	500.0
	107.4	470.0	374.3	500.0	500.0	500.0	500.0	500.0	500.0	500.0
	161.1	155.8	463.1	449.7	500.0	500.0	500.0	500.0	500.0	500.0
	214.8	438.4	334.8	475.2	479.9	500.0	500.0	500.0	500.0	500.0
	375.9	216.3	413.1	407.0	470.2	482.2	495.5	498.7	500.0	500.0

$r = 0.1, 0.15, 0.2, 0.25, 0.3$ and 0.4. For each run with a different value of r the temperatures are given for four times at equal intervals and then for the first five values of r at time $402.5\,\text{s}$ which they have in common. The expected behaviour pattern is that the temperature should gradually fall at the exposed end towards the external temperature and the cooling will move deeper into the bar as time progresses. The temperature should also fall monotonically from the insulated to the exposed end.

At the beginning of the process the form of the equations allows temperatures to change only by one space interval per time step. The number of time steps per output is three for $r = 0.10$, two for $r = 0.15$ and one for the other values of r. The results for $r=0.10$ and $r=0.15$ seem reasonably consistent, with the difference of temperature mostly less than 2 K. However, the results for 402.5 s agree to within 0.6 K. When we examine the results for $r=0.20$ a departure from expected behaviour is observed where it is seen that the temperature at the free end rises between $t=26.8$ s and $t=53.6$ s. The behaviour thereafter is as expected and the results for $t=402.5$ s agree with those for $r=0.10$ to within 1.3 K. The results for $r=0.25$, 0.3 and 0.4 show that as r increases so the initial oscillations of temperature at the free end become more severe but by $t=402.5$ s the temperatures along the bar for $r=0.25$ and $r=0.3$ are not too different from those for $r=0.1$. For $r=0.4$ the temperature at the radiating end of the bar is still oscillating at $t=375.9$ s and, in addition there are still fluctuations up and down along the bar. If the $r=0.4$ case is run for more than $t \sim 1000$ s, the behaviour settles down to that expected although the temperatures are 20 K or more different from those given at corresponding times with $r=0.1$.

In Section 2.5 we found that, for the explicit method, the system was quite stable for $r \leqslant 0.5$. Although we are considering an explicit method here, the nonlinearity in the equations introduced by the radiation from the end of the bar, as expressed in (2.38b), changes the conditions for stability. The equations *are* stable under the conditions we have examined since the solution does not run out of control but does eventually settle down to a reasonable behaviour pattern – even if the accuracy is poor. A good rule of thumb is that if two runs, with values of r differing by a factor of 2, give results at all times within the tolerance required then the results are probably reliable.

2.8 The Dufort–Frankel method

In the explicit method a forward difference is taken for the derivative in time and a central difference for the space derivative. Since central-difference formulae give more precise results it would seem better to replace the time derivative in (2.21) by a central-difference form. Doing so gives

$$\frac{\theta(i,j+1)-\theta(i,j-1)}{2\Delta t} = \frac{\kappa}{\rho c} \frac{\theta(i+1,j)+\theta(i-1,j)-2\theta(i,j)}{(\Delta x)^2}$$

or

$$\theta(i,j+1)=\theta(i,j-1)+2r\{\theta(i+1,j)+\theta(i-1,j)-2\theta(i,j)\}, \qquad (2.41)$$

where r is defined in (2.28).

To use (2.41) to update temperatures at time t_{j+1} requires temperatures at two previous times, t_j and t_{j-1}. The equation shows that the temperature at t_{j+1} is obtained from that at t_{j-1} by adding a quantity derived from temperatures at time t_j. The use of (2.41) is called the *leapfrog* method. It is not self-starting, and one stage of another method must be used to generate temperatures at t_1 from the initial temperatures t_0 before the use of (2.41) is possible.

A program LEAPDF is provided (see p. xv) for implementing the leapfrog process for the problem described in Section 2.5. It is a modification of the HEATEX program and requires a different subroutine CYCLE – which also has provision for another method, shortly to be described. We consider the standard problem, partly provided by the program, where the bar is initially at a uniform temperature of 300 K except at one end which is kept at 500 K. Running this problem soon reveals that the leapfrog method is very unstable. Figure 2.9a shows the graphical solution after 4, 8, 12 and 16 time steps with $r = 0.1$. For the first eight time steps the solutions seem quite normal, but from 12 time steps onwards the solution develops increasingly large, unphysical fluctuations. The situation is improved if a smaller value of r is chosen in that a greater simulated time occurs before the instability manifests itself. With $r = 0.01$, corresponding to one-tenth of the time step used for Fig. 2.9a, the instability shows itself after 160 time steps (Fig. 2.9b), equivalent to 16 time steps for $r = 0.1$. However, no matter how small a time step is taken, eventually the instability sets in and the oscillations grow without limit.

The stability condition can be improved by a modification of (2.41) where the term $2\theta(i,j)$ on the right-hand side is replaced by $\theta(i,j+1) + \theta(i,j-1)$. Putting together like terms then gives

$$\theta(i,j+1) = \frac{1-r}{1+r}\theta(i,j-1) + \frac{r}{1+r}\{\theta(i+1,j) + \theta(i-1,j)\}. \qquad (2.42)$$

The application of this equation is the Dufort–Frankel method, which turns out to be always stable, although it develops limited oscillations for larger values of r. Figure 2.10 shows the results of the problem which gave Fig. 2.9 but run with the Dufort–Frankel method for $r = 1.0$. The method is quite stable, in that if the oscillations appear they do not grow indefinitely, as will be seen in the figure, but the accuracy may not be high.

In considering finite-difference methods we have referred to stability in a fairly intuitive way as describing a method which may not necessarily be accurate but where the errors stay within bounds. In Section 2.10 we deal in a more formal way with the concept of *stability*, but first we turn to another concept, that of *consistency*, which leads eventually to the condition that gives convergence.

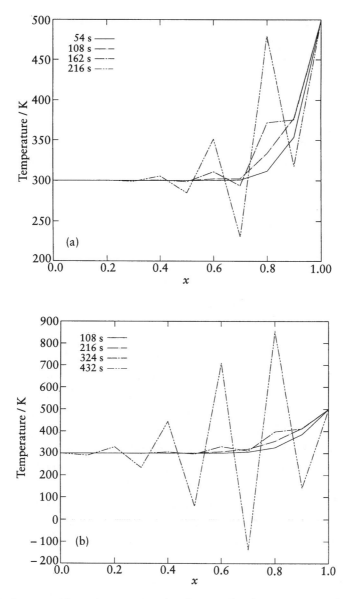

Fig. 2.9 (a) Output with LEAPDF run in leapfrog mode after 4, 8, 12 and 16 cycles with $r = 0.1$; (b) output after 80, 160, 240 and 320 cycles with $r = 0.01$.

2.9 Consistency

In Table 2.9 the temperatures along a cooling bar are shown after a time of 402.5 s as estimated by running RADBAR with different values of r. Intuitively we have more confidence in the temperatures found with the lower values of r,

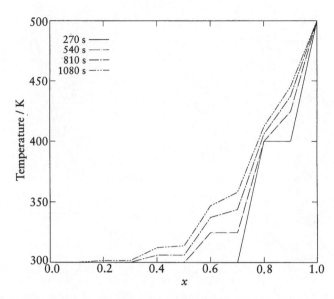

Fig. 2.10   Output from LEAPDF in Dufort–Frankel mode with $r = 1.0$.

corresponding to smaller time steps Δt, and we should also expect that using a larger number of segments in the bar, corresponding to a smaller Δx, should give higher accuracy. Our intuition is reliable here, and a method is said to be *convergent* if as Δt and Δx both approach zero the solution approaches that which would be obtained analytically. However, a necessary condition for convergence is that the finite-difference equations should be *consistent* – so that as Δx and Δt both tend to zero the finite-difference equations should tend towards the exact differential equation.

We shall illustrate the condition of consistency by analysis of the explicit and Crank–Nicholson methods. The mathematical tools we need for this are the Taylor series with its remainder term, dealt with in Section 2.1, together with a simple theorem which states that if a single-valued function $f(x)$ is continuous in the range x_1 to x_2 then one can always write

$$f(x_1) + f(x_2) = 2 f(x_3), \tag{2.43}$$

where x_3 is in the range x_1 to x_2. This theorem can be proved by rigorous mathematical analysis, but for our purpose it will suffice to satisfy ourselves that it is true by looking at a diagram. In Fig. 2.11 the point C, the mid-point of the line PQ, has an ordinate equal to $\frac{1}{2}\{f(x_1) + f(x_2)\}$ and a horizontal line through C cuts the curve at R with abscissa x_3. The reader will not find it possible to draw any single-valued continuous curve between x_1 and x_2 that does not give x_3, or more than one value of x_3, between x_1 and x_2.

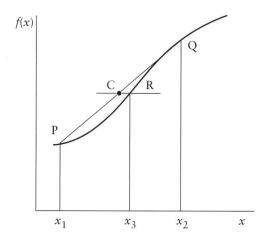

Fig. 2.11 A demonstration of theorem (2.43).

2.9.1 *Consistency for the explicit method*

To consider consistency for the explicit method we start with (2.26), repeated here for convenience:

$$n(i,j+1)=r\{n(i+1,j)+n(i-1,j)\}+(1-2r)n(i,j). \qquad (2.26)$$

These values of n are those actually used in the numerical solution and will differ from the true values, N, which would be found by analysis. We now write

$$n(i,j)=N(i,j)+\varepsilon(i,j), \qquad (2.44)$$

where $\varepsilon(i,j)$ is the error in the value of $n(i,j)$. Substituting for the values of n in (2.26),

$$\varepsilon(i,j+1)=r\{\varepsilon(i+1,j)+\varepsilon(i-1,j)\}+(1-2r)\varepsilon(i,j)$$

$$+r\{N(i+1,j)+N(i-1,j)\}+(1-2r)N(i,j)-N(i,j+1). \quad (2.45)$$

We now use the Taylor expansion (2.1), including the remainder term in the form (2.2), noting that the interval from $i-1$ to i, or from i to $i+1$, is Δx and the interval from j to $j+1$ is Δt (see Fig. 2.5). Thus we may write

$$N(i+1,j)=N(i,j)+\frac{\partial N(i,j)}{\partial x}\Delta x+\frac{\partial^2 N(\eta_1,t_j)}{\partial x^2}\frac{(\Delta x)^2}{2}, \qquad (2.46)$$

where $x_i<\eta_1<x_{i+1}$. In the remainder term the coordinates at the position of the second derivative are given explicitly as (η_1,t_j) rather than in the shorthand

(i,j) notation. Similarly, we find

$$N(i-1,j)=N(i,j)-\frac{\partial N(i,j)}{\partial x}\Delta x+\frac{\partial^2 N(\eta_2,t_j)}{\partial x^2}\frac{(\Delta x)^2}{2},\qquad x_{i-1}<\eta_2<x_i,\quad (2.47)$$

and

$$N(i,j+1)=N(i,j)+\frac{\partial N(x_i,\xi)}{\partial t}\Delta t,\qquad t_j<\xi<t_{j+1}.\qquad (2.48)$$

Substituting (2.46), (2.47), (2.48) and, in part, the expression for r given in (2.27) into (2.45) gives

$$\varepsilon(i,j+1)=r\{\varepsilon(i+1,j)+\varepsilon(i-1,j)\}+(1-2r)\varepsilon(i,j)$$

$$-\Delta t\left[\frac{\partial N(x_i,\xi)}{\partial t}-\frac{D}{2}\left\{\frac{\partial^2 N(\eta_1,t_j)}{\partial x^2}+\frac{\partial^2 N(\eta_2,t_j)}{\partial x^2}\right\}\right].\qquad (2.49)$$

There will be various values of $\varepsilon(i,j)$, for different i, both positive and negative, but we take the largest *magnitude* of the set of values as $E(j)$. Let us consider that in the total calculation where time is advanced to t_{j+1} the maximum magnitude of the square-bracketed quantity in (2.49), for any i and j, is Q. Then, as long as $1-2r$ is non-negative, by putting the maximum positive value for each term on the right-hand side of (2.49), it follows that

$$|\varepsilon(i,j+1)|\leqslant r\{E(j)+E(j)\}+(1-2r)E(j)+Q\Delta t$$

or

$$|\varepsilon(i,j+1)|\leqslant E(j)+Q\Delta t.\qquad (2.50)$$

Since (2.50) is true for any i, including that which gives the maximum magnitude of $\varepsilon(i,j+1)$, then we may write

$$E(j+1)\leqslant E(j)+Q\Delta t.\qquad (2.51)$$

By an extension of (2.51) we find that

$$E(j+1)\leqslant E(j)+Q\Delta t\leqslant E(j-1)+2Q\Delta t\leqslant\cdots\leqslant E(0)+Qt_{j+1}.\qquad (2.52)$$

Since we may assume that the initial values in the calculation are correct, then $E(0)=0$. In addition, if we take both $\Delta t\to 0$ *and* $\Delta x\to 0$, then the quantity in the square brackets in (2.49) tends towards

$$\frac{\partial N}{\partial t}-D\frac{\partial^2 N}{\partial x^2},$$

which, from the original partial differential equation (2.20), equals zero. We have demonstrated that as Δx and Δt tend to zero then, as long as $r \leqslant \frac{1}{2}$, the numerical solution tends towards the analytical solution. This shows that the explicit method is consistent.

2.9.2 Consistency for the Crank–Nicholson method

To examine consistency for the Crank–Nicholson implicit method, we begin with (2.33), again reproduced here for convenience:

$$-rn(i-1,j+1)+2(1+r)n(i,j+1)-rn(i+1,j+1)$$
$$= rn(i-1,j)+2(1-r)n(i,j)+rn(i+1,j). \tag{2.33}$$

Substituting from (2.44),

$$r\varepsilon(i-1,j+1)-2(1+r)\varepsilon(i,j+1)+r\varepsilon(i+1,j+1)$$
$$= -r\varepsilon(i-1,j)-2(1-r)\varepsilon(i,j)-r\varepsilon(i+1,j)$$
$$-rN(i-1,j+1)+2(1+r)N(i,j+1)-rN(i+1,j+1) \tag{2.53}$$
$$-rN(i-1,j)-2(1-r)N(i,j)-rN(i+1,j).$$

Now we expand two of the terms involving N at time t_{j+1} using the Taylor series:

$$rN(i-1,j+1)=rN(i,j+1)-r\frac{\partial N(x_i,t_{j+1})}{\partial x}\Delta x+r\frac{\partial^2 N(\eta_1,t_{j+1})}{\partial x^2}\frac{(\Delta x)^2}{2}, \tag{2.54a}$$

where η_1 is in the range x_{i-1} to x_i; and

$$rN(i+1,j+1)=rN(i,j+1)+r\frac{\partial N(x_i,t_{j+1})}{\partial x}\Delta x+r\frac{\partial^2 N(\eta_2,t_{j+1})}{\partial x^2}\frac{(\Delta x)^2}{2}, \tag{2.54b}$$

where η_2 is in the range x_i to x_{i+1}. Summing the three terms involving N at time t_{j+1} gives

$$S_{j+1}=2N(i,j+1)-r\frac{(\Delta x)^2}{2}\left\{\frac{\partial^2 N(\eta_1,t_{j+1})}{\partial x^2}+\frac{\partial^2 N(\eta_2,t_{j+1})}{\partial x^2}\right\}. \tag{2.55}$$

By a similar process, the sum of the three terms involving N at time t_j is found to be

$$S_j=-2N(i,j)-r\frac{(\Delta x)^2}{2}\left\{\frac{\partial^2 N(\eta_3,t_j)}{\partial x^2}+\frac{\partial^2 N(\eta_4,t_j)}{\partial x^2}\right\}, \tag{2.56}$$

where η_3 is between x_{i-1} and x_i and η_4 is between x_i and x_{i+1}. Hence the sum of all six terms involving N is

$$S = S_j + S_{j+1} = 2N(i, j+1) - 2N(i, j)$$

$$- r \frac{(\Delta x)^2}{2} \left\{ \frac{\partial^2 N(\eta_1, t_{j+1})}{\partial x^2} + \frac{\partial^2 N(\eta_2, t_{j+1})}{\partial x^2} \right.$$

$$\left. + \frac{\partial^2 N(\eta_3, t_j)}{\partial x^2} + \frac{\partial^2 N(\eta_4, t_j)}{\partial x^2} \right\}. \qquad (2.57)$$

All the four terms in the curly brackets on the right-hand side are functions of two variables of the same kind, with the first variable in the range x_{i-1} and x_{i+1} and the second variable with values either t_j or t_{j+1}. From a two-dimensional version of (2.43) we can write

$$S = 2N(i, j+1) - 2N(i, j) - 2r(\Delta x)^2 \frac{\partial^2 N(\eta', \xi')}{\partial x^2}, \qquad (2.58)$$

where η' is between x_{i-1} and x_{i+1} and ξ' is between t_j and t_{j+1}. We now apply the Taylor series to the first term on the right-hand side of (2.58), giving

$$2N(i, j+1) = 2N(i, j) + \frac{\partial N(x_i, \xi)}{\partial t} \Delta t, \qquad (2.59)$$

where ξ is between t_j and t_{j+1}. Combining (2.58) and (2.59) and substituting for r from (2.27) gives the N-dependent part of the right-hand side of (2.53) equal to

$$2\Delta t \left\{ \frac{\partial N(x_i, \xi)}{\partial t} - D \frac{\partial^2 N(\eta', \xi')}{\partial x^2} \right\} = 2Q\Delta t. \qquad (2.60)$$

The original (2.53) now appears as

$$r\varepsilon(i-1, j+1) - 2(1+r)\varepsilon(i, j+1) + r\varepsilon(i+1, j+1)$$

$$= -r\varepsilon(i-1, j) - 2(1-r)\varepsilon(i, j) - r\varepsilon(i+1, j) + 2Q\Delta t. \qquad (2.61)$$

If both $\Delta t \to 0$ and $\Delta x \to 0$ then $Q \to (\partial N/\partial t) - D(\partial^2 N/\partial x^2) = 0$ because of (2.20) and the implicit Crank–Nicholson method is consistent. Since the initial condition is error-free then $\varepsilon(i, 0)$ is zero for all i so that when (2.61) is solved with $Q = 0$ then the solution will be $\varepsilon(i, 1) = 0$ for all i. Clearly the solution for all times will be error-free and the method is also convergent.

2.10 Stability

Although consistency is a necessary condition for convergence, it is not sufficient. The *Lax equivalence theorem* states that for the kind of well-posed initial-value problems we are considering here it is also required that the finite-difference system must be stable. With both consistency and stability there will be a convergent system.

Stability is concerned with the way that errors do or do not grow as the solution progresses. If a small error at some stage grows without limit until it eventually completely swamps the solution then the system is unstable. On the other hand, if the error falls in value, or stays within reasonable bounds, then the system is stable. We shall illustrate the phenomenon of stability, as for consistency, by analysis of the explicit method and the implicit Crank–Nicholson method.

2.10.1 *Stability of the explicit method*

The basic equations of the explicit method, (2.26), may be expressed in matrix form as

$$\mathbf{n}_{j+1} = \mathbf{A}\mathbf{n}_j + \mathbf{b}_j. \tag{2.62}$$

The vector $\mathbf{n}_j = \{n(1,j), n(2,j), \ldots, n(M-1,j)\}$ where the space of the one-dimensional problem has been divided into M segments and the vector $\mathbf{b}_j (= \{rn(0,j), 0, \ldots, rn(M,j)\})$ contains the two boundary conditions at time t_j. The square matrix $\mathbf{A}$, illustrated for the case $M=7$, is of the tridiagonal form

$$\begin{bmatrix} 1-2r & r & 0 & 0 & 0 & 0 \\ r & 1-2r & r & 0 & 0 & 0 \\ 0 & r & 1-2r & r & 0 & 0 \\ 0 & 0 & r & 1-2r & r & 0 \\ 0 & 0 & 0 & r & 1-2r & r \\ 0 & 0 & 0 & 0 & r & 1-2r \end{bmatrix}. \tag{2.63}$$

Let us now suppose that (2.62) represents an error-free calculation, but that we now add errors to all the values of n at time t_j, represented by an error vector $\mathbf{\varepsilon}_j$. This will give rise to errors in the values of n at time t_{j+1} which are the elements of the error vector $\mathbf{\varepsilon}_{j+1}$. Then

$$(\mathbf{n}_{j+1} + \mathbf{\varepsilon}_{j+1}) = \mathbf{A}(\mathbf{n}_j + \mathbf{\varepsilon}_j) + \mathbf{b}_j. \tag{2.64}$$

Subtracting (2.62) from (2.64) gives

$$\mathbf{\varepsilon}_{j+1} = \mathbf{A}\mathbf{\varepsilon}_j, \tag{2.65}$$

which shows that the propagation of errors is entirely controlled by the properties of the matrix $\mathbf{A}$. Once an error is present at one stage – say, at time t_j – then at some subsequent time t_{j+s} the errors will be related by

$$\varepsilon_{j+s} = \mathbf{A}^s \varepsilon_j. \tag{2.66}$$

Here we shall assume knowledge of some of the standard properties of matrices but these are reviewed in Appendix 1. The repeated application of a matrix to an originally arbitrary non-null vector eventually leads to the equation

$$\mathbf{A}\mathbf{x} = \lambda\mathbf{x} \tag{2.67}$$

where λ is the principal eigenvalue of the matrix (that is, the eigenvalue with the greatest magnitude) and $\mathbf{x}$ is the corresponding eigenvector. The application of a matrix of form (2.63) to the initial error vector ε_0 will give a new error vector ε_1, the elements of which will bear no simple relationship to those of ε_0. However, as each new error vector is generated by successive multiplication by $\mathbf{A}$ the pattern will become established whereby each newly-generated error vector differs from the previous one by having each element multiplied by the same factor λ, the principal eigenvalue of $\mathbf{A}$. This indicates the condition for stability; if $|\lambda| > 1$ then the elements of the error vectors increase in magnitude indefinitely and the system is unstable. Conversely if $|\lambda| \leqslant 1$, then the magnitudes of the elements of the error vectors will reduce, or, in the special case of $|\lambda| = 1$, will remain constant, and the system will be stable.

The matrix $\mathbf{A}$ will have $M-1$ eigenvalues, and analysis shows that these are of the form

$$\lambda_m = 1 - 4r\sin^2\left(\frac{m\pi}{2M}\right), \qquad m = 1, \dots, M-1. \tag{2.68}$$

Since the second term must be positive the maximum positive value of any λ is 1 but, depending on the value of r, there is no limit on negative values. It is clear that no eigenvalue can be less than -1 if the condition

$$1 - 4r \geqslant -1, \tag{2.69}$$

that is, $r \leqslant 0.5$, is satisfied, regardless of the values of $\sin^2(m\pi/2M)$. This is consistent with what we have found in numerical experiments with the program HEATEX.

It should be noted that it *is* possible for values of r greater than 0.5 to give stability. For example with $M = 7$ the six values of $\sin^2(m\pi/2M)$ are

$$0.0495 \quad 0.1883 \quad 0.3887 \quad 0.6113 \quad 0.8117 \quad 0.9505$$

and a value of $r = 0.526$ will make the eigenvalue of largest magnitude equal to -1. For larger values of M the possible departure from the condition (2.69) is very small and it is normal to express the conditional for stability of the explicit value as (2.69).

2.10.2 *Stability of the Crank–Nicholson method*

From (2.33) the form of the matrix equation for the Crank–Nicholson method, illustrated with $M=7$, is

$$\mathbf{A}\mathbf{n}_{j+1}+\mathbf{b}_{j+1}=\mathbf{B}\mathbf{n}_j+\mathbf{b}_j, \tag{2.70}$$

where

$$\mathbf{A}=\begin{bmatrix} 2(1+r) & -r & 0 & 0 & 0 & 0 \\ -r & 2(1+r) & -r & 0 & 0 & 0 \\ 0 & -r & 2(1+r) & -r & 0 & 0 \\ 0 & 0 & -r & 2(1+r) & -r & 0 \\ 0 & 0 & 0 & -r & 2(1+r) & -r \\ 0 & 0 & 0 & 0 & -r & 2(1+r) \end{bmatrix},$$

$$\mathbf{B}=\begin{bmatrix} 2(1-r) & r & 0 & 0 & 0 & 0 \\ r & 2(1-r) & r & 0 & 0 & 0 \\ 0 & r & 2(1-r) & r & 0 & 0 \\ 0 & 0 & r & 2(1-r) & r & 0 \\ 0 & 0 & 0 & r & 2(1-r) & r \\ 0 & 0 & 0 & 0 & r & 2(1-r) \end{bmatrix},$$

$$\mathbf{n}_{j+1}=\{n(1,j+1),n(2,j+1),n(3,j+1),n(4,j+1),n(5,j+1),n(6,j+1)\},$$

$$\mathbf{n}_j=\{n(1,j),n(2,j),n(3,j),n(4,j),n(5,j),n(6,j)\},$$

$$\mathbf{b}_{j+1}=\{(n(0,j+1),0,0,0,0,n(7,j+1)\},$$

$$\mathbf{b}_j=\{(n(0,j),0,0,0,0,n(7,j)\}. \tag{2.71}$$

By similar reasoning to that used to obtain (2.65), we find

$$\mathbf{A}\boldsymbol{\varepsilon}_{j+1}=\mathbf{B}\boldsymbol{\varepsilon}_j$$

or

$$\boldsymbol{\varepsilon}_{j+1}=\mathbf{A}^{-1}\mathbf{B}\boldsymbol{\varepsilon}_j. \tag{2.72}$$

and the eigenvalues of $\mathbf{A}^{-1}\mathbf{B}$ are found by analysis to be

$$\lambda_m=\frac{2-4r\sin^2(m\pi/2M)}{2+4r\sin^2(m\pi/2M)}. \tag{2.73}$$

For $r=0$ all values of λ equal 1, while for $r=\infty$ all values of λ are equal to -1. For any positive finite value of r,

$$|\lambda|<1,$$

which shows that the Crank–Nicholson implicit method is unconditionally stable.

It is important not to confuse stability with accuracy. Stability merely ensures that the system will behave in a more or less physically plausible way and that the solutions will remain finite. However, for any system using finite differences there is an inherent error, called *truncation error*, introduced by the remainder of the Taylor series in the approximations used, although this error may be reduced to any required tolerance by taking small enough intervals Δx and Δt.

2.11   Types of partial differential equation

A general second-order differential equation is of the form

$$A\frac{\partial^2\phi}{\partial x^2}+B\frac{\partial^2\phi}{\partial x\partial y}+C\frac{\partial^2\phi}{\partial y^2}+D\frac{\partial\phi}{\partial x}+E\frac{\partial\phi}{\partial y}+F\phi+G=0, \tag{2.74}$$

in which the capital-letter coefficients may be functions of ϕ, x and y. Partial differential equations may be divided into three types: hyperbolic, for which $B^2-4AC>0$; parabolic, for which $B^2-4AC=0$; and elliptic, for which $B^2-4AC<0$. Each type of equation lends itself to different methods of solution using the finite-difference approach.

The diffusion equation

$$D\frac{\partial^2 n}{\partial x^2}-\frac{\partial n}{\partial t}=0$$

is clearly a parabolic equation and the explicit, Crank–Nicholson, leapfrog and Dufort–Frankel methods are suitable to deal with such problems. In the following section we shall consider a two-dimensional problem, that of determining the steady-state distribution of temperature in a thin heated slab of material, which will introduce methods of dealing with elliptic equations. Hyperbolic equations will be encountered when we deal with the wave equation in Chapter 5.

2.12   A heated plate in equilibrium

If we take a thin plate of material, of uniform thickness and well insulated on both sides, then heat can only flow parallel to the surface of the plate and we have essentially a two-dimensional heat-flow problem. We now consider a small element of the plate of thickness z and rectangular area $\delta x \times \delta y$ (Fig. 2.12) the corner of which is at (x, y).

The rate of heat flow into the element along the x direction through the face A of dimension $z\delta y$ is

$$\delta Q_x = -\kappa z \delta y \frac{\partial \theta}{\partial x};$$

and, similarly, the rate of heat flow out of the element through the face B is

$$\delta Q_{x+\delta x} = -\kappa z \delta y \left(\frac{\partial \theta}{\partial x} + \frac{\partial^2 \theta}{\partial x^2} \delta x \right).$$

This gives the net rate of flow in the x direction into the element,

$$\Delta Q_x = \kappa z \delta x \delta y \frac{\partial^2 \theta}{\partial x^2}, \tag{2.75}$$

and the total from both the x and y directions,

$$\Delta Q_x + \Delta Q_y = \kappa z \delta x \delta y \left(\frac{\partial^2 \theta}{\partial x^2} + \frac{\partial^2 \theta}{\partial y^2} \right) = \kappa z \delta x \delta y \nabla^2 \theta, \tag{2.76}$$

where ∇^2 is the Laplacian operator. There may also be some source (or sink) of heat energy in the element, amounting to Q_S per unit volume per unit time, where Q_S is a function of position in the plate. If we are considering the steady-state case then the net flux of heat energy into the element must be zero, so that

$$\kappa z \delta x \delta y \nabla^2 \theta + Q_S z \delta x \delta y = 0. \tag{2.77}$$

This gives Poisson's equation

$$\nabla^2 \theta = -\frac{1}{\kappa} Q_S, \tag{2.78}$$

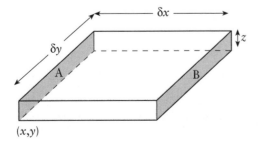

(x,y)

Fig. 2.12   An element of a heated plate.

but the special case $Q_S = 0$ gives Laplace's equation

$$\nabla^2 \theta = 0. \tag{2.79}$$

For either Poisson's or Laplace's equation it will be seen from (2.74) that A and C are finite and equal, with $B = 0$, so that the condition for elliptic equations is satisfied.

From (2.25) we find that

$$\nabla^2 \theta(i,j) = \frac{\theta(i+1,j) + \theta(i-1,j) - 2\theta(i,j)}{\Delta x^2} + \frac{\theta(i,j+1) + \theta(i,j-1) - 2\theta(i,j)}{\Delta y^2},$$

$$\tag{2.80}$$

where i and j now refer to the x and y directions. If we take $\Delta x = \Delta y = h$, then

$$\nabla^2 \theta(i,j) = \frac{1}{h^2} \{\theta(i+1,j) + \theta(i-1,j) + \theta(i,j+1) + \theta(i,j-1) - 4\theta(i,j)\}. \tag{2.81}$$

The pattern of these terms is shown in Fig. 2.13, which is similar to Fig. 2.5 in form, and (2.81) is sometimes referred to as the *five-star formula*. From (2.9) we find that the error in applying this formula is $O(h^2)$.

To illustrate the way that this formula can be used, we treat the problem shown in Fig. 2.14. A square plate of dimensions $20\,\text{cm} \times 20\,\text{cm}$, well insulated on its top and bottom surfaces, has all its edges maintained at fixed temperatures, the so-called *Dirichlet problem*. The plate is divided into square elements of side $5\,\text{cm}$ and the problem is that of finding the nine temperatures, θ_1 to θ_9, at the internal grid-points. There are no sources of heat within the plate, so we have a Laplace problem, and from (2.81) we find the following

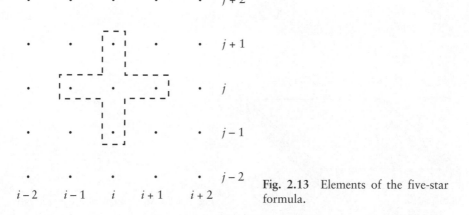

Fig. 2.13 Elements of the five-star formula.

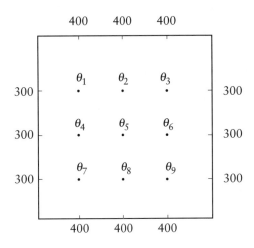

Fig. 2.14 A square plate with constant-temperature edges.

set of equations to solve:

$$300 + \theta_4 + \theta_2 + 400 - 4\theta_1 = 0$$
$$\theta_1 + \theta_5 + \theta_3 + 400 - 4\theta_2 = 0$$
$$\theta_2 + \theta_6 + 300 + 400 - 4\theta_3 = 0$$
$$300 + \theta_7 + \theta_5 + \theta_1 - 4\theta_4 = 0$$
$$\theta_4 + \theta_8 + \theta_6 + \theta_2 - 4\theta_5 = 0 \qquad (2.82)$$
$$\theta_5 + \theta_9 + 300 + \theta_3 - 4\theta_6 = 0$$
$$300 + 400 + \theta_8 + \theta_4 - 4\theta_7 = 0$$
$$\theta_7 + 400 + \theta_9 + \theta_5 - 4\theta_8 = 0$$
$$\theta_8 + 400 + 300 + \theta_6 - 4\theta_9 = 0.$$

These can be expressed in matrix form

$$\mathbf{A\theta} = \mathbf{b}, \qquad (2.83)$$

where

$$\mathbf{A} = \begin{bmatrix}
-4 & 1 & 0 & 1 & 0 & 0 & 0 & 0 & 0 \\
1 & -4 & 1 & 0 & 1 & 0 & 0 & 0 & 0 \\
0 & 1 & -4 & 0 & 0 & 1 & 0 & 0 & 0 \\
1 & 0 & 0 & -4 & 1 & 0 & 1 & 0 & 0 \\
0 & 1 & 0 & 1 & -4 & 1 & 0 & 1 & 0 \\
0 & 0 & 1 & 0 & 1 & -4 & 0 & 0 & 1 \\
0 & 0 & 0 & 1 & 0 & 0 & -4 & 1 & 0 \\
0 & 0 & 0 & 0 & 1 & 0 & 1 & -4 & 1 \\
0 & 0 & 0 & 0 & 0 & 1 & 0 & 1 & -4
\end{bmatrix}, \qquad (2.84)$$

$$\mathbf{\theta} = (\theta_1, \theta_2, \theta_3, \theta_4, \theta_5, \theta_6, \theta_7, \theta_8, \theta_9)$$

and

$$\mathbf{b} = (-700, -400, -700, -300, 0, -300, -700, -400, -700).$$

The matrix $\mathbf{A}$ has a characteristic banded form with a dominant diagonal. The solution can be found from a standard program for dealing with linear equations, but the strong diagonal makes the iterative Gauss–Seidel method a simple alternative.

2.13 Gauss–Seidel, relaxation and conjugate-gradient methods

2.13.1 *The Gauss–Seidel method*

For the Gauss–Seidel method each equation in the set (2.82) is rewritten in a form which expresses the variable with the strong diagonal coefficient in terms of the other variables. Thus the set of equations (2.82) become:

$$\theta_1 = \tfrac{1}{4}(\theta_2 + \theta_4 + 700)$$

$$\theta_2 = \tfrac{1}{4}(\theta_1 + \theta_3 + \theta_5 + 400)$$

$$\theta_3 = \tfrac{1}{4}(\theta_2 + \theta_6 + 700)$$

$$\theta_4 = \tfrac{1}{4}(\theta_1 + \theta_5 + \theta_7 + 300)$$

$$\theta_5 = \tfrac{1}{4}(\theta_2 + \theta_4 + \theta_6 + \theta_8) \qquad\qquad (2.85)$$

$$\theta_6 = \tfrac{1}{4}(\theta_3 + \theta_5 + \theta_9 + 300)$$

$$\theta_7 = \tfrac{1}{4}(\theta_4 + \theta_8 + 700)$$

$$\theta_8 = \tfrac{1}{4}(\theta_5 + \theta_7 + \theta_9 + 400)$$

$$\theta_9 = \tfrac{1}{4}(\theta_6 + \theta_8 + 700).$$

Starting with some initial estimates of all the temperatures – say, each one equal to the average of the boundary temperatures, $350\,\mathrm{K}$ – a new estimate is found for θ_1 – which happens also to be $350\,\mathrm{K}$. Next, a new estimate is found for θ_2 with all the current estimates of temperature on the right-hand side including the new value of θ_1; this estimate is $362.5\,\mathrm{K}$, which is then used in finding a new estimate for θ_3. When the first new estimate for θ_9 is found a second iteration is commenced, starting with θ_1 again. Table 2.10 shows the progression of the process, and it will be seen that in six cycles it converges to the final solution to a tolerance level of 0.001. The convergence is quite fast

Table 2.10 Solution of the problem illustrated in Fig. 2.14, showing the results of successive iterations with (2.85). The process finishes when the greatest difference in any value in two successive cycles is less than the requested tolerance of 0.0001.

Cycle	θ_n for $n=$								
	1	2	3	4	5	6	7	8	9
0	350.000	350.000	350.000	350.000	350.000	350.000	350.000	350.000	350.000
1	350.000	362.500	353.125	337.500	350.000	338.281	346.875	361.719	350.000
2	350.000	363.281	350.391	336.719	350.000	337.598	349.609	362.402	350.000
3	350.000	362.598	350.049	337.402	350.000	337.512	349.951	362.448	350.000
4	350.000	362.512	350.006	337.488	350.000	337.502	349.994	362.498	350.000
5	350.000	362.502	350.001	337.498	350.000	337.500	349.999	362.500	350.000
6	350.000	362.500	350.000	337.500	350.000	337.500	350.000	362.500	350.000
7	350.000	362.500	350.000	337.500	350.000	337.500	350.000	362.500	350.000

because the starting estimated temperatures were not too far from their correct values. However, even starting much further away still gives the solution, for example, starting with all estimated initial temperatures equal to zero gives the solution after 23 cycles. In fact, indicating the elements of matrix (2.84) by $a_{i,j}$, the set of equations (2.82) satisfies the condition that

$$|a_{i,i}| \geqslant \sum_{\substack{j=1 \\ j \neq i}}^{n} |a_{i,j}| \tag{2.86}$$

for all i, a condition known as *diagonal dominance* which ensures that the Gauss–Seidel method will converge to the correct solution no matter what is the initial trial solution vector. Even starting with each element of the initial vector equal to 10 000 gives the solution to the same tolerance level as in Table 2.10 in 28 cycles.

2.13.2 *The relaxation method*

At each stage in the Gauss–Seidel method, when a new estimate for one of the variables is found the equation which gives that estimate is satisfied by the current estimates for all the variables. However, the other equations will, in general, not be satisfied and the residuals of the equations (the differences between the left- and right-hand sides) will be different for each equation. In the Gauss–Seidel method no account is taken of the magnitudes of the residuals and the equations are used in sequence. There is a *relaxation method*, first suggested by Southwell in 1940 before computers were available, which does take account of the residual magnitudes and will accelerate the convergence somewhat. We can illustrate this with a simple system of equations:

$$4x - y + z = 4$$

$$x + 4y - z = 4$$

$$x + y + 2z = 4$$

which are rewritten in the form

$$x - \tfrac{1}{4}y + \tfrac{1}{4}z - 1 = 0$$

$$\tfrac{1}{4}x + y - \tfrac{1}{4}z - 1 = 0 \qquad (2.87)$$

$$\tfrac{1}{2}x + \tfrac{1}{2}y + z - 2 = 0,$$

where all terms are on the left-hand side and the equations are scaled to make the dominant coefficient in each equation equal to 1. Starting with the estimate $x = y = z = 0$ the residuals of the equations are -1, -1, -2, and the last equation gives the greatest residual magnitude. By making $z = 2$ this residual can be reduced to zero and the three residuals, with $x = y = 0$, $z = 2$, are -0.5, -1.5, 0. The residual with largest magnitude is now that for the second equation, and by making $y = 1.5$ this residual can be reduced to zero. This process, where for the equation with the largest residual the dominant variable is assigned a new value to reduce the residual to zero, is repeated until the process converges on the solution. Doing the calculation by hand to three places of decimals gives the progression in Table 2.11, which shows that the solution is obtained in 17 steps. However, a computer solution with a program GAUSSOR, described later, which applies the Gauss–Seidel method with the equations taken sequentially without regard to residuals, gave the solution in 18 steps (six cycles of the three equations) so not much is saved by the relaxation method in this case. There are cases where the relaxation process can lead to considerable savings, but it is a method which is awkward to program and the advantage of requiring fewer cycles can be swallowed up by the process of finding the largest residual.

2.13.3 *The over-relaxation method*

In applying the relaxation method Southwell found that acceleration of the process could sometimes be obtained by *over-relaxation*. This consisted of changing the value of the variable so that it did not just change the residual to zero but took it through zero so that it changed sign. The over-relaxation factor w, the amount by which the shift of value was multiplied, could be between 1.0

Table 2.11 A hand application of the Southwell relaxation method to equations (2.87). The residuals of the three equations are indicated by R_1, R_2 and R_3.

Step	x	y	z	R_1	R_2	R_3
0	0	0	0	−1	−1	−2
1	0	0	2.000	−0.500	−1.500	0
2	0	1.500	2.000	−0.875	0	0.750
3	0.875	1.500	2.000	0	0.219	1.188
4	0.875	1.500	0.813	−0.297	0.516	0
5	0.875	0.985	0.813	−0.169	0	−0.257
6	0.875	0.985	1.156	−0.082	−0.086	0
7	0.875	1.070	1.156	−0.104	0	0.128
8	0.875	1.070	1.027	−0.136	0.032	0
9	1.011	1.070	1.027	0	0.066	0.046
10	1.011	1.004	1.027	0.017	0	0.035
11	1.011	1.004	0.993	0.008	0.009	0
12	1.011	0.995	0.993	0.010	0	−0.005
13	1.001	0.995	0.993	0	−0.003	−0.010
14	1.001	0.995	1.002	0.003	−0.005	0
15	1.001	1.000	1.002	0.002	0	−0.003
16	1.001	1.000	1.000	0.001	0	0
17	1.000	1.000	1.000	0	0	0

and 2.0, but it was difficult to tell in advance what degree of over-relaxation would give the best efficiency. In general, the most effective value of w increases with the number of equations; for a five-equation system $w = 1.2$ might be appropriate, whereas for a 100-equation system $w = 1.8$ could be most effective.

The relaxation method is no longer used, but the over-relaxation idea can be applied to the Gauss–Seidel procedure when it is called the *successive over-relaxation* (SOR) method. In this procedure when a change in the value of a variable is found from the normal Gauss–Seidel process this change is multiplied by a factor w. A program GAUSSOR is available (see p. xv) which carries out the SOR procedure – which is normal Gauss–Seidel if w is made equal to 1. The program asks for a tolerance value, τ; the iterations cease when the largest change in the value of any variable in one complete cycle of operations is less than τ. We apply GAUSSOR to the following set of equations:

$$-5x_1 + x_2 + x_3 + x_4 + x_5 = -5$$

$$x_1 - 5x_2 + x_3 + x_4 + x_5 = -11$$

$$x_1 + x_2 - 5x_3 + x_4 + x_5 = -17 \qquad (2.88)$$

$$x_1 + x_2 + x_3 - 5x_4 + x_5 = 13$$

$$x_1 + x_2 + x_3 + x_4 - 5x_5 = 19,$$

for which the solution is $x_1=1$, $x_2=2$, $x_3=3$, $x_4=-2$ and $x_5=-3$. The tolerance is set at 0.0001, initial values of x_i to zero and values of w are used from 1 to 2 in steps of 0.1. The number of cycles required for solution is shown in Table 2.12. It is clear that a value of w about 1.3 gives the most efficient procedure, but it should not be thought that this value would be best for any set of five equations. For example, the following set of equations

$$-5x_1+x_2+2x_3-x_4=13$$

$$-x_1+6x_2+2x_3+x_4-x_5=3$$

$$2x_1-x_2+5x_3+x_5=2 \tag{2.89}$$

$$x_1+3x_3+7x_4-2x_5=-10$$

$$-2x_1+x_2+x_4+4x_5=-9,$$

run with GAUSSOR, gives the result show in Table 2.13. For this example the straightforward Gauss–Seidel approach with no over-relaxation gives the best results.

The best over-relaxation factor depends on the elements of the coefficient matrix and analysis using the techniques of matrix algebra is capable of giving the optimum value of w for any set of elements. For the two-dimensional version of Laplace's equation and a uniform mesh with N_x cells along x, each of size Δx, and N_y cells along y, each of size Δy, the optimum relaxation coefficient for the resultant linear equations is

$$w_0=2\left\{\frac{1-\sqrt{1-\xi}}{\xi}\right\}, \tag{2.90}$$

Table 2.12 The number of cycles of SOR required for the solution of equations (2.88) with a tolerance 0.0001 and various values of the over-relaxation factor w.

w	1.0	1.1	1.2	1.3	1.4	1.5	1.6	1.7	1.8	1.9	2.0
Cycles	21	17	13	9	11	14	19	26	43	85	>100

Table 2.13 The number of cycles of SOR required for the solution of equations (2.89) with a tolerance 0.0001 and various values of the over-relaxation factor w.

w	1.0	1.1	1.2	1.3	1.4	1.5	1.6	1.7	1.8	1.9	2.0
Cycles	8	11	13	35	>100	Unstable and divergent – no solution					

where

$$\xi = \left\{ \frac{\cos(\pi/N_x) + \beta^2 \cos(\pi/N_y)}{1 + \beta^2} \right\}^2.$$

and

$$\beta = \Delta x / \Delta y.$$

2.13.4 *Conjugate-gradient methods*

With the increasing power of modern computers the SOR method is being displaced by *conjugate-gradient methods*, which are appropriate to use when the coefficient matrix is sparse, as when Laplace's equation is solved. We shall not describe the details of the process here, but just indicate what the methods actually do. The conjugate-gradient solution of the set of equations $\mathbf{Ax} = \mathbf{b}$ minimizes a function such as $g(\mathbf{x}) = |\mathbf{Ax} - \mathbf{b}|^2$. If the solution vector has n elements then $g(\mathbf{x})$ is a function in an n-dimensional space. Starting with a trial solution $\mathbf{x}_0$, a better solution is found by reducing the value of $g(\mathbf{x})$. The conjugate-gradient method does this by finding the gradient in this n-space, $\mathbf{u}_0 = \nabla g(\mathbf{x})$ at $\mathbf{x} = \mathbf{x}_0$, and moving along the gradient by an amount $\lambda \mathbf{u}$ to make $g(\mathbf{x})$ a minimum. This gives the next approximation to the solution as $\mathbf{x}_1 = \mathbf{x}_0 + \lambda \mathbf{u}_0$. This process is repeated until the refinement function $g(\mathbf{x})$ has an acceptably small value. Standard programs exist for applying the conjugate-gradient method which require as input the elements of $\mathbf{A}$, the right-hand-side vector $\mathbf{b}$ and an initial trial solution $\mathbf{x}_0$. For efficient use of the programs it is also necessary to provide subroutines which exploit the sparseness of the matrix to evaluate economically $\mathbf{As}$ and $\mathbf{A}^T\mathbf{s}$, where $\mathbf{s}$ is a vector, and the matrix $\mathbf{A}^T$ is the *transpose* of $\mathbf{A}$ and is obtained from $\mathbf{A}$ by interchanging rows and columns, so that $\mathbf{A}^T(i, j) = \mathbf{A}(j, i)$. A first-principles derivation of a simple conjugate-gradient approach is given in Appendix 2, together with an indication of how the linear equations may be preconditioned to optimize the method.

2.14 The solution of general heated-plate problems

The program HOTPLATE (see p. xv) can be used to solve automatically the plate problem shown in Fig. 2.14. This program defines the plate in terms of a square mesh with up to 11×11 points, corresponding to 10×10 square elements. The plate need not be rectangular, but all the edges must be either along the principal directions of the mesh or make an angle of 45° with a principal direction. In the input, for a boundary point at a fixed temperature the temperature is entered, and for an internal point, the temperature of which has to be found, the symbol U is entered. The input is called for row by row and for the Fig. 2.14 problem the input is of the form

350	400	400	400	350
300	U	U	U	300
300	U	U	U	300
300	U	U	U	300
350	400	400	400	350

At the corners where there is a junction of two boundaries at different temperatures the mean temperature is entered. For this problem the corner points are not involved in the calculation, but there are some circumstances where junction points do get involved. The tolerance, τ, and the over-relaxation factor, w, are also input by the user. The program begins with all the temperatures to be determined set equal to zero; although this is not the most efficient value to take, the calculation is so rapid on modern computers that it makes little difference what are taken as the initial temperature estimates.

HOTPLATE has been applied to the non-rectangular plate shown in Fig. 2.15. The description of the plate is based on a rectangular area and points within the 7×7 grid, but outside the plate, are entered as X. Thus the input data defining the extent of the plate and its boundary temperatures are:

X	X	X	350	400	400	450
X	X	300	U	U	U	500
X	300	U	U	U	U	500
350	U	U	U	U	U	500
400	U	U	U	U	U	500
400	U	U	U	U	U	500
350	300	300	300	300	300	400

It should be noted that, in this instance, the point with temperature 350 K at the left-hand edge, where two fixed-temperature sides come together, *will* be involved in the solution. Running the problem with HOTPLATE for

$w=1.0$ and $\tau=0.0001$ gives the solution shown in Fig. 2.16 in 45 cycles of the Gauss–Seidel process. With SOR the same solution was obtained for all values of w from 1.1 to 1.9, at steps of 0.1, but the solution had not been reached with $w=2.0$ after 1000 cycles, the maximum permitted by HOTPLATE. The number of cycles required for the various values of w are shown in Table 2.14.

Although simple problems of this kind take very little time on modern computers, a time usually dwarfed by the time of manual input of the data, there could still be interest in optimizing the process by a proper choice of w. An application could be envisaged where the initial data were being generated by computer and where a large number of problems were being set up and

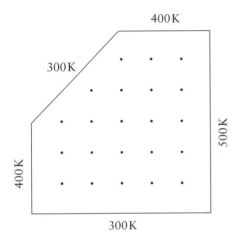

Fig. 2.15 A non-rectangular plate with constant-temperature edges.

```
THE TOLERANCE IS   0.00010
THE OVER-RELAXATION PARAMETER IS   1.00
THE NUMBER OF CYCLES IS   45

 -1.     -1.     -1.     350.    400.    400.    450.

 -1.     -1.     300.    352.    397.    436.    500.

 -1.     300.    327.    362.    401.    445.    500.

 350.    339.    345.    367.    400.    444.    500.

 400.    359.    350.    360.    387.    432.    500.

 400.    348.    334.    337.    355.    397.    500.

 350.    300.    300.    300.    300.    300.    400.
```

Fig. 2.16 HOTPLATE output for the problem shown in Fig. 2.15. Points marked -1 are outside the plate.

Table 2.14 Number of cycles required for solution of the problem described in Fig. 2.14 with $\tau = 0.0001$ and different values of the over-relaxation factor, w.

w	1.0	1.1	1.2	1.3	1.4	1.5	1.6	1.7	1.8	1.9
Cycles	45	36	28	19	19	25	33	47	74	147

run. The best value to take for w is given by (2.90), which has been derived from a theoretical approach. However, for the solution of a HOTPLATE problem defined on a $p \times q$ grid, if $n = (pq)^{1/2}$ then a good rule-of-thumb is that

$$w_{\text{optimum}} = \frac{2n+4}{n+6}. \tag{2.91}$$

For the HOTPLATE problem defined in Fig. 2.15 we have $n = 7$ which gives $w_{\text{optimum}} = 1.38$, while (2.90) gives 1.39, both of which are consistent with the results in Table 2.14.

So far we have considered plates with boundaries at fixed temperatures but without any heat generation within the plate. This has involved the solution of Laplace's equation (2.79) but the addition of heating (or cooling) within the plate will transform the problem into one of solving Poisson's equation (2.78). When translated into finite-difference form, the equation at the point (i, j) becomes

$$\theta(i+1, j) + \theta(i-1, j) + \theta(i, j+1) + \theta(i, j-1) - 4\theta(i, j) = -\frac{h^2}{\kappa} Q(i, j), \tag{2.92}$$

where $Q(i, j)$ is the rate of heat generation per unit volume at the point (i, j). Transformed into a standard form for SOR solution, this equation becomes

$$\theta(i, j) = \tfrac{1}{4} \left\{ \theta(i+1, j) + \theta(i-1, j) + \theta(i, j+1) + \theta(i, j-1) + \frac{h^2}{\kappa} Q(i, j) \right\}. \tag{2.93}$$

The program HOTPLATE makes provision for the extra heating term. It is necessary for the user to provide a function subprogram HEAT (X, Y) which gives the heating rate per unit volume (cooling if negative) at the point (X, Y) such that $X = (i-1)h$ and $Y = (j-1)h$, where the coordinate origin is at the point $(i, j) = (1, 1)$. There is also a DATA statement which must be modified to give the appropriate values of h, the dimension of the square grid, and κ, the conductivity of the material of the plate.

We illustrate the application of this facility by solution of the problem described in Fig. 2.15 with a heating term $Q(X, Y) = 10^6(X+Y) \, \text{W} \, \text{m}^{-3}$ and with $h=0.1$ m and $\kappa=400\,\mathrm{W\,m^{-1}K^{-1}}$. The value of w was taken as 1.38, the optimum value suggested by (2.91), with $\tau=0.0001$. The solution, found after 19 cycles of the SOR process, is shown in Fig. 2.17. Comparison with Fig. 2.16 shows the effect of the heating term which, as expected, gives higher temperatures within the plate.

The final feature which can be introduced into the heated-plate problem is to have differential boundary conditions corresponding to an insulated boundary or one exchanging heat with its environment. These are the kinds of differential boundary conditions dealt with in Section 2.7, where the gradients at the boundary were treated by using false points. In Section 2.7 we assumed that the end of the bar was exposed to a constant-temperature enclosure and

```
THE TOLERANCE IS   0.00010
THE OVER-RELAXATION PARAMETER IS   1.38
THE NUMBER OF CYCLES IS   19

  -1.    -1.    -1.   350.   400.   400.   450.

  -1.    -1.   300.   365.   414.   449.   500.

  -1.   300.   342.   388.   430.   466.   500.

 350.   352.   372.   401.   435.   470.   500.

 400.   376.   378.   396.   422.   458.   500.

 400.   362.   355.   363.   381.   416.   500.

 350.   300.   300.   300.   300.   300.   400.
```

Fig. 2.17 HOTPLATE output for the problem shown in Fig. 2.15, together with heat generation $Q(x,y)=10^6 xy\,\mathrm{W\,m^{-3}}$. The element edge is 0.1 m and the thermal conductivity $\kappa=400\,\mathrm{W\,m^{-1}K^{-1}}$.

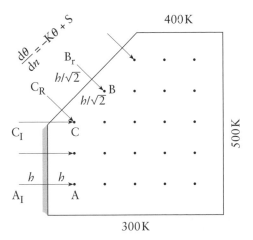

Fig. 2.18 A plate with one insulated edge and one exchanging heat with its surroundings. The external 'false' points have temperatures related to the internal temperatures at the heads of the arrows.

that transfer of heat to and from the bar was by radiation. Another important form of heat exchange is by convection, and in many cases this may be the dominant mode of heat exchange between an exposed surface and its surroundings. The total loss or gain of heat, as expressed by the thermal gradient at the boundary, is often modelled by

$$\kappa \frac{d\theta}{dn} = -K\theta + S, \tag{2.94}$$

where the thermal gradient is along the normal to the boundary and K and S are two constants. The plate shown in Fig. 2.15 is shown again in Fig. 2.18, but this time with one left-hand edge insulated and the other exchanging energy with its surroundings. For the insulated edge the thermal gradient at the insulator must be zero, and that is obtained by making the temperature of the false point A_I, $\theta(A_I) = \theta(A)$, and similarly $\theta(C_I) = \theta(C)$. The radiating edge is at $45°$ to the principal directions of the grid. The given values of K and S in (2.94) enable the thermal gradient to be found and hence the temperature of the false point B_r in terms of the temperature at B. To illustrate the use of HOTPLATE we run the problem of finding the equilibrium temperature in the plate illustrated in Fig. 2.19 which incorporates the use of all the facilities in the program as follows. Side AB is held at a constant temperature of $500\,\mathrm{K}$. Side BC is held at a constant temperature of $700\,\mathrm{K}$. Side CD is exchanging heat

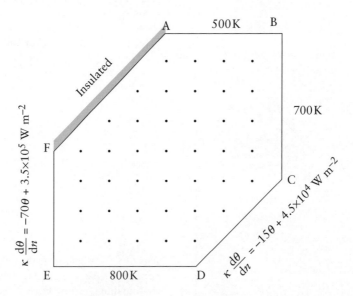

Fig. 2.19 A non-rectangular plate with edges at constant temperature, insulated and exchanging heat with their surroundings.

with its surroundings: the program calls for the input of values of K and S for the points indicated by E when defining this boundary. Side DE is held at a constant temperature of 800 K. Side EF is exchanging heat with its surroundings with a given K and S. Side FA is insulated, indicated by I. The plate heating is given by $H = 10^7 XY(1.0 - X)(1.0 - Y) \, \mathrm{W \, m^{-3}}$, and $h = 0.125 \, \mathrm{m}$, $\kappa = 400 \, \mathrm{W \, m^{-1} K^{-1}}$. The input to HOTPLATE describing the plate within a 9×9 mesh is:

X	X	X	X	500	500	500	500	600
X	X	X	I	U	U	U	U	700
X	X	I	U	U	U	U	U	700
X	I	U	U	U	U	U	U	700
I	U	U	U	U	U	U	U	700
E	U	U	U	U	U	U	U	700
E	U	U	U	U	U	U	E	X
E	U	U	U	U	U	E	X	X
800	800	800	800	800	800	X	X	X

The output of the program is shown in Fig. 2.20 with contours added by hand better to appreciate the overall temperature distribution.

2.15 The Poisson, Laplace and diffusion equations with other geometries

The Laplacian operator ∇^2 which appears in Poisson's and Laplace's equations, (2.78) and (2.79), has so far been treated only in a two-dimensional Cartesian coordinate system where

$$\nabla^2 = \frac{\partial^2}{\partial x^2} + \frac{\partial^2}{\partial y^2}. \tag{2.95a}$$

For three-dimensional problems this may be extended to

$$\nabla^2 = \frac{\partial^2}{\partial x^2} + \frac{\partial^2}{\partial y^2} + \frac{\partial^2}{\partial z^2}. \tag{2.95b}$$

The Laplacian operator also occurs in the three-dimensional form of the diffusion equation, and (2.20) may be generalized to

$$\frac{\partial n}{\partial t} = D\nabla^2 n. \tag{2.96}$$

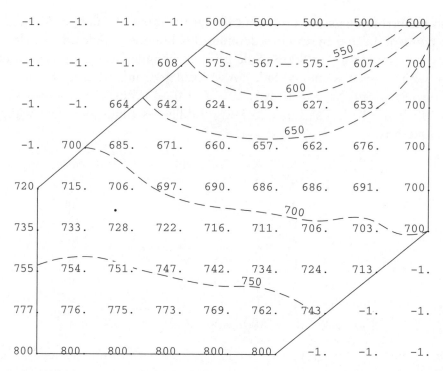

Fig. 2.20 HOTPLATE output for the plate shown in Fig. 2.19. Temperature contours have been added by hand.

The rectangular Cartesian geometry has been suitable for dealing with thermal equilibrium in the plates we have described so far, which are either rectangular or have sides at 45° to principal directions. However, other forms of the Laplacian operator are available for dealing with problems with different geometries – for example, for two-dimensional polar coordinates (r, θ) we have

$$\nabla^2 = \frac{1}{r}\frac{\partial}{\partial r}\left(r\frac{\partial}{\partial r}\right) + \frac{1}{r^2}\frac{\partial^2}{\partial \theta^2} = \frac{\partial^2}{\partial r^2} + \frac{1}{r}\frac{\partial}{\partial r} + \frac{1}{r^2}\frac{\partial^2}{\partial \theta^2}. \tag{2.97}$$

The grid that is appropriate to (2.97) is shown in Fig. 2.21, which shows circular arcs corresponding to constant values of r and radial lines corresponding to constant values of θ.

2.15.1 *The control-volume method*

Many problems are conservative, by which we mean that the total quantity of the field variable is a constant and gains and losses within a particular region of space are balanced by fluxes through the boundary surface. Setting up finite-difference equations which are conservative for generalized geometries can be achieved by the *control-volume method* which applies the conservation law directly to each cell. We take as an example a two-dimensional problem based on the cell structure shown in Fig. 2.21. For the purpose of illustrating the control-volume method we modify the cell to the form shown in Fig. 2.22 so that the field variable is determined at points such as P corresponding to integral values of i and j and half-integral values define the edges of the cell. Assuming that D in (2.96) is constant and isotropic, we can express in

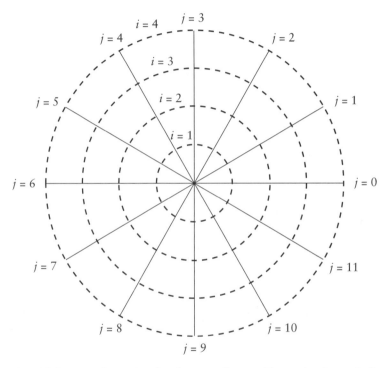

Fig. 2.21 A grid for two-dimensional polar coordinates. To retain the periodic nature of angular measure, values of j should be taken modulo 12.

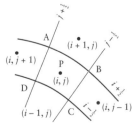

Fig. 2.22 Cells for the control-volume method.

finite-difference form the inward flux into the volume element ABCD in Fig. 2.22 which is assumed to have unit thickness. The cells are defined by constant intervals of r and θ so that $r_i - r_{i-1} = \Delta r$ for all i, $\theta_j - \theta_{j-1} = \Delta\theta$ for all j, and $r_{i+1/2} = \frac{1}{2}(r_i + r_{i+1})$.

The *inward* flux of solute through AB in time Δt is given by

$$F_{AB} = Dl_{AB}\left(\frac{\partial n}{\partial r}\right)_\alpha \Delta t, \tag{2.98}$$

where l_{AB} is the length of the arc AB and the mean radial concentration gradient is assumed to be half-way along the arc from B to A, at the point $(r_{i+1/2}, \theta_j)$. In finite-difference form this becomes

$$F_{AB} = Dr_{i+1/2}\Delta\theta \frac{n^t(i+1,j) - n^t(i,j)}{\Delta r}\Delta t, \tag{2.99a}$$

where the superscript t is an integer indicating the time. Similarly,

$$F_{CD} = Dr_{i-1/2}\Delta\theta \frac{n^t(i-1,j) - n^t(i,j)}{\Delta r}\Delta t. \tag{2.99b}$$

In addition, we find the finite-difference form of the inward flux of solute through the plane faces of the element as

$$F_{CB} = D\Delta r \frac{n^t(i,j-1) - n^t(i,j)}{r_i\Delta\theta}\Delta t \tag{2.99c}$$

and

$$F_{DA} = D\Delta r \frac{n^t(i,j+1) - n^t(i,j)}{r_i\Delta\theta}\Delta t. \tag{2.99d}$$

For conservation this is equated with the finite-difference expression for the increase in solute within the control volume, which is the change of concentration times the volume. If an explicit equation is required, then this is of the form

$$\{n^{t+1}(i,j) - n^t(i,j)\}\Delta r\, r_i\Delta\theta. \tag{2.100}$$

Equating (2.100) to the sum of (2.99a), (2.99b), (2.99c) and (2.99d), we obtain

$$n^{t+1}(i,j) = n^t(i,j) + D\Delta t\left[\frac{r_{i+1/2}\{n^t(i+1,j) - n^t(i,j)\} + r_{i-1/2}\{n^t(i-1,j) - n^t(i,j)\}}{r_i(\Delta r)^2}\right.$$
$$\left. + \frac{n^t(i,j+1) + n^t(i,j-1) - 2n^t(i,j)}{r_i^2(\Delta\theta)^2}\right]. \tag{2.101}$$

Since $r_{i+1/2}=r_i+\frac{1}{2}\Delta r$ and $r_{i-1/2}=r_i-\frac{1}{2}\Delta r$, (2.101) can be put in the form

$$n^{t+1}(i,j)=n^t(i,j)+D\Delta t\left[\frac{n^t(i+1,j)+n^t(i-1,j)-2n^t(i,j)}{(\Delta r)^2}+\frac{1}{r_i}\frac{n^t(i+1,j)-n^t(i-1,j)}{2\Delta r}\right.$$

$$\left.+\frac{1}{r_i^2}\frac{n^t(i,j+1)+n^t(i,j-1)-2n^t(i,j)}{(\Delta\theta)^2}\right]. \tag{2.102}$$

This is exactly the form of relationship which would have been derived from the form of ∇^2 given at the end of (2.97) and shows that this form is conservative. It would be possible to derive a finite-difference equation from the first form of ∇^2 given in (2.97); this would involve terms such as $n^t(i+2,j)$ and $n^t(i-2,j)$ and it would not be conservative.

2.15.2 *A heat-flow problem with axial symmetry*

A problem in which (2.96) might be useful is where fluid is transmitted at constant temperature through a long, thick-walled pipe, the outside of which is also at a fixed temperature. The flow of heat is radially outwards and the problem of finding the temperature distribution within the wall of the pipe is essentially a one-dimensional one, for which the Laplacian operator is

$$\nabla^2=\frac{\partial^2}{\partial r^2}+\frac{1}{r}\frac{\partial}{\partial r}. \tag{2.103}$$

Laplace's equation can be solved analytically in this case and gives

$$\theta=A\ln(r)+B, \tag{2.104}$$

where θ is temperature and A and B are constants which may be determined from the fixed temperatures at the inner and outer walls of the pipe.

The finite-difference form of Laplace's equation for this problem is given by the first two terms within the square brackets in (2.102) and, writing $\Delta r=h$, a set of linear equations is obtained of the form

$$\left(\frac{1}{h}+\frac{1}{2r}\right)\theta(i+1)-\frac{2}{h}\theta(i)+\left(\frac{1}{h}-\frac{1}{2r}\right)\theta(i-1)=0. \tag{2.105}$$

We take the inner and outer radii of the pipe as 0.05 m and 0.10 m respectively, with 10 divisions in the thickness of the pipe, so that $h=0.005$ m, and the temperature of the inner and outer walls is given by $\theta_0=300$ K and $\theta_{10}=500$ K. The equations for the interior points of the wall, which give coefficients

Table 2.15 The matrix coefficients and right-hand-side vector for the equations solving for the temperature within the walls of the pipe.

i	Coefficients of			Right-hand-side vector
	θ_{i-1}	θ_i	θ_{i+1}	
1		−400	209.09	−57 000
2	191.67	−400	208.33	
3	192.31	−400	207.69	
4	192.86	−400	207.14	
5	193.33	−400	206.67	
6	193.75	−400	206.25	
7	194.12	−400	205.88	
8	194.45	−400	205.55	
9	194.74	−400		−102 500

Table 2.16 A comparison of the solution of the problem of temperature within the pipe wall from GAUSSOR with the analytical solution from (2.104).

i	$\theta(i)$ (GAUSSOR)	$\theta(i)$ (analytical)
1	327.5	327.5
2	352.6	352.6
3	375.7	375.7
4	397.1	397.1
5	417.0	417.0
6	435.6	435.6
7	453.1	453.1
8	469.6	469.6
9	485.2	485.2

forming a tridiagonal matrix, are indicated in Table 2.15. The solution of this set of equations, given in Table 2.16, as determined by the program GAUSSOR, agrees exactly with the analytical solution from (2.104).

Finite-difference methods can be used to solve Laplace's or Poisson's equation for any coordinate system as long as the proper form of the Laplacian operator is used. From the pipe problem, where comparison with an analytical solution is possible, it will be seen that the method can be quite precise. As a check, where high precision is important, it is advisable to run the problem twice with intervals h and $2h$ in each of the dimensions. If the two results agree within the required tolerance then the result with the smaller interval can be accepted with confidence.

Problems

2.1 A bar of length 1 m, lagged along its length, has a cross-sectional area varying linearly from $0.0001 \, m^2$ at $x=0$ to $0.0002 \, m^2$ at $x=1.0 \, m$. The material of the bar has thermal conductivity $250 \, W \, m^{-1} K^{-1}$. If the temperature at $x=0$ is $500 \, K$ and at $x=1.0 \, m$ is $400 \, K$ then, by use of the modified program SHOOTEMP, find the heat flow along the bar and the temperature at $x=0.25, 0.50$ and $0.75 \, m$.

2.2 Use the program HEATRI to solve Problem 2.1. It will be necessary to calculate the appropriate coefficients for the tridiagonal matrix and right-hand-side vector and to incorporate these into a modified program.

2.3 A bar of length 2 m with uniform cross-section is lagged along its length but has exposed ends. At time $t=0$ it is at a uniform temperature of $300 \, K$, except for one end which is held at a constant temperature of $400 \, K$. If the material of the bar has thermal conductivity $150 \, W \, m^{-1} K^{-1}$, specific heat capacity $1250 \, J \, kg^{-1} K^{-1}$ and density $3500 \, kg \, m^{-3}$, then find the temperature profile at 20 cm intervals along the bar after $2000 \, s$ using:

  (i) the explicit method with HEATEX;
 (ii) the Crank–Nicholson method with HEATCRNI;
(iii) the Dufort–Frankel method with LEAPDF.

Investigate the instability of the leapfrog method.

2.4 Run the standard RADBAR problem with external temperature (i) $300 \, K$ and (ii) $400 \, K$. Divide the bar into eight segments and use $r=0.2$ ($\Delta t = 26.8 \, s$). Find the temperature profile in the bar after 107.3, 214.7 and 322.0 s.

2.5 Solve the following set of equations with GAUSSOR and find the optimum over-relaxation factor. You will find it convenient to modify GAUSSOR so that different relaxation factors can be tried without restarting the program and re-entering the equation coefficients each time.

$$
\begin{bmatrix}
8 & -1 & 0 & 2 & 3 & 0 & 1 & -1 \\
0 & 6 & 0 & 1 & -1 & 1 & -1 & 1 \\
0 & -2 & 5 & -1 & -1 & 0 & 0 & -1 \\
1 & 3 & 2 & 11 & -1 & 0 & -1 & 0 \\
3 & -1 & -1 & 1 & -9 & 0 & 1 & 1 \\
0 & 1 & 0 & -1 & 1 & 7 & 2 & 1 \\
0 & -1 & 0 & 1 & 0 & 1 & 4 & -1 \\
1 & -1 & 1 & -1 & 1 & -1 & 1 & 7
\end{bmatrix}
\begin{bmatrix}
x_1 \\ x_2 \\ x_3 \\ x_4 \\ x_5 \\ x_6 \\ x_7 \\ x_8
\end{bmatrix}
=
\begin{bmatrix}
28 \\ -10 \\ 6 \\ -2 \\ -23 \\ 7 \\ 4 \\ -8
\end{bmatrix}
$$

2.6   Figure 2.23 has top and bottom faces insulated and the edges at constant temperature, insulated or exchanging heat with the surroundings as shown. The thermal conductivity of the plate is $300\,\mathrm{W\,m^{-1}K^{-1}}$ and, with respect to the origin O, is heated according to $H = 10^7 \sin(\pi x)\sin(\pi y)\,\mathrm{W\,m^{-3}}$, where x and y are in metres. Use the program HOTPLATE to find the distribution of temperature in the plate.

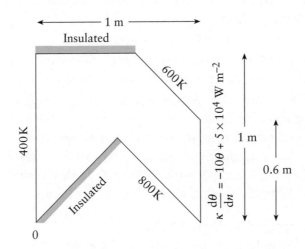

Fig. 2.23   Diagram for Problem 2.6.

3   *Simulation with particles*

3.1   Types of problem

We have already been introduced to particle methods in Section 1.4 and
Section 1.5, where bodies were simulated by point masses. In the case of the
oscillator the motion of only a single mass was followed, but in the case of the
Trojan asteroids there were four masses. These are representative of a class of
problems where the number of bodies is small and there is a one-to-one
correlation between the bodies in the system and those in the simulation.
Examples of few-body problems which fall into this category are: individual
electron orbits in magnetic and/or electric fields, as in the lens system of an
electron microscope; planetary motion with either a single planet or several
planets; and the evolution of small stellar clusters. In particle-interaction
problems it is often necessary to consider interactions between all pairs of
bodies. Assuming that interactions are symmetrical, so that the force on
particle i due to particle j, $\mathbf{F}_{i,j}$, is equal to $-\mathbf{F}_{j,i}$ and that particles do not exert
forces on themselves, then the total number of pair interactions is $\frac{1}{2}N(N-1)$,
where N is the number of bodies. Thus for a cluster of 100 stars there are 4950
pair interactions, which can easily be handled with computers of modest
power.

The astronomical example of the cluster of 100 stars has been suggested
as a few-body system, but astronomy offers much larger systems – for
example, globular stellar clusters with 10^5–10^6 stars. Here the number of
pair interactions is in the range 5×10^9 to 5×10^{11}, which is clearly beyond
the capacity of even the most powerful computers on a reasonable time-scale.
There are systems which are much larger still in terms of the number of
particles they contain. Examples are: liquids containing $\sim 10^{16}$ molecules in
$1\,\mu g$; galaxies containing 10^{11} stars; plasmas, which are intimate mixtures of
positive ions and electrons, the predominant state of matter in the universe;
and electrons in solids, of interest in semiconductor device simulation, for
instance. It is clear that pair interactions cannot be considered in systems of
this size and the study of such systems involves approximations which, while
making the problem manageable, still give results of sufficient precision to
be useful.

3.2   A few particles with inter-particle forces

A body moving in a region where its potential energy at position **r** is $V(\mathbf{r})$ experiences a force

$$F(\mathbf{r}) = -\nabla V(\mathbf{r}) \tag{3.1a}$$

or

$$m\frac{\mathrm{d}^2\mathbf{r}}{\mathrm{d}t^2} = -\nabla V(\mathbf{r}). \tag{3.1b}$$

Equation (3.1b) may be replaced by a pair of first-order equations:

$$\frac{\mathrm{d}\mathbf{r}}{\mathrm{d}t} = \mathbf{v} \tag{3.2a}$$

$$m\frac{\mathrm{d}\mathbf{v}}{\mathrm{d}t} = -\nabla V(\mathbf{r}), \tag{3.2b}$$

where **v** is the velocity of the body. For a single particle in three dimensions this requires the solution of six coupled differential equations:

$$\frac{\mathrm{d}x}{\mathrm{d}t} = v_x, \qquad \frac{\mathrm{d}y}{\mathrm{d}t} = v_y, \qquad \frac{\mathrm{d}z}{\mathrm{d}t} = v_z;$$

$$m\frac{\mathrm{d}v_x}{\mathrm{d}t} = -\frac{\partial V}{\partial x}, \qquad m\frac{\mathrm{d}v_y}{\mathrm{d}t} = -\frac{\partial V}{\partial y}, \qquad m\frac{\mathrm{d}v_z}{\mathrm{d}t} = -\frac{\partial V}{\partial z}. \tag{3.3}$$

In Section 1.5.1 the Runge–Kutta process for the solution of differential equations was applied to the problem of the stability of Trojan asteroids and also the decay of the orbit of a tidally affected satellite. The Runge–Kutta process was generalized for two dependent variables and the principle of extending the process to any number of dependent variables was clearly indicated. Even a simple problem involving two interacting bodies in a three-dimensional space gives 6 dependent variables and the system of equations to be solved is then of the form:

$$\frac{\mathrm{d}x}{\mathrm{d}t} = f_x(x, y, z, v_x, v_y, v_z, t) \qquad \frac{\mathrm{d}y}{\mathrm{d}t} = f_y(x, y, z, v_x, v_y, v_z, t)$$

$$\frac{\mathrm{d}z}{\mathrm{d}t} = f_z(x, y, z, v_x, v_y, v_z, t) \qquad \frac{\mathrm{d}v_x}{\mathrm{d}t} = f_{v_x}(x, y, z, v_x, v_y, v_z, t) \tag{3.4}$$

$$\frac{dv_y}{dt}=f_{v_y}(x,y,z,v_x,v_y,v_z,t) \quad \frac{dv_z}{dt}=f_{v_z}(x,y,z,v_x,v_y,v_z,t)$$

The general strategy for solving a problem with many interacting bodies, where only pair interactions occur, is to consider all pairs of bodies in turn. For the pair of bodies i and j, the contributions to the left hand sides of (3.4) can be found and added into appropriate arrays. When all pairs have been considered the arrays will contain the complete contributions to the right-hand sides of (3.4).

The four step Runge–Kutta process is one member of a family of methods, some of which are simpler than the four-step process and some of which are much more complicated, involving five or more steps. In general the more steps in the process the greater is the accuracy which can be obtained for a given amount of computational effort. Alternatively, for a particular accuracy less computational effort is required. However, for many problems high accuracy is not required and methods are available which are simple in concept, easy to program, and very economical to apply. In the course of this chapter the reader will be introduced to this kind of approach.

3.2.1 *A binary-star system*

Here we shall demonstrate the general principle of handling few-body systems by the simple problem of a binary-star system. The problem is not that of one body orbiting another which is essentially at rest; this would only be true if one of the bodies had a very small mass. With finite mass for both bodies it is more complicated because the two stars are both in orbit around their stationary centre of mass. The situation is illustrated in Fig. 3.1a where the stars, S_1 and S_2, with masses M_1 and M_2, are separated by a distance r. The centre of mass is at O, so that

$$OS_1 = rM_2/(M_1+M_2) \tag{3.5a}$$

and

$$OS_2 = rM_1/(M_1+M_2). \tag{3.5b}$$

The accelerations, shown in Fig. 3.1a, have magnitudes GM_2/r^2 and GM_1/r^2, respectively.

From the representational point of view it is an advantage to transform the problem so that one of the stars is at rest at the origin. This can be done by applying a uniform acceleration to the whole system which brings one of

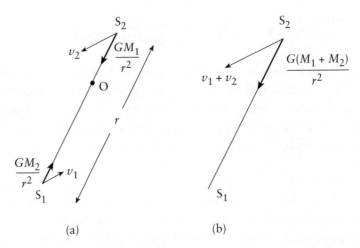

Fig. 3.1 (a) Two bodies orbiting around their centre of mass. (b) An acceleration bringing S_1 to rest changes the acceleration of S_2 to $G(M_1+M_2)/R^2$.

the stars to rest and then taking its position as the origin. This is shown in Fig. 3.1b, where S_1 becomes the origin. Bringing S_1 to rest requires that the acceleration of S_2 now has magnitude $G(M_1+M_2)/r^2$. For a two-body system this is equivalent to using a *reduced mass frame* where the mass $M_1 M_2/(M_1+M_2)$ is subjected to a force with magnitude $GM_1 M_2/r^2$, but the concept of applying a uniform acceleration to bring one body to rest is applicable in many-body systems.

One way of testing the accuracy of the computational process is to check on the conservation of energy, momentum and angular momentum. When the origin is shifted to one of the bodies the conservation of momentum cannot be checked because the assumption has been built in that the centre of mass is given by equations (3.5). If the velocity of S_2 relative to S_1 is $\mathbf{v}_{12}$ then the velocities of S_1 and S_2 relative to the centre of mass are

$$\mathbf{v}_1 = -\frac{M_2}{M_1+M_2}\mathbf{v}_{12} \tag{3.6a}$$

and

$$\mathbf{v}_2 = \frac{M_1}{M_1+M_2}\mathbf{v}_{12}. \tag{3.6b}$$

This implies that the momentum relative to the centre of mass is always zero.

The total energy of the system is given by

$$E = \frac{1}{2} M_1 v_1^2 + \frac{1}{2} M_2 v_2^2 - \frac{GM_1 M_2}{r}; \tag{3.7}$$

from equations (3.6), this can be expressed as

$$E = \frac{1}{2} \frac{M_1 M_2}{M_1 + M_2} v_{12}^2 - \frac{GM_1 M_2}{r}, \tag{3.8}$$

which quantity should be conserved during the progress of the computation. In general, the angular momentum for an *n*-body system can be expressed as

$$\mathbf{H} = \sum_{i=1}^{n} m_i \mathbf{v}_i \times \mathbf{r}_i. \tag{3.9}$$

This can be written in component form as

$$\mathbf{H} = H_x \hat{\mathbf{i}} + H_y \hat{\mathbf{j}} + H_z \hat{\mathbf{k}}, \tag{3.10}$$

where the symbol ^ indicates the unit vectors in the *x*, *y* and *z* directions. For the binary-star problem, which is two-dimensional, the motion can be defined in the *x*–*y* plane so that the angular momentum vector points along *z*. The quantity to be conserved in this case is

$$H_z = M_1 (v_{x1} y_1 - v_{y,1} x_1) + M_2 (v_{x2} y_2 - v_{y,2} x_2), \tag{3.11a}$$

where the coordinates of the stars are with respect to the centre of mass. Using equations (3.6), this becomes

$$H_z = \frac{M_1 M_2}{M_1 + M_2} (v_{x12} y - v_{y12} x), \tag{3.11b}$$

where the velocity components and coordinates are those of S_2 relative to S_1 as origin.

We can illustrate the conservation of energy and angular momentum with results for a binary-star simulation run with a modification of the program NBODY. The two stars had masses $0.75 M_\odot$ and $0.25 M_\odot$ and were separated by a distance 5.2 AU. One star was initially at rest, with the other moving perpendicular to the separation vector at speed of $2.755\,359\,\mathrm{AU\,yr^{-1}}$ in the astronomical system of units described in Section 1.5.1. This gives a circular motion of each of the planets around the centre of mass. The program was

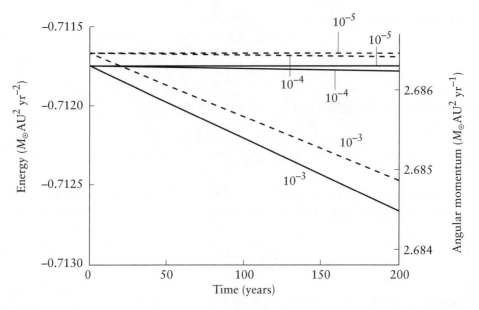

Fig. 3.2 Changes of energy (full line) and angular momentum (dashed line) with different tolerances.

run with different tolerances and the variation of energy and angular momentum with time is shown in Fig. 3.2. For a simulated time of 200 years there was no change in energy or angular momentum to one part in 10^5 for a tolerance of 10^{-5} or less, but for tolerances of 10^{-4} and 10^{-3} there were significant changes.

The tolerance required for any particular problem will depend on the aim of the simulation. It is clear from Fig. 3.2 that a tolerance of 10^{-3} is leading to large errors, which increase as the simulation time increases. A tolerance level of 10^{-6} would give no detectable change of energy and angular momentum over 200 years, but if it was intended to look at the long-term development of the binary system – over, say, 10^8 years – then even this tolerance would probably be inadequate. To decrease the tolerance even further would involve a heavy penalty in computation time and bring increasing danger of significant error due to computational round-off, so the answer to the problem is to use a better integration routine. The Runge–Kutta process we have shown here is a four-step process. There are other routines of similar type with more steps for each advance of the independent variable which, although they take longer per time step, allow longer time steps and are more economical for a given accuracy. A very detailed treatment of such methods has been given by Dormand (1996).

3.3 An electron in a magnetic field

The basic equation for the motion of an electron in a magnetic field is

$$m\frac{d^2\mathbf{r}}{dt^2} = e\mathbf{v} \times \mathbf{B},\qquad(3.12)$$

where e is the charge of the electron and $\mathbf{B}$ the magnetic field. This may be factorized into the pair of equations

$$\frac{d\mathbf{r}}{dt} = \mathbf{v}\qquad(3.13a)$$

and

$$\frac{d\mathbf{v}}{dt} = \frac{e}{m}\mathbf{v} \times \mathbf{B},\qquad(3.13b)$$

which leads to the set of differential equations

$$\frac{dx}{dt} = v_x,\qquad \frac{dy}{dt} = v_y,\qquad \frac{dz}{dt} = v_z;$$

$$\frac{dv_x}{dt} = \frac{e}{m}(v_y B_z - v_z B_y),\qquad \frac{dv_y}{dt} = \frac{e}{m}(v_z B_x - v_x B_z),\qquad(3.14)$$

$$\frac{dv_z}{dt} = \frac{e}{m}(v_x B_y - v_y B_x).$$

If we take a simplified system with two-dimensional motion $\mathbf{v} = (v_x, v_y, 0)$ perpendicular to a magnetic field $\mathbf{B} = (0, 0, B_z)$ then the equations to be solved are

$$\frac{dx}{dt} = v_x \quad\text{and}\quad \frac{dy}{dt} = v_y,$$

together with

$$\frac{dv_x}{dt} = \frac{e}{m}v_y B_z \quad\text{and}\quad \frac{dv_y}{dt} = -\frac{e}{m}v_x B_z.\qquad(3.15)$$

For an electron moving with speed v in a circular orbit perpendicular to a uniform magnetic field $\mathbf{B}$, equating central force to mass times centripetal acceleration gives

$$\frac{v^2}{r} = \frac{e}{m}vB$$

or

$$\frac{v}{r} = \omega = \frac{e}{m} B.$$

This value of ω, which is independent of the radius of the orbit and therefore is characteristic of the field at a point, is called the *local cyclotron frequency* and usually represented by the symbol Ω. This quantity, like the field itself, can vary in both space and time. The two final equations in (3.15) can now be written

$$\frac{dv_x}{dt} = \Omega v_y \quad \text{and} \quad \frac{dv_y}{dt} = -\Omega v_x. \tag{3.16}$$

The four coupled differential equations describing the motion of the electron could be solved using the Runge–Kutta method, but here we shall show a solution process involving finite differences. Using j to represent the time, with time step Δt, similar to the notation developed in Section 2.4, the four equations now appear in the form

$$\frac{x(j+1)-x(j)}{\Delta t} = \frac{1}{2}\{v_x(j)+v_x(j+1)\}, \tag{3.17a}$$

$$\frac{y(j+1)-y(j)}{\Delta t} = \frac{1}{2}\{v_y(j)+v_y(j+1)\}, \tag{3.17b}$$

$$\frac{v_x(j+1)-v_x(j)}{\Delta t} = \frac{1}{2}\Omega\{v_y(j+1)+v_y(j)\}, \tag{3.17c}$$

$$\frac{v_y(j+1)-v_y(j)}{\Delta t} = -\frac{1}{2}\Omega\{v_x(j+1)+v_x(j)\}. \tag{3.17d}$$

On the right-hand side of these equations the averages of v_x and v_y in the interval $t(j)$ to $t(j+1)$ are used.

Equations (3.17c) and (3.17d) can be solved for $v_x(j+1)$ and $v_y(j+1)$, giving

$$v_x(j+1) = \left(\frac{1-\psi^2}{1+\psi^2}\right)v_x(j) + \left(\frac{2\psi}{1+\psi^2}\right)v_y(j) \tag{3.18a}$$

and

$$v_y(j+1) = \left(\frac{1-\psi^2}{1+\psi^2}\right)v_y(j) - \left(\frac{2\psi}{1+\psi^2}\right)v_x(j), \tag{3.18b}$$

where $\psi = \frac{1}{2}\Omega\Delta t$, which is half the cyclotron angle through which the electron rotates in time Δt. Inserting results (3.18) in (3.17a) and (3.17b), we find

$$x(j+1) = x(j) + \Delta t \left\{ \left(\frac{1}{1+\psi^2} \right) v_x(j) + \left(\frac{\psi}{1+\psi^2} \right) v_y(j) \right\} \qquad (3.19a)$$

and

$$y(j+1) = y(j) + \Delta t \left\{ \left(\frac{1}{1+\psi^2} \right) v_y(j) - \left(\frac{\psi}{1+\psi^2} \right) v_x(j) \right\}. \qquad (3.19b)$$

If the field, which is restricted to the z direction, is a function of x, y and t then the value of ψ used in (3.19) should correspond to the field at the average position and average time. This will be

$$\psi = \frac{1}{2} \Delta t \frac{e}{m} B_z \left\{ x(j) + \frac{1}{2} \Delta t v_x(j), y(j) + \frac{1}{2} \Delta t v_y(j), t(j) + \frac{1}{2} \Delta t \right\}. \qquad (3.20)$$

Equations (3.18) and (3.19) enable the motion of the electron to be followed.

From equations (3.18) it is readily found that if B_z is a constant, so that ψ is the same at times t_j and t_{j+1}, the kinetic energy, E_K, of the electron remains constant since

$$E_K = \frac{1}{2} m \{ v_x^2(j) + v_y^2(j) \} = \frac{1}{2} m \{ v_x^2(j+1) + v_y^2(j+1) \}. \qquad (3.21)$$

If this were not so then the electron would gradually spiral inwards or outwards in order to change its energy and no stable closed motion in a constant magnetic field would be possible.

If an electric field is added with direction in the x–y plane, then equations (3.16) become

$$\frac{dv_x}{dt} = \Omega v_y + \frac{e}{m} E_x \quad \text{and} \quad \frac{dv_y}{dt} = -\Omega v_x + \frac{e}{m} E_y. \qquad (3.22)$$

The equations corresponding to the previous equations (3.17c) and (3.17d) are now

$$v_x(j+1) - v_x(j) = \psi \{ v_y(j+1) + v_y(j) \} + \frac{e}{m} E_x \Delta t \qquad (3.23a)$$

and

$$v_y(j+1) - v_y(j) = -\psi \{ v_x(j+1) + v_x(j) \} + \frac{e}{m} E_y \Delta t. \qquad (3.23b)$$

Equations (3.17a), (3.17b), (3.23a) and (3.23b) may be solved to give position and velocity at time $t(j+1)$ in terms of the corresponding quantities at time $t(j)$. The equations giving the velocities are of the form

$$v_x(j+1)=\left(\frac{1-\psi^2}{1+\psi^2}\right)v_x(j)+\left(\frac{2\psi}{1+\psi^2}\right)v_y(j)+\frac{e}{m}\Delta t\,\frac{1}{1+\psi^2}\,(E_x+\psi E_y) \quad (3.24a)$$

and

$$v_y(j+1)=\left(\frac{1-\psi^2}{1+\psi^2}\right)v_y(j)-\left(\frac{2\psi}{1+\psi^2}\right)v_x(j)+\frac{e}{m}\Delta t\,\frac{1}{1+\psi^2}\,(E_y-\psi E_x). \quad (3.24b)$$

The first two terms in each of these equations are just those which appear in equations (3.18), and the final terms give the extra components of velocity due to the presence of the electric field. Part of these extra components added to $v_x(j+1)$ and $v_y(j+1)$ is in the direction of the electric field, but another part, proportional to E_y and $-E_x$ respectively, is perpendicular to the electric field. Thus an important effect of the electric field, which can be observed, is to give a slow drift of the electron's motion perpendicular to the direction of the electric field. This pattern of motion is also found if more precise ways of solving the differential equations are used.

3.3.1 *The electron-microscope lens*

An important application of the motion of electrons in magnetic fields is in the design of lenses for various types of electron microscope. Here we shall illustrate the principle by which focusing is achieved with a two-dimensional example. We consider electrons moving in the x–y plane starting at position $(0, Y)$ fairly close to the origin and moving in a direction making a small angle with the x-axis. There is a magnetic field along the z direction with magnitude

$$B_z = cy, \quad (3.25)$$

where c is a constant. The trajectories of such electrons can be followed with the computer program MAGELEC (see p. xv). We consider 1 keV electrons, for which the corresponding speed is $1.785 \times 10^7\,\mathrm{m\,s^{-1}}$. It is evident that electrons starting at the origin and moving along the x-axis will not be deflected because they are in zero field. We now take an electron starting at the origin for which the initial components of velocity in the x and y directions are $v_x = 1.785 \times 10^7\,\mathrm{m\,s^{-1}}$ and $v_y = 1.785 \times 10^5\,\mathrm{m\,s^{-1}}$. The constant c in (3.25) is taken as $0.5\,\mathrm{T\,m^{-1}}$ and the time step for solving equations (3.18) and (3.19)

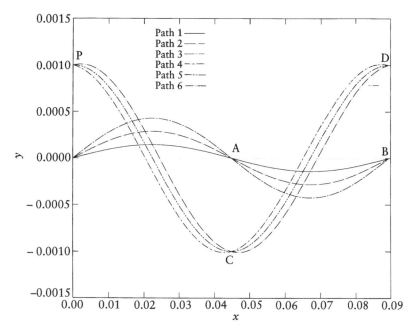

Fig. 3.3 The trajectories of electrons in a magnetic field $B_z = cy$.

is fixed at 5×10^{-11} s. The trajectory found is the one shown as path 1 in Fig. 3.3, which is seen to cut the axis at points A and B. Path 2 also starts from the origin but in this case the component of velocity v_y is doubled to $3.570 \times 10^5 \, \mathrm{m \, s^{-1}}$ and it too crosses the x-axis at the points A and B. Electrons which set out from the origin in directions making a small angle to the x-axis will all pass through A and B, which clearly shows a focusing effect. Next we start the electrons from a point P at a distance 1 mm from the origin and consider trajectories of electrons all of which have the same x component of velocity, $1.785 \times 10^7 \, \mathrm{m \, s^{-1}}$ but with y components 1.785, 0 and $-1.785 \times 10^5 \, \mathrm{m \, s^{-1}}$ (paths 4–6). These are shown in Fig. 3.3, and it is found that they all pass through the points C and D, with the same x coordinates as A and B, respectively. A one-dimensional object situated on the y-axis would form an inverted image on the line AC and an upright image on the line BD.

3.4 N-body problems

We have already mentioned the difficulties associated with the solution of problems involving a large number of interacting bodies. If there are N bodies interacting gravitationally then the system of equations to be solved is

$$\frac{d\mathbf{r}_i}{dt} = \mathbf{v}_i, \qquad \frac{d\mathbf{v}_i}{dt} = \sum_{\substack{k=1 \\ k \neq i}}^{N} \frac{Gm_k(\mathbf{r}_k - \mathbf{r}_i)}{|\mathbf{r}_k - \mathbf{r}_i|^3}. \tag{3.26}$$

For $N=2$ there is an analytical solution, as there also is for some special three-body problems such as the Trojan asteroids. For larger values of N numerical methods must be used.

We have seen that such problems can be tackled by using the Runge–Kutta method which is incorporated in the program NBODY. However, in equations (3.26) it can be seen that the changes in position depend on velocity and the changes of velocity depend upon position, and this enables the leapfrog method (Section 2.8) to be used. While this will be much less accurate than the Runge–Kutta method, it will be much faster and also require much less computer memory for large systems. If the interest is in the general behaviour pattern of a system rather than in determining the precise position of every body then it may be adequate. The form of the leapfrog equations corresponding to (3.26) is as follows:

$$x(i,j+1) = x(i,j-1) + 2v_x(i,j)\Delta t \tag{3.27a}$$

and

$$v_x(i,j+2) = v_x(i,j) + 2\Delta t \sum_{\substack{k=1 \\ k \neq i}}^{N} \frac{Gm_k\{x(k,j+1) - x(i,j+1)\}}{|r(k,j+1) - r(i,j+1)|^3}, \tag{3.27b}$$

with corresponding equations for the y and z components.

3.4.1 *Evolution of a stellar cluster*

The problem with the leapfrog method, apart from its lack of precision, is that its continual use depends upon a constant time step, and this may lead to complete failure of the computation for systems which are unpredictable in their behaviour. Thus if two bodies come so close together such that the distance between them is less than the distance moved in one time step then the results may become meaningless. The program CLUSTER is designed to integrate the motions of a cluster of solar-mass stars from a quasi-stable initial condition using the leapfrog method. The chosen number, N, of stars is randomly placed in a spherical volume of radius R. Each star is given the same speed V but in a randomly chosen direction; the speed is found from the virial theorem (Appendix 3). Small corrections are made to the randomly chosen positions and velocities to put the centre of mass at the origin and to give zero momentum. Since the leapfrog method is not self-starting it is initiated with one step of a simple Euler predictor-corrector process (Section 1.3). The initial time step is estimated as 0.01 times the minimum distance between stars divided by the maximum speed of any star. This ensures that the distance between any pair of stars should not change by more than 2 per cent during the time step. At the beginning of each time step the ratio of minimum distance to maximum velocity times time step is found. If this is outside the range 50 to 150 then a new beginning is made with the leapfrog method using an initial predictor-corrector step and a resetting of the time step as previously described. In this simple, albeit not the most efficient, way the conditioning of the leapfrog method is kept as favourable as possible.

Table 3.1 shows the results of running CLUSTER for $N=40$ and $R=40\,000$ AU for various simulation times from approximately 10 000 years to 320 000 years. Since the force on star i due to star j is equal and opposite to that on star j due to star i, the leapfrog process should conserve momentum. From the columns COM and $\langle V \rangle$ in the table it will be seen that the mean position and the zero momentum of the stars is preserved for all simulation times to within the precision of the computation. Something which is not necessarily conserved by the algorithm is energy, and it will be seen that the total energy does change and by almost 5 per cent for the longest simulation time. The table shows a clear tendency for the total energy to increase (that is, become less negative) with time. In fact it can be shown that for this type of calculation and with nearly random truncation errors energy will progressively increase in a random fashion. For a system with potential and kinetic energy satisfying the virial theorem the mean square distance of particles from

Table 3.1 The results from CLUSTER with 40 solar-mass stars initially within a spherical volume of radius 40 000 AU and with initial speeds given by the virial theorem.

Time (years)	ΣR^2 (AU^2)	COM (AU)	$\langle V \rangle$ (AU yr^{-1})	TOTEN $(M_\odot \, \text{AU}^2 \, \text{yr}^{-2})$
0	3.89×10^{10}	3.68×10^{-4}	2.72×10^{-9}	-0.4650
10 037	3.91×10^{10}	1.34×10^{-3}	1.59×10^{-9}	-0.4643
20 158	3.94×10^{10}	1.25×10^{-3}	2.68×10^{-9}	-0.4643
40 122	4.00×10^{10}	2.37×10^{-3}	5.61×10^{-9}	-0.4643
80 041	4.12×10^{10}	1.67×10^{-3}	1.72×10^{-8}	-0.4649
160 330	4.42×10^{10}	6.79×10^{-3}	2.93×10^{-8}	-0.4641
320 017	5.17×10^{10}	9.41×10^{-3}	2.87×10^{-8}	-0.4438

ΣR^2 is a measure of the geometrical moment of inertia (Appendix 3); COM is the distance of the centre of mass from the origin; $\langle V \rangle$ is the speed of the centre of mass; and TOTEN is the total energy of the system.

the origin, $\langle R^2 \rangle$, should be invariant with time. It will be seen that this is not true, especially for the longer simulation times, but this is linked to the previously mentioned non-conservation of energy.

In this application, as time progresses, the leapfrog method is showing instability, as mentioned in Section 2.8. It is not recommended for N-body problems demanding precision – for example, following the motions of a system of planets for millions of years or more. For such applications it is necessary to use the very accurate integration algorithms described by Dormand (1996).

3.5   Molecular dynamics

Molecular dynamics is a very powerful and widely used technique for a large range of applications involving solid-atom systems, molecular structure and liquids. The general principle is very simple. The dynamics of a single particle i of position $\mathbf{r}_i$ and velocity $\mathbf{v}_i$, subject to a total force $\mathbf{F}_i$, is computed by the numerical integration of the kinematic equation of motion,

$$\frac{d\mathbf{r}_i}{dt} = \mathbf{v}_i, \tag{3.28a}$$

and Newton's second law,

$$\frac{d\mathbf{v}_i}{dt} = \frac{\mathbf{F}_i}{m_i}, \tag{3.28b}$$

where m_i is the mass of the particle. The force $\mathbf{F}_i$ is the sum of the external forces and the mutual interactions. As we have already noted, the total force, in principle, contains too many terms to be calculated on a repetitive basis. However, in problems where molecular dynamics is used the short-range nature of the forces allows these sums to be greatly curtailed. This occurs in two ways:

1. The general structural arrangement of particles is fixed, so that each individual particle has a set of clearly identifiable neighbours. Examples of this are models of chemical compounds, widely used in the pharmaceutical industry to design drugs; surface behaviour (for example, the study of catalysts); models of chemical reactions.
2. The medium is effectively infinite, but uniform, so that any one region is similar to any other. This allows the use of periodicity to restrict the number of particles required, as illustrated in the following example.

3.5.1 *Simulation of a liquid by molecular dynamics*

A liquid is a state of matter where the potential energy of the system, arising from the inter-molecular forces, has a magnitude similar to that of the kinetic energy of the molecular motion. Individual molecules may acquire enough kinetic energy to leave the surface of the liquid, forming a vapour, but the bulk of the material will be bound together so that the volume is fixed. Within the liquid the molecules move around forming small ordered aggregations which are constantly breaking up and reforming in new arrangements. By contrast, in a solid, potential energy dominates and the molecules will be rigidly bound in a lattice. While the individual molecules or atoms will possess energy of vibration around their mean positions, this energy is insufficient to disrupt the bonds binding the system together. Finally, for a gas, with much greater distances between molecules, the kinetic energy is dominant and molecules move freely, occupying all the space available to them.

An obvious approach to creating a model of liquid behaviour is to use molecular dynamics where the motions of individual molecules are followed. It is necessary to know the force law between molecules but, if this is known, then an N-body simulation can be carried out – at least in principle. From the molecular motions and the changing pattern of molecular positions it may then be possible to derive the properties of the liquid by statistical means. However, for such a model, where it is required to deduce the properties of the *bulk* fluid it is necessary to escape from the restriction of having a boundary. One obvious way of doing this is to have a very large system with very many molecules and then to make the estimate of properties from the behaviour of the molecules at the centre of the system well away from the boundary. This would require an enormous number of particles – too many to follow by any precise method of integration of the equations of motion. However, as previously mentioned, another way to simulate an effectively infinite liquid without needing to consider a very large number of particles is by using a periodic cell structure, illustrated in Fig. 3.4 in two dimensions. The centre cell in Fig. 3.4 contains 15 particles representing atoms or molecules, and this cell is reproduced on a lattice to give the eight similar neighbouring cells. All normal force laws are, in principle, infinite in their range but in practice it is nearly always possible to terminate them at a finite distance. There are two reasons for this: first, beyond a certain distance the actual magnitudes of the forces will be small; and second, forces due to the infinite region beyond a certain distance will, by symmetry, tend to cancel each other. Thus in our two-dimensional case only the particles within some circle of radius r_L need to be considered in determining the forces on particle A.

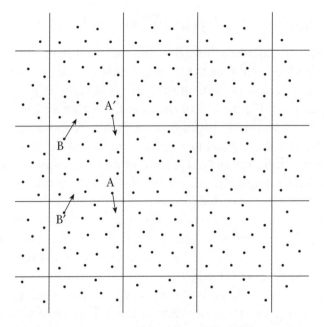

Fig. 3.4 Simulation of a two-dimensional liquid by a cell model.

A condition for this cell method to work satisfactorily is that the side of the cell should be greater than the accepted range of the force – two or three times greater gives a very satisfactory system. The repeated-cell model has the property that the number of particles in each cell remains constant as the dynamics is followed. If particles A and B move out of the cell as shown then the *ghost* particles A′ and B′ move in to take their place. This also ensures that the density of the liquid remains fixed, which is required in most, but not all, simulations.

3.5.2 *The equation of state of a liquid*

Before embarking on a description of methods of modelling liquids, we should first consider some basic theory concerning the equation of state of a liquid, because deducing that is an important goal of the modelling. We consider a cubical container, with an origin of coordinates at its centre, of side L, containing N molecules each of mass m. The ith molecule has coordinates (x_i, y_i, z_i), a velocity c_i with components (u_i, v_i, w_i), and experiences a force F_i with components $(F_{x,i}, F_{y,i}, F_{z,i})$. Then we may write

$$F_{x,i} = m \frac{d^2 x_i}{dt^2}, \tag{3.29a}$$

with similar equations for the other two components. We now note the relationship

$$\frac{d}{dt}\left(\frac{dx_i^2}{dt}\right) = \frac{d}{dt}\left(2x_i\frac{dx_i}{dt}\right) = 2u_i^2 + 2x_i\frac{d^2x_i}{dt^2}. \tag{3.29b}$$

Combining the results of (3.29a) and (3.29b), we find

$$F_{x,i}x_i = mx_i\frac{d^2x_i}{dt^2} = \frac{1}{2}m\frac{d}{dt}\left(\frac{dx_i^2}{dt}\right) - mu_i^2. \tag{3.30}$$

Adding the components in the other directions and summing over all molecules,

$$\frac{1}{2}m\sum_{i=1}^{N}\frac{d}{dt}\left\{\frac{d}{dt}(x_i^2+y_i^2+z_i^2)\right\} = \sum_{i=1}^{N}(F_{x,i}x_i+F_{y,i}y_i+F_{z,i}z_i) + \sum_{i=1}^{N}mc_i^2. \tag{3.31}$$

Since the molecules are confined in the box the quantity on the left-hand side, although it will slightly fluctuate, must average to zero. The second term on the right-hand side is twice the total translational kinetic energy of the molecules. Since each molecule has three degrees of translational freedom, each with average energy $\frac{1}{2}kT$, where k is the Boltmann constant and T the absolute temperature, then the value of this final term is $3NkT$.

The first term on the right-hand side of (3.31) is known as the *virial of Clausius*, and we shall now see how to express it in a more convenient way. The forces on the molecules are of two kinds – those of the molecules on each other and those due to the walls of the container. If we take the molecules very close to the wall at $x=\frac{1}{2}L$ then each of these will exert a force on the wall and the wall will exert an equal reaction force on the molecule. The total force on the wall in the x direction is PL^2, where P is the pressure on the wall. This is therefore the magnitude of the sum of the forces exerted by the wall on the molecules near the wall, all with coordinate $\frac{1}{2}L$. The contribution to the virial term is thus $-\frac{1}{2}PL^3$, and there will be the same contribution from each of the six walls – giving a total contribution $-3PL^3 = -3PV$, where V is the volume of the container.

If the x component of the force on molecule i due to molecule j is $F_x(r_{ij})$, where r_{ij} is the distance between the two molecules, then

$$F_{x,i} = \sum_{\substack{j=1\\i\neq j}}^{N} F_x(r_{ij}), \tag{3.32}$$

which gives the x component of the molecule–molecule contribution to the virial term as

$$C_x = \sum_{i=1}^{N} \left\{ \sum_{\substack{j=1 \\ j \neq i}}^{N} F_x(r_{ij}) x_i \right\}. \tag{3.33}$$

The terms in the summation C_x involve interactions between all pairs of molecules. For the pair of molecules i and j the net contribution to C_x is

$$F_x(r_{ij}) x_i + F_x(r_{ji}) x_j = F_x(r_{ij}) x_i - F_x(r_{ij}) x_j = F_x(r_{ij})(x_i - x_j), \tag{3.34}$$

since the force on i due to j is equal and opposite to that on j due to i. If the force on i due to j is directed along the line joining the two molecules then we can write

$$F_x(r_{ij}) = F(r_{ij}) \frac{x_i - x_j}{r_{ij}}, \tag{3.35}$$

and hence the total contribution of the pair of molecules i and j, for all three components, is

$$F(r_{ij}) \frac{(x_i - x_j)^2 + (y_i - y_j)^2 + (z_i - z_j)^2}{r_{ij}} = F(r_{ij}) r_{ij}. \tag{3.36}$$

With the values we have found for all the terms in equation (3.31) it now appears as

$$PV = NkT + \frac{1}{3} \left\langle \sum_{\text{pairs}} F(r_{ij}) r_{ij} \right\rangle, \tag{3.37}$$

where the averaging bracket round the final term is to allow for the fluctuations with time of all the terms in the equation. Without the second term on the right-hand side we just have the equation of state for a perfect gas where the individual molecules do not interact. The liquid equation of state contains in addition the final term which is completely concerned with molecule–molecule interactions.

3.5.3 *The equation of state from molecular dynamics*

A molecular dynamics program FLUIDYN, based on a cell model, is available (see p. xv). It is assumed that pairs of molecules separated by a distance r give a Lennard-Jones potential of the form

$$\phi(r) = \frac{a}{r^{12}} - \frac{b}{r^6}. \tag{3.38}$$

The second term represents a long-range attraction and the first a convenient way of representing a short-range repulsion when the molecules approach each other too closely. The form of this potential is shown in Fig. 3.5a, and the corresponding force–distance relationship in Fig. 3.5b. At distance r_c the force is zero and at distance σ the potential is zero. The depth of the potential well is ε. Other forms of (3.38) can then be found as

$$\phi(r) = \varepsilon\left\{\left(\frac{r_c}{r}\right)^{12} - 2\left(\frac{r_c}{r}\right)^6\right\} \tag{3.39a}$$

or

$$\phi(r) = 4\varepsilon\left\{\left(\frac{\sigma}{r}\right)^{12} - \left(\frac{\sigma}{r}\right)^6\right\}. \tag{3.39b}$$

The constants ε and σ provided for the Lennard-Jones potential in FLUIDYN are those for argon, and constants for other inert gases and for nitrogen are given in Table 3.2. The cell contains 125 molecules which are initially placed on a regular grid and then slightly displaced in a random fashion. The molecules of an actual fluid would actually have a distribution of speeds given by the Maxwell–Boltzmann distribution, which is what happens when a system of particles undergoes perfectly elastic interactions. In FLUIDYN the particles are all given an initial speed equal to the root-mean-square speed appropriate to their temperature but in random directions. It is assumed that

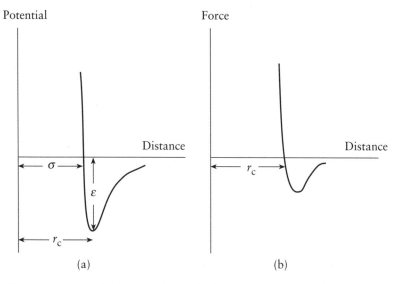

Fig. 3.5 The variation of (a) potential and (b) force for a pair of molecules with a Lennard-Jones potential.

Table 3.2 The Lennard-Jones constants σ and ε (in the form $T_0 = \varepsilon/k$, where k is the Boltzmann constant) for some inert gases and nitrogen.

Constant	Neon	Krypton	Xenon	Nitrogen
σ (nm)	0.275	0.360	0.410	0.370
$T_0 = \varepsilon/k$ (K)	36	171	221	95

by the time the particles have interacted for 50 time steps the velocity distribution will be approaching the correct form.

The integration of the molecular paths is carried out by the Runge–Kutta method and at each step after the first 50 steps the contributions to the virial term in (3.37) are found and accumulated. The value of the virial term finally taken is the average found for all the steps after the first 50. Again after each step the radial distribution function, $\rho(r)$, is found. This is the average density as a function of distance taking one of the molecules as origin, relative to the average density in the complete cell taken as unity. Clearly, because of the strong repulsion at small distances, the value of $\rho(r)$ is zero for $r \ll \sigma$. It peaks at the average separation of molecules and then has other fluctuations at greater distances. A classical solid at absolute zero with the same average molecule separation would have a radial density distribution consisting of a series of delta functions. The radial density distribution for a fluid will be a blurred version of this since the molecules are able to move, so giving a greater variety of inter-molecule distances. The peaks will be sharper at high fluid densities as the molecules cannot depart too far from the arrangement of a solid without some very close interactions between molecules.

The results of running FLUIDYN for argon at a temperature of 329 K, for which experimental results are available, are shown in Fig. 3.6. The dimensionless quantity V^* is given by

$$V^* = \frac{V}{N\sigma^3}, \tag{3.40}$$

where N molecules are contained in a cell of volume V, so that the larger the value of V^* the smaller is the density of the fluid. The quantity determined as a function of V^* is PV/NkT, which would be unity for a perfect gas. It can be seen that the results from the cell model are a little low but in reasonable agreement with experiment. The radial distribution functions for $V^* = 0.9$ and $V^* = 1.25$ are given in Fig. 3.7; the increasing fuzziness with decreasing density is evident.

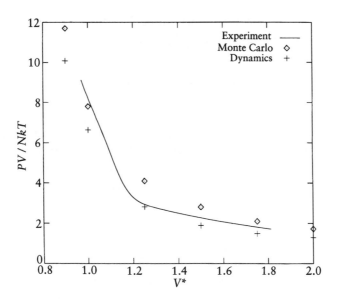

Fig. 3.6 *PV/NkT* for argon from experiment and from the programs FLUIDYN and METROPOL (see Section 4.4).

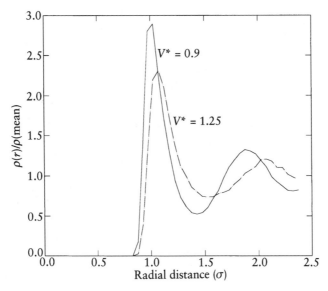

Fig. 3.7 Radial distribution functions for argon from FLUIDYN with two values of V^*.

There is an alternative Monte Carlo approach to the study of the properties of liquids which will be described in Section 4.4.

## 3.6	Considerations in modelling plasmas

Plasmas are often called the fourth state of matter, the others being solids, liquids and gases. They consist of mixtures of ions and electrons together with some neutral atoms if the material is only partially ionized. For many-electron atoms there can be different degrees of ionization which will in general depend on the temperature and the density of the material. There will be quasi-neutrality in the plasma, with

$$n_e = Zn_i \tag{3.41}$$

where n_e and n_i are the electron and ion density respectively, and Z the average ion charge number. Approximate neutrality is caused by the large space-charge fields which are generated by any significant imbalance of charges. Most plasmas are at temperatures above 10^4 K and temperatures of interest go up to 10^8 K and beyond, which is the thermal regime for research into energy generation by fusion.

The individual ions of a plasma placed in an electric or magnetic field, or a combination of the two, will experience forces which were described for electrons in Section 3.3. In one class of problems, described by the term *magnetohydrodynamics*, the motions of the electrons and ions can be described in terms of currents and the behaviour is dominated by the forces on the current elements due to magnetic fields, both imposed externally and also generated by the currents themselves. As the currents can be regarded as flowing in closed circuits there is little or no charge separation in such a system. The behaviour of such a system is governed by fluid dynamics and by Maxwell's equations of electromagnetism. Another class of problems is where electrostatic fields are dominant, which may partly be externally applied and partly space-charge fields. In one-dimensional systems where current loops do not exist there are no current-generated magnetic fields; it is this latter class of problems which we shall deal with here; the equations which describe the motion of the jth individual particle, with mass m_j and charge q_j, are

$$m_j \frac{d\mathbf{v}_j}{dt} = q_j(\mathbf{E} + \mathbf{v}_j \times \mathbf{B}), \tag{3.42}$$

$$\mathbf{E} = -\nabla\phi \tag{3.43}$$

and

$$\nabla^2 \phi = -\frac{\rho}{\varepsilon_0}, \tag{3.44}$$

where **E** and **B** are the total electric and magnetic fields at the position of the particle and ρ the total charge density. As previously indicated, it is assumed here that any magnetic field is imposed externally and not generated by currents within the plasma.

It is clear that, in view of the large numbers of charged particles involved, there would be no way of modelling such systems using individual particles, one for each ion or electron. In a plasma, motions are coherent over the whole system so that we are interested in the collective behaviour of a plasma, the way that streams of electrons and ions move relative to one another or themselves. Collective effects mean that the individual charges are lost into a continuum description which enables us to simplify the problem by the use of *superparticles* which represent large numbers of electrons or ions and possess the combined mass and the combined charge of the group of particles they represent. For a good simulation, if the continuous nature of the charge distribution is to be well represented, then it is necessary that there should be many superparticles. In a particular model the number of superparticles being handled might typically be in the range 10^4–10^7, with each superparticle representing 10^7–10^9 electrons or ions.

Even with the reduction in number by the use of superparticles, dealing with the simulation by particle–particle interactions is still not practicable. In the case of the Lennard-Jones potential in the liquid simulation considered in Section 3.5, it was permissible to consider that the forces were short-range and that they could be terminated at a certain distance from the particles. However, this approximation is not applicable for long-range inverse-square forces. For example, one cannot say that the gravitational field at the Earth's surface is mainly due to nearby material: the centre of action is at the centre of the Earth and distant material at the far side of the Earth is having a significant effect. Nevertheless, it is evident that distant particles do not have to be dealt with individually but that a reasonably small cluster of them will have almost the same effect as the combined charge at the centre of mass of the cluster. Although in the method to be described the field experienced by individual particles is *not* calculated by dividing the combined charge of a cluster by the square of its distance, it is instructive to see what errors might come about from such an approximation. In Fig. 3.8 we show in two dimensions a square box of unit side with centre at coordinates (m, n). Using a

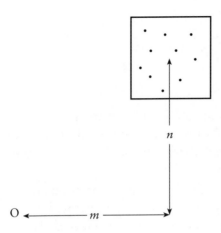

Fig. 3.8 Ten equal charges randomly placed in a unit-side square box with the box centre at (m, n) with respect to the origin.

random number generator, 10 equal charges are positioned in the box and the components of field at the origin due to the 10 individual charges are found. For each value of (m, n) 100 different random configurations are generated and the mean and standard deviation of the components of field at the origin are calculated. These results are shown in Table 3.3, compared with the approximate field components calculated by assuming that all the 10 charges were at the centre of the box. It will be seen that there is a systematic difference between the mean and approximate values which can be summarized by the statement that 'the average of inverse squares is greater than the inverse square of the average'. This effect is small for the larger distances but, as appears from a comparison of the mean and approximate values, can be as much as 10 per cent for very small distances. The standard deviations show that the random fluctuations can be even larger, as much as 20 per cent or even more, at close distances. The errors would be smaller, but similar in size, if the combined charge were taken at the centre of mass of the charges rather than at the centre of the box.

The way in which the distribution of electrons and ions is transformed into electric fields in the method to be described is not by the direct process we have used in this test. However, one part of the method does involve the approximation that all particles act as though they were placed at the nearest point of a grid and the errors we have found here will still appear, albeit in a less transparent way. For the errors to be small the cells defined by the grid should contain ~ 100 particles; another condition, if the coherent motions of electrons are to be properly represented, is that the cell size should be small compared with the characteristic coherence length. In Section 3.7 we shall

Table 3.3 Testing the approximation that 10 charges in a unit-side square box may be replaced by the combined charge at the centre of the box. The coordinates of the box centre are (m, n).

m	n	Approx. E_x	Mean E_x	σ_x	Approx. E_y	Mean E_y	σ_y
10	10	0.0354	0.0354	0.0006	0.0354	0.0354	0.0006
10	6	0.0631	0.0631	0.0011	0.0378	0.0378	0.0008
10	2	0.0943	0.0943	0.0018	0.0189	0.0188	0.0010
8	8	0.0552	0.0554	0.0011	0.0552	0.0553	0.0011
8	4	0.1118	0.1120	0.0025	0.0559	0.0559	0.0017
8	0	0.1562	0.1563	0.0038	0.0000	−0.0001	0.0019
6	6	0.0982	0.0985	0.0025	0.0982	0.0983	0.0025
6	2	0.2372	0.2378	0.0074	0.0791	0.0789	0.0043
4	4	0.2210	0.2223	0.0087	0.2210	0.2217	0.0085
4	0	0.6250	0.6283	0.0300	0.0000	−0.0012	0.0158
3	3	0.3928	0.3967	0.0208	0.3928	0.3953	0.0202
3	1	0.9487	0.9608	0.0602	0.3162	0.3169	0.0351
2	2	0.8839	0.9027	0.0727	0.8839	0.8981	0.0698
2	1	1.7888	1.8430	0.1751	0.8944	0.9090	0.1080
2	0	2.5000	2.5641	0.2426	0.0000	−0.0129	0.1419
1	1	3.5355	3.8746	0.7075	3.5355	3.8488	0.6740
1	0	10.0000	10.9798	2.1222	0.0000	−0.1879	1.5704

'Approx. E_x' and 'approx. E_y' are the field components with the combined charge at the box centre. 'Mean E_x' and σ_x are the mean and standard deviation of the x component of the field for 100 random arrangements of charges; there are similar quantities for the y component.

describe the *cloud-in-cell* method in which each particle is spread out over several cells, which reduces the errors.

The forces acting on a charged particle can be divided into two types: those due to distant charges, which give a slowly varying field in the vicinity of the particle and so contribute to collective motion of the particles in its region; and those due to nearby particles which cause it to move relative to its neighbours in an uncorrelated way. The correlated motions are governed by a time-scale which is known as the *plasma period*, t_P, which is the time-scale for natural oscillations in the plasma. Consider a slab of plasma, as illustrated in Fig. 3.9a, that is then subjected to a brief electric field which slightly separates the charges and creates two thin layers of opposite polarity, each of thickness x, as shown in Fig. 3.9b. An infinite sheet of uniform charge density σ per unit area gives rise to a uniform field $\sigma/2\varepsilon$ in its vicinity. Since the surface density of charge in each layer has magnitude nex and they reinforce one another within the plasma, the total field is nex/ε_0 in an upward direction.

Each electron, of mass m, experiences a force $-ne^2x/\varepsilon_0$ and thus undergoes simple harmonic motion with angular frequency, known as the *plasma frequency*,

$$\omega_{\mathrm{P}} = \left(\frac{ne^2}{m\varepsilon_0}\right)^{1/2}, \tag{3.45}$$

corresponding to a plasma period

$$t_{\mathrm{P}} = 2\pi\left(\frac{m\varepsilon_0}{ne^2}\right)^{1/2}. \tag{3.46}$$

The distance within which the uncorrelated particle–particle interactions are regarded as important is called the *Debye length*, which we denote by λ_{D}. If we consider the *Debye sphere*, a sphere of radius λ_{D} surrounding the particle, then the effect of the distribution of charge beyond a distance λ_{D} is substantially reduced by screening. To understand the role of screening consider a test charge q at the origin surrounded by electrons in thermal equilibrium. Time-averaged over the statistical fluctuations the electron density, n, at a position with potential ϕ will be governed by the Boltzmann probability and will be $n_{\mathrm{e}} \exp(e\phi/kT)$, where e is the electron charge and T the temperature. Since the plasma is globally quasi-neutral the electron space charge is on average

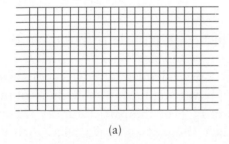

(a)

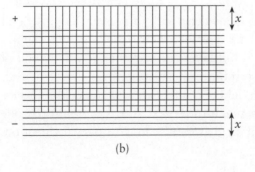

(b)

Fig. 3.9 (a) A neutral plasma with equal positive ion charge (vertical lines) and negative electron charge (horizontal lines). (b) Two slabs of charge, each of thickness x, due to the separation of the charges.

balanced by that of the ions, so that the average electron density, n_e, is Z times that of the ions, n_i, where Z is the mean ion charge.

Thus in the neighbourhood of the test charge there exists a space charge, due to the electron-density fluctuation resulting from the potential, given by

$$\rho(r) = Zen_i - en = en_e[1 - \exp(e\phi/kT)] \approx -\frac{e^2 n}{kT}\phi + \cdots. \tag{3.47}$$

The potential ϕ is determined by the space charge from Poisson's equation (3.44) which in this context, with the appropriate spherically-symmetric form of the Laplacian operator, is

$$\frac{1}{r^2}\frac{d}{dr}\left(r^2\frac{d\phi}{dr}\right) = -\frac{1}{\varepsilon_0}\rho(r) = \frac{e^2 n}{\varepsilon_0 kT}\phi \tag{3.48}$$

subject to $\phi \to q/4\pi\varepsilon_0 r$ as $r \to 0$, the local test charge field. The solution of (3.48) with the imposed boundary condition is

$$\phi = \frac{q}{4\pi\varepsilon_0 r}\exp\left(-\frac{r}{\lambda_D}\right), \tag{3.49a}$$

where

$$\lambda_D = \sqrt{\frac{\varepsilon_0 kT}{e^2 n}} \tag{3.49b}$$

is the Debye length. It is evident that for $r \ll \lambda_D$ the field is due to the test charge, but for r of order λ_D or greater the field is substantially reduced (screened) by the electrons (and also by an equivalent, but neglected, term due to the ions).

For distances less than the Debye length the fields due to *individual* charged particles are effective and the plasma behaves as a collection of individual uncorrelated particles. Over large distances the individual behaviour is screened out by the collective action of many particles. Indeed, over these lengths only *collective* behaviour, in which the particles behave coherently, usually in the form of a plasma wave, can occur. It is in this latter region that particle-in-cell simulation is appropriate.

Particle behaviour in the short-range (individual) regime is characterized by collisional effects, distinguished from those in gases by the importance of the simultaneous interaction of the test particle with many other bodies. Now the question is to decide how important are the induced motions due to local particle–particle interactions compared to the collective motions due to the more distant particles. To do this we consider an interaction between two particles, each with magnitude of charge e, as shown in Fig. 3.10. The distance

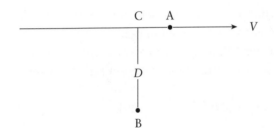

Fig. 3.10 Relative motion of two charged particles with B at rest.

of nearest approach of the two bodies is D and the speed of A relative to B is V. It can be shown (Appendix 4) that the effect of the interaction is to give to A a component of velocity along the direction CB of magnitude

$$\delta v = \frac{e^2}{2\pi\varepsilon_0 mDv} \qquad (3.50a)$$

where m is the mass of particle A. This corresponds to an angular deflection of its path by

$$\delta\theta = \frac{e^2}{2\pi\varepsilon_0 mDv^2}. \qquad (3.50b)$$

A collision time-scale, t_c, is defined which is the expected time for a particle to be deflected through an angle of $\pi/2$. Since the individual deflections are randomly oriented in space then N deflections, each with a root-mean-square magnitude of deviation $\langle\delta\theta^2\rangle^{1/2}$, will give an expected total deviation of magnitude $N^{1/2}\langle\delta\theta^2\rangle^{1/2}$. Based on this relationship, it is shown in Appendix 4 that the ratio t_c/t_P is of the order of the number of particles in the Debye sphere. If the number of particles in the Debye sphere is very large, which it normally is, then the modelling of a plasma may be carried out over several plasma periods without collision effects being important. Under these conditions the system can be regarded as collisionless and the modelling done on the basis of calculating smoothed-out average fields in the vicinity of each particle.

3.7   The collisionless particle-in-cell model

Modelling of plasmas can be done in one, two or three dimensions. The physical reality is that any plasma must be three-dimensional, so when we study a two-dimensional plasma – say, in the x–y plane – we are assuming that all sections of constant z are similar and also that the system has infinite extent in the z direction. The latter condition can never be true but may be a reasonable assumption if the z dimension is large compared with the scale of the fluctuations in particle densities. Each superparticle in a two-dimensional simulation represents a rod of charge and mass density per unit distance parallel to z. Whereas point charges give a $1/r^2$ force law for fields, charge rods give a $1/r$, law although this relationship is not explicitly used in the computations. For a one-dimensional plasma each superparticle represents an infinite sheet of charge and mass density per unit area perpendicular to x. Infinite charge sheets give a uniform field independent of distance from the sheet.

In the collisionless particle-in-cell (PIC) model the particles are placed in a mesh, which is usually cubical in three dimensions and square in two dimensions. What is needed from the distribution of charges is the electric field at the position of each electron or ion so that its acceleration can be found and its motion followed. The steps in the process for purely electrostatic fields are:

1. Construct a convenient grid in the one-, two- or three-dimensional space within which the system can be defined. As examples, in one dimension 250 cells may be used, in two-dimensions 60×60 cells and in three dimensions $30 \times 30 \times 30$ cells. The number of cells will depend on the problem and the computing power available.

2. Decide on the number of superparticles, both electrons and ions, and allocate positions to them. To obtain as little random fluctuation in the fields as possible it is required to have as many particles as possible per cell. Between 25 and 100 particles per cell is desirable but with the limitation that the cell dimension must be less than a Debye length. The superparticles may be initially uniformly positioned within the cells. For some modelling problems a perturbation away from a uniform distribution is required and this can be imposed.

3. If there is a uniform drift velocity then this can be given to all particles. A drift velocity requires an open system otherwise particles will pile up at one closed end and a particle vacuum will be created at the other. Where there is a drift velocity then periodic boundary conditions are usually used as described for liquid models in Section 3.5. Another possibility is for the boundary to reflect the particles back into the system. The size of the space being modelled must be larger than the scale of the largest significant feature in the phenomenon being investigated.

4. A 'cold' plasma is one in which there is no random thermal motion of the particles. This is very rarely used as numerical energy generation heats the particles because the Debye length is very small. For the more usual 'warm' plasma model, velocities must be chosen randomly from a Maxwellian

distribution and allocated to the particles in random fashion. Due to statistical fluctuations with small numbers of superparticles, 'hot-spots' or 'cold-spots' may develop within the plasma, and in some codes correction procedures are built in to avoid this.

5. Assign the charge of each superparticle to the nearest grid-point, or grid-points, and calculate the charge densities at the grid-points.
6. Using the densities at grid-points, Poisson's equation

$$\nabla^2 \phi = -\rho/\varepsilon_0 \qquad (3.51)$$

is solved to find the potential at each grid-point using techniques similar to those described in Section 2.12 or otherwise (see Section 3.71).

7. From the potentials, field components are found at the grid-points by the finite-difference approximation

$$E_x(i) = -\frac{\phi_x(i+1) - \phi_x(i-1)}{2\Delta x} \qquad (3.52)$$

or otherwise (see the one-dimensional example which follows). Alternatively, this can be done by Fourier differentiation (see (3.73)).

8. Move the superparticles by numerical solution of (3.42). This can be done by any suitable method; a leapfrog procedure is often used for speed of application. For complex problems a combination of computer storage and time will often dictate the method to be used. The time step for the integration should be about 0.03 or so of the shortest time of interest in the system – which in the electrostatic case we are considering here would be the cell crossing time or, less likely, the plasma period.
9. Calculate and store any characteristics of the plasma which are required. Output numerically or graphically at required intervals.
10. If the total simulation time is not exceeded then return to 5.

3.7.1 *A one-dimensional plasma program*

We shall describe a simple one-dimensional program for investigating aspects of plasma behaviour. One simplification that can be imposed is in the way that the ions are handled. Although in general ions and electrons must be treated as distinct kinds of particles with different charge-to-mass ratios, it is obvious that, because of their large mass, ions move much less than do electrons. For some kinds of problem it is sufficient to consider the ions as a stationary background just contributing to the net charge density, and this is the assumption for this program.

The one-dimensional cell structure for a total of N cells is set up as shown in Fig. 3.11, where the centres of cells are at

$$x_i = (i + \tfrac{1}{2})\Delta x, \qquad 0 \leqslant i \leqslant N, \tag{3.53}$$

and the boundaries of cells at

$$x_{i+1/2} = (i+1)\Delta x, \qquad -1 \leqslant i \leqslant N. \tag{3.54}$$

For one dimension, Poisson's equation can be simplified to give fields directly from charge density by

$$\nabla^2 \phi = \frac{d^2\phi}{dx^2} = -\frac{dE}{dx} = -\frac{\rho}{\varepsilon_0}. \tag{3.55}$$

A finite-difference form for the field at the cell boundary is (Gauss's theorem)

$$\frac{E_{i+1/2} - E_{i-1/2}}{\Delta x} = \frac{\rho_i}{\varepsilon_0}$$

or

$$E_{i+1/2} = E_{i-1/2} + \frac{\rho_i \Delta x}{\varepsilon_0}, \tag{3.56a}$$

and the field at a cell centre is then given as

$$E_i = \frac{1}{2}(E_{i-1/2} + E_{i+1/2}). \tag{3.56b}$$

The recurrence relationship (3.56a) for the fields at boundaries can be initiated either by some field boundary condition imposed by the problem, such as $E_{-(1/2)} = 0$, or by some known potential drop across the system, such as

$$\phi_{N+1/2} - \phi_{-1/2} = -\sum_{i=0}^{N} E_i \Delta x = 0. \tag{3.57}$$

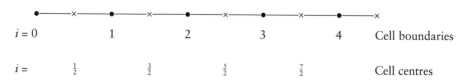

| | $i = 0$ | 1 | 2 | 3 | 4 | Cell boundaries |

| $i =$ | $\frac{1}{2}$ | $\frac{3}{2}$ | $\frac{5}{2}$ | $\frac{7}{2}$ | Cell centres |

Fig. 3.11 A one-dimensional cell structure with cell boundaries at integral values of i and cell centres at half-integral values.

The charges at cell centres are found from the positions of the individual particles by

$$\rho_i = \sum_j w_i(x_j) q_j, \tag{3.58}$$

where the summation is over all the particles, particle j has coordinate x_j and charge q_j, and where the weighting function $w_i(x)$ gives the proportion of the charge of a particle at position x that is allocated to the centre of cell i. There are various weighting schemes, the simplest being to allocate all charge to the nearest grid-point, for which the weighting function is

$$w_i(x) = \begin{cases} 1 & \text{if } |x - x_i| < \tfrac{1}{2}\Delta x \\ 0 & \text{otherwise.} \end{cases} \tag{3.59a}$$

The cloud-in-cell method is another simple scheme, where the charge is assumed to be uniformly distributed over a length Δx and each part of the charge is then allocated to the nearest cell centre. This is illustrated in Fig. 3.12; the vertically-shaded portion of the charge is allocated to cell centre i and the horizontally-shaded portion to cell centre $i+1$. The weighting function is:

$$w_i(x) = \begin{cases} 1 - |x - x_i|/\Delta x & \text{if } |x - x_i| < \Delta x \\ 0 & \text{otherwise.} \end{cases} \tag{3.59b}$$

Since changes in velocity depend on the positions of the particles through the fields they generate and changes of position depend upon velocities, it is convenient to solve the equations of motion by a leapfrog process. For the jth electron (the ions are not moved) this is of the form

$$x_j^n = x_j^{n-1} + v_j^{n-(1/2)}\Delta t \tag{3.60a}$$

$$v_j^{n+(1/2)} = v_j^{n-(1/2)} + \frac{q_j}{m_j} E_j^n \Delta t, \tag{3.60b}$$

where the superscript n represents the number of time steps from the beginning of the calculation. To find the field at any particle position the same weighting

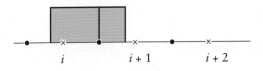

$$i \qquad\qquad i+1 \qquad\qquad i+2$$

Fig. 3.12 The cloud-in-cell method. The vertically shaded part of the charge is allocated to cell with centre at i and the horizontally-shaded part to cell with centre at $i+1$.

functions used for the charge density, described in (3.59), *must* be used so that

$$E_j^n = \sum_{i=0}^{N} w_i(x_j^n) E_i,$$ (3.61)

which involves either taking the field at the nearest cell centre or linearly interpolating from the flanking cell centres in the two cases we have considered.

With computations of this kind the use of an appropriate time step is very important. Since the natural period of disturbances in the plasma will be of the order of the plasma period, a time step which is some small fraction of that period is an obvious requirement, and stability requires that $\Delta t \leqslant 0.2 t_P$. What usually turns out to be a more important requirement is that in a single time step no particle should be able to travel more that one cell length so that it cannot cross more than one cell boundary. This depends on the maximum speed of any particle, and for a one-dimensional case we can safely set v_{max} equal to four times the root-mean-square speed of the electrons. The limitation of the time step by this condition may be found to be given by the relationship

$$\Delta t < 0.25 \frac{\Delta x}{v_{rms}} = 0.25 \frac{\Delta x}{\lambda_D} \frac{1}{\omega_P}.$$ (3.62)

Since the scale length of events in the plasma will be of order λ_D and the cell length must be less than the Debye length, (3.62) will then be the critical relationship for determining the time step.

The program PIC (see p. xv) models the dynamic boundary of a plasma layer. The initial ion density is set up as shown in Fig. 3.13, where the density is constant for the first X_1 Debye lengths, then falls linearly over the next X_2

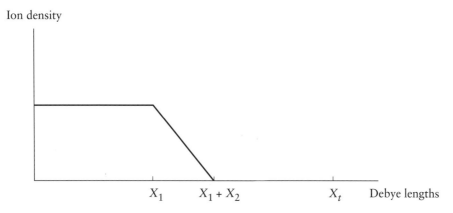

Fig. 3.13 An initial configuration of ion density of PIC. The total extent of the mesh is X_t Debye lengths.

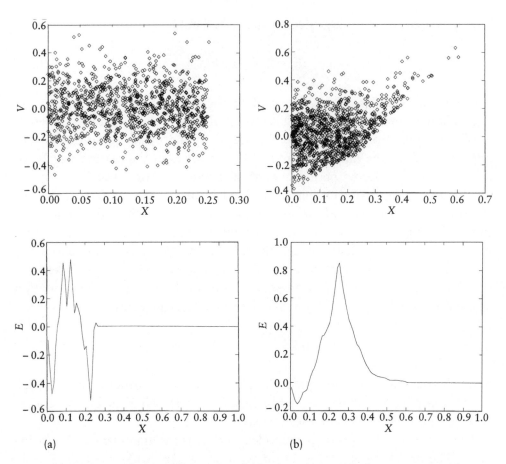

Fig. 3.14 Position–velocity and position–field plots from PIC for: (a) $t=0$ s; (b) $t=6.727 \times 10^{-15}$ s; (c) $t=2.018 \times 10^{-14}$ s; (d) $t=2.691 \times 10^{-14}$ s.

Debye lengths, and then is zero to the end of the mesh which has a total extent of X_t Debye lengths. For the program as given $X_t = 10$, $X_1 = 2.5$ and $X_2 = 0$. The number of cells in the mesh is 100, so each cell is one-tenth of a Debye length. The temperature of the plasma is set at 10^4 K and the density of ions in the constant-density body of the plasma is 10^{25} m^{-3}. The program generates 10 000 random electron positions using a generator which gives the required distribution and also assigns velocities to these electrons following a Maxwell–Boltzmann distribution, which in one dimension is a normal distribution with zero mean and standard deviation $(kT/m)^{1/2}$. The initial positions are those for zero time and the calculated velocities are taken as those for time $= \frac{1}{2}\Delta t$ to get the leapfrog process started. To keep the plasma electrically neutral on average, particles which leave the mesh region are returned. Any leaving at

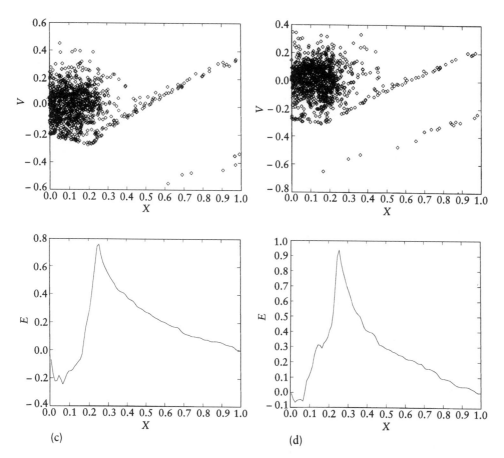

Fig. 3.14 (cont) Position–velocity and position–field plots from PIC for: (a) $t = 0$ s; (b) $t = 6.727 \times 10^{-15}$ s; (c) $t = 2.018 \times 10^{-14}$ s; (d) $t = 2.691 \times 10^{-14}$ s.

$x = 0$, at the dense plasma boundary, are returned with their directions of motion reversed and speeds randomly chosen from a Maxwell–Boltzmann distribution. Those leaving at the other boundary, $x = x_t$ are reflected back into the system with reversed velocity.

The results this kind of model are best understood from graphical output and we show a number of stages in Fig. 3.14. The top diagrams show the position–velocity coordinates of each particle with dimensionless velocities expressed as fractions of v_{max}. The bottom diagrams show the variation of field throughout the mesh where the field is given in a dimensionless form as $E/(E_{max} - E_{min})$. Since each particle represents an infinite sheet of charge, which gives a constant field independent of distance from the sheet, the field at a point is just a measure of the total imbalance of charge up to that point.

From Fig. 3.14a, which shows the situation at $t=0$, it is clear that the net charge seen by a test particle at the right-hand end of the mesh is zero, so there is no net field. As the test particle moves towards the origin this situation is still true, until it enters that part of the region initially occupied by the plasma. Within the plasma the fluctuations in field are just due to the statistical nature of the distribution of the electrons.

The top diagram of Fig. 3.14b shows the transient effect of the faster thermal electrons leaving the dense plasma and moving into the vacuum, leading to a positive field everywhere outside the ion boundary. This positive field also exists in most of the ion region except near the left-hand reflecting boundary, where a local accumulation of electrons reverses the field. Eventually, as seen in Fig. 3.14c, electrons are reflected back from outside the mesh on the right-hand side, seen as the lower negative-velocity band. As time progresses so this band moves upwards as slower electrons move into and across the vacuum region (Fig. 3.14d). Eventually this fills and the particle distribution and field settle down into a nearly quiescent state – dynamic equilibrium. A careful study of simulations of this kind can lead to a good understanding of plasma behaviour.

3.8   Galaxy simulation

Another system which can be modelled by the collisionless PIC method is a galaxy. A photograph of a spiral galaxy, similar to our own Milky Way system, is shown in Fig. 3.15a, and a simplified model of it in Fig. 3.15b. A real galaxy contains of the order 10^{11} stars of varying masses but with an average mass similar to that of the Sun. Some of the mass is in the central bulge, the halo, which is simulated by a uniform distribution of stars in a spherical non-rotating region. It plays no part in the simulation except to provide a constant external gravitational field in which the other stars move. This external field will vary as r^{-2} outside the halo but will be proportional to r inside the halo. The remaining stars are in a thin disc and one of the parameters of the model is the proportion, f, of the total number of stars in the disc. A value of $f=0.2$ corresponds to a heavy halo and $f=0.7$ a light one. If the radius of the disc is r_d and the radius of the halo is r_h, then another parameter of the model is $\alpha=r_d/r_h$. A compact halo would correspond to $\alpha=3$, and a diffuse halo to $\alpha=1$. The radius of a galaxy will be typically 6×10^{20} m (20 kpc), with a disc of thickness 2×10^{19} m (~ 0.7 kpc). The period of rotation varies little with radial distance, because of the way the mass is distributed in the galaxy, and for the Milky Way the period is estimated as 2×10^8 years.

(a)   (b)

Fig. 3.15 (a) A photograph of the 'Sombrero hat' galaxy M104. (b) A model galaxy with halo radius r_h and disc radius r_d.

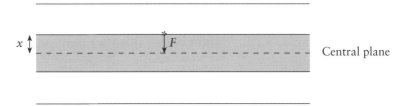

Fig. 3.16 A star displaced from the central plane of the disc experiences a restoring force, F, due to the stars in the shaded region, of thickness $2x$.

The disc stars can be represented by 10^4–10^5 superstars distributed in a thin disc with the gravitational contribution of the stationary halo calculated from its configuration as a uniform-density sphere. What is of interest is to determine for how many rotational periods the simulation can be followed so that the collisionless PIC assumption is valid. To do this, we need quantities which are analogous to the plasma frequency and the Debye length. The quantity equivalent to the plasma frequency is the period of oscillation of a star due to the gravitational field gradient in the disc. Figure 3.16 shows a cross-section of the disc, assumed to be infinite in extent. A star displaced from the central plane by a distance x experiences a net restoring force due to the gravitational field of the stars in the shaded slab. For an infinite slab the field is found to be $2\pi G\sigma$, where σ is the mass per unit area of the slab. Replacing σ by $2x\rho$, where ρ is the density in the disc, assumed uniform, we see that the field per unit displacement is $4\pi G\rho x$. The motion of the star across the disc is therefore a simple harmonic oscillation with frequency

$$\omega_s = (4\pi G\rho)^{1/2}. \tag{3.63}$$

This is equivalent to equation (3.45) with m replacing e and ε_0 replaced by $1/(4\pi G)$, which is the way that the electrostatic force law is transformed into the gravitational force law. Taking the number of stars in the disc as 5×10^{10}, each of solar mass (2×10^{30} kg) it is found that the period of the oscillations through the disc, t_s, is 1.04×10^8 years or about one half of the rotational period, t_r. By analogy with the result found for a plasma in Appendix 4, the ratio t_c/t_s will be approximately the number of superparticles in the Debye sphere so that the ratio t_c/t_r, will be about one-half of that number. Making the transformation from electrostatic to gravitational forces, the Debye length for gravitational forces is

$$^g\lambda_D = \left(\frac{kT}{4\pi Gnm^2}\right)^{1/2}. \tag{3.64}$$

The temperature in this equation is a measure of the random translational motion of the stars (as it is for ions and electrons), so we may substitute

$$v_{ran}^2 = \frac{kT}{m}$$

to give

$$^g\lambda_D = \left(\frac{v_{ran}^2}{4\pi Gnm}\right)^{1/2}. \tag{3.65}$$

Thus the ratio

$$\frac{t_c}{t_P} = \frac{2\pi}{3}n\left(\frac{v_{ran}^2}{4\pi Gnm}\right)^{3/2}. \tag{3.66}$$

The product nm is the mass of stars (or superstars) per unit volume and we can replace n by N/V, where N is the total number of superstars in the simulation and V the volume of the disc. Taking v_{ran} as $40\,\mathrm{km\,s^{-1}}$, an observational figure, we find

$$\frac{t_c}{t_P} = \frac{N}{1204}. \tag{3.67}$$

This suggests that in order to stay within the collisionless assumption it is necessary to have more than 1200 superparticles per rotation of the galaxy.

Using a different basis, Hockney and Eastwood (1988) come to a figure of 140 superparticles per rotation. However, the difference is not important; if 100 000 superparticles are used then, on either basis, this is adequate to preserve the collisionless assumption for 40–60 rotations, which covers the range of estimates for the lifetime of the universe.

Figure 3.17 shows the calculated evolution of a galaxy with $f=0.2$, $\alpha=1$ and with no random velocity imposed on the original superstar motions (Berman *et al.*, 1978); the results show striking similarities to some photographs of spiral galaxies.

3.9 Fourier series methods of solving Poisson's equation

For galaxy simulation, or plasma simulation in more than one dimension by a PIC method, it is necessary to solve Poisson's equation repeatedly in two or three dimensions and on a very extensive grid. For this reason it is desirable to find a more efficient method than those described in Section 2.12 and, to this end, very effective methods based on Fourier series have been devised. We shall describe the basis of such methods for a particular example where there is a two-dimensional grid within a square region of side L defined by $n \times n$ square cells, each of side $\Delta(=L/n)$, and where the boundary condition is everywhere $\phi=0$ or a constant. For such a situation the potential may be described over the square area as a half-sine-wave discrete Fourier series plus a constant

$$\phi(x,y) = \sum_{h=1}^{n-1} \sum_{k=1}^{n-1} C_{hk} \sin\left(\frac{\pi h x}{L}\right) \sin\left(\frac{\pi k y}{L}\right) + \phi_B, \tag{3.68}$$

where ϕ_B is the constant potential of the boundary. From Poisson's equation we find

$$\rho(x,y) = -\varepsilon_0\left(\frac{\partial^2 \phi}{\partial x^2} + \frac{\partial^2 \phi}{\partial y^2}\right) = \varepsilon_0 \frac{\pi^2}{L^2} \sum_{h=1}^{n-1} \sum_{k=1}^{n-1} (h^2 + k^2) C_{hk} \sin\left(\frac{\pi h x}{L}\right) \sin\left(\frac{\pi k y}{L}\right), \tag{3.69}$$

from which it is clear that ρ must be zero along all boundaries. Thus it is possible to represent the charge density as a half-sine-wave series, but we use the discrete form

$$\rho(i,j) = \sum_{h=1}^{n-1} \sum_{k=1}^{n-1} D_{hk} \sin\left(\frac{\pi h i}{n}\right) \sin\left(\frac{\pi k j}{n}\right), \tag{3.70}$$

Simulation with particles

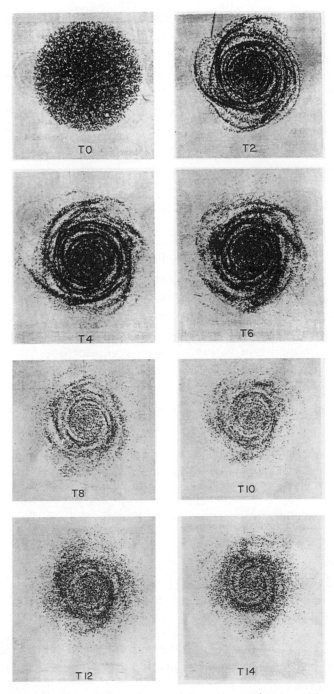

Fig. 3.17 A particle-in-cell simulation of an evolving galaxy. The times (*t*) are in units of rotation periods (Berman *et al.*, 1978).

where (i, j) represents a grid-point and where $i/n = x/L$ and $j/n = y/L$. The coefficients D_{hk} can be found from the charge densities at the grid-points from

$$D_{hk} = \frac{4}{n^2} \sum_{i=1}^{n-1} \sum_{j=1}^{n-1} \rho(i, j) \sin\left(\frac{\pi H i}{n}\right) \sin\left(\frac{\pi K j}{n}\right) \tag{3.71}$$

(Appendix 5). The Ds may thus be determined from the charge-density distribution at the grid-points and, from (3.69) and (3.70),

$$C_{hk} = \frac{L^2 D_{hk}}{\varepsilon_0 \pi^2 (h^2 + k^2)}. \tag{3.72}$$

With the C coefficients known the potential may be calculated in the $L \times L$ region. In addition, as an alternative to finding field components by a finite-difference approach, as in (3.52), one may use

$$E_x = -\frac{\partial \phi}{\partial x} = -\frac{\pi}{L} \sum_{i=1}^{n-1} \sum_{j=1}^{n-1} h C_{hk} \cos\left(\frac{\pi h x}{L}\right) \sin\left(\frac{\pi k y}{L}\right). \tag{3.73}$$

The Fourier summations required in (3.68), (3.71) and (3.73) can be carried out by the fast Fourier transform (FFT) algorithms (see Press *et al.*, 1986) which were pioneered by Cooley and Tukey (1965) and give a great advantage in time in dealing with large grids in two or three dimensions. The principle underlying the FFT process is explained in one dimension in Section 5.6.

Although the process has been described for two dimensions and particular boundary conditions, it can be generalized. If the gradient of the potential is zero at the boundary then a half-cosine series is required to describe the density and for more general periodic boundary conditions it is necessary to use a full Fourier series with both sine and cosine terms.

Problems

3.1   Make a copy of MAGELEC and modify it to simulate a magnetic lens for which $B = Dy$ for $0.02 \leqslant x \leqslant 0.03$ and $B = 0$ otherwise. By computational experiments find the value of D which gives a magnification of two for 1 keV electrons.

3.2   Make a copy of CLUSTER and modify it so that the initial total energy is zero and so that kinetic energy rather than total energy is output. Also change FORMAT statement 300 so that the geometrical moment of inertia, R^2, is output with E11.5. Run the program for 50 stars with an initial radius of 50 000 AU and for times up to 100 000 years at intervals of 10 000 years. Use the finite-difference expression (2.9) to find $d^2(R^2)/dt^2$ over the time range and confirm that, within the accuracy of the computation, it equals twice the kinetic energy. Show that this follows from the virial theorem.

3.3   Modify the data statements in FLUIDYN to find PV/NkT for xenon at 600 K and 800 K for V^* values of 0.9, 1.0, 1.1, 1.2, 1.4, 1.6, 1.8 and 2.0. The values of σ and ε/k are given in Table 3.2.

3.4   Examine a listing of PIC to understand what it does. Run PIC with the following parameters:

$$XT = 12, \quad IT = 100, \quad NT = 600, \quad DT = 0.2,$$

$$X1 = 3, \quad X2 = 3, \quad DENS = 10^{24}\,m^{-3}, \quad TEMP = 2 \times 10^4 K.$$

Produce graphical output for the velocity of the electrons and the field within the space for times close to 5×10^{-14} s and 1×10^{-13} s and comment upon your results.

4 *The Monte Carlo method*

4.1 Applications of Monte Carlo simulations

In Section 1.6.1 the Monte Carlo method was introduced by describing its very first application to the penetration of barriers by neutrons and also two kinds of random-walk problem. The physics of many real problems is stochastic, that is, dependent on chance; examples are the behaviour of a small number of radioactive atoms and the outcome of an interaction between an electron and an atom. For radioactivity we know the probability of disintegration of a single atom per unit time but we do not know for certain what will be the fate of any particular atom. Repeated experiments with the same initial number of atoms for a fixed period of time will give a variety of final states. For electron collisions there are competing processes of X-ray emission or ejection of an Auger electron with known probabilities for each. However, with both these examples if we take a very large system – say, 10^{20} radioactive atoms or bombardment of a sample by an intense beam of electrons – then possible outcomes will have very small fluctuations about the average so that for all practical purposes the system can be regarded as deterministic, meaning that the final outcome is exactly determined by the initial conditions of the system.

There are two types of problem to which we can apply Monte Carlo methods. The first type is that of purely stochastic problems where it seems natural that a solution may be found by making random number selection mimic the inherent randomness of the physical behaviour. The second type is where we replace a deterministic problem, or one with no obvious random behaviour, with a stochastic model whose average over many trials gives the same solution. Another important application of the Monte Carlo process, which is often related to the solution of a physical problem, is the evaluation of multi-dimensional integrals. In this application what is obtained is not only an estimate of the integral but also a standard deviation which is a measure of the uncertainty of the estimate. This is a characteristic of all Monte Carlo calculations; one always obtains an estimate and a deviation, and the reduction of the standard deviation, or variance, is an important aspect of the application of the method.

4.2 The generation of random numbers *is having rectangular distribution* – uniform deviates

In Section 1.6.1 a simplified random-walk problem was developed in which the steps could only be on a square grid in the $\pm x$ directions or the $\pm y$ directions. The four directions had equal probability and the decision was made by generating a random number with a uniform probability density in the interval 0 to 1 and using its value in one or other of the ranges 0 to 0.25, 0.25 to 0.5, 0.5 to 0.75 and 0.75 to 1 to decide on the direction of the step.

The generation of truly random numbers is more complicated than it might seem on first consideration. One infallible way, which is used to select the winners of Premium Bond prizes in the UK, is to use a random noise generator, essentially a device emitting random electrical discharges which are interpreted as the bits of a binary number. With a properly designed generator this gives truly random numbers, but it is inconvenient for most scientific calculations where the preference is for pseudo-random number generators. These generate the succession of numbers by some numerical algorithm which gives the advantage that numerical models can be repeated with the same sequences of numbers if required. Thus in the DRUNKARD program it will be seen in the listing that the random number generator is of the form

$$IR = MOD(IR * IX + IY, IM)$$

$$R = FLOAT(IR)/FLOAT(IM)$$

This kind of random number generator is called a *linear congruential generator*. The integers IR can be anywhere in the range 0 to $IM - 1$, and with a proper choice of IX, IY and IM a sequence of IM integers will contain all possible values. Clearly the sequence that follows will then be a repetition of what has gone previously. If IM is sufficiently large, 53125 in the DRUNKARD program, then the random numbers will be discrete but with very small intervals between allowed values – which will cause no difficulties for most modelling problems. However, if more than IM random numbers are required then the randomness of the sequence of numbers will be lost.

4.2.1 *Sequential correlation*

Another problem which afflicts linear congruential generators is that of *sequential correlation*. Users of standard system-provided random number generators should be aware that they may present this problem. If the requirement for randomness is very demanding, a specialized subroutine designed to avoid sequential correlation should be used. Sequential correlation is a difficult concept to describe in an abstract way but can be illustrated with a simple example. We consider the linear congruent generator $IR = MOD(7 \times IR + 3, 11)$. Starting with $IR = 1$ the sequence generated is 1, 10, 7, Mod 8, 4, 9, 0, 3, 2, 6, 1, 10, ... It is not a totally efficient sequence because use 5 is $(7 \times 5 + 3, 11)$ missing (just as well, because it generates itself!) but the principle can still be $= 5$. illustrated. We now take successive pairs of values as (x, y) coordinates and plot them in a coordinate system where the x coordinate is repeated cyclically. The values shown plotted in Fig. 4.1 are of all adjacent pairs in the sequence $(1, 10)$, $(10, 7)$, $(7, 8)$, $(8, 4)$, $(4, 9)$, $(9, 0)$, $(0, 3)$, $(3, 2)$, $(2, 6)$ and $(6, 1)$. The sequential correlation is shown by the points lying on sets of parallel lines in the two-dimensional space. In general, with sequential correlation, if sets of s successive points are taken then they will fall on $(s-1)$-dimensional planes in an s-dimensional coordinate system. To avoid this phenomenon, the random numbers can be generated several at a time and then shuffled by use of a second random-number generator to change their order of acceptance. Excellent programs for doing this will be found in Press *et al.* (1986). *change of range*

So far we have considered only random numbers with a uniform probability *of uniform* density between 0 and 1, i.e. the probability of a value between x and $x + dx$ *deviates* is dx, which are described as *uniform deviates* (0–1). By a simple linear *from (0,1)* transformation the range can be changed; for example, if a set of uniform *by linear* deviates (0–1), r, are generated then the values of $2r - 1$ will have a uniform *tfmn*. distribution between -1 and $+1$. The extension of this principle to other ranges is straightforward.

4.2.2 The selection of random points within a sphere

A problem which often occurs in a Monte Carlo calculation is that of selecting random points within a sphere with rectangular Cartesian coordinates based

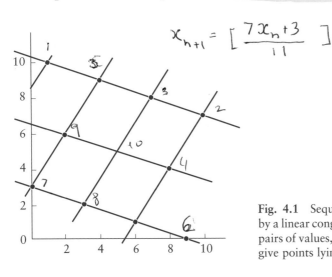

$$x_{n+1} = \left[\frac{7x_n + 3}{11} \right]$$

Fig. 4.1 Sequential correlation produced by a linear congruential generator. Adjacent pairs of values, treated as (x, y) coordinates, give points lying on a set of straight lines.

on an origin at the sphere's centre. This may occur in an astrophysical problem in which the motion of stars in a spherical cluster is to be followed under their mutual gravitational interactions. To select a random point within a unit sphere we first select three uniform deviates (0–1), r_1, r_2 and r_3, and then transform them to the range -1 to $+1$ by $x=2r_1-1$, $y=2r_2-1$, $z=2r_3-1$. These can be thought of as Cartesian coordinates within a cube of side 2 units centred on the origin. The quantity $s^2=x^2+y^2+z^2$ is calculated and if it is greater than unity then the selection is discarded. Another requirement for the astrophysical problem would be the selection of a random direction for the initial motion of each star. A method of generating a random set of angles (θ, ϕ) from two uniform deviates is given in Section 4.7.

4.3 The generation of random numbers – non-uniform deviates

4.3.1 The transformation method

Sometimes there is a need to generate variables with a particular non-uniform probability density. Figure 4.2 shows the probability density $P(x)$, normalized to give $\int_{-\infty}^{\infty} P(x)\,dx=1$, so that the probability of values between x and $x+dx$ is $P(x)\,dx$. The integral $\Phi(x)=\int_{-\infty}^{x} P(x')\,dx'$ is the *cumulative distribution function*, namely the probability of generating a value $\leq x$. To obtain the required distribution the probability of generating a value less than x_r, the value of x at the point C in Fig. 4.2, must be $r=\Phi(x_r)$. For a uniform distribution (0–1) the probability of a value $\leq r$ is just r. Hence if we generate a uniform deviate r and find the corresponding x such that the cumulative probabilities are the same, then the values of x so generated will have the required distribution

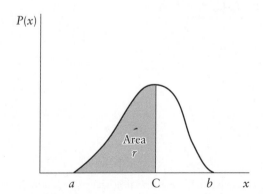

Fig. 4.2   Points C, such that the shaded area is a uniform deviate (0–1), will be deviates of the normalized probability density, $P(x)$.

distribution $P(x)$. The values of x_r are found from $r = \Phi(x_r)$ or $x_r = \Phi^{-1}(r)$. The process for choosing successive values of x is as follows:

1. Generate r, a uniform deviate (0–1).
2. Since the probability of a value less than r is just r, this is equated to the cumulative value to give the required value of x. This is equivalent to finding the x value of the point C in Fig. 4.2 such that the shaded area equals r.

Let us see how to do this for the normalized distribution $P(x) = \frac{1}{2}\pi \sin \pi x$ in the range $0 \leqslant x \leqslant 1$. The area under the curve from $x = 0$ to $x = X$ is $\frac{1}{2}(1 - \cos \pi X)$. If a uniform deviate (0–1), r, is chosen then we need the value of X which satisfies

$$\frac{1}{2}(1 - \cos \pi X) = r \qquad (4.1)$$

which is

$$X = \frac{1}{\pi} \arccos(1 - 2r). \qquad (4.2)$$

Handwritten annotations:

$\therefore 1 - \cos \pi X = 2r$
$\therefore 1 - 2r = \cos \pi X$
$\therefore \pi X = \cos^{-1}(1-2r)$
$\therefore X = \frac{1}{\pi}\cos^{-1}(1-2r)$

Figure 4.3 shows a histogram of values of X chosen by this algorithm, together with the theoretical distribution.

$\frac{\pi}{2}\int_0^1 \sin \pi x = \left[-\frac{\cos \pi x}{2}\right]_0^1 = \frac{1}{2}[\cos 0 - \cos \pi]$
$= \frac{1}{2}[1 - (-1)] = 1.$

Mode is obtained by solving $P'(x) = \frac{\pi^2}{2}\cos \pi x = 0$

Hence $x = \frac{1}{2}$

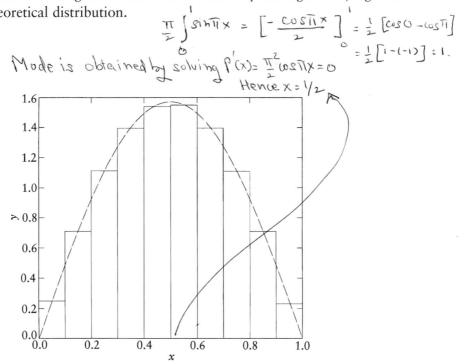

Fig. 4.3 A histogram of values of x derived from (4.3) compared with the theoretical curve (broken line) $y = \frac{1}{2}\pi\sin(\pi x)$.

Handwritten: 4·2

4.3.2 *The normal distribution – the Box–Müller algorithm*

A very common requirement in Monte Carlo calculations is to produce random numbers having a normal (or Gaussian) distribution with zero mean and a particular standard deviation, σ. If numbers can be produced having a normal distribution with zero mean and unit standard deviation then just multiplying those numbers by σ gives what is required. For a non-zero mean all that is necessary is to add the required mean to the generated numbers. The normalized distribution with zero mean and unit standard deviation is of the form

$$P(x) = \frac{1}{\sqrt{2\pi}} \exp\left(-\frac{x^2}{2} \right). \tag{4.3}$$

A straightforward application of the transformation method is not possible since areas under the curve involve the so-called *error function* whose inverse is not normally provided as an intrinsic function. Figure 4.4 shows a small rectangular block of sides dx and dy in the x–y plane. If the probability distribution for x values is given by (4.3) and for y values is given by (4.3) with y replacing x, then the probability of finding a point in the box is

$$P(x, y)\, dx\, dy = \frac{1}{2\pi} \exp\left(-\frac{x^2 + y^2}{2} \right) dx\, dy. \tag{4.4}$$

Since $x^2 + y^2 = r^2$ and (4.4) gives the probability per unit area, it can be seen that the probability of finding the particle at a distance between r and $r + dr$

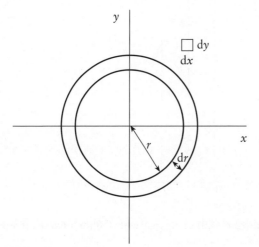

Fig. 4.4 Areas in the x–y plane for deriving normal variates.

from the origin is

$$P(r)2\pi r\,dr = \exp\left(-\frac{r^2}{2}\right)r\,dr. \tag{4.5}$$

Thus the probability of finding a point somewhere between infinity and distance R from the origin is

$$\int_R^\infty r\exp\left(-\frac{r^2}{2}\right)r\,dr = \exp\left(-\frac{R^2}{2}\right). \tag{4.6}$$

We now require s, a uniform deviate $(0-1)$, but for this purpose it is convenient to derive it in an unusual way. Two uniform deviates $(0-1)$, t_1 and t_2, are chosen such that $s = t_1^2 + t_2^2 \leqslant 1$ (readers may confirm that s is a uniform deviate between 0 and 1 either analytically or with a computer program). A value of R is now found from (4.6) such that the area under the curve $P(r)$ between infinity and a distance R from the origin is s. This is

$$R = \sqrt{-2\ln s}. \tag{4.7}$$

A random point on the circle of radius R will give two independent random numbers from a normal distribution of unit standard deviation (normal deviate, $\sigma = 1$). Because of the way that s was chosen we can now avoid the use of computer-expensive trigonometric functions to find the random point on the circle, and the two normal deviates are found from

$$r_1 = t_1\sqrt{-\frac{2\ln s}{s}}, \qquad r_2 = t_2\sqrt{-\frac{2\ln s}{s}}. \tag{4.8}$$

This is known as the *Box–Müller method* for generating normal deviates.

4.3.3 The rejection method

A useful and quite efficient general method of developing variables with a particular distribution is the *rejection method* devised by von Neumann. To give a simple illustration of the principle of the rejection method in Fig. 4.5 we show the distribution function $P(x)$ which is restricted to the interval $a < x < b$ and has a maximum value of P_m. We also show the distribution function $U(x)$, which gives a uniform distribution in the interval and is shown scaled to a maximum value of P_m. If we select a uniform deviate in the interval then the probability that it falls in the interval x to $x + dx$ is dx. We now find another uniform deviate $(0-1)$, x', and compare the values of $P_m x'$ and $P(x)$. The probability that $P_m x' \leqslant P(x)$ is proportional to $P(x)$. If that condition is

We find two independent uniform variates x & x' in $(0,1)$
If $136 \int_m \cdot x' \leq P(x)$
then x is accepted.

satisfied then the variate x is accepted – otherwise it is discarded and next x is generated and tested in the same way. From this we can see that the probability of accepting a value between x and $x+dx$ will be $P(x)dx$, which will give the required distribution.

From Fig. 4.5 we can see that the rejection method as described might be a rather inefficient process in that the proportion of variates accepted will be the area under $P(x)$ divided by the area of the reactangle ABCD. It becomes far more efficient if instead of choosing the variates x from a uniform distribution we chose them from a distribution very similar to the one of interest for which variables can be easily derived. Figure 4.6 again shows the distribution $P(x)$ together with $S(x)=C\sin\{\pi(x-a)/(b-a)\}$, which has been scaled to have a maximum value of P_m so that $S(x) \geqslant P(x)$ for all x – a necessary condition. The variates for this distribution are just linearly transformed versions of those given in (4.2). We now choose a variate from this distribution; the probability that its

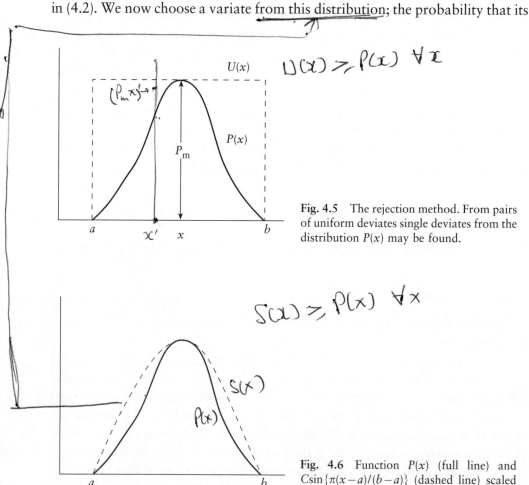

$U(x) \geqslant P(x)\ \forall x$

Fig. 4.5 The rejection method. From pairs of uniform deviates single deviates from the distribution $P(x)$ may be found.

$S(x) \geqslant P(x)\ \forall x$

Fig. 4.6 Function $P(x)$ (full line) and $C\sin\{\pi(x-a)/(b-a)\}$ (dashed line) scaled to have the same maximum value.

value is between x and $x + dx$ is $S(x)dx$. If we make the probability of accepting this value of x proportional to $P(x)/S(x)$ then the retained values of x will have the required distribution. A uniform variate, x', in the range 0 to 1 is now selected. If $P(x)/S(x) > x'$ then the value of x is accepted, otherwise it is rejected and the retained values of x will have the required distribution. If $P(x)$ and $S(x)$ have similar values over most of the range then the values of $P(x)/S(x)$ will be close to unity over most of the range and the rejection rate will be low – which makes the process more efficient.

4.3.4 *Markov chain methods*

In the study of physical systems, where the ideas of statistical mechanics are involved, for example, it is sometimes desirable to generate configurations of a many-particle system such that some property – such as the potential energy – of the system has a required distribution. To achieve this end it may be possible to use a *Markov chain* method provided each separate event is independent of the preceeding ones. We shall illustrate the idea with some simple examples involving a single variable which may take discrete values with particular probabilities. From each of the possible values a stochastic operator is applied to generate the next value. The successive operations should be able to generate all possible values of the variable and, if the process is to be useful, their probability distribution should eventually settle down to, and remain at, the one required.

Consider a variable which may only have one of two values, x_1 and x_2. When the variable has value x_1 the probabilities that the next variable will be either x_1 or x_2 are $P_{1,1}$ and $P_{1,2}$, respectively. Similarly, when the variable has a value x_2 the probabilities that the next variable will be either x_1 or x_2 are $P_{2,1}$ and $P_{2,2}$, respectively. The values of P can be thought of as the elements of a *stochastic matrix*

$$\mathbf{P} = \begin{pmatrix} P_{1,1} & P_{1,2} \\ P_{2,1} & P_{2,2} \end{pmatrix}. \tag{4.9}$$

We take the values $P_{1,1} = \frac{1}{2}$, $P_{1,2} = \frac{1}{2}$, $P_{2,1} = \frac{1}{3}$ and $P_{2,2} = \frac{2}{3}$, where the sum of the probabilities in each row of the matrix equals unity. Starting with either of the values and generating each successive value by applying the appropriate probabilities it is found that the final probabilities of obtaining x_1 and x_2 are $\frac{2}{5}$ and $\frac{3}{5}$, respectively after many trials.

The usual situation is that the probability distribution is known and the need is to find the stochastic matrix which generates it. For the simple situations we are considering here there are three conditions to be satisfied for the generation of variables to settle down to the required distribution:

(1) that the sum of the elements in a row should equal unity;
(2) that $p(x_i)P_{i,j}=p(x_j)P_{j,i}$, where $p(x_i)$ is the required probability for variable x_i;
(3) that the elements should allow all variables to be accessed.

We now illustrate the development of a stochastic matrix by the requirement $p(x_1)=0.2$, $p(x_2)=0.3$ and $p(x_3)=0.5$. From condition (2), $P_{2,1}=\frac{2}{3}P_{1,2}$, $P_{3,1}=\frac{2}{5}P_{1,3}$ and $P_{3,2}=\frac{3}{5}P_{2,3}$. We may start by assigning arbitrary values to $P_{1,1}$ and $P_{1,2}$, subject to their sum being less than unity. Their sum could be equal to unity but zeros in the matrix tend to slow down the acquisition of the steady-state distribution. Let us choose $P_{1,1}=P_{1,2}=\frac{1}{3}$. From condition (1) we must have $P_{1,3}=\frac{1}{3}$. From condition (2) we now have $P_{2,1}=\frac{2}{9}$ and $P_{3,1}=\frac{2}{15}$. We now make another arbitrary assignment $P_{2,2}=\frac{4}{9}$ which, by (1), gives $P_{2,3}=\frac{1}{3}$. From (2) we must have $P_{3,2}=\frac{1}{5}$ and hence from (1) $P_{3,3}=\frac{2}{3}$. The full matrix is thus

$$\begin{bmatrix} \frac{1}{3} & \frac{1}{3} & \frac{1}{3} \\ \frac{2}{9} & \frac{4}{9} & \frac{1}{3} \\ \frac{2}{15} & \frac{1}{5} & \frac{2}{3} \end{bmatrix}.$$

These values may be inserted in the program MARKOV3 (see p. xv) to confirm that the required distribution for the values of x_1, x_2 and x_3 are obtained. In finding the stochastic matrix three elements were chosen arbitrarily. Another possible matrix, giving the same distribution, is the following:

$$\begin{bmatrix} \frac{1}{6} & \frac{1}{3} & \frac{1}{2} \\ \frac{2}{9} & \frac{1}{9} & \frac{2}{3} \\ \frac{1}{5} & \frac{2}{5} & \frac{2}{5} \end{bmatrix}.$$

The Markov chain principle can be applied in much more complicated forms to finding configurations of systems, usually systems of particles, for which the energy conforms to some theoretical distribution. We now describe one such application.

4.4   Simulation of a fluid by a Monte Carlo method

It is known from statistical mechanics that the probability of finding an arrangement of interacting particles for which the total potential energy is Φ is proportional to $\exp(-\Phi/kT)$, where k is the Boltzmann constant and T the absolute temperature. Thus, for example, if there were some quantity Q associated with the collection of particles then the average value of Q for all possible arrangements of the system would be

$$\langle Q \rangle = \frac{\sum_a Q \exp(-\Phi/kT)}{\sum_a \exp(-\Phi/kT)}, \tag{4.10}$$

where Φ is the potential energy of the system and the summation over a implies that it is over *all* possible arrangements. It should be possible in principle to find a good approximation for $\langle Q \rangle$ by generating a very large number of random configurations and evaluating the two summations for them but, in practice, this will not work. Virtually all the arrangements will have one or more pairs of particles very close together so that Φ for the arrangement is very large, thus making the probability vanishingly small.

4.4.1 *The Metropolis algorithm – the equation of state of a liquid*

A way of overcoming this difficulty was found by Metropolis *et al.* (1953), whereby a succession of configurations can be generated by a Markov chain process in such a way that the probability of generating a configuration with potential energy Φ is proportional to $\exp(-\Phi/kT)$. The configurations which are most probable are produced most often and $\langle Q \rangle$ can be found just from an unweighted average of Q from the generated configurations. Different variants of the process can be devised. One approach is as follows:

1. Generate an initial configuration. This can be a uniform distribution since the process eventually randomizes the distribution. The total potential energy Φ is found.
2. Select a molecule at random. This is done by first selecting r, a uniform variate (0–1). If there are N molecules then the molecule selected is indicated by the integer $\text{INT}(rN) + 1$.
3. A random direction is chosen in which to move the molecule. This is done by the process described in Section 4.7 involving the selection of two uniform variates (0–1).
4. The molecule is moved in the chosen direction a distance δ which is itself chosen from a uniform distribution between 0 and Δ, where Δ can be of order 0.05 of the average distance between molecules.
5. Calculate the new potential Φ' and the change of potential $\Delta\Phi = \Phi' - \Phi$.
6. If $\Delta\Phi$ is negative, which means that the potential energy has been reduced by moving the molecule, then the new configuration is accepted as one of those from which the value of $\langle Q \rangle$ will eventually be found. Then return to step 2 to find the next configuration.

7. If $\Delta\Phi$ is positive then the quantity $\exp(-\Delta\Phi/kT)$, which will be between 0 and 1, is calculated. A uniform variate $(0-1)$, r, is selected and then

   (a) if $\exp(-\Delta\Phi/kT) \geqslant r$, the new configuration is accepted and contributes to $\langle Q\rangle$;

   (b) if $\exp(-\Delta\Phi/kT) < r$, the new configuration is rejected and the original contribution makes a further contribution to $\langle Q\rangle$.

Then return to step 2 to find the next configuration.

This algorithm achieves the desired end of generating configurations with the required probabilities. It is incorporated in the program METROPOL (see p. xv) which, as provided, deals with 125 molecules per cell. Starting from the uniform configuration it ignores the first 20 000 configurational changes to eliminate any initial bias and then calculates the virial term in (3.37) and inter-molecule distances every 20 configurations for the next 80 000 configurations. Then, as for FLUIDYN (Section 3.5.2), it gives the value of PV/NkT and the radial density distribution.

The variation of PV/NkT with V^* for the Monte Carlo method is shown in Fig. 3.6, and it is seen to give values higher than the molecular-dynamics model and also higher than experiment. The radial distribution functions for $V^* = 0.9$ and $V^* = 1.25$ are given in Fig. 4.7, which are similar to those found from the molecular dynamics approach in Fig. 3.7.

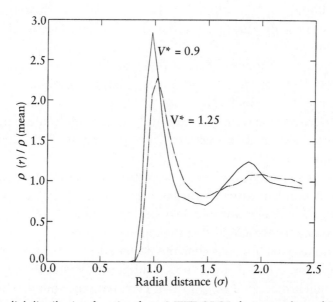

Fig. 4.7   Radial distribution function from METROPOL for two values of V^*.

There are ways of modelling liquids other than those of molecular dynamics (Section 3.5.2) and the Monte Carlo approach. In practice, the modelling processes we have examined are inadequate in that they assume that only two-body effects are important – in other words, that the force between two bodies is independent of the presence of a nearby third body. This is not actually true because of polarization effects. The third body will modify the electron distribution in each of the other two and thereby change the forces between them. There are ways of modelling such many-body effects, but they are time-consuming and difficult to apply.

4.5   Integration by Monte Carlo methods

In some scientific problems multi-dimensional integrals may occur which would be extremely expensive to evaluate by conventional quadrature techniques. If there is a system of n particles with pair potential energy $\phi(r_{i,j})$ then the classical partition function

$$Z = \int\int \cdots \int\int \exp\left\{\sum_{\text{pairs}} \phi(r_{i,j})/kT\right\} d^3r_1 \cdots d^3r_n \qquad (4.11)$$

involves integration in $3n$ dimensions. If $n=20$ and coordinates were taken at two points in each dimension then the number of points at which the integrand is evaluated is 2^{60}. With a supercomputer which could carry out 10^9 function evaluations per second this task would take about 40 years. A description of the commonly used methods of quadrature is given in Appendix 6. A quite efficient procedure is Gauss quadrature, and if a ten-dimensional integral were to be evaluated with an integrand requiring five Gauss points per dimension then this would require about 10^7 function evaluations – which is feasible but expensive in time on desktop computers. There is an alternative approach using Monte Carlo ideas based on the concept that since the value of (4.11) is actually

$$Z = \overline{\exp\left\{-\sum_{\text{pairs}} \phi(r_{i,j})/kT\right\}} V^n, \qquad (4.12)$$

where V is the volume of the system, then Monte Carlo methods can be used to find the average value of the integrand.

This principle will now be illustrated in one dimension. We consider the function $f(x)$ shown in Fig. 4.8 which is defined in the range a to b. The integral of the function over the range, which is the area under the curve, equals the

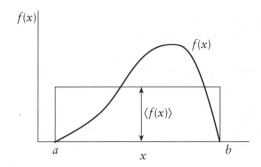

Fig. 4.8 The area under $f(x)$ between a and b equals $(b-a)\langle f(x)\rangle$.

average value of $f(x)$ over the range multiplied by the range, in this case

$$I=\int_a^b f(x)\,\mathrm{d}x=(b-a)\langle f(x)\rangle. \tag{4.13}$$

In the trapezium, Simpson and Romberg methods of numerical quadrature (Appendix 6) the values of $f(x)$ are sampled at uniform intervals of x in order to estimate the value of $\langle f(x)\rangle$. An alternative, albeit seemingly inferior, method is to select random values of x by a Monte Carlo procedure in the range of the integrand. We illustrate this process with

$$I=\int_0^1 \frac{1}{1+x^2}\,\mathrm{d}x=\frac{\pi}{4}=0.785\,40. \tag{4.14}$$

The second column of Table 4.1 shows the value of the integral found as the average of $(1+x^2)^{-1}$ from n different random values of the uniform variate x in the range 0 to 1. The estimate is clearly better as n increases, which is to be expected. If the Monte Carlo integration were repeated several times with n function evaluations but with a different seed for the random number generator each time, there would be a range of different estimates. It is possible to evaluate the variance of the estimates from sampling theory. We envisage a situation where there is a large, effectively infinite, set of variables x_i with a mean $\langle X\rangle$ and variance σ_U^2. A random sample of n of these variables is selected and has a mean $\langle x\rangle$ and variance σ_S^2. From the sample the best estimates of the mean and variance of the whole population are $\langle x\rangle$ and $n\sigma_S^2/(n-1)$ respectively, the latter being approximately σ_S^2 if n is sufficiently large. If many different estimates from samples of n are found then these samples would have a variance of σ_U^2/n which gives a measure of the reliability of an estimate from a single sample. Normally, with a population of unknown character, the variance of the estimate would be estimated as σ_S^2/n. For the present example the standard deviation of the estimate $(\sigma_S/n^{1/2})$ is given in the third column of Table 4.1.

Table 4.1 Monte Carlo estimates of $\int_0^1 1/(1+x^2)\,\mathrm{d}x$ and standard deviations without variance reduction and with variance reduction using $Q(x) = \frac{1}{3}(4-2x)$.

n	Without variance reduction		With variance reduction	
	Estimate	σ	Estimate	σ
10	0.753 097	0.057 005	0.780 962	0.006 259
100	0.810 334	0.016 174	0.784 293	0.001 954
1000	0.792 977	0.005 059	0.785 572	0.000 621
10 000	0.786 674	0.001 607	0.785 446	0.000 200
100 000	0.785 470	0.000 508	0.785 407	0.000 063
1 000 000	0.785 399	0.000 161	0.785 399	0.000 020

There are ways of finding an estimate of the integral with a much smaller variance if an integrable function is known with similar shape to the function to be numerically integrated. The general idea behind this technique is similar to that used in the rejection method of finding random variables described in Section 4.3.3. We suppose that we have a function $Q(x)$, the form of which has some similarity to that of $f(x)$ and is normalized in the range a to b. We express (4.13) in the form

$$I = \int_a^b \frac{f(x)}{Q(x)} Q(x)\,\mathrm{d}x. \tag{4.15}$$

A change is made to a variable s such that

$$\frac{\mathrm{d}s}{\mathrm{d}x} = Q(x)$$

and

$$s = \int_a^x Q(x')\,\mathrm{d}x'. \tag{4.16}$$

From (4.16) the transformation from x to s is found and since the range of s is from 0 to 1 the integral (4.15) now appears as

$$I = \int_0^1 \frac{f(x)}{Q(x)}\,\mathrm{d}s. \tag{4.17}$$

This is now evaluated from values of s chosen as uniform variates in the range 0 to 1. Since $Q(s)$ has been deliberately chosen to have a similar form to $f(s)$ the values of the integrand in (4.17) will have little variation and hence the variance of the estimate of I will be correspondingly smaller. We illustrate this for the example in (4.14); the form of $Q(x)$ we take is

$$Q(x) = \tfrac{1}{3}(4 - 2x) \tag{4.18}$$

which is normalized in the range of the integral and falls linearly over the range from $\frac{4}{3}$ to $\frac{2}{3}$ which is in the same ratio as the fall in the values of the integrand in (4.14) between $x = 0$ and $x = 1$. From (4.16) we have

$$s = \frac{1}{3} \int_0^x (4 - 2x)\, dx = \frac{x}{3}(4 - x), \tag{4.19}$$

from which we find

$$x = 2 - \sqrt{4 - 3s}. \tag{4.20}$$

The integral is now transformed to

$$I = \int_0^1 \frac{f(2 - \sqrt{4 - 3s})}{Q(2 - \sqrt{4 - 3s})}\, ds. \tag{4.21}$$

The Monte Carlo estimates of I and their standard deviations are shown in the fourth and fifth columns of Table 4.1. It is clear that the estimates are better and the standard deviations are smaller.

All the above is just for illustrative purposes, as in practice one would not evaluate a one-dimensional integral in this way – a much better sample of the integral range is found by taking values of the variable systematically, as in the methods in Appendix 6, rather than randomly. An important feature of the Monte Carlo method is that the expected error is $O(n^{-1/2})$ so that increasing the number of integrand evaluations by a factor of 100 decreases the expected error by a factor of 10. The Monte Carlo method can be applied to a multi-dimensional integral by evaluating the integrand at random points in the multi-dimensional space where each coordinate is a uniform variate in the range of that coordinate. If it turns out that an integrable model function similar to the one being evaluated is available then a solution with smaller standard deviation may be found. Regardless of the number of dimensions, of the integral the error will still be $O(n^{-1/2})$.

Suppose, however, that the n integrand evaluations are used for an m-dimensional integral; then the number of points for each coordinate range is n/m. The expected error for standard methods usually depends on some power of the integration interval, say α, and so will be $O([m/n]^\alpha)$ which will also be the order of error of the total m-dimensional integral. For a particular n, at some value of m the balance of favour will switch from factorized conventional integration to the Monte Carlo procedure. As an example, a somewhat artificial one but it illustrates the principle, we consider the integral

$$I = \int_0^1 \int_0^1 \int_0^1 \int_0^1 \int_0^1 \int_0^1 \int_0^1 \int_0^1 \int_0^1 \int_0^1 2^{10} \prod_{i=1}^{10} \{ \sin^3(\pi x_i) \, dx_i \}. \qquad (4.22)$$

The integral can be factorized into a product of 10 similar integrals and its true value is easily found as 0.1942. A Monte Carlo estimate based on 3^{10} (59 049) points, without variance reduction, gave a reasonable estimated value 0.1943 with a standard deviation of 0.0117. A ten-dimensional Gauss integration with three points in each dimension gives a poor estimated value, 0.5117.

Because of the simplicity of programming the Monte Carlo method is often used for multi-dimensional integration $(n \geqslant 4)$ when its use would not be justified by considerations of precision alone.

4.6 Monte Carlo solution of Poisson's equation

In Section 2.13 a finite-difference approach was used to solve Poisson's equation in the form

$$\theta(i,j) = \frac{1}{4} \{ \theta(i+1,j) + \theta(i-1,j) + \theta(i,j+1) + \theta(i,j-1) \} + \frac{h^2}{\kappa} Q(i,j). \qquad (2.93)$$

If we write $Q'(i,j) = (h^2/4\kappa) Q(i,j)$ then we can now look at this equation in another way by considering that the four quantities $\theta(i+1,j) + Q'(i,j)$, $\theta(i-1,j) + Q'(i,j)$, $\theta(i,j+1) + Q'(i,j)$ and $\theta(i,j-1) + Q'(i,j)$ are estimates of the temperature at the point (i,j), each with a probability of 0.25. If we made Monte Carlo selections of the four quantities with equal probabilities then the average of a large number of selections would give the required temperature. However, unless a neighbouring point is a boundary point at fixed temperature, its temperature is also unknown but it too can be estimated from its neighbouring points in the same way as described above. In Fig. 4.9 P is the point for which the temperature $\theta(P)$ is required. A neighbouring point S_1 is selected and, assuming our probability interpretation and a change of notation, we can say that $\theta(S_1) + Q'(P)$ is an estimate of $\theta(P)$. If now S_2, a neighbouring point to S_1, is selected then $\theta(S_2) + Q'(S_1)$ may be considered as an estimate of $\theta(S_1)$ and hence $\theta(S_2) + Q'(P) + Q'(S_1)$ becomes an estimate of $\theta(P)$. Eventually, after m, steps a boundary point will have been reached where the temperature is known as $\theta(B)$ and there will then be an estimate of $\theta(P)$ given by

$$\varepsilon\{\theta(P)\} = \theta(B) + Q'(P) + \sum_{i=1}^{m-1} Q'(S_i). \qquad (4.23)$$

A single estimate will not be very reliable but by repeating the process many times the average of the estimates will give a reasonable measure of $\theta(P)$. If n Monte Carlo trials are made then the average of the individual estimates will be the overall estimate of $\theta(P)$ and the standard deviation of the overall estimate will be the standard deviation of the individual estimates divided by $n^{1/2}$. The Monte Carlo program MCPLATE (see p. xv) is a modification of HOTPLATE (Section 2.14) and solves the Dirichlet problem where the boundaries are all at fixed temperatures. The input is similar to that for HOTPLATE except that the user must specify the number of Monte Carlo trials per point whose temperature is to be determined. The problem described in Fig. 2.15 is solved with 1000 trials per point, and the solution is shown in Fig. 4.10 together with the standard deviations. The solution compares favourably with that shown in Fig. 2.16 although it took somewhat longer to obtain. In general, problems of this sort would not be solved by the Monte Carlo method unless there were special circumstances. If, for example, the geometry of the surface was very complicated and the temperature was required at only one point then the Monte Carlo method could be an attractive alternative to finite-difference, finite-element (Chapter 6) or other methods.

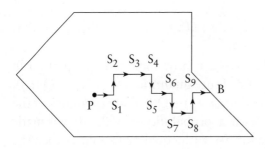

Fig. 4.9 A random walk from point P to a boundary point in the Monte Carlo method of solving the Dirichlet problem.

-1.	-1.	-1.	350.	400.	400.	450.	0.0	0.0	0.0	0.0	0.0	0.0	0.0
-1.	-1.	300.	352.	400.	433.	500.	0.0	0.0	0.0	1.9	2.2	2.1	0.0
-1.	300.	326.	361.	402.	443.	500.	0.0	0.0	1.7	2.4	2.6	2.5	0.0
350.	339.	344.	365.	402.	443.	500.	0.0	1.6	2.1	2.6	2.8	2.6	0.0
400.	358.	348.	363.	388.	432.	500.	0.0	1.7	2.1	2.5	2.9	2.9	0.0
400.	348.	335.	338.	357.	397.	500.	0.0	1.7	1.9	2.2	2.7	3.1	0.0
350.	300.	300.	300.	300.	300.	400.	0.0	0.0	0.0	0.0	0.0	0.0	0.0

Fig. 4.10   (a) The Monte Carlo solution of the Dirichlet problem shown in Fig. 2.15. These results should be compared with the finite-difference solution in Fig. 2.16. (b) Standard deviations of the temperature estimates.

4.7   The Monte Carlo method applied to a nuclear reactor

We shall conclude our description of the use of the Monte Carlo technique with a detailed case study of the operation of a nuclear reactor, which is a good illustration of the power of the method. Natural uranium contains two isotopes: ^{238}U, the major component; and ^{235}U, the minor component which accounts for 0.7194 per cent of the mixture. When a slow neutron is absorbed by a ^{235}U nucleus fission may occur, with the release of energy and the production of fast neutrons with an energy distribution with mean 2 MeV. The average number of fast neutrons produced per fission process is 2.47. In order for these fast neutrons to be slowed down so that they can interact with ^{235}U, a *moderator* is present. This is a light-atom material, graphite (carbon) or heavy water (deuterium), which takes energy from the fast neutrons by elastic collisions while at the same time being a poor absorber of neutrons. However, in competition with the moderating process, while the neutrons are slowing down, there is a loss of neutrons by resonance absorption, principally in ^{238}U. This peaks in a number of well-defined energy bands which would make resonance absorption rather expensive to simulate in detail, but fortunately it is possible to average over the resonances to give an average cross-section in the slowing-down regime.

Since many of the fission-produced neutrons are absorbed either within the reactor or by the walls of the reactor, it is clear that for the energy production to be self-sustaining at least one neutron per fission process must itself go on to produce another fission process. The average number of neutrons per fission that go on to produce further fission is called the *multiplication factor* for the reactor. The multiplication factor must be greater than unity for continuous energy production; on the other hand, if the multiplication factor is greater than unity then feedback control will be necessary where extra control rods of boron, a heavily absorbing material, are introduced when required to prevent a runaway increase in energy production leading to an explosion.

If natural uranium is used in a reactor then it is necessary to separate the fuel into a series of comparatively slender rods separated by the moderator. With this geometry a large proportion of the fission neutrons will be able to leave the rods and be slowed down to thermal energy by the moderator before entering another rod with the possibility of producing a fission event. On the other hand, if the uranium is enriched in ^{235}U then it is possible to have an intimate mixture of fuel and moderator and still to have a multiplication factor greater than unity. Here we shall consider the program REACTOR (see p. xv) which gives a simulation of an enriched-fuel reactor in a spherical container. Various aspects of the simulation will now be described and will be found within the program itself.

Neutron production

The distribution of energies (in MeV) of fission-produced neutrons, the *Watt spectrum*, is approximately given by

$$N(E) = C \sinh\{(2E)^{1/2}\}e^{-E}, \tag{4.24}$$

where C is a normalization constant and the proportion of neutrons with energies between E and $E + dE$ is $N(E)\,dE$. This distribution is illustrated in Fig. 4.11. The neutrons are emitted isotropically; the mean energy of the distribution is 2 MeV and the peak of the distribution is at 0.72 MeV.

Interaction cross-sections

In moving through the moderator–fuel mixture the neutrons are capable of interacting with nuclei in various ways. Associated with each type of reaction there is a *cross-section* which is defined as the effective area that the nucleus places in the path of the neutron for the interaction to take place. The natural unit in which to express cross-sections in particle interactions is the *barn*: 1 barn $= 10^{-28}\,\text{m}^2$. A type of interaction that a neutron can have with any type of nucleus is elastic scattering, with scattering cross-sections $\sigma_{sm} = 4.8$, $\sigma_{s35} = 10$ and $\sigma_{s38} = 8.3$ barns for C (graphite), ^{235}U and ^{238}U nuclei, respectively. An elastic collision which results in the neutron being deflected through an

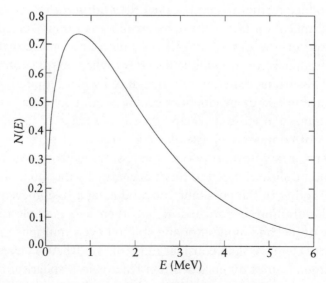

Fig. 4.11 The energy distribution of fission neutrons from ^{235}U.

angle θ gives a ratio of final neutron energy, E', to initial energy, E, as

$$\frac{E'}{E} = \frac{1 + 2A\cos\theta + A^2}{1 + A^2},\tag{4.25}$$

where A is the mass number of the scattering nucleus. Since the mass numbers of uranium nuclei are so large they do not greatly effect the energy of the scattered neutrons. On the other hand, the neutrons are slowed down from initial MeV energies to thermal energies ($\sim 0.025\,\text{eV}$) by elastic collisions with moderator atoms; for C this requires of the order of 100 collisions.

An important aspect of the behaviour of a neutron in a reactor is its scattered path through the material, for one way it can become ineffective as a fission producer is to be absorbed by the walls of the reactor. If there were only a single type of scatterer with scattering cross-section σ_s and number density n_s then the scattering probability per unit path would be $n_s \sigma_s$. For the mixture in the reactor the scattering probability per unit path is

$$\Sigma_s = n_m \sigma_{sm} + n_{35} \sigma_{s35} + n_{38} \sigma_{s38}.\tag{4.26}$$

Another type of interaction is where the neutron is absorbed by the nucleus and is lost as a potential fission-producing neutron. Absorption by moderator material is very low and, indeed, moderators are chosen to have this property; for carbon $\sigma_{am} = 3.2 \times 10^{-3}$ barn. Absorption by ^{238}U is a resonance phenomenon, and therefore a very strongly varying function of the neutron energy during the slowing-down process. To follow this in detail in the Monte Carlo process would require extensive sampling in the resonance region and following a large number of neutron paths to obtain meaningful statistics. Fortunately, it is possible to average over the resonances and to produce an average cross-section in the slowing-down regime. This is of the form

$$\bar{\sigma}_{a38} = \left(\int_{E_{th}}^{E_0} \frac{\sigma_e}{E}\,dE \right) \Big/ \ln\left(\frac{E_0}{E_{th}}\right),\tag{4.27}$$

where E_0 is the initial neutron energy which comes from (4.24) and E_{th} is the thermal energy, taken as 0.025 eV. The quantity σ_e is defined by

$$\sigma_e = \frac{\sigma_{a38} \times (\Sigma_s/n_{38})}{\sigma_{a38} + (\Sigma_s/n_{38})}\tag{4.28}$$

with $\sigma_{a38} = 2.73$ barns. The results of this calculation are given in Table 4.2.

Finally, we come to the absorption cross-section of ^{235}U, σ_{a35}. For fast neutrons it is very small but for thermal neutrons it is extremely high, 694 barns, but of this 582 barns is σ_f, the cross-section for fission.

Table 4.2 The absorption cross-section σ_{a38} derived from (4.28) and (4.29) as a function of Σ_s/n_{38}.

Σ_s/n_{38}	8.3	50	100	300	500	800	1000	2000	∞
σ_{a38}	0.601	1.066	1.506	2.493	3.096	3.754	4.138	5.400	15.936

The total probability per unit path of some interaction or other will be

$$\Sigma = \Sigma_s + \Sigma_a = (n_m\sigma_{sm} + n_{35}\sigma_{s35} + n_{38}\sigma_{s38}) + (n_m\sigma_{am} + n_{35}\sigma_{a35} + n_{38}\sigma_{a38}) \quad (4.29)$$

and the mean free path, λ, between interactions will be Σ^{-1}. The probability of a free path between l and $l+dl$ is then

$$p_L(l)dl = \frac{1}{\lambda}\exp\left(-\frac{l}{\lambda}\right)dl. \quad (4.30)$$

The following procedure follows a particular neutron through the spherical reactor of radius R.

1. Calculate an initial random neutron energy from the distribution (4.24) using the generator DISDEV provided in REACTOR. This uses the rejection method (Section 4.3.3).
2. Choose a random direction for the resultant speed, to give velocity **v**, and place the neutron at some distance from the centre of the reactor (see step 5).
3. From distribution (4.30) select a distance for the neutron to travel to the next interaction. If x is a uniform deviate (0–1) then

$$l = -\lambda\ln x. \quad (4.31)$$

If the initial distance of the neutron from the centre of the reactor is r and the angle between the radius vector and **v** is ψ_0, then after travelling a distance l the new values are r_1 and ψ_1, where

$$r_1^2 = r_0^2 + l^2 + 2r_0l\cos\psi_0 \quad (4.32)$$

and

$$\cos\psi_1 = \frac{r_1^2 + l^2 - r_0^2}{2r_1l} \quad (4.33)$$

(see Fig. 4.12). If $r_1 \geqslant R$ then the neutron has been absorbed by the walls of the container and that particular neutron gives no fission.

4. Select the next interaction as either absorption or scattering with branching probabilities Σ_a/Σ and Σ_s/Σ, respectively. This is done by comparison with x, a uniform variate (0–1). If absorption is selected and the neutron has thermal energy then the probability of fission is σ_f/Σ_a and the neutron path

concludes with the production of 2.47 fast neutrons. Otherwise the neutron path concludes without production of further neutrons.

For scattering, account must be taken of the three-dimensional geometry of the reactor. Figure 4.13 shows, in the centre-of-mass frame of the neutron and scatterer, the initial velocity **v**, the new velocity **v′** and the radius vector **r**. The angle of deflection, θ, is the angle between **v** and **v′** and we take ϕ as the angle between the plane defined by **v** and **r** and the plane defined by **v** and **v′**. The angles θ and ϕ have the same relationship as the angles defining direction in a spherical polar coordinate system where θ has a normalized probability density $P(\theta) = \frac{1}{2}\sin\theta$ and ϕ is a uniform variate $(0-2\pi)$. The values of $\cos\theta$ and ϕ may be selected from two uniform variates x_1 and x_2 $(0-1)$, where $\cos\theta = 2x_1 - 1$ and $\phi = 2\pi x_2$. If, prior to the scattering, in the laboratory frame of reference, the angle between **v** and **r** was ψ_0 and after scattering the angle between **v′** and **r** is $\psi′$ then it can be shown that

$$\cos\psi' = \frac{(1 + A\cos\theta)\cos\psi_0 + A\sin\theta\sin\psi_0\cos\phi}{\sqrt{1 + 2A\cos\theta + A^2}}, \tag{4.34}$$

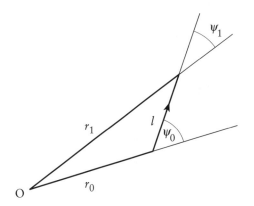

Fig. 4.12 Changes of distance from reactor centre, O, and of angle between radius vector and direction of motion after neutron moves a distance *l*.

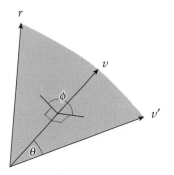

Fig. 4.13 The angle of deflection is θ, and ϕ is the angle between the shaded planes.

and the energy loss is as given by (4.25). If the neutrons have been thermalized and are in equipartition equilibrium with the other particles, then there is no longer any *net* energy change, and this is simulated by keeping the energy constant regardless of the scattering conditions.

5. Once the neutron has been launched on its journey the above steps 1–4 will enable it to be followed to its conclusion of either being absorbed or producing a fission – from which the multiplication factor can be found. Where to start the neutron has still to be decided. There are computationally expensive ways of doing this which come from the results of computation itself, but the best and most economical way is to use an analytical result that the neutron density profile will be given by

$$n(r) = \frac{n_0}{r} \sin\left(\frac{\pi r}{R + \lambda/\sqrt{2}}\right), \tag{4.35}$$

where r is the distance from the centre of the spherical reactor.

The fall-off at the boundary of function (4.35) is due to diffusion loss in that region. In REACTOR the random number generator DENDEV yields deviates with distribution (4.35). This also uses the rejection method.

The output from REACTOR gives not only the multiplication factor but also the thermalization probability, the proportion of neutrons slowed down to thermal speeds before being absorbed, and also the fission probability, the proportion of neutrons giving fission. Figure 4.14 shows the multiplication

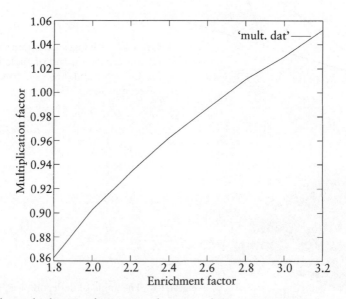

Fig. 4.14 The multiplication factor as a function of the enrichment factor for a spherical reactor of radius 6 m with $U/C = 0.001$.

factor as a function of the enrichment factor for

Uranium : graphite atomic ratio	1:1000
Radius of reactor	6 m
Number of trial neutrons	10 000.

It will be seen that the multiplication factor reaches unity at an enrichment factor of about 2.7.

Monte Carlo programs, much more complex than REACTOR and including control rod simulation, exist to model the working of nuclear reactors and no reactor would ever be built until a simulation had shown that it could be operated efficiently and safely.

Problems

4.1. Write a program to:

(i) generate N uniform deviates (0–1);
(ii) find the average of the N values and the departure, δ_N, from the expected value, 0.5;
(iii) repeat this process 100 times and find $\langle \delta_N^2 \rangle$.

Plot $\log \langle \delta_N^2 \rangle$ against $\log N$ for $N = 10, 20, 40, 80, 160$ and 320 and hence find a relationship linking $\langle \delta_N^2 \rangle$ and N.

4.2. According to the *central limit theorem* the sum of N random variables with means x_i and variances V_i will have a normal distribution with mean $\sum_{i=1}^{N} x_i$ and variance $\sum_{i=1}^{N} V_i$ if N is large (theoretically infinite). A uniform variate between -1 and $+1$ has a variance of $\frac{1}{3}$ so that sums of 27 such deviates should have a normal distribution with mean zero and standard deviation $\sigma = 3$. Using a uniform-deviate generator find 100 000 such sums and find the proportions within σ, 2σ and 3σ from the mean. For a normal distribution these should be 0.6826, 0.9545 and 0.9973.

4.3. Use the rejection method to generate 1 000 000 deviates for the probability distribution $P(x) = Ce^{-3x}$ in the range $x = 0$ to $x = 1$, where C is the normalizing constant. Use the comparison function $Q(x) = D(1 - 0.95x)$, where D is the normalizing constant. Find the numbers of deviates in ranges of 0.1 from $x = 0$ to $x = 1$ and compare with the theoretical values.

4.4. Develop a 4×4 stochastic matrix $\mathbf{P}$ such that the four probabilities generated are $p(x_1) = 0.1$, $p(x_2) = 0.2$, $p(x_3) = 0.3$ and $p(x_4) = 0.4$. You may choose the first three elements in the top row arbitrarily and thereafter you will need to choose arbitrarily the middle two elements in the second row and the third element in the third row. Write a program to use the matrix in a

Markov chain process to generate 1 000 000 variables and check that the correct probabilities are found.

4.5. Repeat Problem 3.3 using METROPOL. Since this program takes much longer than FLUIDYN you might wish to modify the program so that it will complete all values of V^* in a long single run.

4.6. Write a program to evaluate

$$\int_0^{\pi/8}\int_0^{\pi/8}\int_0^{\pi/8}\int_0^{\pi/8}\int_0^{\pi/8}\int_0^{\pi/8}\int_0^{\pi/8}\int_0^{\pi/8} \sin(x_1+x_2+x_3+x_4+x_5+x_6+x_7+x_8)\,dx_1\,dx_2\,dx_3\,dx_4\,dx_5\,dx_6\,dx_7\,dx_8$$

by the Monte Carlo method using the number of samples, $N = 10$, 100, 1000, 10 000 and 100 000. Give the result for one run of the program for each value of N. Modify the program to run 25 times for each value of N and by comparing the 25 results with the analytical result $70 - 16\sin\frac{\pi}{8} + 56\sin\frac{\pi}{4} - 112\sin\frac{3\pi}{8} = 5.371\,873 \times 10^{-4}$, find the standard deviation, σ_N, for each value of N. Plot $\log\sigma_N$ against $\log N$ and hence show that $\sigma_N \propto N^{-(1/2)}$. Make sure that the program is so designed that for each of the 25 runs the seed of the random number generator is different.

4.7. A thin plate, as shown in Fig. 4.15, is insulated on its top and bottom surfaces and had edges maintained at the temperatures indicated. With respect to the origin shown, it also is heated according to $H = 10^7\sin(\pi x)\sin(\pi y)\,\mathrm{W\,m^{-3}}$, where x and y are in metres. The square grid within the plate has side 0.1 m and the thermal conductivity of the plate is $500\,\mathrm{W\,m^{-1}K^{-1}}$. Modify the program MCPLATE to find the temperature distribution within the plate using 1000 trials per point.

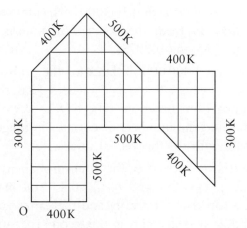

Fig. 4.15   Diagram for Problem 4.7.

4.8. Run the program REACTOR with the following data:

ratio of atomic fuel to graphite	0.001
fuel enrichment factor	2.7
number of trial neutrons	10 000
radius of reactor	1.0 to 9.0 m in steps of 1.0 m.

Find how the multiplication constant varies with reactor radius and comment on your results.

5 *The wave equation*

5.1 General solutions of the wave equation

Wave motions occur commonly in problems in physics, in vibrations on strings or as electromagnetic waves, as solutions to the Schrödinger equation and in the behaviour of plasmas, to give a few examples. The general form of the wave equation in one dimension is

$$\frac{\partial^2 \eta}{\partial t^2} = c^2 \frac{\partial^2 \eta}{\partial x^2}, \tag{5.1}$$

where c is the velocity of the wave motion, assumed constant. It is a linear equation with two independent variables, x and t, and one dependent variable, the displacement η, and from Section 2.11 it will be seen that it is a hyperbolic partial differential equation.

A general solution of (5.1) is

$$\eta = f(x \pm ct), \tag{5.2}$$

where f is any function. If several individual solution functions, $f_1, f_2, \ldots, f_n$, exist then any linear combination of these,

$$\eta = \sum_{i=1}^{n} w_i f_i(x \pm ct), \tag{5.3}$$

will also be a solution. Simple solutions of the wave equation are often expressed as sine or cosine waves or in complex exponential form, thus enabling the power of the Fourier series or of the Fourier transform to be exploited in dealing with the problem.

To give some physical picture of the wave equation we illustrate in Fig. 5.1 some regular waves moving down a canal with an observer standing on the bank. The observer sees the waves with wavelength λ, and v waves pass him per second. The velocity of the waves moving along the canal is clearly a product of the wavelength λ and the frequency v, or

$$c = \lambda v. \tag{5.4}$$

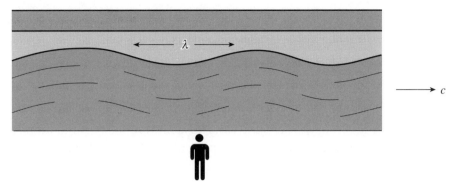

Fig. 5.1 Waves along a canal as seen by an observer on the bank.

If the waves are simple sine waves then they can be described by

$$\eta = A\sin\left\{2\pi\left(\frac{x}{\lambda} - vt\right) + \phi\right\}, \tag{5.5}$$

where ϕ is a phase angle which may be adjusted to give the required value of η for any chosen origins of x and t. At a fixed position x – for example, the position of the stationary observer – the water oscillates up and down with amplitude A and frequency v. At a fixed time, as may be recorded by a photograph, the water surface has a sinusoidal profile with amplitude A and wavelength λ.

The wave in the canal is a *progressive wave* that moves continuously without any boundaries – at least in theory. There are also *standing waves* that exist in a restricted region and where some kind of boundary conditions exist. Such a wave occurs in a taut plucked string fixed at both ends, where the velocity of the wave is given by

$$c = \sqrt{\frac{T}{m}}, \tag{5.6}$$

in which T is the tension in the string and m its mass per unit length. The motion of the string can be a simple sine wave, as shown in Fig. 5.2, or much more complex, as is usually the case with the plucked string of a musical instrument. For a simple sine wave the standing-wave pattern can be thought of as two superimposed wave motions moving in opposite directions, or

$$\eta_{sw} = \frac{1}{2}A\sin\left\{2\pi\left(\frac{x}{\lambda} + vt\right)\right\} + \frac{1}{2}A\sin\left\{2\pi\left(\frac{x}{\lambda} - vt\right)\right\} = A\sin\left(2\pi\frac{x}{\lambda}\right)\cos(2\pi vt).$$
$$\tag{5.7}$$

Fig. 5.2 A standing wave consisting of three half-waves.

At a fixed position along the string it vibrates with frequency v and amplitude $A|\sin(2\pi x/\lambda)|$ and at a fixed time the displacements form a wave with wavelength λ and amplitude $A|\cos(2\pi v t)|$. If the string is fixed at both ends then it is clear that for simple sine-wave vibrations the length of the string, L, must contain a whole number, n, of half-wavelengths, so that

$$L = n\lambda/2. \tag{5.8}$$

Any complex displacement of the string will be expressible in the form of a sum of half-sine waves (see, for example Section 3.9). Since the velocity is the same for all components and the wavelengths are of the form $2L/m$ ($m = 1, 2, 3, \ldots$), then, from (5.4), the frequencies are of the form $cm/(2L)$. Thus when the component of longest wavelength $2L$ has completed one complete vibration the component of wavelength $2L/m$ would have undergone m complete vibrations and the string would have returned to its original condition. This shows that, without any damping processes, the mixture of frequencies, or harmonic composition, of plucked string would remain unchanged with time; in practice, the damping rate differs for the different components so that the harmonic composition of the note changes as it becomes quieter.

5.2   A finite-difference approach

We can express the differential terms in the wave equation (5.1) in finite-difference form, as given in Section 2.4, as

$$\frac{\eta(i,j+1) + \eta(i,j-1) - 2\eta(i,j)}{(\Delta t)^2} = c^2 \frac{\eta(i+1,j) + \eta(i-1,j) - 2\eta(i,j)}{(\Delta x)^2}, \tag{5.9}$$

where i and j represent increments in space and time, respectively. This can be rearranged as

$$\eta(i,j+1) = \left(\frac{c\Delta t}{\Delta x}\right)^2 \{\eta(i+1,j) + \eta(i-1,j) - 2\eta(i,j)\} + 2\eta(i,j) - \eta(i,j-1). \tag{5.10}$$

The solution process for this finite-difference equation is not self-starting since, to advance knowledge of the displacements to time t_{j+1} requires knowledge of the displacements at two previous times.

The equation can be somewhat simplified by setting Δt and Δx such that $c\Delta t / \Delta x = 1$ since this eliminates the terms involving $\eta(i, j)$. However, what is required to initiate the solution is to define not only the initial displacement of the string when $j = 0$ but also the motion of the string, $\dot{\eta}(i, 0)$ for all i. We can write, in finite-difference notation,

$$\dot{\eta}(i, j) = \frac{\eta(i, j+1) - \eta(i, j-1)}{2\Delta t}. \tag{5.11}$$

The interpretation is now made that the initial motion of the string can be described from (5.11) in terms of its displacements at time $j = 1$ and hypothetical displacements at time $j = -1$. On this basis, we find by substitution in (5.11)

$$\eta(i, -1) = \eta(i, 1) - 2\Delta t \dot{\eta}(i, 0), \tag{5.12}$$

and it is these hypothetical displacements that allow the process of solution from (5.10) to be started. If, as is often the case, the initial configuration is a static one, so that $\dot{\eta}(i, j) = 0$ for all i, then the initial condition is that $\eta(i, -1) = \eta(i, 1)$. Substituting this in (5.10),

$$\eta(i, 1) = \frac{1}{2}\left(\frac{c\Delta t}{\Delta x}\right)^2 \{\eta(i+1, 0) + \eta(i-1, 0)\} + \left\{1 - \left(\frac{c\Delta t}{\Delta x}\right)^2\right\}\eta(i, 0). \tag{5.13}$$

The program WAVE (see p. xv) uses equations (5.13) and (5.10) to solve the vibrating-string problem. Numerical output can be on the computer screen and/or printed, and there is a facility to produce output files for subsequent input to a graphics package. Figure 5.3 shows the output of such a package for an initial displacement of the string such that

$$\eta(x, 0) = \begin{cases} \alpha x, & 0 \leqslant x \leqslant L/4, \\ \alpha L/4, & L/4 < x < 3L/4, \\ \alpha(L-x), & 3L/4 \leqslant x \leqslant L, \end{cases}$$

where the string is released from rest. The simplification $c\Delta t / \Delta x = 1$ has been used and the output configurations are for every second time step. The string is divided into 12 segments for the purpose of the calculation, and the solution shows this in the non-smooth representation of the motion. By using many more segments the motion of the string may be represented somewhat better. In obtaining this solution no information has been employed relating to the tension in the string, its length and its mass per unit length. Such information enables a time-scale to be attached to the calculated results. For example, if

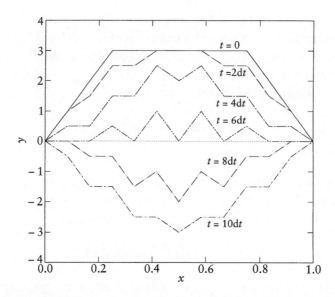

Fig. 5.3   Output from WAVE showing the vibration of a string under tension.

the tension in the string is 400 N and the mass per unit length of the string is
0.01 kg m^{-1} then, from (5.6), the wave velocity is 200 m s^{-1}. If the length of
the string is 1 m then $\Delta x = 0.0825$ m which, combined with the wave velocity,
gives $\Delta t = 4.125 \times 10^{-4}$ s. The interval between the stages of output in Fig. 5.3
is therefore 8.25×10^{-4} s.

5.2.1   *Stability of the finite-difference equations*

The wave equation can be expressed in the form of a pair of coupled first-
order partial differential equations involving the gradient of the displacement,
$u = \partial\eta/\partial x$, and the velocity of the displacement $v = \partial\eta/\partial t$:

$$\frac{\partial u}{\partial t} = \frac{\partial v}{\partial x}, \tag{5.14a}$$

$$\frac{\partial v}{\partial t} = c^2 \frac{\partial u}{\partial x}. \tag{5.14b}$$

A leapfrog formulation of the solution of these equations is

$$u(i,j+1) = u(i,j) + \frac{\Delta t}{\Delta x}\left\{v\left(i+\frac{1}{2},j+\frac{1}{2}\right) - v\left(i-\frac{1}{2},j+\frac{1}{2}\right)\right\}, \tag{5.15a}$$

centred on $(i, j+\frac{1}{2})$, and

$$v\left(i+\frac{1}{2}, j+\frac{1}{2}\right) = v\left(i+\frac{1}{2}, j-\frac{1}{2}\right) + \frac{c^2 \Delta t}{\Delta x}\{u(i+1, j) - u(i, j)\}, \quad (5.15b)$$

centred on $(i+\frac{1}{2}, j)$. Reverting to displacements, for example,

$$u(i, j+1) = \frac{\eta(i, j+3/2) - \eta(i, j+1/2)}{\Delta x}$$

and

$$v\left(i+\frac{1}{2}, j+\frac{1}{2}\right) = \frac{\eta(i+1/2, j+1) - \eta(i+1/2, j)}{\Delta t},$$

makes (5.15a) an identity and (5.15b) equivalent to (5.10) but centred on $(i+\frac{1}{2}, j)$. Form (5.15) is convenient if the wave motion is expressed as a pair of dynamic equations involving a restoring force dependent on displacement and a damping term involving velocity.

To investigate the properties of this system of equations, we consider the travelling-wave solution of (5.1)

$$\eta(x, t) = A_0 \exp\{i(kx \pm \omega t)\},$$

where $\omega = ck$. Since $v(x, t) = \partial \eta / \partial t$, it follows that

$$v(x, t) = V_0 \exp\{i(kx \pm \omega t)\}, \quad (5.16a)$$

where

$$V_0 = \pm i\omega A_0,$$

and similarly

$$u(x, t) = U_0 \exp\{i(kx \pm \omega t)\}, \quad (5.16b)$$

where

$$U_0 = ikxA_0.$$

The solution represents the familiar backward and forward travelling sinusoidal waves. With $U(t) = U_0 \exp(\pm i\omega t)$ and $V(t) = V_0 \exp(\pm i\omega t)$, another form of the equations is

$$u(x, t) = U(t)\exp(ikx) \quad (5.17a)$$

and

$$v(x, t) = V(t)\exp(ikx). \quad (5.17b)$$

In the finite-difference representation (5.17) has the discrete formulation

$$u(I, J) = U(J)\exp(ikI\Delta x) \tag{5.18a}$$

$$v(I + \tfrac{1}{2}, J + \tfrac{1}{2}) = V(J + \tfrac{1}{2})\exp\{ik(I + \tfrac{1}{2})\Delta x\}. \tag{5.18b}$$

Substituting from (5.18) into (5.15), we obtain

$$U(J+1) = U(J) + 2i\frac{\Delta t}{\Delta x}\sin\left(\frac{k\Delta x}{2}\right)V\left(J + \frac{1}{2}\right) \tag{5.19a}$$

and

$$V\left(J + \frac{1}{2}\right) = V\left(J - \frac{1}{2}\right) + 2i\frac{c^2\Delta t}{\Delta x}\sin\left(\frac{k\Delta x}{2}\right)U(J). \tag{5.19b}$$

Substituting the right-hand side of (5.19b) for $V(J + \tfrac{1}{2})$ in (5.19a) gives

$$U(J+1) = U(J)\left\{1 - 4\left(\frac{c\Delta t}{\Delta x}\right)^2\sin^2\left(\frac{k\Delta x}{2}\right)\right\} + 2i\frac{\Delta t}{\Delta x}\sin\left(\frac{k\Delta x}{2}\right)V\left(J - \frac{1}{2}\right).$$
$$\tag{5.19c}$$

Equations (5.19b) and (5.19c) can be expressed in the form

$$\begin{pmatrix} U(J+1) \\ V(J+\tfrac{1}{2}) \end{pmatrix} = \begin{pmatrix} 1 - a^2 & ia/c \\ iac & 1 \end{pmatrix}\begin{pmatrix} U(J) \\ V(J-\tfrac{1}{2}) \end{pmatrix}, \tag{5.20a}$$

where

$$a = \frac{2c\Delta t}{\Delta x}\sin\left(\frac{k\Delta x}{2}\right). \tag{5.20b}$$

The complex matrix

$$G = \begin{pmatrix} 1 - a^2 & ia/c \\ iac & 1 \end{pmatrix}$$

is called the *amplification matrix*. Its eigenvalues contain information on the time dependence of the waves generated in the finite-difference calculation. From (A1.18) in Appendix 1 the eigenvalues are the roots of the equation

$$\begin{vmatrix} 1 - a^2 - \lambda & ia/c \\ iac & 1 - \lambda \end{vmatrix} = \lambda^2 - (2 - a^2) + 1 = 0. \tag{5.21}$$

In Appendix 1 it was shown that if a non-null vector was repeatedly multiplied by a given square matrix then eventually the principal eigenvector of the matrix is produced and each new vector generated by the process is the previous vector multiplied by the principal eigenvalue. Hence if the principal eigenvector of G is greater than 1 then solutions for u and v (and hence η) grow exponentially without limit and the process is unstable. From (5.21), if $|a|>2$ then the eigenvalues are real and of magnitude greater than 1, so giving instability. This treatment is the basis of the von Neumann stability condition (Section 7.4) which requires that the amplification factor for all the Fourier modes must have amplification factors not greater than 1.

If in (5.21) $a \leqslant 2$ then the roots are complex. The quadratic equation (5.21) can also be put in the form

$$(\lambda - \lambda_1)(\lambda - \lambda_2) = 0,$$

where λ_1 and λ_2 are the eigenvalues. Comparing coefficients, it is clear that

$$\lambda_1 + \lambda_2 = 2 - a^2 \tag{5.22a}$$

and

$$\lambda_1 \lambda_2 = 1. \tag{5.22b}$$

Since the right-hand sides of (5.22a) and (5.22b) are real it follows that $\lambda_1 = \lambda_2^*$, and hence that $\lambda_1 \lambda_2 = |\lambda_1|^2 = |\lambda_2|^2 = 1$ – giving a stable process. From this result we also find from (5.22a) that

$$2 \cos \phi = 2 - a^2$$

or

$$\phi = \arccos\left(1 - \frac{a^2}{2}\right), \tag{5.22c}$$

where $\phi = \arg(\lambda_1) = -\arg(\lambda_2)$.

From (5.20b) the condition for stability, $a \leqslant 2$, is satisfied for any k if

$$C = \frac{c\Delta t}{\Delta x} \leqslant 1, \tag{5.23}$$

an important result derived in a classic paper by Courant *et al.* (1928). This paper established the general concept that explicit finite-difference solutions of wave problems are stable *provided* the wave propagates no more than one mesh interval in one time step; it is known as the Courant–Friedrich–Lewy condition and C is the *Courant number*.

Since the eigenvalues have magnitude 1 the displacement gradient, velocity and amplitude remain constant. The phase change per time step is $\phi = \pm \arccos[1 - C^2\{1 - \cos(k\Delta x)\}]$ instead of the exact value $kc\Delta t = kC\Delta x$.

The phase change is therefore correct if $C=1$ or if $k\Delta x$ is very small. The former case represents a transformation of one cell per time step with no interpolation; the latter case corresponds to having wavelengths that are long compared with the mesh spacing. For short wavelengths, comparable with the mesh spacing, the phase errors are significant and the wave speed differs from c. As a consequence the numerical solution suffers from dispersion – that is, different propagation speeds for different wavelengths – unless a suitably large mesh with small spacing is used.

5.3   Two-dimensional vibrations

The equivalent of (5.1) where there are two space dimensions is

$$\frac{\partial^2 \eta}{\partial t^2} = c^2 \left(\frac{\partial^2 \eta}{\partial x^2} + \frac{\partial^2 \eta}{\partial y^2} \right). \tag{5.24a}$$

However, if the system and its vibrations have circular symmetry then the corresponding equation is

$$\frac{\partial^2 \eta}{\partial t^2} = c^2 \left\{ \frac{\partial^2 \eta}{\partial r^2} + \frac{1}{r} \frac{\partial \eta}{\partial r} \right\} = \frac{c^2}{r} \frac{\partial}{\partial r} \left(r \frac{\partial}{\partial r} \right). \tag{5.24b}$$

This equation can be used to find the circularly-symmetrical vibrations of a circular drumskin. The velocity, c, is given by an expression of form (5.6) where the mass is per unit area of the drumskin and T, its tautness, is in units of force per unit length.

In finite-difference form (5.24b) appears as

$$\frac{\eta(i,j+1) + \eta(i,j-1) - 2\eta(i,j)}{(\Delta t)^2}$$

$$= c^2 \left\{ \frac{\eta(i+1,j) + \eta(i-1,j) - 2\eta(i,j)}{(\Delta r)^2} + \frac{\eta(i+1,j) - \eta(i-1,j)}{2r(i)\Delta r} \right\}, \tag{5.25a}$$

where i indicates increments in the radial space domain and j increments in the time domain. The updating of displacements comes from

$$\eta(i,j+1) = \left(\frac{c\Delta t}{\Delta r} \right)^2 \left[\eta(i+1,j) \left\{ 1 + \frac{\Delta r}{2r} \right\} + \eta(i-1,j) \left\{ 1 - \frac{\Delta r}{2r} \right\} \right]$$

$$+ 2 \left\{ 1 - \left(\frac{c\Delta t}{\Delta r} \right)^2 \right\} \eta(i,j) - \eta(i,j-1) \tag{5.25b}$$

Assuming an initial stationary start, for the first step we take $\eta(i, -1) = \eta(i, 1)$ so that for the first time step only we use

$$\eta(i, 1) = \frac{1}{2}\left(\frac{c\Delta t}{\Delta r}\right)^2\left[\eta(i+1, 0)\left\{1 + \frac{\Delta r}{2r}\right\} + \eta(i-1, 0)\left\{1 - \frac{\Delta r}{2r}\right\}\right]$$

$$+\left\{1 - \left(\frac{c\Delta t}{\Delta r}\right)^2\right\}\eta(i, 0). \tag{5.26}$$

The simplification that $c\Delta t/\Delta r = 1$ gives good results in general.

Equations (5.25b) and (5.26) are incorporated in the program TWODWAVE (see p. xv) which enables the circularly-symmetric vibrations of a circular drumskin to be investigated. Figure 5.4 shows the output for a drumskin of radius 0.25 m with $m = 0.01\,\mathrm{kg\,m^{-2}}$ and $T = 200\,\mathrm{N\,m^{-1}}$, where the initial displacement is of the form

$$\eta_0(s) = \exp(-16s^2)\cos(2\pi s). \tag{5.27}$$

From general principles it would be expected that the drumskin would always be horizontal at its centre, but this is not apparent in Fig. 5.4. By taking smaller intervals Δr and Δt, but keeping the ratio of the two constant, the calculated behaviour pattern is seen to resemble that expected better.

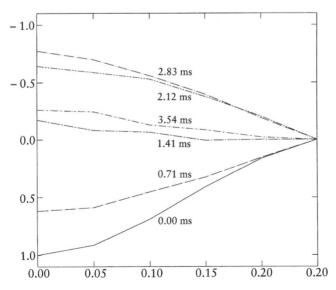

Fig. 5.4 Output from TWODWAVE showing the radial profile of a drumskin making circularly-symmetric vibrations.

5.4 Optical diffraction

Electromagnetic waves, which can propagate through a vacuum, manifest their wave properties most strikingly in the phenomenon of diffraction. Optical diffraction patterns are very easy to observe. A street lamp at some distance seen through a handkerchief held close to the eye will show satellites around the main image due to diffraction by the rectangular grid of apertures produced by the warp and weft of the fabric. In Fig. 5.5 we consider a small area dQ, in a plane, P_1, illuminated by coherent light; the coherence could come from having all the oncoming light radiating from a very small source or from an extended intrinsically coherent source such as a laser. For simplicity we shall consider a small point source of light at A of source strength S, and we shall take the *transmission function* of a point in the plane P_1 as $t(\mathbf{r})$, where $\mathbf{r}$ is the vector position relative to some origin within the plane. The amplitude of the light wave falling on area dQ will be S/d_1 and its phase, relative to the wave motion at A, will be $2\pi d_1/\lambda$. The disturbance at the position of dQ may thus be described in amplitude and phase by

$$\eta_P = \frac{S}{d_1} \exp\left(2\pi i \frac{d_1}{\lambda} \right). \tag{5.28}$$

A proportion $f(\mathbf{r}_Q)$ is transmitted by the plane P_1 and this scatters in all directions with the area dQ acting as a secondary source. A point B, on the other side of the plate from A, receives from A via the small area dQ a wave disturbance which may be described in amplitude and phase as

$$d\eta_B = \frac{Sf(\mathbf{r})}{d_1 d_2} \exp\left(2\pi i \frac{d_1 + d_2}{\lambda} \right) dQ. \tag{5.29}$$

The total disturbance at B will be obtained by integrating (5.29), giving

$$\eta_B = S \int_{P_1} \frac{f(\mathbf{r})}{d_1 d_2} \exp\left(2\pi i \frac{d_1 + d_2}{\lambda} \right) dQ, \tag{5.30}$$

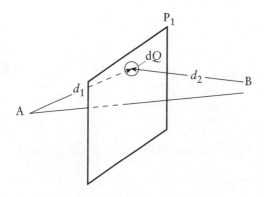

Fig. 5.5 Light travelling from A to B via scattering from a small area dQ.

where the integral is over the illuminated part of the plane P$_1$. An obliquity factor should be included in (5.29) and (5.30) to allow for the fact that the secondary scattering is most effective in the direction of the incident radiation and falls off with increasing angle from that direction. However, we shall restrict ourselves to situations where the angle between the two directions is small so that the factor is essentially unity.

In optics two simplified types of diffraction are recognized, associated with the names *Fresnel* and *Fraunhofer*. In Fig. 5.6 the plane P$_1$ is perpendicular to the z direction and passes through the origin, and the point source A has coordinates $(0, 0, -D_A)$. The coordinates of the point B are (x_B, y_B, D_B) and the coordinate of a scattering point in the plane P$_1$ is given by $(x, y, 0)$. We now express the quantities d_1 and d_2, which occur in a very sensitive way in the phase term of (5.30), in terms of the coordinates. Making the usual binomial approximations,

$$d_1 = D_A + \frac{x^2 + y^2}{2D_A} \tag{5.31a}$$

and

$$d_2 = D_B + \frac{(x - x_B)^2 + (y - y_B)^2}{2D_B} \tag{5.31b}$$

If terms involving higher than the first powers of x and y can be ignored in the phase term of (5.30), then we have Fraunhofer diffraction; otherwise, if quadratic terms are significant and higher-order terms can be neglected, then we have Fresnel diffraction. With R as the radius of the scattering region in P$_1$

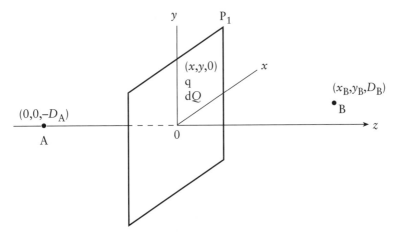

Fig. 5.6 Points shown in Fig. 5.5 with Cartesian coordinates.

the condition for Fraunhofer diffraction is, from (5.31),

$$\frac{R^2}{2D} \ll \lambda, \tag{5.32}$$

where the condition must hold for both $D = D_A$ and $D = D_B$.

There is no sharp division between Fraunhofer and Fresnel diffraction, and they merge one into the other. However, if $R^2/(2D) \geqslant \lambda/2$ then certainly the diffration would be in the Fresnel regime.

5.5 Fraunhofer diffraction

A simple experimental way of producing Fraunhofer diffraction is illustrated in Fig. 5.7. The diffracting mask is illuminated by parallel light, effectively a point source at infinity, and the diffraction pattern is observed at the focal plane of the lens L so that the diffracted image is equivalent to that at infinity without the lens. The phase lag of radiation scattered from Q, relative to that scattered at the origin O, is given by

$$\alpha_Q = \frac{2\pi}{\lambda}(MQ + QN)$$

$$= \frac{2\pi}{\lambda}(\mathbf{r} \cdot \mathbf{S} - \mathbf{r} \cdot \mathbf{S}_0)$$

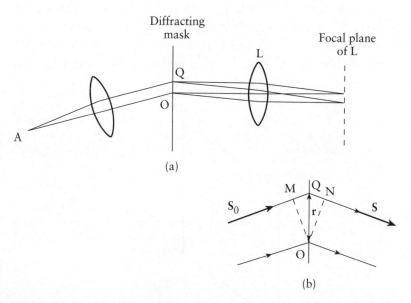

Fig. 5.7 (a) An arrangement for producing Fraunhofer diffraction. (b) The path difference for scattering from Q relative to that from O is MQ + QN.

where $\mathbf{r}$ is the vector position of Q relative to the origin O and S and S_0 are unit vectors in the incident beam and scattered beam directions, respectively. We now make the simplifying assumption that S_0 is perpendicular to the diffracting mask so that $\mathbf{r} \cdot S_0 = 0$. All the radiation scattered from different points of the mask which moves along the direction S is combined by the lens to fall on a screen in its focal plane. The scale of the diffraction pattern on the screen will depend on the focal length of the lens, but its actual form will not depend on the focal length. Representing S by its direction cosines (l, m, n), then the position on the screen will be $(u, v) = (cl, cm)$, where c is a scaling constant. Since $\mathbf{r} \cdot S = (x, y, 0) \cdot (l, m, n) = lx + my$, then

$$\alpha_Q = \frac{2\pi}{\lambda} (lx + my) = \frac{2\pi}{\lambda c} (xu + yv). \tag{5.33}$$

With a suitable choice of scaling factor, $\lambda c = 1$ and the disturbance on the screen can be described as

$$F(u, v) = \iint f(x, y) \exp\{2\pi i(xu + yv)\} \, dx \, dy, \tag{5.34}$$

where any overall scaling constants have been absorbed in $f(x, y)$. The integrals are carried out over the whole infinite plane of the diffracting mask, although in practice they are limited to the transmitting region. As defined in (5.34), $F(u, v)$ is the *Fourier transform* of $f(x, y)$, and theory shows that $f(x, y)$ is the *inverse Fourier transform* of $F(u, v)$ and is given by

$$f(x, y) = \iint F(u, v) \exp\{-2\pi i(ux + vy)\} \, du \, dv. \tag{5.35}$$

Both $f(x, y)$ and $F(u, v)$ are continuous functions within the planes in which they are defined, and in computational work the functions must be sampled over grids which are fine enough to reveal all the detail they contain. Such calculations are normally carried out very efficiently by fast Fourier transform (FFT) algorithms, which were mentioned in Section 3.9. The basic principles of the FFT process will now be described.

5.6 Discrete Fourier transforms

The implementation of FFT algorithms for multi-dimensional transforms is very complicated, but here we shall restrict the discussion to one dimension with a function defined within a region from $x = 0$ to $x = 1$. This range can always be imposed by a suitable change of scale and origin, and doing this gives no loss of generality in the analysis which follows. The Fourier transform we wish to find can now be expressed as the finite integral

$$F(u) = \int_0^1 f(x)\exp(2\pi i x u)\,dx, \tag{5.36}$$

and this can be approximated by a trapezium-rule summation as

$$F(u) = \sum_{j=0}^{N} w(j)f\left(\frac{j}{N}\right)\exp\left(2\pi i \frac{j}{N}u\right), \tag{5.37}$$

where $N+1$ values are taken on a uniform grid in the range of x, $w(0)= w(N)=0.5$ and all other ws equal unity. If $f(x)$ is a periodic function, so that $f(0)=f(1)$, or if $f(x)=0$ at $x=0$ and $x=1$, then the summation appears as

$$F(u) = \sum_{j=0}^{N-1} f\left(\frac{j}{N}\right)\exp\left(2\pi i \frac{j}{N}u\right). \tag{5.38}$$

In this form the $F(u)$s would be called the discrete Fourier coefficients of the periodic function. From the form of (5.38) it is easily seen that $F(u+N)=F(u)$ and that $F(-u)=F^*(u)$ where '*' indicates the *complex conjugate*. Hence it is only necessary to find the complex quantities $F(u)$ for $u=0, 1 \ldots\ldots \mathrm{int}(N/2)$, where $\mathrm{int}(n)$ means the integral part of n since all other Fourier coefficients may be determined from this set.

5.6.1 *Fast Fourier transforms*

The N values of $F(u)$ are linear combinations of the values of $f(x)$ at the grid-points. We now make a simplification in notation by writing

$$Z_k = \exp\left(2\pi i \frac{k}{N}\right) \tag{5.39}$$

and, because of the nature of the right-hand side function,

$$Z_{k_1}Z_{k_2}=Z_{k_1+k_2} \quad \text{and} \quad Z_{k+N}=Z_k. \tag{5.40}$$

Expressed in matrix notation, the N values of $F(u)$, for $N=8$, are given by

$$
\begin{bmatrix} F(0) \\ F(1) \\ F(2) \\ F(3) \\ F(4) \\ F(5) \\ F(6) \\ F(7) \end{bmatrix} = \begin{bmatrix}
Z(0) & Z(0) & Z(0) & Z(0) & Z(0) & Z(0) & Z(0) & Z(0) \\
Z(0) & Z(1) & Z(2) & Z(3) & Z(4) & Z(5) & Z(6) & Z(7) \\
Z(0) & Z(2) & Z(4) & Z(6) & Z(0) & Z(2) & Z(4) & Z(6) \\
Z(0) & Z(3) & Z(6) & Z(1) & Z(4) & Z(7) & Z(2) & Z(5) \\
Z(0) & Z(4) & Z(0) & Z(4) & Z(0) & Z(4) & Z(0) & Z(4) \\
Z(0) & Z(5) & Z(2) & Z(7) & Z(4) & Z(1) & Z(6) & Z(3) \\
Z(0) & Z(6) & Z(4) & Z(2) & Z(0) & Z(6) & Z(4) & Z(2) \\
Z(0) & Z(7) & Z(6) & Z(5) & Z(4) & Z(3) & Z(2) & Z(1)
\end{bmatrix} \begin{bmatrix} f(0/8) \\ f(1/8) \\ f(2/8) \\ f(3/8) \\ f(4/8) \\ f(5/8) \\ f(6/8) \\ f(7/8) \end{bmatrix}.
$$

$$(5.41)$$

To evaluate an element of the left-hand side vector involves eight product operations and seven additions, and to evaluate the complete left-hand-side vector would involve $8 \times 15 = 120$ operations in total. The general expression for the number of operations would be $N(2N-1)$ which, for large N, is proportional to N^2. Cooley and Tukey (1965) gave an algorithm which needed fewer operations which therefore speeded up the calculation. Here we shall just explain the concepts of the fast Fourier transform process and for simplicity assume that N is a power of 2 – which makes it easier to program, although it is not a necessary condition to apply the method.

The main step in the process is the factorization of the matrix in (5.41) into a product of two simpler matrices. The forms of the component matrices are simplified if the equations (5.41) are reordered to give

$$
\begin{bmatrix} F(0) \\ F(2) \\ F(4) \\ F(6) \\ F(1) \\ F(3) \\ F(5) \\ F(7) \end{bmatrix} = \begin{bmatrix}
Z(0) & Z(0) & Z(0) & Z(0) & 0 & 0 & 0 & 0 \\
Z(0) & Z(2) & Z(4) & Z(6) & 0 & 0 & 0 & 0 \\
Z(0) & Z(4) & Z(0) & Z(4) & 0 & 0 & 0 & 0 \\
Z(0) & Z(6) & Z(4) & Z(2) & 0 & 0 & 0 & 0 \\
0 & 0 & 0 & 0 & Z(0) & Z(1) & Z(2) & Z(3) \\
0 & 0 & 0 & 0 & Z(0) & Z(3) & Z(6) & Z(1) \\
0 & 0 & 0 & 0 & Z(0) & Z(5) & Z(2) & Z(7) \\
0 & 0 & 0 & 0 & Z(0) & Z(7) & Z(6) & Z(5)
\end{bmatrix}
$$

$$
\times \begin{bmatrix}
Z(0) & 0 & 0 & 0 & Z(0) & 0 & 0 & 0 \\
0 & Z(0) & 0 & 0 & 0 & Z(0) & 0 & 0 \\
0 & 0 & Z(0) & 0 & 0 & 0 & Z(0) & 0 \\
0 & 0 & 0 & Z(0) & 0 & 0 & 0 & Z(0) \\
Z(0) & 0 & 0 & 0 & Z(4) & 0 & 0 & 0 \\
0 & Z(0) & 0 & 0 & 0 & Z(4) & 0 & 0 \\
0 & 0 & Z(0) & 0 & 0 & 0 & Z(4) & 0 \\
0 & 0 & 0 & Z(0) & 0 & 0 & 0 & Z(4)
\end{bmatrix} \begin{bmatrix} f(0/8) \\ f(1/8) \\ f(2/8) \\ f(3/8) \\ f(4/8) \\ f(5/8) \\ f(6/8) \\ f(7/8) \end{bmatrix}.
$$

$$(5.42)$$

Writing (5.42) as $\mathbf{F} = \mathbf{ABf}$, the product $\mathbf{Bf}$ involves 16 multiplications and 8 additions. The matrix $\mathbf{A}$ is in block-diagonal form so the equation for evaluating $\mathbf{F}$ can be broken into separate parts for odd and even values of u:

$$\begin{bmatrix} F(0) \\ F(2) \\ F(4) \\ F(6) \end{bmatrix} = \begin{bmatrix} Z(0) & Z(0) & Z(0) & Z(0) \\ Z(0) & Z(2) & Z(4) & Z(6) \\ Z(0) & Z(4) & Z(0) & Z(4) \\ Z(0) & Z(6) & Z(4) & Z(2) \end{bmatrix} \begin{bmatrix} f(0/8) + f(4/8) \\ f(1/8) + f(5/8) \\ f(2/8) + f(6/8) \\ f(3/8) + f(7/8) \end{bmatrix} \tag{5.43a}$$

and

$$\begin{bmatrix} F(1) \\ F(3) \\ F(5) \\ F(7) \end{bmatrix} = \begin{bmatrix} Z(0) & Z(1) & Z(2) & Z(3) \\ Z(0) & Z(3) & Z(6) & Z(1) \\ Z(0) & Z(5) & Z(2) & Z(7) \\ Z(0) & Z(7) & Z(6) & Z(5) \end{bmatrix} \begin{bmatrix} f(0/8) + Z(4)f(4/8) \\ f(1/8) + Z(4)f(5/8) \\ f(2/8) + Z(4)f(6/8) \\ f(3/8) + Z(4)f(7/8) \end{bmatrix}. \tag{5.43b}$$

The evaluation of each of (5.43a) and (5.43b) requires 16 multiplications and 12 additions. The total evaluation using the factorization of the original 8×8 matrix thus takes 80 operations rather than the 120 from directly using (5.41). However, this is not the only economy of effort: the 4×4 matrices occurring in (5.43a) and (5.43b) can also be factorized as products of two simple 4×4 matrices, thus:

$$\begin{bmatrix} Z(0) & Z(0) & Z(0) & Z(0) \\ Z(0) & Z(2) & Z(4) & Z(6) \\ Z(0) & Z(4) & Z(0) & Z(4) \\ Z(0) & Z(6) & Z(4) & Z(2) \end{bmatrix} = \begin{bmatrix} Z(0) & Z(0) & 0 & 0 \\ 0 & 0 & Z(0) & Z(2) \\ Z(0) & Z(4) & 0 & 0 \\ 0 & 0 & Z(0) & Z(6) \end{bmatrix}$$

$$\times \begin{bmatrix} Z(0) & 0 & Z(0) & 0 \\ 0 & Z(0) & 0 & Z(0) \\ Z(0) & 0 & Z(4) & 0 \\ 0 & Z(0) & 0 & Z(4) \end{bmatrix} \tag{5.44a}$$

and

$$\begin{bmatrix} Z(0) & Z(1) & Z(2) & Z(3) \\ Z(0) & Z(3) & Z(6) & Z(1) \\ Z(0) & Z(5) & Z(2) & Z(7) \\ Z(0) & Z(7) & Z(6) & Z(5) \end{bmatrix} = \begin{bmatrix} Z(0) & Z(0) & 0 & 0 \\ 0 & 0 & Z(0) & Z(3) \\ Z(0) & Z(4) & 0 & 0 \\ 0 & 0 & Z(0) & Z(7) \end{bmatrix}$$

$$\times \begin{bmatrix} Z(0) & 0 & Z(2) & 0 \\ 0 & Z(1) & 0 & Z(3) \\ Z(0) & 0 & Z(6) & 0 \\ 0 & Z(0) & 0 & Z(6) \end{bmatrix}. \tag{5.44b}$$

The reader may confirm that the use of the factorized 4×4 matrices again gives a saving in the number of operations to be performed. Applying the FFT algorithm when N is a power of 2 involves a number of operations proportional to $N \log_2 N$, whereas the straightforward multiplication in the form (5.41) requires a number of operations proportional to N^2. The saving for large N can be considerable: for $N = 128$ the number of operations required would be reduced by a factor of about 18.

There are many standard FFT programs available. Examples can be found in Press *et al.* (1986). They give a one-dimensional subroutine FOUR1 and a general multi-dimensional subroutine FOURN, and the programs can give either the Fourier transform or the inverse Fourier transform as described in (5.35). The function being transformed, which can be either real or complex, is presented to the subroutines as arrays with sample values of the function at points of a grid. As an example the array of numbers, forming a letter X as shown in Table 5.1, was input to FOURN. Within the function space $x = 0$ to 1 and $y = 0$ to 1 the function is centrosymmetric, which is to say that $f(x, y) = f(1 - x, 1 - y)$. Under this condition the Fourier transform is real and Table 5.2

Table 5.1   The function $f(x, y)$ forming a letter X.

y	x							
	0/8	1/8	2/8	3/8	4/8	5/8	6/8	7/8
0/8	0	0	0	0	0	0	0	0
1/8	0	1	0	0	0	0	0	1
2/8	0	0	1	0	0	0	1	0
3/8	0	0	0	1	0	1	0	0
4/8	0	0	0	0	1	0	0	0
5/8	0	0	0	1	0	1	0	0
6/8	0	0	1	0	0	0	1	0
7/8	0	1	0	0	0	0	0	1

Table 5.2   The Fourier transform $F(u, v)$ of the function shown in Table 5.1.

v	u							
	0	1	2	3	4	5	6	7
0	13.0	−1.0	−3.0	−1.0	−3.0	−1.0	−3.0	−1.0
1	−1.0	5.0	−1.0	−3.0	−1.0	−3.0	−1.0	5.0
2	−3.0	−1.0	5.0	−1.0	−3.0	−1.0	5.0	−1.0
3	−1.0	−3.0	−1.0	5.0	−1.0	5.0	−1.0	−3.0
4	−3.0	−1.0	−3.0	−1.0	13.0	−1.0	−3.0	−1.0
5	−1.0	−3.0	−1.0	5.0	−1.0	5.0	−1.0	−3.0
6	−3.0	−1.0	5.0	−1.0	−3.0	−1.0	5.0	−1.0
7	−1.0	5.0	−1.0	−3.0	−1.0	−3.0	−1.0	5.0

Table 5.3 The function $f(x,y)$ forming a letter C.

y				x				
	0/8	1/8	2/8	3/8	4/8	5/8	6/8	7/8
0/8	0	0	0	0	0	0	0	0
1/8	0	0	0	1	1	1	0	0
2/8	0	0	1	0	0	0	1	0
3/8	0	0	1	0	0	0	0	0
4/8	0	0	1	0	0	0	0	0
5/8	0	0	1	0	0	0	0	0
6/8	0	0	1	0	0	0	1	0
7/8	0	0	0	1	1	1	0	0

Table 5.4 The Fourier transform $F(u,v)$ of the function shown in Table 5.3. The imaginary component is shown below the real component.

v					u			
	0	1	2	3	4	5	6	7
0	13.000	−4.828	−5.000	0.828	5.000	0.828	−5.000	−4.828
	0.000	3.000	0.000	−3.000	0.000	3.000	0.000	−3.000
1	1.828	−3.414	3.828	0.586	−3.828	0.586	3.828	−3.414
	0.000	−2.414	0.000	2.414	0.000	−2.414	0.000	2.414
2	−3.000	0.000	3.000	0.000	−3.000	0.000	3.000	0.000
	0.000	1.000	0.000	−1.000	0.000	1.000	0.000	−1.000
3	−3.828	3.414	−1.828	−0.586	1.828	−0.586	−1.828	3.414
	0.000	0.414	0.000	−0.414	0.000	0.414	0.000	−0.414
4	−3.000	4.828	−5.000	−0.828	5.000	−0.828	−5.000	4.828
	0.000	−1.000	0.000	1.000	0.000	−1.000	0.000	1.000
5	−3.828	3.414	−1.828	−0.586	1.828	−0.586	−1.828	3.414
	0.000	0.414	0.000	−0.412	0.000	0.414	0.000	−0.414
6	−3.000	0.000	3.000	0.000	−3.000	0.000	3.000	0.000
	0.000	1.000	0.000	−1.000	0.000	1.000	0.000	−1.000
7	1.828	−3.414	3.828	0.586	−3.828	0.586	3.828	−3.414
	0.000	−2.414	0.000	2.414	0.000	−2.414	0.000	2.414

gives the values found from FOURN. An inverse transform using the values shown in Table 5.2 exactly reproduced the original function shown in Table 5.1.

To illustrate a Fourier transform of a non-centrosymmetric function, the array shown in Table 5.3 was input, defining a letter C. The Fourier transform of this function is complex, and is shown in Table 5.4. Applying the inverse Fourier transformation to these complex values of $F(u,v)$ gives precisely the values shown in Table 5.3.

The theory and practice of Fourier transforms we have illustrated here for one and two dimensions can be carried over into any number of dimensions. An important application of Fourier transforms occurs in the theory of X-ray crystallography where X-rays are diffracted from crystals. Crystals are effectively infinite three-dimensional periodic arrays of scatterers and the Fourier transforms of such arrangements have finite values only at the grid-points of a *reciprocal lattice* – corresponding to having only integer values of three quantities equivalent to u and v in (5.25). A full treatment of the theory of this kind of scattering will be found in Woolfson (1997).

5.7 Fresnel diffraction

For Fresnel diffraction it is necessary to evaluate the integral in (5.30), including the quadratic terms in (5.31a) and (5.31b). Ignoring terms higher than quadratic in x and y is valid if the scattering region in the plane P_1 and the point B at which the diffraction is observed (Fig. 5.5) are both fairly close to the axis. While the quadratic terms in the expansion of d_1 and d_2 will be important in the phase part of the integrand, the value of the divisor $d_1 d_2$ will vary very little for different values of (x, y) and so can be replaced by $D_A D_B$ and taken outside the integral. With these conditions in place, the disturbance at point B is found as

$$\eta_B = \frac{S}{D_A D_B} \exp\left\{\frac{2\pi}{\lambda} i(D_A + D_B)\right\} \exp\left\{\frac{2\pi}{\lambda D_B} i(x_B^2 + y_B^2)\right\}$$

$$\times \iint f(x, y) \exp\left\{\frac{2\pi}{\lambda Z} i(x^2 + y^2)\right\} \exp\left\{-\frac{2\pi}{\lambda D_B} i(x x_B + y y_B)\right\} dx\, dy, \quad (5.45)$$

where

$$\frac{1}{Z} = \frac{1}{2}\left(\frac{1}{D_A} + \frac{1}{D_B}\right).$$

The phase-component terms outside the integral can be ignored if only the intensity of the diffraction pattern is required since they have unit magnitude. We now write

$$g(x, y) = f(x, y) \exp\left\{\frac{2\pi}{\lambda Z} i(x^2 + y^2)\right\},$$

$$u = \frac{1}{\lambda D_B} x_B, \qquad v = \frac{1}{\lambda D_B} y_B,$$

$$G(u, v) = \iint g(x, y) \exp\{-2\pi i(xu + yv)\}\, dx\, dy. \quad (5.46)$$

Since $G(u,v)$ is the inverse Fourier transform of $g(x,y)$, we can use the power of the FFT to calculate a Fresnel diffraction pattern. The steps are as follows:

1. Multiply the mask transmission function $f(x,y)$ by $\exp\{2\pi i(x^2+y^2)/\lambda Z\}$ to give the complex function $g(x,y)$.
2. Use an FFT to calculate $G(u,v)$, the inverse Fourier transform of $g(x,y)$.
3. The value of the inverse transform at (u,v), where u and v are integers, is the value of the integral at the point $(x_B, y_B) = (\lambda D_B u, \lambda D_B v)$.
4. $|G(u,v)|^2$ gives intensities on a relative scale. If the amplitude and phase of the diffraction pattern are required then $(2\pi/\lambda)\{D_A + D_B + (x_B^2+y_B^2)/2D_B\}$ is added to the phase of $G(u,v)$.

As an example, Fig. 5.8 shows a transparent annular aperture illuminated by a point source A. The external diameter of the aperture is 0.5 mm and the internal diameter is 0.1875 mm. The distances D_A and D_B are 60 mm and 120 mm respectively, which gives $Z = 80$ mm; under the conditions of geometrical optics the image of the aperture on the screen B would have an external diameter of 1.5 mm and an internal diameter of 0.5625 mm. The aperture is modelled in a 1 mm square region divided into a 128×128 mesh with the origin at the centre. Grid-points corresponding to opaque parts of the mesh have a value of zero and those at clear parts have a value $\exp\{(2\pi/\lambda Z)i(x^2+y^2)\}$, where λ was taken as 5×10^{-4} mm. The real and imaginary parts of $g(x,y)$ were calculated and stored in two separate tables for input to FOURN. The output Fourier transform gave real and imaginary values on a grid for (x_B, y_B) at increments of distance in each direction of λD_B, or 0.06 mm. The radial intensity,

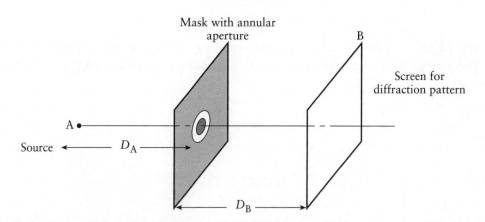

Fig. 5.8 An arrangement for observing Fresnel diffraction.

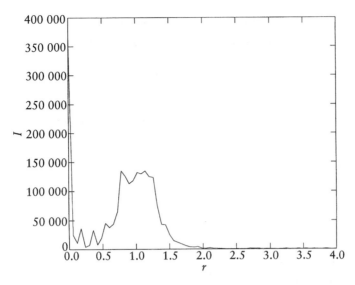

Fig. 5.9 The computed radial intensity profile for Fresnel diffraction from an annular aperture.

obtained from the sum of the squares of the real and imaginary parts of the output, is shown in Fig. 5.9. It will be seen that transmission through the aperture does not give a sharp shadow image but that edges are blurred and there are clear diffraction rings. A very notable feature is the high intensity at the centre of the diffraction pattern. Such a high intensity occurs at the centre of a Fresnel diffraction pattern of any round object and the experimental observation of this by Fresnel and Arago in 1818 was the final proof that led to general acceptance of the wave theory of light.

Problems

5.1. Run the program WAVE with the standard parameters provided. Write a subroutine WAVIN.FOR which gives an initial wave profile $\eta = \sin^3(\pi x/L)$. Obtain either printed or data-file output at times corresponding to $10n\Delta t$, with n from 0 to 6. Plot the solution by hand, or input the data files to a graphics package, to view the wave profile as a function of time.

5.2. A circular drumskin of radius R, with the standard parameters given by the program TWODWAVE, is struck dead centre so that the depression at $t = 0$ is $\exp\{-20(r/R)^2\}$, where r is the distance from the centre. Produce output to plot the displacement of the drumskin at times corresponding to $10n\Delta t$, with n from 0 to 6. Plot the solution by hand, or input the data files to a graphics package, to view the drumskin profiles as a function of time.

5.3. With the program FOURN from Press *et al.* (1986), or some similar program, find the Fourier transform of the 'arrow' shown below.

y				x				
	0/8	1/8	2/8	3/8	4/8	5/8	6/8	7/8
0/8	0	0	0	0	1	0	0	0
1/8	0	0	0	1	1	1	0	0
2/8	0	0	1	0	1	0	1	0
3/8	0	1	0	0	1	0	0	1
4/8	0	0	0	0	1	0	0	0
5/8	0	0	0	0	1	0	0	0
6/8	0	0	0	0	1	0	0	0
7/8	0	0	0	0	1	0	0	0

  (i) Fourier transform the arrow and then carry out the inverse transform to obtain the arrow again.
 (ii) Do an inverse transform just using the real part of the transform of the arrow and find the corresponding intensity.
(iii) Do an inverse transform just using the imaginary part of the transform of the arrow and find the corresponding intensity.

Also examine the amplitude/phase distribution in the inverse transforms in parts (ii) and (iii), and interpret them in terms of the original arrow.

6 *The finite-element method*

6.1 Introduction

There is a alternative complementary approach to formulating numerical solutions to multi-dimensional partial differential equations, based on error minimization rather than consistent representation as in the finite-difference methods we have thus far explored. This is the so-called *finite-element approach*, which may be formulated in a number of different ways depending on our definition of the error. It is particularly useful for handling irregular multi-dimensional domains in which the physical problem can be expressed in terms of a quantity minimization – a variational problem. Typical examples are the principles of least energy, least action and least time and the variational principle in quantum mechanics. Such problems are usually stationary and in their differential form must be of second order. The former condition implies that time-marching is not involved, and stability is not a consideration, and the latter condition implies that not *all* problems can be solved by this variational approach. The method is widely used for solving for equilibria in structural mechanics and Laplace's equations in engineering configurations.

6.2 Differential equations and functionals

There is a class of problems, which arise either in a scientific context or as a part of a branch of mathematics known as the *calculus of variations*, which involve *functionals* or 'functions of functions'. A common type of functional is

$$I(\phi) = \int_a^b f(x, \phi, \phi') \, dx, \tag{6.1}$$

where ϕ is a function of x which satisfies Dirichlet boundary conditions $\phi(a) = \alpha$ and $\phi(b) = \beta$ and $\phi' = d\phi/dx$. The calculus of variations is concerned with finding the function ϕ which will optimize the value of the functional, and in our application we shall be concerned with minimization.

Consider the graphical representation of some function $\phi(x)$ between $x = a$ and $x = b$ as shown in Fig. 6.1. Each point of the curve gives x, ϕ and ϕ' and hence a value of $f(x, \phi, \phi')$ which can all be expressed in terms of x. We now need to find the condition that the function ϕ is such that when $f(x, \phi, \phi')$

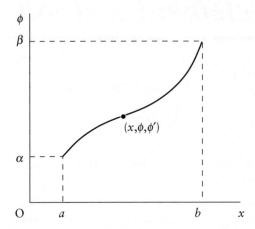

Fig. 6.1 A curve with boundary conditions.

is integrated between $x=a$ and $x=b$ it gives a minimum value. If a slightly different function, $\phi+\delta\phi$, is chosen which satisfies the same boundary conditions then

$$I(\phi+\delta\phi) = \int_a^b \left(f + \frac{\partial f}{\partial\phi}\,\delta\phi + \frac{\partial f}{\partial\phi'}\,\delta\phi' \right) dx, \tag{6.2}$$

where f is written for $f(x, \phi, \phi')$. If $I(\phi)$ is at a minimum then its rate of change with respect to changes of ϕ should be zero, or

$$\int_a^b \left(\frac{\partial f}{\partial\phi}\,\delta\phi + \frac{\partial f}{\partial\phi'}\,\delta\phi' \right) dx = 0. \tag{6.3}$$

It should be noted that $\delta\phi$ is a function of x which has very small values in the range $x=a$ to $x=b$ and $\delta\phi'$ is its derivative with respect to x. The function $\delta\phi$ must be zero at $x=a$ and $x=b$ in order that the boundary conditions should be satisfied by $\phi+\delta\phi$.

We now take a special form of $f(x, \phi, \phi')$ which leads to an equation of interest in the solution of physical problems. This is

$$f(x, \phi, \phi') = \tfrac{1}{2}c(\phi')^2 - \tfrac{1}{2}G\phi^2 + F\phi, \tag{6.4}$$

where c is a constant and G and F may be functions of x. For this function

$$\frac{\partial f}{\partial\phi} = -G\phi + F \quad \text{and} \quad \frac{\partial f}{\partial\phi'} = c\phi'. \tag{6.5}$$

The condition for the functional to be a minimum is thus, from (6.3),

$$\int_a^b \{(-G\phi+F)\delta\phi+c\phi'\,\delta\phi'\}\,dx=0. \tag{6.6}$$

The last term in the integrand is now integrated by parts to give

$$\int_a^b c\phi'\delta\phi'\,dx=|c\phi'\delta\phi|_a^b-\int_a^b c\phi''\delta\phi\,dx. \tag{6.7}$$

The first term on the right-hand side is zero since $\delta\phi$ is zero at both limits, so that the condition for a minimum of the functional can be written as

$$\int_a^b (-c\phi''-G\phi+F)\delta\phi\,dx=0. \tag{6.8}$$

This condition will certainly be met if the integrand is zero over the whole range of x or

$$c\frac{d^2\phi}{dx^2}+G\phi-F=0 \tag{6.9}$$

from $x=a$ to $x=b$. A function which satisfies (6.9) with the boundary conditions $\phi(a)=\alpha$ and $\phi(b)=\beta$ will make

$$\int_a^b \left\{\frac{1}{2}c\left(\frac{d\phi}{dx}\right)^2-\frac{1}{2}G\phi^2+F\phi\right\}dx \quad \text{a minimum.} \tag{6.10}$$

The task of solving the differential equation (6.9) can be achieved by finding a function which satisfies (6.10) and also has the required boundary conditions. However, it seems that the problem of solving the differential equation has just been transformed into what is, apparently, an equally difficult problem of finding a function which minimizes the integral. If a precise solution of the differential equation was required that would be true; in fact we have good techniques for numerically solving the differential equation, while it is more difficult to find a precise numerical solution satisfying the condition (6.10). However, there are analogues of the differential equation in two and three dimensions where it is somewhat more difficult to find a numerical solution, although finite-difference methods may be applicable, but there may be comparatively simple methods for finding an *approximate* function for minimizing the integral. The main advantage of obtaining a solution through minimization of a functional comes when problems are in more than one dimension and where the boundaries of the problem are irregular.

The technique which is used to solve the integral minimization problem approximately is the *variational method*, which finds applications in many areas of physics. Often the approximate form of the solution may be known or can be guessed and some analytical expression with adjustable parameters can be found with the right general shape. Alternatively, the solution can be approximated by a polynomial expression with a limited number of terms which, by adjusting the coefficients (parameters) can take on a variety of forms. The essence of the variational method is as follows:

1. Decide on the analytical function which contains adjustable parameters.
2. Evaluate the functional in terms of the unknown parameters or coefficients.
3. Find the values of the parameters which minimize the functional.
4. Insert these parameters into the analytical function to give the required approximate solution.

Clearly the success of this method will depend on the extent to which the *variational function* can take on a form similar to the correct one and the skill in getting the best from the variational method is in choosing a good variational function. We shall now illustrate the principle of the variational method with a simple example.

We wish to find y in the range $x=0$ to $x=\pi/2$ where

$$\frac{d^2y}{dx^2} + y = 2\cos x,\tag{6.11}$$

with boundary conditions $x=0$, $y=0$ and $x=\pi/2$, $y=\pi/2$.

Comparing (6.9) and (6.11) we find $c=1$, $G=1$ and $F=2\cos x$. We shall use a variational function of the form

$$y = ax + bx^2,\tag{6.12}$$

which satisfies the boundary condition at $x=0$. For the other boundary condition

$$a\frac{\pi}{2} + b\left(\frac{\pi}{2}\right)^2 = \frac{\pi}{2},$$

which gives

$$b = \frac{2}{\pi}(1-a).\tag{6.13}$$

This leaves one variational parameter, a, to minimize the functional. With this value of b

$$y = ax + \frac{2}{\pi}(1-a)x^2 \quad \text{and} \quad y' = a + \frac{4}{\pi}(1-a)x.$$

Table 6.1 Comparison of the variational method solutions based on the quadratic function (6.12) and the two-straight-line function (6.16a) with the analytical solution.

x	y_{quad}	y_{anal}	y_{tsl}
0	0.000	0.000	0.000
$\pi/12$	0.138	0.067	0.189
$\pi/6$	0.325	0.262	0.379
$\pi/4$	0.563	0.555	0.569
$\pi/3$	0.849	0.907	0.903
$5\pi/12$	1.185	1.264	1.237
$\pi/2$	1.571	1.571	1.571

We now find a by minimizing the integral (6.10) which, for this problem, is

$$I(a) = \int_0^{\pi/2} \left\{ \frac{1}{2}\left[a + \frac{4}{\pi}(1-a)x \right]^2 - \frac{1}{2}\left[ax + \frac{2}{\pi}(1-a)x^2 \right]^2 \right.$$

$$\left. + 2\cos x \left[ax + \frac{2}{\pi}(1-a)x^2 \right] \right\} dx. \tag{6.14}$$

The minimization requires that $dI(a)/da = 0$ and we can differentiate each of the terms in the integrand with respect to a before integrating. This leads to

$$\frac{\pi}{6}(a-1) + \frac{\pi^3}{40}\left(\frac{a}{6} + \frac{1}{4} \right) + 2\left(\frac{\pi}{2} - 1 \right) - \left(\pi - \frac{8}{\pi} \right) = 0$$

which gives $a = 0.4333$ and hence, from (6.14), $b = 0.3607$. The approximate solution of the differential equation (6.11) from the application of the variational principle with function (6.12) is

$$y = 0.4333x + 0.3607x^2. \tag{6.15}$$

Table 6.1 shows this solution, y_{quad}, compared with the analytical solution $y = x\sin x$. The solution is not a very good one because the variational function was not flexible enough to give a good match. A better result could be obtained with a higher-order polynomial; indeed, by choosing a polynomial of sufficiently high order a result as close to the analytical result within any desired tolerance could be obtained.

6.3 Linear variational functions

The match of the variational function (6.15) to the correct solution of the differential equation is shown in Fig. 6.2 and is not a very close one. What can be seen just by visual inspection is that a pair of straight lines, shown as

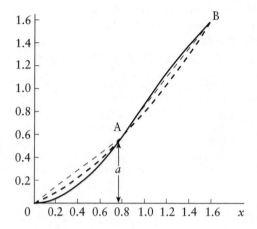

Fig. 6.2 Full line – the analytical solution of (6.11). Dashed line – the quadratic variational function estimate. Dash-dotted line – a two-straight-line estimate. For this estimate a is the variational parameter.

OA and AB, would probably give just as good a match taking the range of x as a whole. Given that boundary conditions at O and B have to be satisfied such a pair of straight line lines would be defined by a single parameter a, the ordinate of point A if its x coordinate is fixed at, say, $\pi/4$. We shall now apply the variational method to find the equations of the two straight lines and hence find an approximate solution of the differential equation (6.11).

To match the straight lines to the points O, A and B their forms are

$$y = \frac{4}{\pi} ax \qquad\qquad 0 \leqslant x < \frac{\pi}{4} \qquad (6.16a)$$

and

$$y = \left(2a - \frac{\pi}{2}\right) + \left(2 - \frac{4}{\pi}a\right)x \qquad \frac{\pi}{4} \leqslant x \leqslant \frac{\pi}{2}. \qquad (6.16b)$$

The corresponding derivatives are

$$y' = \frac{4a}{\pi} \quad \text{and} \quad y' = 2 - \frac{4a}{\pi}. \qquad (6.17)$$

The functional which is to be minimized is

$$I(a) = \int_0^{\pi/4} \left(\frac{8a^2}{\pi^2} - \frac{8a^2}{\pi^2}x^2 + \frac{8a}{\pi}x\cos x\right)dx + \int_{\pi/4}^{\pi/2}\left[\frac{1}{2}\left(2 - \frac{4a}{\pi}\right)^2 - \frac{1}{2}\left\{\left(2a - \frac{\pi}{2}\right)\right.\right.$$

$$\left.\left. + \left(2 - \frac{4a}{\pi}\right)x\right\}^2 + 2\cos x\left\{\left(2a - \frac{\pi}{2}\right) + \left(2 - \frac{4a}{\pi}x\right)\right\}\right]dx. \qquad (6.18)$$

The minimization condition $dI(a)/da = 0$ leads to $a = 0.569$ and the variational function as the two straight lines

$$y = 0.724x \qquad 0 \leqslant x < \frac{\pi}{4}$$

and

$$y = 1.276x - 0.433 \qquad \frac{\pi}{4} < x \leqslant \frac{\pi}{2}. \tag{6.19}$$

As seen in Table 6.1, the average deviation of the two-straight-line solution, y_{tsl}, from the correct values is similar to that for the quadratic function, but the quadratic function is to be preferred because the deviations are more uniform over the range.

6.3.1 *Many-straight-line variational functions*

Figure 6.3 shows a many-straight-line piece-wise continuous linear variational function where the variational parameters are the ordinates at equally spaced values of x. If each straight line corresponded to a short, approximately linear part of the true solution then linear interpolation between the values of x would define the true function well. We shall introduce the following terminology: each straight-line section is called an *element* and each junction of elements is called a *node*. Then the y coordinate for some value of x in the element between nodes x_i and x_{i+1} is given by

$$y = \frac{x_{i+1} - x}{x_{i+1} - x_i} a_i + \frac{x - x_i}{x_{i+1} - x_i} a_{i+1}$$
$$= N_i(x) a_i + N_{i+1}(x) a_{i+1}. \tag{6.20}$$

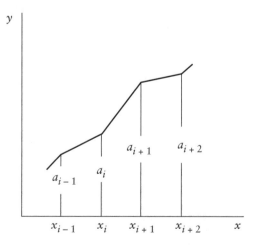

Fig. 6.3 A many-straight-line variational function.

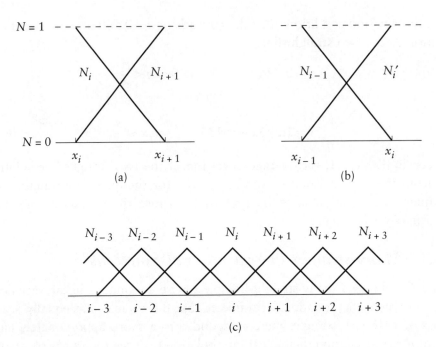

Fig. 6.4 (a) $N_i(x)$ and $N_{i+1}(x)$ in the range x_i to x_{i+1}. (b) $N_{i-1}(x)$ and $N'(x)$ in the range x_{i-1} to x_i. (c) The tent-shaped functions $N(x)$.

N_i is known as the *shape function*. It gives the contribution of the value a_i at node i to the value, y, at point x. The form of N_i and N_{i+1} in the range x_i to x_{i+1} is shown in Fig. 6.4a, and the form of N_{i-1} and N_i in the range x_{i-1} to x_i in Fig. 6.4b. Taking all the ranges together, N_i is a tent-shaped function which is non-zero over the pair of elements covering x_{i-1} to x_{i+1} and is zero elsewhere. This is shown in Fig. 6.4c, where the N is at the apex of each corresponding tent, and it will be seen that there is only one-half of a 'tent' for the two end-points. With such a definition of the Ns the value of y at any point in the total range x_0 to x_n can be written as

$$y = \sum_{i=0}^{n} N_i(x) a_i. \tag{6.21}$$

From (6.21) we can also write

$$y' = \sum_{i=0}^{n} N_i'(x) a_i$$

$$y^2 = \sum_{i=0}^{n} \sum_{j=0}^{n} N_i(x) N_j(x) a_i a_j \tag{6.22a}$$

and

$$(y')^2 = \sum_{i=0}^{n} \sum_{j=0}^{n} N_i'(x) N_j'(x) a_i a_j. \tag{6.22b}$$

Within the double summation (6.22a) some of the terms will disappear since

$$N_i(x) N_j(x) = 0, \qquad \text{for } |i-j| > 1. \tag{6.23}$$

In addition, if the spacing of the x values is h then the slopes of the tent sides are $1/h$ and $-1/h$ on the left- and right-hand sides respectively, from which

$$N_i'(x) N_j'(x) = 0, \qquad |i-j| > 1, \tag{6.24a}$$

$$N_i'(x) N_{i+1}'(x) = -\frac{1}{h^2} \tag{6.24b}$$

and

$$\{N_i'(x)\}^2 = \frac{1}{h^2}. \tag{6.24c}$$

We now use these results to find a four-element solution to the differential equation (6.11), where the functional to be minimized is

$$I(a_1, a_2, a_3) = T_1(a_1, a_2, a_3) - T_2(a_1, a_2, a_3) + T_3(a_1, a_2, a_3),$$

with

$$T_1(a_1, a_2, a_3) = \frac{1}{2} \int_0^{\pi/2} (y')^2 \, dx = \frac{1}{2} \int_0^{\pi/2} \left\{ \sum_{i=1}^{4} N_i'(x) a_i \right\}^2 dx, \tag{6.25a}$$

$$T_2(a_1, a_2, a_3) = \frac{1}{2} \int_0^{\pi/2} y^2 \, dx = \frac{1}{2} \int_0^{\pi/2} \left\{ \sum_{i=1}^{4} N_i(x) a_i \right\}^2 dx \tag{6.25b}$$

and

$$T_3(a_1, a_2, a_3) = 2 \int_0^{\pi/2} y \cos x \, dx = 2 \int_0^{\pi/2} \cos x \left\{ \sum_{i=1}^{4} N_i(x) a_i \right\} dx. \tag{6.25c}$$

The variational parameters (ordinates) a_1, a_2 and a_3 correspond to $x = \pi/8$, $\pi/4$ and $3\pi/8$, so that $h = \pi/8$ and $1/h^2 = 64/\pi^2$. Since $a_0 = 0$ it is not included in the summations, but the other boundary value $a_4(=\pi/2)$ is included. The method of approach is to make $\partial I(a_1, a_2, a_3)/\partial a_i = 0$ for $i = 1, 2$ and 3 and then to solve the resulting equations for a_1, a_2 and a_3. This gives the approximate solution of the differential equation at the nodal values. Using relationships

Table 6.2 Nodal values with the four-element variational method compared to the analytical solution.

x	a_{var}	a_{anal}
$\pi/8$	0.1540	0.1503
$\pi/4$	0.5592	0.5554
$3\pi/8$	1.0901	1.0884

(6.24) the integrals are straightforward to evaluate and the full calculation is given in Appendix 7. From $\partial I/\partial a_1 = 0$ we find

$$4.831\,16a_1 - 2.611\,93a_2 = -0.716\,34. \tag{6.26a}$$

The other two equations, from $\partial I/\partial a_2 = 0$ and $\partial I/\partial a_3 = 0$, are found to be

$$-2.611\,93a_1 + 4.831\,16a_2 - 2.611\,93a_3 = -0.548\,26 \tag{6.26b}$$

and

$$-2.611\,93a_2 + 4.831\,16a_3 = 3.806\,09. \tag{6.26c}$$

The solution of the set of equations is given in Table 6.2, together with the corresponding analytical values. The agreement is quite good at the nodal points but would be less good if interpolated values were taken along the straight lines defining the approximate solution. However, if function values were required between nodal points then finding a polynomial fit to the nodal points would give better estimates. Again, if more elements were taken then obviously the approximation can be made as close as required to the analytical solution.

Although equal intervals of x were used to define the elements there is no reason why unequal intervals should not be used. Elements could be longer where the function changed slowly and shorter where the function changed more rapidly. However, the use of such a strategy implies pre-knowledge of the form of the solution which is not always available.

The system of equations (6.26) can be expressed in matrix form as

$$\begin{pmatrix} 4.831\,16 & -2.611\,93 & 0 \\ -2.611\,93 & 4.831\,16 & -2.611\,93 \\ 0 & -2.611\,93 & 4.831\,16 \end{pmatrix} \begin{pmatrix} a_1 \\ a_2 \\ a_3 \end{pmatrix} = \begin{pmatrix} -0.716\,34 \\ -0.548\,26 \\ 3.806\,09 \end{pmatrix}, \tag{6.27}$$

and it will be noticed that the tridiagonal matrix on the left-hand side has the same coefficients in each row. This comes about because G in (6.9) is not a function of x; we shall now represent it by g. With T_1, T_2 and T_3 as given previously and with n elements, we find

$$\frac{\partial T_1}{\partial a_i} = c \int_0^{x_{max}} N_i'(N_{i-1}'a_{i-1} + N_i'a_i + N_{i+1}'a_{i+1}) dx$$

$$= c \left[-a_{i-1} \int_{x_{i-1}}^{x_i} \frac{1}{h^2} dx + a_i \int_{x_{i-1}}^{x_{i+1}} \frac{1}{h^2} dx - a_{i+1} \int_{x_i}^{x_{i+1}} \frac{1}{h^2} dx \right]$$

$$= \frac{c}{h}(-a_{i-1} + 2a_i - a_{i+1}). \tag{6.28}$$

Similarly,

$$\frac{\partial T_2}{\partial a_i} = g \int_0^{x_{max}} N_i(N_{i-1}a_{i-1} + N_i a_i + N_{i+1}a_{i+1}) dx$$

$$= g \left[a_{i-1} \int_{x_{i-1}}^{x_i} N_i N_{i-1} dx + a_i \int_{x_{i-1}}^{x_{i+1}} N_i^2 dx + a_{i+1} \int_{x_i}^{x_{i+1}} N_i N_{i+1} dx \right]. \tag{6.29}$$

For the first term, from (6.20), in the range x_{i-1} to x_i, $N_i = (x - x_{i-1})/h$ and $N_{i-1} = (x_i - x)/h$. Hence for the first term, the coefficient of a_{i-1} is

$$\int_{x_{i-1}}^{x_i} N_i N_{i-1} dx = \frac{1}{h^2} \int_{x_i}^{x_{i+1}} (x - x_{i-1})(x_i - x) dx = \frac{h}{6}. \tag{6.30}$$

This is also the coefficient of a_{i+1}. The coefficient of a_i is

$$\int_{x_{i-1}}^{x_{i+1}} N_i^2 dx = \frac{1}{h^2} \int_{x_i}^{x_{i+1}} (x_{i+1} - x)^2 dx + \frac{1}{h^2} \int_{x_{i-1}}^{x_i} (x - x_{i-1})^2 dx = \frac{2h}{3}. \tag{6.31}$$

This gives

$$\frac{\partial T_2}{\partial a_i} = \frac{gh}{6}(a_{i+1} + 4a_i + a_{i-1}). \tag{6.32}$$

It will be seen from (6.31) that $\partial T_3/\partial a_i$ does not add anything to the elements of the matrix in (6.27) so in the equation produced by partial differentiation with respect to a_i the terms are

$$-\left(\frac{c}{h} + \frac{gh}{6}\right)a_{i-1} + \left(\frac{2c}{h} - \frac{2gh}{3}\right)a_i - \left(\frac{c}{h} + \frac{gh}{6}\right)a_{i+1}. \tag{6.33}$$

For the differential equation (6.11) $c=1$ and $g=1$ and for the four-straight-line variational function $h=\pi/8$. Substituting these values in (6.39) gives

$$-2.611\,93a_{i-1}+4.831\,16a_i-2.611\,93a_{i+1},$$

which confirms the matrix elements in (6.27).

The right-hand-side vector in (6.27) depends on the functional form of F in (6.9) and also on the contributions from the boundary conditions. The application of the variational method with discrete elements spanning the domain is the basis of the finite-element method. The matrix which appears in (6.27) is referred to as the *stiffness matrix* and the right-hand-side vector is called the *load vector*, these terms arising because the finite-element method was first applied to engineering mechanical-structure problems.

6.4 Applications of the finite-element method in one dimension

6.4.1 *Time-dependent heat flow*

The time-dependent diffusion equation applied to heat flow in one dimension – as, for example, in heat flow along a bar with insulated walls – is given by (2.21) as

$$\frac{\partial\theta}{\partial t}=\frac{\kappa}{c\rho}\frac{\partial^2\theta}{\partial x^2}. \tag{6.34}$$

This problem is one which is better solved by the finite-difference method and is used here simply to provide an example for illustrating principles. The problem can be transformed into a form suitable for solution by the finite-element method if the left-hand side is expressed in a forward-difference form as

$$\frac{\partial\theta}{\partial t}=\frac{\theta-\theta_{\text{prev}}}{\Delta t}, \tag{6.35}$$

where the temperature θ is that to be determined at points in the bar and θ_{prev} is the known temperature at the previous time step. Inserting (6.35) in (6.34) and rearranging,

$$\frac{\kappa}{c\rho}\frac{\partial^2\theta}{\partial x^2}-\frac{1}{\Delta t}\theta+\frac{1}{\Delta t}\theta_{\text{prev}}=0. \tag{6.36}$$

Equation (6.36) has the same form as (6.9) with $c=\kappa/c\rho$, $G=-1/\Delta t$ and $F=-(1/\Delta t)\theta_{\text{prev}}$. Given that the boundary conditions are fixed, or are known as a function of time, then the method described in Section 6.2 may be used for each time step in calculating the evolving temperature profile. The nodes can be chosen in the same way as for the finite-difference method, although unequal elements are usually chosen for the finite-element method if it is suspected that the temperature profile justifies this. If unequal elements are used then, although the stiffness matrix stays symmetric, it does not have the uniformity shown in (6.27).

6.4.2 *Heat flow with differential boundary conditions*

The problem to be considered is that described in Section 2.7 where a uniform bar, insulated along its length, has one or both ends either insulated or exchanging heat with the environment either by radiation or convection. For the finite-element method the linear functions within elements which have one end at a boundary point define the rate of change of temperature at the boundary.

There are three basic types of boundary condition which naturally occur. Expressed in one-dimensional terms, these are as follows:

1. ϕ is specified on the boundary – the Dirichlet condition.
2. $\partial \phi / \partial x$ is specified on the boundary – the von Neumann condition.
3. $\partial \phi / \partial x = -M\phi + S$ on the boundary – a mixture of conditions 1 and 2.

Conditions (1) and (3) have been encountered already in a two-dimensional form as in the problem illustrated in Fig. 2.18. Condition (2) may occur in a problem dealing with potentials where the field, $E = -\partial \phi / \partial x$, is fixed at a boundary.

Returning to our one-dimensional thermal problem, if one end is insulated so that, say, $(d\theta / dx)_0 = 0$, then this implies that $\theta_0 = \theta_1$ so that θ_0 does not appear explicitly in the linear equations; the notation used here is that the variational parameters are θ_1 to θ_{n-1}.

For a boundary exchanging radiation with a constant-temperature enclosure, the gradient at the end of the bar is, from (2.39),

$$\kappa \frac{\partial \theta}{\partial x} = -\sigma(\theta_n^4 - \theta_{ext}^4), \tag{6.37}$$

where θ_n is the temperature at the end of the bar and θ_{ext} the temperature of the enclosure. Where the problem is time-dependent (implied by the use of partial differentiation in (6.37)) then the right-hand side can be estimated from the previous time step. This will give, in the finite-difference notation of Chapter 2,

$$\theta(n, j+1) = \theta(n-1, j+1) - h\frac{\sigma}{\kappa}\{\theta(n, j)^4 - \theta_{ext}^4\}, \tag{6.38}$$

where h is the length of the element. In this way the temperature at the end is given explicitly in terms of the temperature of the neighbouring node and again the equations found are linear in the internal nodal values – which are the variational parameters. Very often the heat loss from an exposed end is modelled as

$$\kappa \frac{\partial \theta}{\partial x} = -M\theta + S, \tag{6.39}$$

which is an approximate description of convective exchange with the surroundings.

For a steady-state problem where Laplace's equation is valid the solution of conducting bar problems are always obvious. If the ends are at fixed temperatures then the final state is a linear variation along the bar between the fixed temperatures. If one end is in radiation equilibrium with an enclosure then eventually that end attains a temperature such that the uniform gradient along the bar gives a heat flow equal to the net gain or loss of heat from the radiating end. If one end of the bar is insulated then eventually the whole bar has the temperature of the non-insulated end. However, if there is temperature generation along the bar, so that Poisson's equation is applied in its general form, then the solutions may not be so obvious. If an end of the bar is radiating into an enclosure then the unknown temperature at that end will appear to the fourth power so that the linearity of the equation system to be solved will be destroyed. In problems of this kind it is customary to transform to an exchange-of-heat equation based on Newton's law of cooling rather than a fourth-power radiation law. Newton's law of cooling takes the form

$$H = CA(\theta - \theta_{ext}), \tag{6.40}$$

where H is the rate of loss of heat, A the area of the surface and C a constant. This is an approximation to the radiation-law formula (2.35)

$$H = A\sigma(\theta^4 - \theta_{ext}^4). \tag{6.41a}$$

If θ and θ_{ext} are not too different, then (6.41a) can be written as

$$H = 4A\sigma\theta_{ext}^3(\theta - \theta_{ext}), \tag{6.41b}$$

which is of the same form as (6.40) with $C = 4\sigma\theta_{ext}^3$. The Newton's law approximation is very imprecise if the absolute temperatures θ and θ_{ext} differ by more than 10 per cent or so. From (6.40) the condition at the end of the bar is

$$\kappa \frac{d\theta}{dx} = -C(\theta - \theta_{ext}),$$

which gives for the nodal values

$$\theta_n = \theta_{n-1} - \frac{Ch}{\kappa} \{\theta_n - \theta_{\text{ext}}\}$$ (6.42)

or

$$\theta_n = \frac{\kappa}{\kappa + Ch} \left\{ \theta_{n-1} + \frac{Ch}{\kappa} \theta_{\text{ext}} \right\},$$ (6.43)

which maintains the linearization of the equations to be solved. Losses by both convection and radiation are usually lumped together in the form given by (6.38).

6.4.3 *Heat generation, point sources and sinks*

For a bar with heat generation the differential equation to be solved in the steady-state situation is

$$\frac{d^2\theta}{dx^2} - \frac{1}{\kappa} Q(x) = 0,$$ (6.44)

where $Q(x)$ is the rate of energy generation per unit volume at the position x in the bar. Comparing (6.44) with (6.9), $c = 1$, $G = 0$ and $F = Q(x)/\kappa$, and the solution can be found using the finite-element method in a straightforward way. The heat generation term will contribute to the ith element of the load vector of (6.27) an amount

$$\frac{\partial T_3}{\partial a_i} = \frac{1}{\kappa} \int_{x_{i-1}}^{x_{i+1}} N_i Q(x) \, dx.$$ (6.45)

In many real physical situations there occurs an input of some quantity – for example, heat energy – over such a highly localized region that it can be considered a point source. In this case, if the point source is at position x_P, the function $Q(x)$ in (6.44) may be written in the form

$$Q(x) = Q_P \, \delta(x - x_P)$$ (6.46)

where δ is the *Dirac delta function* which has the properties

$$\delta(x - x_P) = 0, \qquad x \neq x_P,$$

and

$$\int_a^b \delta(x - x_P) \, dx = 1,$$ (6.47)

where x_P is in the range a to b. A property of a delta function which follows from (6.47) is that

$$\int_a^b f(x)\,\delta(x-x_P)\,dx = f(x_P),\qquad\qquad (6.48)$$

where x_P is in the range a to b. The function $f(x)$ has the constant value $f(x_P)$ in the finite region of $\delta(x-x_P)$ and so can be taken outside the integral. Result (6.48) then follows from (6.47).

If a point source arises in a problem then it simplifies matters if the elements are so chosen as to put it at a node – say, at x_j. The contribution of the source to the element i of the load vector in (6.27) will be

$$\frac{1}{\kappa}\int_{x_{i-1}}^{x_{i+1}} N_i Q_P\,\delta(x-x_j)\,dx,\qquad\qquad (6.49)$$

which, from (6.48) equals $N_i(x_j)Q_P/\kappa$. At node j, $N_j=1$, and all the other Ns are zero – from which it follows that the source will contribute Q_P/κ to the jth element of the load vector in (6.27) and nothing elsewhere.

The discussion above has been in terms of a point source providing a positive heating effect. It is also possible to have a *sink* which would be some kind of cooling mechanism which takes heat out of the system at a particular rate. A sink, like a source, can be concentrated and effectively a point or extended. The treatment given above is also valid for sinks but the sign of the contributions to the load vector in (6.27) will be negative.

6.4.4   *A one-dimensional finite-element program*

The one-dimensional finite-element program HEATELEM (see p. xv) calculates the temperature distribution in a uniform conducting bar, insulated along its length, with boundary conditions which can be a fixed temperature, an insulated boundary or one exchanging radiation with its surroundings. It includes the linearization of the radiating condition, as in (6.41), although this may not be very precise. There is also provision for an extended heating (or cooling) function and/or point heating and cooling. We now show the results for various situations: in each case the bar was divided into ten elements.

1. Length of bar $1\,\mathrm{m}$, thermal conductivity $400\,\mathrm{W\,m^{-1}\,K^{-1}}$. Lower boundary $300\,\mathrm{K}$, upper boundary $500\,\mathrm{K}$. The result is shown in Fig. 6.5 and is the expected one where there is a uniform temperature gradient along the bar.

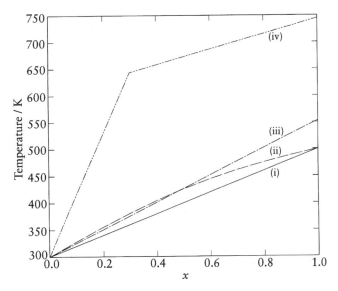

Fig. 6.5 Results from HEATELEM for a bar of length 1 m and thermal conductivity $400\,\mathrm{W\,m^{-1}K^{-1}}$. (i) Lower boundary 300 K, upper boundary 500 K. (ii) As (i) but with an extended source $Q(x) = 2 \times 10^5 x(1-x)\,\mathrm{W\,m^{-3}}$. (iii) As (i) but radiating into an enclosure at 1000 K at upper boundary. (iv) As (iii) but with point source $4 \times 10^5\,\mathrm{W}$, 0.3 m from 300 K end.

2. This is as situation 1, but with the addition of an extended source of heating of the form

$$Q(x) = 2 \times 10^5 x(1-x)\,\mathrm{W\,m^{-3}}.$$

The function $Q(x)$ gives the greatest heating effect at the centre of the bar, and this is evident from the form of the temperature profile.

3. This is as situation 1, except that the end originally at 500 K is now in an enclosure with a constant temperature 1000 K. Figure 6.5 shows that the temperature gradient is uniform along the bar and has adjusted itself so that the rate of heat flow along the bar equals the net rate of gain of heat from the enclosure.

4. This is as situation 3 but with a point source of strength $4 \times 10^5\,\mathrm{W\,m^{-3}}$ situated at a distance of 0.3 m from the 300 K end. It is seen to give a discontinuity of slope at the position of the heat input.

The reader is advised to study the listing of HEATELEM to see how boundary conditions and the heating terms influence the stiffness matrix and the load vector in the linear equations which give the variational parameters.

6.5 The general finite-element approach

The preceeding simple one-dimensional example illustrates the general principles underlying the finite-element approach. Here we describe how this is
accomplished by a series of steps, which are conveniently expressed within the
program structure.

1. Discretization of the domain: the physical space is broken down into a
   series of finite elements filling the 'volume' whose size and shape vary
   to reflect the boundaries and the expected form of the solution. The geometrical form of the elements will vary but typically will be the simplest
   consistent with the dimension of the space – line segment in one dimension,
   triangle in two and tetrahedron in three.
2. Choice of nodes: the form of the interpolation is chosen, and determines
   the number of nodes, in each element – for example, linear interpolation
   requires 2, 3 or 4 nodes in 1, 2 or 3 dimensions, respectively. The nodes
   are positioned conveniently within the element – for example, at vertices.
3. Evaluation of the functional in each element: using the interpolation form,
   the functional is evaluated in each element in terms of bilinear forms
   involving the nodal values. Differentiating yields the stiffness matrix and
   load vector for each element.
4. Summation of the stiffness matrix and load vectors: summing the contribution to the total stiffness matrix and load vector from each element enables
   the full set of simultaneous equations for the nodal values to be developed.
5. Inclusion of the boundary conditions: at present all the nodal values are free
   and the set of simultaneous equations is incomplete (singular). In fact some
   nodes have values fixed by boundary conditions. These must now be
   included and the set of equations modified where appropriate by adjusting
   elements of the stiffness matrix and load vector.
6. The stiffness matrix is usually a band symmetric matrix, which may be
   solved by a standard method – for example, the Cholesky method.

Within this general arrangement some additional steps can be taken further
to reduce the computational load. In particular the stiffness matrix will, in
general, be quite sparse as each element contains only a limited number of
nodes and matrix elements only exist between nodes in the same element. By
judicious selection of the node numbers the stiffness matrix can be arranged
into a symmetric band of finite width about the diagonal with zeros elsewhere.
This can be used to reduce both the required memory and the computational
load of solving the simultaneous equations.

6.6 Laplace's equation in a two-dimensional space

We set up a linear interpolation scheme based on a set of triangular elements spanning the entire domain as in Fig. 6.6. Each element has three nodes i, j, k at its corners (Fig. 6.7). The linear interpolation shape function for element i is then

$$N_i^{(e)} = \frac{1}{2A}(a_i + b_i x + c_i y), \tag{6.50a}$$

where

$$a_i = x_j y_k - x_k y_j, \quad b_i = y_j - y_k \quad \text{and} \quad c_i = x_k - x_j, \tag{6.50b}$$

and A is the area of the triangle given by

$$2A = \begin{vmatrix} 1 & x_i & y_i \\ 1 & x_j & y_j \\ 1 & x_k & y_k \end{vmatrix} = (x_j y_k - x_k y_j) + (x_k y_i - x_i y_k) + (x_i y_j - x_j y_i). \tag{6.50c}$$

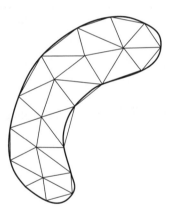

Fig. 6.6 A boomerang-shaped figure modelled with triangular elements.

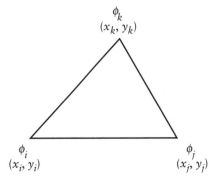

Fig. 6.7 A triangular element.

The shape functions $N_j^{(e)}$ and $N_k^{(e)}$ are obtained by circular permutation of the symbols (i, j, k). Within the element $\nabla N_i^{(e)}$ is a constant given by

$$\nabla N_i^{(e)} = \frac{1}{2A}(b_i\hat{\mathbf{i}} + c_i\hat{\mathbf{j}}), \qquad (6.50d)$$

where $\hat{\mathbf{i}}$ and $\hat{\mathbf{j}}$ are unit vectors in the x and y directions, respectively. For any point within the element a linearly interpolated value of the dependent variable is

$$\phi^{(e)}(x, y) = N_i^{(e)}(x, y)\phi_i + N_j^{(e)}(x, y)\phi_j + N_k^{(e)}(x, y)\phi_k = \sum \phi_l N_l^{(e)}(x, y). \qquad (6.51)$$

It is easily confirmed that, for $x = x_i$ and $y = y_i$, $N_i^{(e)} = 1$ and $N_j^{(e)} = N_k^{(e)} = 0$, from which (6.51) gives $\phi = \phi_i$ as it should. In a single triangular element, contours of constant $N_i^{(e)}$ are straight lines parallel to the side jk as shown in Fig. 6.8a; the lines corresponding to $N_i^{(e)} = 0.0, 0.2, 0.4, 0.6, 0.8$ and a parallel line through the apex $i(N_i^{(e)} = 1.0)$ are equispaced. Another useful geometrical interpretation of the Ns is shown in Fig. 6.8b, where it is seen that they are proportional to the areas of triangles formed by the point in question and the apexes of the triangular element. This result is easily derived. Within the triangle the shape function $N_i^{(e)}$ varies linearly from 1 at i to zero on jk and is proportional to the distance from jk to the point P and therefore to the area A_i. Since $N_i + N_j + N_k = 1$ and $A_i + A_j + A_k = A$, then $N_i = A_i/A$.

The functional corresponding to Laplace's equation is complicated to derive but is

$$I = \frac{1}{2}\int|\nabla\phi|^2\,d\tau + \int_s\left(\frac{1}{2}M\phi^2 - S\phi\right)ds, \qquad (6.52)$$

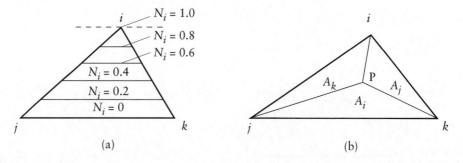

Fig. 6.8   (a) Lines of constant N_i. (b) For the point P, $N_i : N_j : N_k = A_i : A_j : A_k$, where the As are the areas shown.

where s is that part of the boundary of the domain on which the normal gradient of ϕ is specified in the form $\partial\phi/\partial n = -M\phi + S$, that is, the free or natural boundary conditions.

We now find the contribution of the element (e) to the functional. Given (6.51),

$$\nabla\phi^{(e)} = \phi_i\nabla N_i^{(e)} + \phi_j\nabla N_j^{(e)} + \phi_k\nabla N_k^{(e)}, \tag{6.53}$$

from which the contribution to the functional from the first integral in (6.53) is, from (6.50d),

$$\frac{1}{2}\int|\nabla\phi^{(e)}|^2\,d\tau = \sum_l\sum_m\phi_l\phi_m\int\nabla N_l^{(e)}\cdot\nabla N_m^{(e)}\,d\tau$$

$$= \frac{1}{4A^{(e)}}\sum_l\sum_m\phi_l\phi_m(b_lb_m + c_lc_m), \tag{6.54}$$

where each of l and m range over the points i, j and k.

If one or more sides of the triangular element forms part of the boundary, then there is a contribution to the functional from the second integral in (6.52). Any value of ϕ or $\partial\phi/\partial n$ involved in the integral will involve only two of the components in (6.51) – say, corresponding to the line joining point l to point m. A common situation – where, for example, there is thermal equilibrium in a plate with isotropic thermal conductivity – is where $\nabla\phi$ is perpendicular to the boundary, and we shall restrict our discussion to that simple case. For

$$\frac{\partial\phi}{\partial n} = -M\phi + S, \tag{6.55}$$

the second integral in (6.52) is

$$\int_{lm}\left(\frac{1}{2}M\phi^2 - S\phi\right)ds, \tag{6.56}$$

where the integral is along the element edge lm, of length L. Along that edge

$$\phi = N_l^{(e)}\phi_l + N_m^{(e)}\phi_m, \tag{6.57}$$

and, with origin at the point l, $N_l^{(e)}$ goes from 1 to 0, and $N_m^{(e)}$ goes from 0 to 1, as s goes from 0 to L or

$$N_l^{(e)} = 1 - \frac{s}{L} \quad \text{and} \quad N_m^{(e)} = \frac{s}{L};$$

from which the contribution of the edge *lm* to the functional is

$$\frac{1}{2}M\int_0^L\left\{\left(1-\frac{s}{L}\right)\phi_l+\frac{s}{L}\phi_m\right\}^2 ds - S\int_0^L\left\{\left(1-\frac{s}{L}\right)\phi_l+\frac{s}{L}\phi_m\right\}ds$$

$$=\left(\frac{1}{6}\phi_l^2+\frac{1}{12}\phi_l\phi_m+\frac{1}{6}\phi_m^2\right)ML-\frac{1}{2}(\phi_l+\phi_m)SL. \tag{6.58}$$

It is clear from (6.54) and (6.58) that when all the contributions from all elements and all edges of elements forming boundaries are added together the functional is of the form

$$I=\sum_{ij}K_{ij}\phi_i\phi_j-\sum_i P_i\phi_i. \tag{6.59}$$

The condition for minimizing the functional is that

$$\frac{\partial I}{\partial\phi_i}=\sum_j K_{ij}\phi_j-P_i=0, \tag{6.60}$$

for all *i*, and this yields a set of simultaneous linear equations, the solution of which gives the required values of ϕ at the nodes. It is evident that the quantities K_{ij} form the elements of the stiffness matrix, **K**, while the quantities P_i define the load vector, **P**.

   If all the values of ϕ have to be determined then the matrix **K** is symmetrical and *positive definite*, meaning that all its eigenvalues are positive. Such matrices give well-conditioned sets of linear equations for the various solution techniques we have previously mentioned. However, some of the nodal values, say the set Φ_I, have prescribed values and cannot be varied in the minimization procedure. These are called *forced*, *essential* or *geometric* boundary conditions. Thus the corresponding equations in the set (6.60) do not exist. It is very convenient to maintain the overall symmetry of the matrix and this is done by changing **K** and **P** thus:

$$K'_{II}=1:K'_{Ij}=0:P'_I=\phi_I;$$

and to maintain the symmetry of **K**,

$$K'_{jI}=0:P'_j=P_j-K_{jI}\phi_I.$$

6.6.1 *The time-independent heated-plate problem*

We now consider a time-independent heated two-dimensional plate problem, insulated on its top and bottom surfaces, with edges exchanging heat with the surroundings or insulated and with either point or extended sources of heating within it. The differential equation describing the equilibrium of the plate is of the form

$$\nabla^2\theta(x,y) - \frac{1}{\kappa}Q(x,y) - \frac{1}{\kappa}Q_i\delta(\mathbf{r}-\mathbf{r}_i) = 0, \tag{6.61}$$

and the boundary temperatures are of the form (6.55). If in (6.55) M and S are non-zero then we have a boundary exchanging heat with its surroundings. If M and S are both zero then this corresponds to an insulated boundary, but it is clear that this will make no contribution to either the stiffness matrix or the load vector. In (6.61) there is provision for an extended heating source and/or a point source located at vector position $\mathbf{r}_i$ which is assumed to be at a node. Excluding the point-source term, which is straightforward and can be treated separately, the functional to be minimized is

$$I = \int_A \int \frac{1}{2}\left[\left(\frac{\partial\theta}{\partial x}\right)^2 + \left(\frac{\partial\theta}{\partial y}\right)^2\right]dx\,dy$$
$$+ \int_A \int \frac{1}{\kappa}Q\theta\,dx\,dy + \int_s \left(\frac{1}{2}M\theta^2 - S\theta\right)ds, \tag{6.62}$$

where A indicates integration over the whole domain. We have previously dealt with all terms in the functional except for the second integral which, for an individual triangular element, gives, with (6.51),

$$V_{(e)} = \int_{(e)} \int \frac{1}{\kappa}Q(N_i^{(e)}\theta_i + N_j^{(e)}\theta_j + N_k^{(e)}\theta_k)\,dx\,dy. \tag{6.63}$$

If Q is a constant then the integral (6.63) is readily evaluated since, from the form of the function N_i within the triangle (Fig. 6.8a) it can be shown that

$$\int_{(e)} \int N_i^{(e)}\,dx\,dy = \frac{1}{3}A. \tag{6.64}$$

For simplicity it is usually assumed that Q is constant within an element with mean value

$$Q_{(e)} = \frac{1}{3}(Q_i + Q_j + Q_k),$$

which gives

$$V_{(e)} = \frac{Q_{(e)}A}{3\kappa}(\theta_i + \theta_j + \theta_k), \tag{6.65}$$

which provides contributions to components i, j and k of the load vector.

Finally, we come to the contribution of a point source, say Q_p acting at node p. By reasoning similar to that given in the one-dimensional case this gives a contribution $Q_p\theta_p/\kappa$ to the load vector.

The steps outlined above will give the complete stiffness matrix and load vector defining the equations which give estimates of temperature at the nodes. Here we have taken a rather special case of temperature variation in a two-dimensional plate; other problems involving, say, the flow of fluids, the bending of elastic structures or finding distributions of electrical potential will have features not considered here. There are various complex packages capable of dealing with generalized finite-element problems but the temperature-distribution example illustrates the general principles quite well. A program specifically designed to deal with the two-dimensional temperature-distribution problem is now described.

6.7 A two-dimensional finite-element program

The two-dimensional finite-element program FINELEM2 (see p. xv) will deal with the kinds of heated-plate problem solved by HOTPLATE, described in Section 2.14. FINELEM2 has provision for point sources, which must be located at nodes, and triangular elements are used which can be arranged to simulate irregular shapes far better than does fitting a square grid which is all that HOTPLATE offers. An example of a problem solved by FINELEM2 is shown in Fig. 6.9. The plate is square, of side 0.375 m, and is divided into 18 similar triangular elements defined by 16 nodes. Figure 6.10 shows the FINELEM2 output. The first section is an echo-print of the input data giving the elements defined by the corner nodes. The second section gives the coordinates of the nodes and the third section the nodes with fixed temperatures. The fourth section shows that there are two point sources situated at nodes 6 and 11 with strengths 2×10^5 and $3 \times 10^5 \, \mathrm{W\,m^{-3}}$, respectively. Not included in the output is information on distributed heating, defined by a FUNCTION statement which has to be inserted in the source program before it is compiled and run. In this application the form of heating is represented by

$$Q(x,y) = 10^6 xy(0.375-x)(0.375-y)\,\mathrm{W\,m^{-3}}, \qquad (6.66)$$

which is zero at the plate edges and a maximum at the centre of the plate.

Edges with differential boundary conditions which are exchanging energy with their surroundings are described by the nodes at the two ends, and the values of M and S as defined in (6.55). The stiffness matrix is quite heavily populated with non-zero elements and has not been modified as described

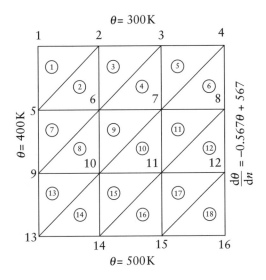

Fig. 6.9 The 18 elements and 16 nodes of the heated plate problem. There is a distributed source of heating $Q(x) = 10^6 xy \times (0.375 - x)(0.375 - y)\,\mathrm{W\,m^{-3}}$ and point sources at nodes $6(2 \times 10^5\,\mathrm{W\,m^{-3}})$ and $11(3 \times 10^5\,\mathrm{W\,m^{-3}})$.

```
CONDUCTIVITY IS   400.0 W m**[-1] K**[-1]

NODE NUMBERS ASSOCIATED WITH EACH ELEMENT
        1    5    2      1    2    6      2    5      3    2    6    3
        4    7    3      6    5    3      7    4      6    4    7    8
        7    5    9      6    8    6      9   10      9    6   10    7
       10    7   10     11   11    7     11    8     12    8   11   12
       13    9   13     10   14   10     13   14     15   10   14   15
       16   14   15     11   17   11     15   12     18   12   15   16

COORDINATES OF NODES
        1 0.0000 0.3750      2 0.1250 0.3750      3 0.2500 0.3750
        4 0.3750 0.3750      5 0.0000 0.2500      6 0.1250 0.2500
        7 0.2500 0.2500      8 0.3750 0.2500      9 0.0000 0.1250
       10 0.1250 0.1250     11 0.2500 0.1250     12 0.3750 0.1250
       13 0.0000 0.0000     14 0.1250 0.0000     15 0.2500 0.0000
       16 0.3750 0.0000

NODES WITH FIXED TEMPERATURES
        1   350.0      2   300.0      3   300.0      4   300.0
        5   400.0      9   400.0     13   450.0     14   500.0
       15   500.0     16   500.0

POSITIONS AND STRENGTHS OF POINT SOURCES
        6      0.2000E+06
       11      0.3000E+06

DIFFERENTIAL BOUNDARY EDGES AND PARAMETERS
  NODE1 NODE2      M          S
        4     8   0.567    567.000
        8    12   0.567    567.000
       12    16   0.567    567.000

  NODE   TEMP
        1   350.      2   300.      3   300.      4   300.
        5   400.      6   565.      7   533.      8   500.
        9   400.     10   528.     11   766.     12   633.
       13   450.     14   500.     15   500.     16   500.
```

Fig. 6.10 Output from FINELEM2.

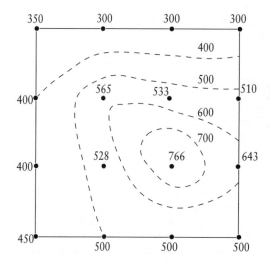

Fig. 6.11 A contoured plot of the output from Fig. 6.9 given in Fig. 6.10.

previously to a symmetric positive-definite form. For small-scale problems amenable to FINELEM2 a general linear-equation solver to determine the variational parameters is adequate and a subroutine employing the Gauss–Jordan elimination method, GAUSSJ, which comes from Press *et al.* (1986), is provided. Finally, in the output from FINELEM2, the solution is given as a list of the nodes with the temperature at each of them. Figure 6.11 shows this result plotted on a grid and contoured; the influence of the point sources gives a local maximum at node 11 and a tongue of higher temperature extending towards node 6. The effect of the distributed heating is masked by the contributions of the point sources.

The data for a large finite-element application can be rather extensive, and it is usually better to enter it through a data file so that if there are errors the file can simply be amended and then tried again. A program FINDATA is available (see p. xv) for preparing such a data file. As a back-up FINELEM2 includes provision for data correction after the data have all been entered but before the main calculation commences.

6.8 Applications of the finite-element method

We have chosen here to restrict our description of the finite-element method to two dimensions and to steady-state heat transfer problems, except for a brief reference to time-dependent problems in Section 6.4.1. There we saw that the time dependence is treated as a finite difference while retaining the finite-element form for the spatial part. If this is done the normal stability

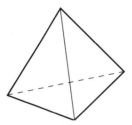

Fig. 6.12 A tetrahedral element.

constraints associated with temporal differencing (Section 2.9) will still apply. If the spacial terms are explicitly treated then a time-step limit must be imposed. However, since this is determined by the eigenvalues of the stiffness matrix, which are not known in advance, it is not very convenient to treat time dependence in this way. It is therefore usual to difference the problem implicitly; the resultant extra matrix terms are already included in the stiffness matrix, so that no extra computational burden is introduced.

Finite-element methods have been applied to a wide range of problems other than those of heat transfer. Some examples are: the twisting of bars of non-circular cross-section; the irrotational flow of fluids around obstacles; finding patterns of acoustic vibrations within finite volumes; mechanical structure analysis; and finding energy levels from the Schrödinger equation. Some of these applications require three-dimensional treatment and, just as triangles can be used for elements in two dimensions, so tetrahedra (Fig. 6.12) can be used in three dimensions. The development of the theory for three dimensions very closely parallels that for two dimensions. In (6.52) the first integral is over the volume contained by the surface and the second integral is over that surface. With tetrahedral elements the surface is simulated by a series of planes from contiguous triangular faces. The constants M and S then describe the derivatives of ϕ along the normals to the triangular faces.

There are formulations of the finite-element method other than the variational approach which has been described here. The variational approach is fairly straightforward and illustrates the general principles of the finite-element method quite well, although it does have the disadvantage that it cannot handle differential equations with a first-derivative term. We now describe other finite-element approaches which can be applied to more general problems.

6.9 The residual formulation of finite-element methods

As we have already pointed out, only a limited class of problems can be expressed in a variational form. Although a large number of the characteristic equations in physics, such as Laplace's equation and Schrödinger's equation, can always be handled in this way, it is restricted to second-order differential equations. In addition, it may not be possible to identify the functional for particular cases. It is therefore important to have an alternative finite-element formulation which can be applied directly to the original partial differential equation and the more familiar and available differential operator which it contains.

The philosophy which is adopted for these calculations is similar to that described previously in that we set up an approximate solution to the problem based on a set of arbitrary values (the nodal values or *displacements*).[1] Using this approximation, we evaluate an error in some appropriate function and minimize its value by varying the values of the displacements. These methods are known as *weighted residual methods*. The residual that gives the error is defined as a weighted integral of the differential operator with respect to the approximation. Thus, suppose our differential equation can be written

$$\mathscr{A}\,\Phi = 0, \tag{6.67}$$

where $\mathscr{A}$ is the differential operator and Φ the field variable. Then we set up the approximation for Φ in terms of the set of displacements ϕ_i. The value of the residual $\mathscr{A}\phi \neq 0$ gives a measure of how well the approximation ϕ fits the required equation (6.67). By introducing a series of weight functions w_j and integrating over the domain we can define a set of errors

$$E_j = \int w_j\, \mathscr{A}\phi\, d\tau, \tag{6.68}$$

which we minimize by finding the set of ϕ_i which either (and usually) zeroes the set E_j or minimize a single residual.

The various methods are characterized by the choice of w_j.

1. Least squares: by taking $w = \mathscr{A}\phi$ the overall error is the least-square value of the residual over the entire domain. Only a single error is obtained, in a bilinear form, and its value is minimized by differentiating. The method is little used.
2. Point collocation: this takes $w_j = \delta(\mathbf{r} - \mathbf{r}_j)$ where $\mathbf{r}_j$ is the position of the node j. This form zeroes the residual at each node, and is simple to apply, although it is little used.
3. Volume collocation: here $w_j = W(\mathbf{r} - \mathbf{r}_j)$, which spreads the residual over a zone around the node j. It is widely used in the form of the Galerkin method (see 4).

---

[1] The nomenclature of finite-element methods – *nodes, displacements, stiffness matrix* and *load vector* – stems from their origins in numerical stress analysis.

4. The Galerkin method: this uses $w_j = N(\mathbf{r} - \mathbf{r}_j)$, where N is the shape function used in the interpolation giving ϕ. The weight used in the residual is therefore complementary to that used in the interpolation. The residual associated with each node is zeroed. This method is very widely used. For self-adjoint equations[2] it is exactly equivalent to the variational method, provided analytic integration by parts is used to reduce the second derivatives to a first-order form. The reader may well find this the most convenient approach.

6.9.1 *Laplace's equations with the Galerkin method*

We now consider the problem we examined in Section 6.6, solving Laplace's equation

$$\mathscr{A}\,\Phi = \nabla^2\Phi = \frac{\partial^2\Phi}{\partial x^2} + \frac{\partial^2\Phi}{\partial y^2} = 0. \tag{6.69}$$

We set up a series of triangular elements (e) with three nodes i, j and k and linear interpolation as before. The shape functions in the element (e) are those described in Section 6.6 and within the element (e) the interpolating function is that given by (6.51).

Since $\phi^{(e)}$ is linear in the coordinates then $\nabla^2\phi = 0$ within the element, which automatically satisfies Laplace's equation no matter what are the values ϕ_i, ϕ_j and ϕ_k. However, we can circumvent this problem by calculating the residue associated with node j within element (e):

$$R_j^{(e)} = \int_{(e)} N_j \nabla^2\phi \, d\tau. \tag{6.70}$$

By using the idendity

$$\nabla \cdot (N\nabla\phi) = N\nabla^2\phi + \nabla N \cdot \nabla\phi,$$

we find

$$R_j^{(e)} = -\int_{(e)} \nabla N_j \cdot \nabla\phi \, d\tau + \int_{(e)} \nabla \cdot (N_j \nabla\phi) d\tau. \tag{6.71}$$

---

[2]This implies equations for which the coefficient matrix is *self-adjoint* (typically *Hermitian* so that matrix element $a_{ij} = a_{ji}^*$; this includes a symmetric matrix with real coefficients). The eigenvalues of such a matrix are real; if, in addition, the eigenvalues are all positive then the matrix is *positive-definite*. Solutions of many physical problems involve such matrices.

Here we apply Gauss's theorem, which states that the surface integral of the divergence of a vector field equals the line integral of the normal component of the field around the boundary, so that

$$\int_{(e)} \nabla \cdot (N_j \nabla \phi) \, d\tau = \int_{(e)} (N_j \nabla \phi) \cdot ds,$$

giving

$$R_j^{(e)} = -\int_{(e)} \nabla N_j \cdot \nabla \phi \, d\tau + \int_{(e)} N_j \nabla \phi \cdot ds, \tag{6.72}$$

where the surface integral is taken over the surface of the element (e). For internal elements the boundary terms cancel in the sums over the elements and so can be omitted, but must be retained at the domain boundaries if the gradient normal $\partial \Phi / \partial n$ is defined and is non-zero. Performing the integrations, the residual for the element (e) for the node j is of the form

$$R_j^{(e)} = -\frac{\phi_j}{4A^{(e)}} \sum_l^{(e)} (b_l b_j + c_l c_j) + \frac{1}{2} \sum_{l \neq j}^{(e)} \left(\frac{\partial \phi}{\partial n}\right)_{jl} l_{jl}$$

$$= -\sum_l K_{lj}^{(e)} \phi_l + P_j^{(e)} = 0, \tag{6.73}$$

where the constants b_i, c_i are given in (6.50b) and l_{lj} is the length of the boundary edge between nodes j and l. The load vector is thus seen to be associated with one kind of boundary condition, that when the gradient is specified (natural or free boundary conditions). The final result is identical to that which has already been obtained using the variational method.

Problems

6.1   Use the variational method with variational function $y = ax + bx^2$ to solve numerically the differential equation

$$\frac{d^2 y}{dx^2} - y - 2e^x = 0,$$

with boundary conditions $x = 0$, $y = 0$ and $x = 1$, $y = e$. From the variational function find the estimated values of $y(x)$ for x from 0 to 1 by steps of $\frac{1}{6}$.

6.2   Use the variational method to find a three-straight-line solution to the differential equation in Problem 6.1 with the variation parameters taken at $x = \frac{1}{3}$ and $x = \frac{2}{3}$. By fitting a parabola to the (x, y) values you find at

$x = 0, \frac{1}{3}$ and $\frac{2}{3}$ (see equation (A6.5) in Appendix 6), estimate the value of y at $x = \frac{1}{2}$.

6.3   A bar 2 m long, with material of thermal conductivity $300\,\mathrm{W\,m^{-1}K^{-1}}$, is insulated along its length and at one end. The other end is in an enclosure at a temperature of 800 K. There is a source of extended heating described by $Q(x) = 3 \times 10^3 x\,\mathrm{W\,m^{-3}}$, where x is in metres, and a point source of heating $1 \times 10^4\,\mathrm{W\,m^{-3}}$ situated 0.5 m from the insulated end. Use the program HEATELEM to determine the temperature distribution along the bar. Compare the result with that obtained by removing the extended source of heating.

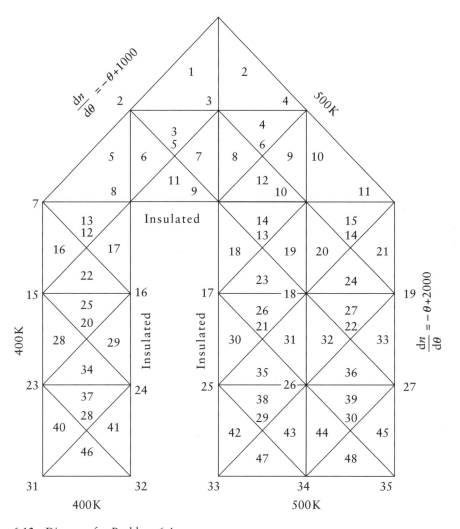

Fig. 6.13   Diagram for Problem 6.4.

6.4   A plate with insulated top and bottom surfaces is shown in Fig. 6.13 with boundary conditions indicated. It has thermal conductivity $400\,\mathrm{W\,m^{-1}K^{-1}}$. A network of finite elements is shown and point heat sources are situated as follows:

Node:	3	20	21	22
Strength ($\mathrm{W\,m^{-3}}$)	8×10^5	2×10^5	2×10^5	2×10^5

There is a uniform extended source of heating of strength $Q(x, y) = 10^3\,\mathrm{W\,m^{-3}}$ throughout the plate. Using FINELEM2 find the temperature distribution within the plate. (*Note*: A data-preparation program, FINDATA, is available and you are advised to use it. By editing the data file you will be able quickly to run modifications of the problem given here and so explore the influence of the various parameters.)

7 *Computational fluid dynamics*

7.1 A general description of fluid dynamics

The flow of fluids is something which happens all around us constantly and in a variety of different ways. Examples are the flow of a river, the winds that blow and the flow of gas through pipes that feed home appliances. In these few examples we can see that a variety of different characteristics are possible in fluid flow. The fluid can be a gas which is easily compressed or a liquid which is not. The flow can be in an effectively infinite space, such as the movement of air in the atmosphere, or can be restricted, as in flow through a river bed or a pipe. It can also be turbulent flow, where there is a random component to the motion leading to energy transfer into heating the fluid, or laminar flow, which is well ordered. To define a particular problem we need know the physical characteristics of the fluid, the forces which act upon it and the space in which it moves. Then if we can find its density, velocity and temperature as a function of position and time the problem has been solved. We shall be looking at particle methods for solving the equations of fluid dynamics. The difference between this kind of problem and the plasma and galactic problems of previous chapters is that the fluid case is dominated by collisions, so that within any small region the particles (molecules and the superparticles that represent them) are constantly sharing their properties by collisions and can be assumed to be in local thermodynamic equilibrium at any time. The condition for a fluid description is that the mean free path is short compared with the characteristic lengths in the problem and the mean time between collisions is short compared to the characteristic time.

A fluid in motion is a macroscopic manifestation of the behaviour of matter at a molecular level. When a model boat is placed in a smoothly flowing river the motion of the boat is governed by the average force generated by water molecules bombarding it from all directions, and their net effect is to move it with the flow of the water. However, the water molecules are not all moving with a uniform velocity equal to that of the river as a whole. Relative to the river velocity they will be moving in random directions, with a distribution of speeds given by a Maxwell distribution appropriate to their temperature. Another way to visualize this situation is to imagine that a bucket of red dye is inserted into the water, forming a circular patch. The centre of the red patch flows down-stream with the speed of the smoothly-flowing river but, at the same time, its radius gradually increases as the dye diffuses outwards from the centre of the patch. Fluid flow transports the properties of the fluid – in the present case 'redness' – and we can recognize two different kinds of transport. The first is *advection*, corresponding to the macroscopic motion of the fluid and describing the motion of the centre of the red patch. The second kind, *diffusion*, is that which describes the spreading of the patch as it flows downstream.

In this chapter we shall first deal with computational aspects of the transport of properties of a fluid by advection and diffusion and then deal with fluid flow as the movement of the fluid itself.

7.2   The equations of transport of fluid properties

The phenomenen of diffusion was encountered in Chapter 2 and the one-dimensional *diffusion equation* (2.20) in terms of transport of some conserved quantity q can be written

$$\frac{\partial q}{\partial t} - D\frac{\partial^2 q}{\partial x^2} = 0, \tag{7.1}$$

where D is the diffusion coefficient. They are many methods available for the solution of this parabolic equation, for example, the explicit method (Section 2.5), the Crank–Nicholson method (Section 2.6) and the Dufont–Frankel method (Section 2.8).

For advection we consider the one-dimensional flow of a fluid which contains some conserved quantity Q with a concentration $q(x, t)$ (that is, the amount of Q per unit volume) which changes in both space and time. In Fig. 7.1 we show a tube of the flowing liquid of unit cross-sectional area with two planes, A and B, perpendicular to the flow and a distance δx apart. In a time δt the amount of Q entering the volume at A is

$$\delta Q_A = qv\delta t, \tag{7.2a}$$

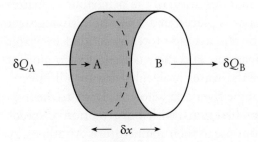

Fig. 7.1   A tube of flowing liquid of unit cross-sectional area.

where v is the constant velocity of the fluid. In the same time the amount of Q leaving at B is

$$\delta Q_B = \left(q + \frac{\partial q}{\partial x} \delta x \right) v \delta t. \tag{7.2b}$$

The net change in concentration in the volume δx in the time δt is thus

$$\delta q = \frac{\delta Q_A - \delta Q_B}{\delta x} = -v \frac{\partial q}{\partial x} \delta t. \tag{7.3}$$

Taking the limit $\delta t \to 0$ gives the *advection equation*

$$\frac{\partial q}{\partial t} + v \frac{\partial q}{\partial x} = 0. \tag{7.4}$$

In the case where both diffusion and advection occur then (7.1) and (7.4) can be combined into the *advection–diffusion equation*

$$\frac{\partial q}{\partial t} + v \frac{\partial q}{\partial x} - D \frac{\partial^2 q}{\partial x^2} = 0. \tag{7.5}$$

We shall now describe several numerical methods for solving (7.5), some successful and some not. The results of using them are found with the program ADVDIF (see p. xv) which contains all the algorithms which are described.

7.3 Numerical studies of diffusion and advection

The application of the explicit method to pure diffusion, using ADVDIF, is illustrated in Fig. 7.2. The initial distribution of q has a triangular form, and Fig. 7.2a illustrates the concentration at 5 s intervals with a diffusion coefficient of $0.1 \, \mathrm{m^2 \, s^{-1}}$, the x interval $\Delta x = 1 \, \mathrm{m}$ and the time interval $\Delta t = 5 \, \mathrm{s}$, which gives the value of r in (2.27) equal to 0.5, the critical value. The solution is quite stable but has an unphysical waviness which shows lack of precision. Taking $\Delta x = 0.5 \, \mathrm{m}$ and $\Delta t = 1.25 \, \mathrm{s}$, again giving $r = 0.5$, gives a somewhat improved appearance (Fig. 7.2b) although the overall diffusion spread is not very different.

We now see what happens when the advection equation (7.4) is converted into an explicit finite-difference form by taking a forward difference in time and a central difference in space. This gives

$$\frac{q(i,j+1) - q(i,j)}{\Delta t} + v \frac{q(i+1,j) - q(i-1,j)}{2\Delta x} = 0$$

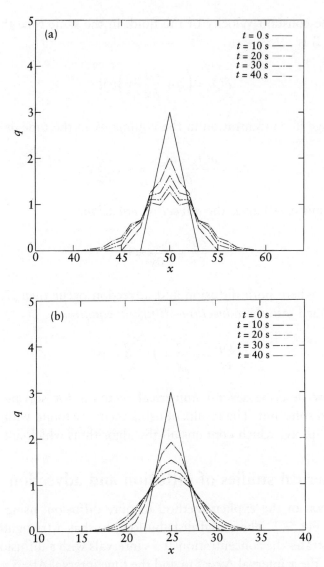

Fig. 7.2 Explicit method applied to the diffusion of a triangular distribution with $D = 0.1\,\mathrm{m^2\,s^{-1}}$ for: (a) $\Delta x = 1\,\mathrm{m}$, $\Delta t = 5\,\mathrm{s}$; (b) $\Delta x = 0.5\,\mathrm{m}$, $\Delta t = 1.25\,\mathrm{s}$.

or

$$q(i, j+1) = q(i,j) - \frac{v\Delta t}{2\Delta x}\{q(i+1, j) - q(i-1, j)\}. \tag{7.6}$$

The quantity $v\Delta t/\Delta x$ is a dimensionless quantity which is called the Courant number, C, and its value controls the behaviour of finite-difference equations in which it occurs. Equation (7.6), applied through ADVDIF, was used to study the advection of a triangular distribution of q; the result with $C=1$, $\Delta x=1$ m and $\Delta t=1$ s is given in Fig. 7.3a. It is a poor outcome which is not improved by taking smaller intervals (Fig. 7.3b). It is an example of an *absolute instability* which cannot be controlled by time step adjustment.

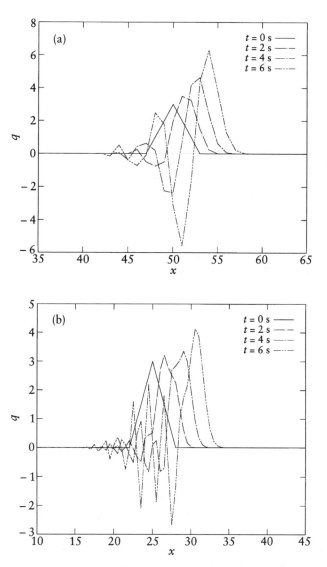

Fig. 7.3 Advection of a triangular distribution using forward difference in time and central difference in space, with: (a) $C=1$, $\Delta x=1$ m, $\Delta t=1$ s; (b) $C=0.5$, $\Delta x=0.5$ m, $\Delta t=0.25$ s.

We now explore another way of setting up an explicit finite-difference solution for advection, but this time using a backward-difference representation of $\partial q/\partial x$ – or *upwind difference*, as it is often called – which might be expected to give an answer inferior to that obtained with the central-difference representation. The finite-difference equation now appears as

$$q(i,j+1)=(1-C)q(i,j)+Cq(i-1,j). \tag{7.7}$$

The result of applying ADVDIF to (7.7) with the triangular distribution with $C=1$, $\Delta x=1$ m and $\Delta t=1$ s is shown in Fig. 7.4a, and is seen to preserve the triangular distribution without any distortion whatsoever. This is not surprising, as from (7.7) it will be seen that with $C=1$ the first term on the right-hand side disappears and in each time step the whole distribution is displaced through a distance Δx. Using $C=0.5$, $\Delta x=1$ and $\Delta t=0.5$ gave the results in Fig. 7.4b, where the distribution spreads out as it progresses. This kind of behaviour, when spreading occurs which should not be there and which is due to the numerical process being used, is called *numerical diffusion*.

Finally, we examine what happens when (7.5) is transformed into finite-difference form. From the experience of dealing with diffusion and advection separately, it would appear to be expedient to express the diffusion term on the right-hand side in the usual central-difference way but the advection term with a backward-difference formulation as has been found to give good results for advection alone. The combination of these two features gives the finite-difference equation

$$q(i,j+1)=(1-C-2r)q(i,j)+(C+r)q(i-1,j)+rq(i+1,j). \tag{7.8}$$

From experience with advection and diffusion treated in isolation, it might be expected that if values of Δx and Δt can be found which give $C=1$ and $r=0.5$ then good results might be obtained. In fact the results are completely unstable under these conditions, and with $C=1$ the value of r has to be reduced to 0.1 before the results, found with ADVDIF, can even be displayed for a short simulated time, as seen in Fig. 7.5. Even then it is clear that the results are not very useful.

Before further consideration of the advection–diffusion problem, it would be wise to see if some sense can be made of the results already found. Procedures found on an intuitive basis seem not to be successful, while using the upwind difference for advection alone, which might seem not to be a good thing to do, actually works. We shall now find out how the behaviour of a finite-difference equation may be understood and predicted.

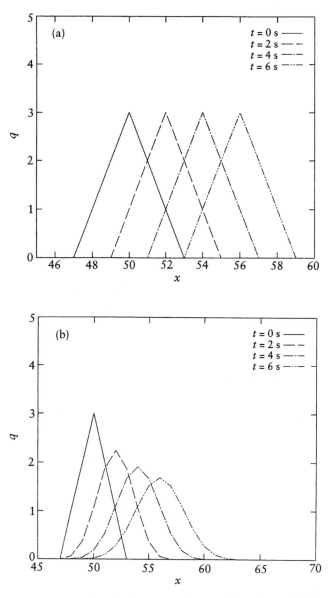

Fig. 7.4 Advection for a triangular distribution with upwind (backward) differencing for space and forward differencing for time, with: (a) $C=1$, $\Delta x=1\,\mathrm{m}$, $\Delta t=1\,\mathrm{s}$; (b) $C=0.5$, $\Delta x=1\,\mathrm{m}$, $\Delta t=0.5\,\mathrm{s}$.

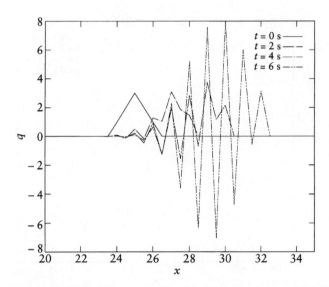

Fig. 7.5 Advection plus diffusion for a triangular distribution using central differencing for the diffusion term, backward difference for advection and forward difference for time. Instability is seen for $C = 1$ and $r = 0.1$.

7.4 Stability conditions

Analytical solutions of the advection–diffusion equation can be found of the form

$$q(x, t) = A \exp[i(ax + bt)]. \tag{7.9}$$

Substituting this into (7.5) gives

$$b = -av + iDa^2$$

or

$$q(x, t) = A \exp[ia(x - vt)]\exp(-Da^2 t). \tag{7.10}$$

This is the form of a decaying progressive wave and is a solution for any value of a. It is helpful to imagine that we are looking for a solution within the range $x = 0$ to L with cyclic boundary conditions, and then we can write a general solution of (7.5) in the form

$$q(x, t) = \sum_{k=0}^{\infty} f(k)\exp\left[2\pi i\left(\frac{kx}{L} - v_k t\right)\right]\exp\left(-\frac{4\pi^2 D k^2}{L^2} t\right). \tag{7.11}$$

For each term the *wave index*, k, is the number of waves which fit into the distance L so that the wavelength $\lambda_k = L/k$. The frequency associated with each term $v_k = v/\lambda_k$. The initial disturbance profile, for $t=0$, is

$$q(x,0) = \sum_{k=0}^{\infty} f(k) \exp\left(2\pi i \frac{kx}{L}\right), \qquad (7.12)$$

and by inverse Fourier transformation (Appendix 5) the coefficients $f(k)$ may be found from

$$f(k) = \int_0^L q(x,0) \exp\left(-2\pi i \frac{kx}{L}\right) dx. \qquad (7.13)$$

In the process of applying a finite-difference equation to advance the time by Δt the coefficients $f(k)$ will, in general, change and von Neumann has given a condition for stability of the finite-difference procedure – which is that amplification of the magnitude of the term of index k, $g(k)$, should be less than or equal to unity for all k. Even if only one of the terms increases its amplitude without limit, then clearly the solution will be unstable. It should be noted that this is *not* a condition for accuracy but just for stability (see Section 2.9), although it clearly has some relation with the 'accuracy' of the representation of a particular problem.

Writing

$$c(k)_i^j = f(k)^j \exp\left(2\pi i \frac{kx_i}{L}\right) \qquad (7.14)$$

as the contribution to $q(x_i, t_j)$ of the term with wave index k, it is found that

$$c(k)_{i+1}^j = c(k)_i^j \exp(i\Delta_k) \quad \text{and} \quad c(k)_{i-1}^j = c(k)_i^j \exp(-i\Delta_k), \qquad (7.15)$$

where $\Delta_k = 2\pi k \Delta x / L$.

This result is now applied to the term of index k for the finite-difference equation (7.6) which was found to be unstable. This gives

$$c(k)_i^{j+1} = c(k)_i^j - \tfrac{1}{2} C\{c(k)_{i+1}^j - c(k)_{i-1}^j\}. \qquad (7.16)$$

Inserting (7.15) in (7.16) gives

$$c(k)_i^{j+1} = c(k)_i^j - \tfrac{1}{2} C c(k)_i^j (e^{ik\Delta_k} - e^{-ik\Delta_k}) = c(k)_i^j \{1 - iC\sin(k\Delta_k)\}. \qquad (7.17)$$

The instability of (7.6) is shown by von Neumann's condition since

$$|c(k)_i^{j+1}| = |c(k)_i^j| \times \{1 + C^2 \sin^2 k\Delta_k\}^{1/2}$$

so that the *amplification factor* $g(k) \geqslant 1$.

We now apply the same treatment to (7.8) which was found to be unstable with $C=1$ and two values of r, 0.5 and 0.1. Applying (7.15) to the term of index k of (7.8)

$$c(k)_i^{j+1}=c(k)_i^j\{1-C-2r+(C+r)e^{-i\Delta_k}+re^{i\Delta_k}\}. \tag{7.18}$$

The quantity in curly brackets is the amplification factor, and its properties can be considered by a graphical approach. If $C+2r>1$ then, in Fig. 7.6a, we see the quantity $1-C-2r$ indicated along the negative real axis of an Argand diagram. Since $C+r$ and r are both positive, the maximum magnitude of the amplification factor is when $\Delta_k=\pi$ and the total contribution, shown in Fig. 7.6a, is

$$|g(k)_{max}|=C+2r+C+r+r-1=2(C+2r)-1>1, \tag{7.19}$$

so the solution is not stable.

We now consider the situation when $C+2r\leqslant1$. As shown in Fig. 7.6b, the quantity $1-C-2r$ now points along the positive real axis and the maximum value of $g(k)$ is when $\Delta_k=0$. Now we have

$$g(k)_{max}=1-C-2r+(C+r)+r=1, \tag{7.20}$$

so the solution is stable. The output for an application of (7.8) with $C=0.5$ and $r=0.25$ $(C+2r=1)$ is given in Fig. 7.7; it is quite a good representation of advection plus diffusion, although some of the diffusion will be numerical and not that implied by the diffusion term in (7.5).

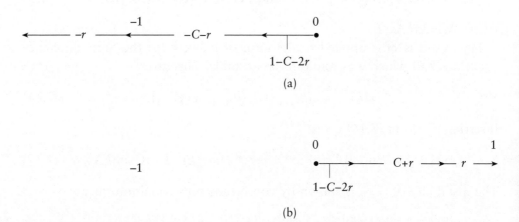

(a)

(b)

Fig. 7.6 The maximum amplification factor for the algorithm leading to Fig. 7.5 with: (a) $C+2r>1$; (b) $C+2r\leqslant1$.

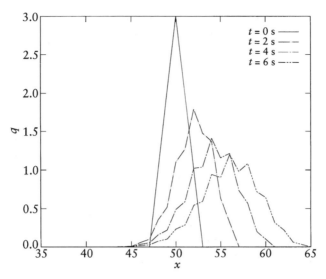

Fig. 7.7 An application of (7.8) with $C=0.5$ and $r=0.25$ showing stability.

7.5 Central difference for advection and diffusion

It might be expected that better results would be obtained for advection and diffusion by using central-difference forms for both of the space terms. This gives

$$q(i,j+1)=(1-2r)q(i,j)+(r-C/2)q(i+1,j)+(r+C/2)q(i-1,j). \quad (7.21)$$

and before showing the results of its use we find the conditions for stability. The amplification factor for the contribution of wave index k is

$$g(k)=1-2r+2r\cos\Delta_k-iC\sin\Delta_k \quad (7.22)$$

The condition for stability is thus

$$(1-2r-2r\cos\Delta_k)^2+C^2\sin^2\Delta_k\leqslant 1,$$

which leads to the condition

$$C^2\leqslant\frac{2r(1-2r\cos^2(\Delta_k/2))}{1-\cos^2(\Delta_k/2)}. \quad (7.23)$$

Since C^2 must be positive and $\cos^2\frac{1}{2}\Delta_k$ can take its maximum value of unity for some k this shows a necessary condition $r\leqslant\frac{1}{2}$. It is also readily confirmed by differentiation that the right-hand side of (7.23) monotonically increases as $\cos^2\frac{1}{2}\Delta_k$ goes through its permitted range of 0 to 1, so that the minimum value

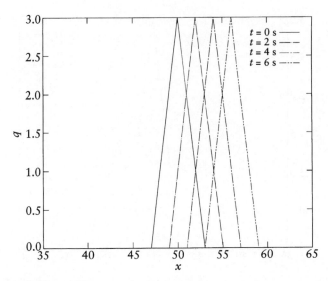

Fig. 7.8 An application of (7.21) with $C=1$ and $r=0.5$ which suppresses diffusion.

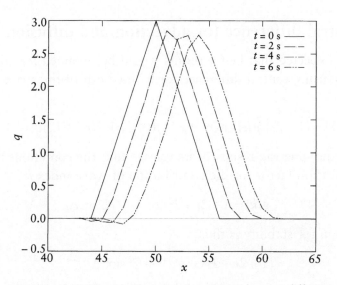

Fig. 7.9 An application of (7.21) with $C=0.7$ and $r=0.245$ showing diffusion.

of the right-hand side is $2r$. This gives the stability condition

$$C \leqslant \sqrt{2r},\qquad\qquad(7.24)$$

which permits $C=1$ and $r=0.5$ which were used in applying ADVDIF to
(7.21) as shown in Fig. 7.8. The result is pure advection with no diffusion, and
by inserting $C=1$ and $r=0.5$ in (7.21) the reason for this will become obvious.

By changing to $C=0.7$ and $r=0.245$, which just satisfies (7.24), the result in Fig. 7.9 is obtained which restores diffusion – but the uncertain contribution of numerical diffusion to the result reduces its usefulness.

7.6 The Lax–Wendroff method

The Lax–Wendroff method is one which was formerly very widely used and forms the basis of many modern methods because it gives comparatively little numerical diffusion. It can be applied to the general differential equation

$$\frac{\partial q}{\partial t} + \frac{\partial F(q)}{\partial x} = 0, \tag{7.25}$$

but we shall illustrate its use with simple advection, for which $F(q)=vq$. We begin by expressing (7.25) for a point in space–time which is at the point i in space and half-way between points j and $j+1$ in time thus:

$$\left(\frac{\partial q}{\partial t}\right)_i^{j+1/2} = -v\left(\frac{\partial q}{\partial x}\right)_i^{j+1/2}. \tag{7.26}$$

Expressing both sides in central finite-difference form using half-way points in space,

$$\frac{q_i^{j+1} - q_i^j}{\Delta t} = v\frac{q_{i-1/2}^{j+1/2} - q_{i+1/2}^{j+1/2}}{\Delta x},$$

or

$$q_i^{j+1} = q_i^j + C\left(q_{i-1/2}^{j+1/2} - q_{i+1/2}^{j+1/2}\right). \tag{7.27}$$

We now find approximations for the terms in parentheses on the right-hand side from

$$\left(\frac{\partial q}{\partial t}\right)_{i+1/2}^j = -v\left(\frac{\partial q}{\partial x}\right)_{i+1/2}^j$$

from which, by taking a forward-difference time derivative over a half time step, we obtain

$$q_{i+1/2}^{j+1/2} = q_{i+1/2}^j + \tfrac{1}{2}C(q_i^j - q_{i+1}^j).$$

Next, by taking the first term on the right-hand side as the average of the two flanking points in space,

$$q_{i+1/2}^{j+1/2} = \tfrac{1}{2}(1-C)q_{i+1}^j + \tfrac{1}{2}(1+C)q_i^j. \tag{7.28}$$

Finally, by inserting (7.28) into (7.27), the Lax–Wendroff advection equation is found as

$$q_i^{j+1} = \tfrac{1}{2}C(1+C)q_{i-1}^j + (1-C^2)q_i^j - \tfrac{1}{2}C(1-C)q_{i+1}^j. \qquad (7.29)$$

Running our standard advection problem using ADVDIF with $C=1$ gives the equivalent result to upwind differencing, as seen in Fig. 7.10a. However, with $C=0.8$ (Fig. 7.10b) some numerical diffusion occurs. Clearly the Lax–Wendroff process offers only a limited advantage over upwind differencing in

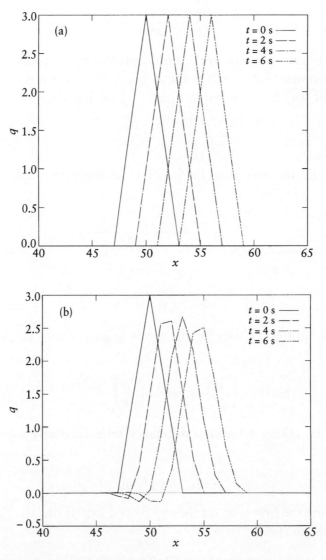

Fig. 7.10 Application of the Lax–Wendroff advection equation with (a) $C=1$ and (b) $C=0.8$ showing numerical diffusion.

this simple advection case, but it is very useful for general functions $F(q)$ where backward differencing would not give such a good result even if applicable. In addition, it gives substantially less numerical diffusion.

7.7 The QUICKEST method

A very successful and accurate process for dealing with the one-dimensional advection–diffusion equation has been developed by Leonard (1979). Its name, QUICKEST, stands for Quadratic Upstream Interpolation for Convective Kinematics with Estimated Streaming Terms, but here we shall just develop the associated finite-difference equation without interpreting it in terms of the name. The general approach is to take each of the terms in (7.5) and to develop it up to and including the third partial derivative with respect to x. Thus, starting with the first term, we use Taylor's theorem to give

$$q_i^{j+1} = q_i^j + \Delta t \left(\frac{\partial q}{\partial t}\right)_i^j + \frac{(\Delta t)^2}{2!}\left(\frac{\partial^2 q}{\partial t^2}\right)_i^j + \frac{(\Delta t)^3}{3!}\left(\frac{\partial^3 q}{\partial t^3}\right)_i^j + \cdots. \tag{7.30}$$

From (7.5) we see that we can convert from partial differentiation with respect to t to partial differentiation with respect to x by the operator transformation

$$\frac{\partial}{\partial t} = -v\frac{\partial}{\partial x} + D\frac{\partial^2}{\partial x^2}. \tag{7.31}$$

Given that we are only interested in terms up to the third partial derivative with respect to x, we find

$$\frac{\partial^2}{\partial t^2} = v^2\frac{\partial^2}{\partial x^2} - 2Dv\frac{\partial^3}{\partial x^3} \quad \text{and} \quad \frac{\partial^3}{\partial t^3} = -v^3\frac{\partial^3}{\partial x^3}. \tag{7.32}$$

Substituting from (7.31) and (7.32) in (7.30) and rearranging,

$$\left(\frac{\partial q}{\partial t}\right)_i^j = \frac{q_i^{j+1} - q_i^j}{\Delta t} - \frac{v^2\Delta t}{2}\left(\frac{\partial^2 q}{\partial x^2}\right)_i^j + \left\{vD\Delta t + \frac{1}{6}v^3(\Delta t)^2\right\}\left(\frac{\partial^3 q}{\partial x^3}\right). \tag{7.33}$$

From another application of Taylor's theorem,

$$q_{i+1}^j = q_i^j + \Delta x\left(\frac{\partial q}{\partial x}\right)_i^j + \frac{(\Delta x)^2}{2!}\left(\frac{\partial^2 q}{\partial x^2}\right)_i^j + \frac{(\Delta x)^3}{3!}\left(\frac{\partial^3 q}{\partial x^3}\right)_i^j + \cdots$$

and

$$q_{i-1}^j = q_i^j - \Delta x\left(\frac{\partial q}{\partial x}\right)_i^j + \frac{(\Delta x)^2}{2!}\left(\frac{\partial^2 q}{\partial x^2}\right)_i^j - \frac{(\Delta x)^3}{3!}\left(\frac{\partial^3 q}{\partial x^3}\right)_i^j + \cdots.$$

Subtracting the second equation from the first and rearranging gives

$$\left(\frac{\partial q}{\partial x}\right)_i^j = \frac{q_{i+1}^j - q_{i-1}^j}{2\Delta x} - \frac{(\Delta x)^2}{3}\left(\frac{\partial^3 q}{\partial x^3}\right)_i^j. \tag{7.34}$$

No modification of the term $(\partial^2 q/\partial x^2)_i^j$ in (7.33) is needed as any correction to the usual finite-difference form (2.9) involves partial differentials of order higher than 3.

It is found that the finite-difference form of the third partial derivative which gives the best stability of the final equation is that based on the four points $i+1$, i, $i-1$ and $i-2$, and is

$$\left(\frac{\partial^3 q}{\partial x^3}\right)_i^j = \frac{q_{i+1}^j - 3q_i^j + 3q_{i-1}^j - q_{i-2}^j}{(\Delta x)^3}. \tag{7.35}$$

Substituting (7.35) in (7.33) and (7.34) and then (7.33) and (7.34) in (7.5) with the final term expressed according to (2.9) gives the final equation,

$$q_i^{j+1} = \{r(1-C) - \tfrac{1}{6}C^3 + \tfrac{1}{2}C^2 - \tfrac{1}{3}C\}q_{i+1}^j + \{1 + r(3C-2) + \tfrac{1}{2}C^3 - C^2 - \tfrac{1}{2}C\}q_i^j$$

$$+ \{r(1-3C) - \tfrac{1}{2}C^3 + \tfrac{1}{2}C^2 + C\}q_{i-1}^j + \{rC + \tfrac{1}{6}C^3 - \tfrac{1}{6}C\}q_{i-2}^j. \tag{7.36}$$

The advection–diffusion problem of the initial triangular profile run with the QUICKEST option in ADVDIF is shown in Fig. 7.11 with two different Courant numbers, 1.0 and 0.5 and $r=0.5$. The results, which are for

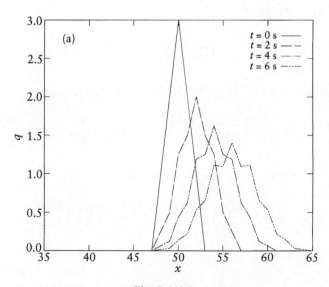

Fig. 7.11(a)

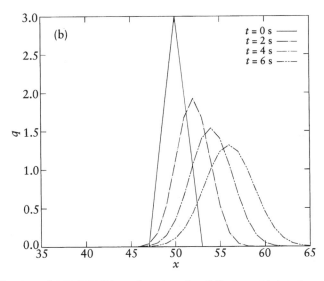

Fig. 7.11 Application of QUICKEST to advection plus diffusion with (a) $C=1$ and (b) $C=0.5$.

equivalent times, are seen to agree reasonably well with each other and with Fig. 7.7. However, it is found that QUICKEST results show less unphysical fluctuations which are a feature of the simple finite-difference equations we have been considering. The stability conditions are very complicated and Fig. 7.12 shows the (r, C) stability field. The system can be stable for $1 \leqslant C \leqslant 2$, but not if $r=0$. Experience indicates that the region around $(0.5, 0.5)$ gives both stability and accuracy in most situations.

This concludes our treatment of the transport of the properties of a fluid by advection and diffusion, and we now consider the motion and behaviour of the fluid itself.

7.8 The basic equations of fluid dynamics

In order to analyse the behaviour of the fluid there are two basic ways of observing it. One is to imagine that we have a fixed frame of reference and that we consider how the properties of the fluid vary with time at fixed positions in the frame. Since the fluid is moving, we are looking at different elements in the fluid at each point as time progresses. This gives us the *Eulerian* formulation of hydrodynamics. The other way to observe the fluid behaviour is to travel with a fixed element of the fluid and to observe the variation of its properties with time. This constitutes the *Lagrangian* formulation of hydrodynamics. Now we shall derive the basic equations of fluid dynamics in

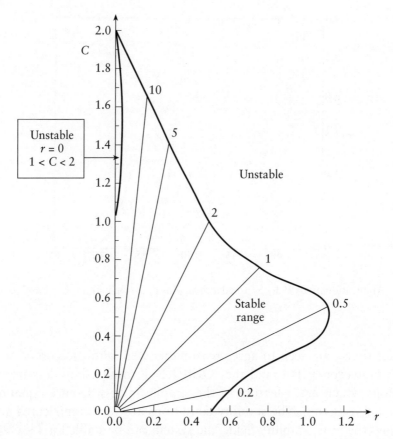

Fig. 7.12   Stability conditions for QUICKEST.

one dimension and then generalize the equations to a three-dimensional form. We shall do this for both the Eulerian and Lagrangian formulations, and also find out how to transform from one form to the other.

7.8.1   *Conservation of mass – Eulerian form*

In Fig. 7.13 we see two parallel plane surfaces, A and B, each of unit area, separated by a distance δx and normal to the direction of flow of a fluid, defined as the x direction. In time δt the mass flowing through the plane A into the volume between the planes is

$$\delta m_A = \rho v \delta t, \qquad\qquad (7.37a)$$

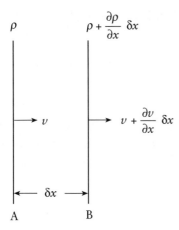

ρ

$\rho + \dfrac{\partial \rho}{\partial x} \, \delta x$

v

$v + \dfrac{\partial v}{\partial x} \, \delta x$

δx

A

B

Fig. 7.13 Flow of a compressible fluid across two unit-area planes A and B in the Eulerian formulation.

where ρ is the density and v the speed of the fluid at the position of plane A. Similarly, the mass flowing out of the volume through plane B is

$$\delta m_\mathrm{B} = \left\{ \rho v + \frac{\partial (\rho v)}{\partial x} \delta x \right\} \delta t. \tag{7.37b}$$

Hence the net flow into the region is

$$\delta m = \delta m_\mathrm{A} - \delta m_\mathrm{B} = - \frac{\partial (\rho v)}{\partial x} \delta x \, \delta t.$$

The volume of the region is δx, and by going to the limit $\delta x \to 0$, $\delta t \to 0$, we find the equation for conservation of mass

$$\frac{\partial \rho}{\partial t} + \frac{\partial (\rho v)}{\partial x} = 0. \tag{7.38a}$$

The three-dimensional form of this equation is

$$\frac{\partial \rho}{\partial t} + \nabla \cdot (\rho \mathbf{v}) = 0. \tag{7.38b}$$

7.8.2 *Conservation of momentum – Eulerian form*

The rate of change of momentum of the material between the surfaces A and B in Fig. 7.13 is due first to the rate at which momentum is transported by the fluid into and out of the volume through the two surfaces and also to the change of pressure between the two surfaces. With only pressure forces operating, and in the absence of gravity and viscosity, the fluid transport of momentum per unit time is

$$\delta h_1 = \rho v \times v - \left\{ \rho v^2 + \frac{\partial(\rho v^2)}{\partial x}\delta x \right\} = -\frac{\partial(\rho v^2)}{\partial x}\delta x. \tag{7.39}$$

The momentum generated within the volume due to the pressure difference between A and B can be visualized by noting that pressure equals force per unit area or rate of change of momentum per unit area. Hence the momentum generated per unit mass within the volume due to the pressure change across it will be

$$\delta h_2 = P - \left(P - \frac{\partial P}{\partial x}\delta x \right) = -\frac{\partial P}{\partial x}\delta x. \tag{7.40}$$

Hence the rate of change of momentum within the volume δx is given by

$$\frac{\partial(\rho v)}{\partial t}\delta x = \delta h_1 + \delta h_2 = -\frac{\partial(\rho v^2)}{\partial x}\delta x - \frac{\partial P}{\partial x}\delta x,$$

or

$$\frac{\partial(\rho v)}{\partial t} + \frac{\partial(\rho v^2)}{\partial x} + \frac{\partial P}{\partial x} = 0, \tag{7.41a}$$

which is the one-dimensional equation for conservation of momentum. To transform this equation into a three-dimensional form we note that

$$\frac{\partial(\rho v^2)}{\partial x} = \frac{\partial(\rho v \times v)}{\partial x} = \rho v \frac{\partial v}{\partial x} + v \frac{\partial(\rho v)}{\partial x}.$$

The three-dimensional form of the equation for conservation of momentum is not simply related to the one-dimensional form, since it involves tensor-related quantities. It is

$$\frac{\partial(\rho \mathbf{v})}{\partial t} + (\rho \mathbf{v} \cdot \nabla)\mathbf{v} + (\nabla \cdot \rho \mathbf{v})\mathbf{v} + \nabla P = 0. \tag{7.41b}$$

Before moving on to the conservation of internal energy, we shall first consider the Lagrangian equations for the conservation of mass and momentum.

7.8.3 *Conservation of mass and momentum – Lagrangian form*

We now consider again the conservation of mass in one dimension, but this time we focus our attention on a fixed element of the fluid. In Fig. 7.14 A and B are

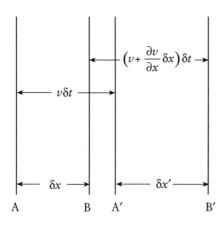

Fig. 7.14 After time δt the element of fluid between unit-area planes at A and B has moved to the region between A' and B'.

two parallel unit-area planes, separated by a distance δx, which define an element of the fluid. After a time δt the fluid originally at A has moved to A' and that originally at B has moved to B'; the element of fluid between A' and B' is just that originally between A and B. The distance AA' is $v\delta t$, where v is the velocity of the fluid at A and the distance BB' is $(v+(\partial v/\partial x)\delta x)\delta t$, so that the distance A'B' is

$$\delta x' = \delta x + \left(v + \frac{\partial v}{\partial x}\delta x\right)\delta t - v\delta t = \delta x + \frac{\partial v}{\partial x}\delta x\,\delta t, \qquad (7.42)$$

that is,

$$\frac{\delta x' - \delta x}{\delta x} = \frac{\partial v}{\partial x}\delta t. \qquad (7.43)$$

The left-hand side of equation (7.43) is just the negative of the fractional change of density, so that

$$-\frac{\delta\rho}{\rho} = \frac{\partial v}{\partial x}\delta t.$$

Taking $\delta t \to 0$ gives the Lagrangian form of the conservation of mass equation,

$$\frac{d\rho}{dt} = -\rho\frac{\partial v}{\partial x}. \qquad (7.44a)$$

The total (Lagrangian) derivative on the left-hand side reflects what an observer sees when travelling with the element – that the mean density within it just varies with time. However, the same observer can detect a velocity within the infinitesimal element that varies both in position and time – hence the partial derivative on the right-hand side.

Rewriting (7.38a) as

$$\left(\frac{\partial}{\partial t} + v\frac{\partial}{\partial x}\right)\rho = -\rho\frac{\partial v}{\partial x},$$

we can see that a transformation from the Eulerian to Lagrangian form is obtained by replacing the operator $\partial/\partial t + v(\partial/\partial x)$ by d/dt. The corresponding transformation in three dimensions is to replace $\partial/\partial t + \mathbf{v}\cdot\nabla$ by d/dt. The three-dimensional form of the Lagrangian equation derived from (7.44a) is

$$\frac{d\rho}{dt} = -\rho\nabla\cdot\mathbf{v}. \tag{7.44b}$$

As an exercise the reader should confirm that the same transformation gives, from (7.41a), the Lagrangian form of the one-dimensional equation for momentum conservation,

$$\rho\frac{dv}{dt} = -\frac{dP}{dx} \tag{7.45a}$$

and in three dimensions, from (7.41b),

$$\rho\frac{d\mathbf{v}}{dt} = -\nabla\cdot P. \tag{7.45b}$$

7.9 The incompressible fluid

Liquids are often regarded as incompressible because they require such high pressures to compress them appreciably. However, it is quite legitimate in many applications to consider even a gaseous medium such as the atmosphere to be incompressible. The characteristic of a gas that causes it to resist compression is its pressure, which is its thermal energy density per unit volume. This is characterized by the mean square thermal speed of the molecules and for, say, nitrogen, the major component of the atmosphere, at $300\,\mathrm{K}$ this is $2.66\times 10^5\,\mathrm{m}^2\,\mathrm{s}^{-2}$. If we now consider the energy of motion of the air moving at $60\,\mathrm{km}\,\mathrm{h}^{-1}$, then this corresponds to a speed squared of $277\,\mathrm{m}^2\,\mathrm{s}^{-2}$. Thus the internal energy of the atmosphere greatly exceeds that of its mass motion and flow cannot appreciably compress it unless it is moving rapidly.

For an incompressible fluid we may write $d\rho/dt = 0$ and, inserting this in (7.38), we find

$$\nabla\cdot\mathbf{v} = 0. \tag{7.46}$$

Incompressible flows are inherently two- or three-dimensional, since the one-dimensional case has only the trivial solution $\mathbf{v}$=constant. Having a zero divergence of the velocity is a well-known condition for incompressibility. Again, given a constant density and (7.46), equation (7.41b) becomes

$$\frac{\partial \mathbf{v}}{\partial t} + (\mathbf{v} \cdot \nabla)\mathbf{v} = -\frac{1}{\rho}\nabla P. \qquad (7.47\text{a})$$

One factor which has so far been ignored is that of viscosity. Including the kinematic viscosity v gives the Navier–Stokes equation

$$\frac{\partial \mathbf{v}}{\partial t} + (\mathbf{v} \cdot \nabla)\mathbf{v} = -\frac{1}{\rho}\nabla P + v\nabla^2 \mathbf{v}. \qquad (7.47\text{b})$$

Equations (7.46) and (7.47b) are all that is required to deal with incompressible fluids and no equation which deals with internal energy is required. We now describe a finite-difference approach to the numerical solution of the equations of incompressible motion and eventually, using some of the ideas from that, a particle method which enables the movement of surfaces of incompressible liquids to be modelled.

7.10 The pressure method for incompressible fluids

By rearranging (7.47b) and taking the divergence of all terms, we find, for constant v,

$$\frac{1}{\rho}\nabla \cdot \nabla P = -\nabla \cdot \frac{\partial \mathbf{v}}{\partial t} - \nabla \cdot (\mathbf{v} \cdot \nabla)\mathbf{v} + v\nabla \cdot \nabla^2 \mathbf{v}. \qquad (7.48)$$

Since the divergence of the velocity is zero so is its rate of change, and the first term on the right-hand side vanishes. In addition $\nabla \cdot \nabla^2 \mathbf{v} = \nabla^2 \nabla \cdot \mathbf{v}$, so the final term also disappears, giving

$$\nabla^2 P = -\rho\nabla \cdot (\mathbf{v} \cdot \nabla)\mathbf{v}. \qquad (7.49)$$

We now consider a two-dimensional problem where at each point in the fluid there is a pressure and a velocity described by its components (u,v). From (7.46) we find

$$\frac{\partial u}{\partial x} + \frac{\partial v}{\partial y} = 0. \qquad (7.50)$$

Expanding (7.49) gives

$$\frac{\partial^2 P}{\partial x^2} + \frac{\partial^2 P}{\partial y^2} = -\rho\left\{\left(\frac{\partial u}{\partial x}\right)^2 + 2\left(\frac{\partial u}{\partial y}\right)\left(\frac{\partial v}{\partial x}\right) + \left(\frac{\partial v}{\partial y}\right)^2\right\}$$

$$-\rho\left\{u\frac{\partial^2 u}{\partial x^2} + v\frac{\partial^2 u}{\partial x \partial y} + u\frac{\partial^2 v}{\partial x \partial y} + v\frac{\partial^2 v}{\partial y^2}\right\}.$$

The second term on the right-hand side is $(u(\partial/\partial x) + v(\partial/\partial y))(\partial u/\partial x + \partial v/\partial y)$, which is zero because of (7.50). The expansion of (7.49) then gives

$$\frac{\partial^2 P}{\partial x^2} + \frac{\partial^2 P}{\partial y^2} = -\rho\left\{\left(\frac{\partial u}{\partial x}\right)^2 + 2\left(\frac{\partial u}{\partial y}\right)\left(\frac{\partial v}{\partial x}\right) + \left(\frac{\partial v}{\partial y}\right)^2\right\}. \tag{7.51}$$

The general form of (7.51) also applies in three dimensions. With $\mathbf{r} = (x_1, x_2, x_3)$ and $\mathbf{v} = (v_1, v_2, v_3)$, the condition for incompressible flow is

$$\sum_{i=1}^{3} \frac{\partial v_i}{\partial x_i} = 0, \tag{7.52}$$

which, together with (7.49), gives

$$\sum_{i=1}^{3} \frac{\partial^2 P}{\partial x_i^2} = -\rho \sum_{i=1}^{3}\sum_{j=1}^{3} \frac{\partial v_i}{\partial x_j}\frac{\partial v_j}{\partial x_i}. \tag{7.53}$$

For the x component of (7.47b) we find

$$\frac{\partial u}{\partial t} = -u\frac{\partial u}{\partial x} - v\frac{\partial u}{\partial y} - \frac{1}{\rho}\frac{\partial P}{\partial x} + v\left(\frac{\partial^2 u}{\partial x^2} + \frac{\partial^2 u}{\partial y^2}\right)$$

Because of (7.50) it is possible to replace $-u(\partial u/\partial x) - v(\partial u/\partial y)$ by $-\partial u^2/\partial x - \partial uv/\partial y$, so the x-component equation now appears as

$$\frac{\partial u}{\partial t} = -\frac{\partial u^2}{\partial x} - \frac{\partial uv}{\partial y} - \frac{1}{\rho}\frac{\partial P}{\partial x} + v\left(\frac{\partial^2 u}{\partial x^2} + \frac{\partial^2 u}{\partial y^2}\right) \tag{7.54a}$$

with a corresponding y-component equation

$$\frac{\partial v}{\partial t} = -\frac{\partial v^2}{\partial y} - \frac{\partial uv}{\partial x} - \frac{1}{\rho}\frac{\partial P}{\partial y} + v\left(\frac{\partial^2 v}{\partial x^2} + \frac{\partial^2 v}{\partial y^2}\right). \tag{7.54b}$$

We can now use these equations to solve for the variables u, v and P in the space defined by the square Eulerian mesh of side Δx, illustrated in Fig. 7.15. Harlow and Welch (1965) applied a simple method, which gives stability, and it requires that u, v and P are defined at the points of three interlocking meshes. Thus, in Fig. 7.15, P is defined at the cell centres, points such as (i, j)

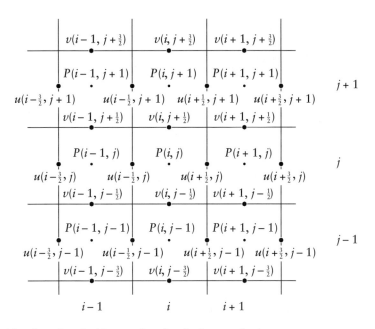

Fig. 7.15 The three interlocking meshes for the Lax method.

where both coordinates are integers; u is defined at face mid-points such as $(i+\frac{1}{2},j)$; and v at points such as $(i,j+\frac{1}{2})$. Referring to Fig. 7.15, we see that the condition similarly for the divergence to be zero for the central cell at time $t+1$ is

$$D_0 = \frac{u^{t+1}(i+\frac{1}{2},j) - u^{t+1}(i-\frac{1}{2},j)}{\Delta x} + \frac{v^{t+1}(i,j+\frac{1}{2}) - v^{t+1}(i,j-\frac{1}{2})}{\Delta y}. \quad (7.55)$$

An approach by Amsden and Harlow (1970) gives a much less diffusive result than earlier methods and makes use of *ZIP differencing*, for which, as an example, $[u(i,j)]^2 = u(i-\frac{1}{2},j)u(i+\frac{1}{2},j)$. Another part of the finite-difference representation transforms the viscous term in (7.54a) by using (7.50) to give

$$\nu\left(\frac{\partial^2 u}{\partial x^2} + \frac{\partial^2 u}{\partial y^2}\right) = \nu\left[\frac{\partial^2 u}{\partial y^2} + \frac{\partial}{\partial x}\left(-\frac{\partial v}{\partial y}\right)\right] = \nu\frac{\partial}{\partial y}\left(\frac{\partial u}{\partial y} - \frac{\partial v}{\partial x}\right). \quad (7.56)$$

This form allows the viscous term to satisfy the numerical condition of $\nabla \cdot \mathbf{v} = 0$. Equations (7.54a) and (7.54b) are used in a finite-difference form to find the velocity components at time $t+1$ from the velocity components and the pressure at time t. The Amsden–Harlow formulation of (7.54a) is now given, where, for brevity, $u^t(i+\alpha,j+\beta)$ is written as $u(\alpha,\beta)$ on the right-hand side although the time superscript, $t+1$, is retained on the left-hand side:

$$u^{t+1}\left(\frac{1}{2},0\right)=u\left(\frac{1}{2},0\right)-\Delta t\left[\frac{u(\frac{3}{2},0)u(\frac{1}{2},0)-u(\frac{1}{2},0)u(-\frac{1}{2},0)}{\Delta x}\right]$$

$$-\Delta t\left[\frac{\{u(\frac{1}{2},1)+u(\frac{1}{2},0)\}\{v(1,\frac{1}{2})+v(0,\frac{1}{2})\}-\{u(\frac{1}{2},-1)+u(\frac{1}{2},0)\}\{v(1,-\frac{1}{2})+v(0,-\frac{1}{2})\}}{4\Delta y}\right]$$

$$-\frac{\Delta t}{\rho\Delta x}[P(1,0)-P(0,0)]+v\Delta t\left[\frac{u(\frac{1}{2},1)-2u(\frac{1}{2},0)+u(\frac{1}{2},-1)}{(\Delta y)^2}\right]$$

$$-v\Delta t\left[\frac{v(1,\frac{1}{2})-v(1,-\frac{1}{2})-v(0,\frac{1}{2})+v(0,-\frac{1}{2})}{\Delta x\Delta y}\right].$$

(7.57)

This is a forward-difference equation giving $u^{t+1}(i+\frac{1}{2},j)$ from known values of u, v and P at time step t. Similar equations can be found for the other velocity components on the right-hand side of (7.55). If the values found for the right-hand side terms are substituted into (7.57) it will be found, in general, that D_0 is non-zero. The form of the equation giving D_0 at the advanced time is

$$D_0=F(u,v)-\frac{\Delta t}{\rho}\left[\frac{P(i+1,j)+P(i-1,j)-2P(i,j)}{\Delta x}\right.$$

$$\left.+\frac{P(i,j+1)+P(i,j-1)-2P(i,j)}{\Delta y}\right],$$

(7.58)

where $F(u,v)$ is a sum of the velocity component dependent part of (7.57) and those from three similar equations. The solution of the set of equations

$$\frac{P(i+1,j)+P(i-1,j)-2P(i,j)}{\Delta x}+\frac{P(i,j+1)+P(i,j-1)-2P(i,j)}{\Delta y}=\frac{\rho}{\Delta t}F(u,v)$$

(7.59)

determines the new pressures and ensures continual zero divergence of the velocity. These values of the pressure are then used to recalculate the velocities from (7.57).

In this method the time step is once again limited by a Courant–Friedrichs–Lewy condition. A safe condition is that if u_{max} and v_{max} are the greatest components of velocity for any cell, then

$$\Delta t\leqslant\frac{\Delta x}{(u_{max}^2+v_{max}^2)^{1/2}}$$

(7.60)

Because of the viscosity term another condition on the time step is involved:

$$\Delta t \leqslant \frac{(\Delta x)^2}{2v}, \tag{7.61}$$

and the more stringent of the time-step constraints is applied.

The pressure method enables the solution of problems in which the fluid is completely enclosed by fixed boundaries – for example, in a pipe. However, if there is a free boundary the method must be extended to take account of the surface and, in particular, it is necessary to identify the location of the interface.

7.11 The marker-and-cell method

This class of modelling problems concerns the way that liquids behave when there is a dynamic liquid–air interface – for example, the breaking of waves on a beach, the flow of water through a sluice-gate or the splash formed when a projectile falls into a liquid. It is necessary to add gravitational forces to the previously derived equation of hydrodynamics; modifying (7.47b) to include gravity, we have

$$\frac{\partial \mathbf{v}}{\partial t} + \mathbf{v} \cdot \nabla \mathbf{v} = -\frac{1}{\rho} \nabla P + v \nabla^2 \mathbf{v} + \mathbf{g}. \tag{7.62}$$

As a simplification, in some circumstances viscosity can be removed, especially where the liquid is water, for which the kinematic viscosity is comparatively small.

The objective of the marker-and-cell method is to define the surface of the fluid as it moves by means of marker particles. Initially marker particles are placed in Eulerian cells to define the space occupied by the fluid, which will include some cells which define the boundary of the fluid. Such a distribution of particles is shown in Fig. 7.16 for water in a sluice before the gate is opened. There are two types of boundary – first, where the fluid is in contact with the rigid walls of a container (fixed); and second, where the surface is in contact with the air (free). The fixed boundaries give boundary conditions on both pressure and velocity. If the wall is horizontal, then the pressure gradient normal to it is ρg. On the other hand, if the boundary wall is vertical then there is no pressure gradient normal to it. The general constraint which applies to horizontal walls, vertical walls or inclined walls is

$$\frac{1}{\rho} \nabla P \cdot \mathbf{n} = \mathbf{g} \cdot \mathbf{n}, \tag{7.63}$$

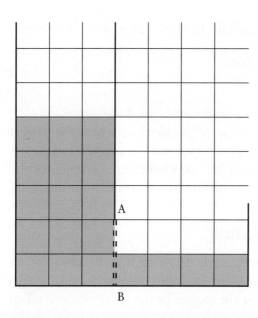

Fig. 7.16 A marker-and-cell configuration for a sluice-gate. When the gate is opened water moves from left to right.

where **n** is the unit normal to the wall. In the immediate vicinity of a rigid wall the velocity can only be parallel to the wall, and we shall indicate it by v_P. Two extreme assumptions can be made – the first (no-slip condition) that the fluid sticks to the wall so that $v_P = 0$; and the second that the fluid moves freely relative to the wall so that there is no drag on it and in the absence of viscosity $\partial v_P / \partial r = 0$ (r parallel to **n**). Intermediate assumptions are also possible.

The general approach in the marker-and-cell process is to solve for the motion of the fluid by the pressure method and to interpolate from the velocity components so found to move the individual particles. Dealing with boundary conditions at the surface is clearly an important part of this process, and for this we define a *surface cell* as one which contains marker particles but is in contact with an empty cell, which we call a *vacuum cell*. In two dimensions a surface cell may have one, two, three or four neighbouring vacuum cells, as shown in Fig. 7.17. The velocity of the fluid relative to the moving surface can only be parallel to the surface, and for this reason the velocity gradient perpendicular to the surface must be zero. This condition is approximately represented in Fig. 7.17a by the condition $v(i, j+\frac{1}{2}) = v(i, j-\frac{1}{2})$, although this really depends on the surface being truly horizontal. Similarly, with two neighbouring vacuum cells, as shown in Fig. 7.17b, the conditions are $v(i, j+\frac{1}{2}) = v(i, j-\frac{1}{2})$ and $u(i+\frac{1}{2}, j) = u(i-\frac{1}{2}, j)$. For the arrangement of vacuum cells in Fig. 7.17c

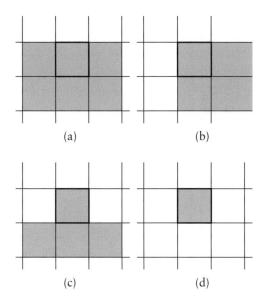

(a)   (b)

(c)   (d)

Fig. 7.17 Possible environments of a surface cell in two dimensions: (a) one neighbouring vacuum cell; (b) two neighbouring vacuum cells; (c) three neighbouring vacuum cells; (d) four neighbouring vacuum cells.

there are no horizontal accelerating forces on the cell, giving conditions $v(i, j+\tfrac{1}{2}) = v(i, j-\tfrac{1}{2})$, $u^{t+1}(i+\tfrac{1}{2}, j) = u^t(i+\tfrac{1}{2}, j)$ and $u^{t+1}(i-\tfrac{1}{2}, j) = u^t(i-\tfrac{1}{2}, j)$. Finally, for an isolated cell, as in Fig. 7.17d, there are no horizontal forces but there is an acceleration due to gravity in a veritcal direction, giving $u^{t+1}(i+\tfrac{1}{2}, j) = u^t(i+\tfrac{1}{2}, j)$ and $u^{t+1}(i-\tfrac{1}{2}, j) = u^t(i-\tfrac{1}{2}, j)$, together with $v^{t+1}(i, j+\tfrac{1}{2}) = v^t(i, j+\tfrac{1}{2}) + g\Delta t$ and $v^{t+1}(i, j-\tfrac{1}{2}) = v^t(i, j-\tfrac{1}{2}) + g\Delta t$. This method was pioneered by Harlow and coworkers, and Fig. 7.18 shows some results obtained by the method. A comparatively simple marker-and-cell program, MAC, is provided (see p. xv). Output from it, shown in Fig. 7.19, illustrates the opening of a sluice-gate where the gate is instantaneously removed and the block of water is suddenly released to move under gravitational forces. In the marker-and-cell method only the behaviour of the surface is indicated and the positions of marker particles within the body of the fluid are not indicative of fluid properties – for example, density. The case illustrated in Fig. 7.19 assumes free movement parallel to the walls of the enclosure. Since the calculation of components of the fluid velocity by (7.57) implies knowledge of velocities outside the rigid boundary, these hypothetical velocities can be provided by the boundary conditions. A useful way of visualizing this is to imagine that there are mirror fluid systems with common boundaries. Thus in Fig. 7.20 the mirror system A has mirror-image related points with horizontal components such that $U_A = -U$ and vertical

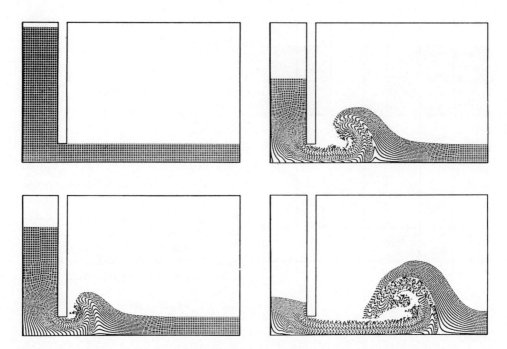

Fig. 7.18 Marker-and-cell simulation of water coming through a sluice gate (Harlow, Shannon, and Welch, 1965). © American Association for the Advancement of Science.

components such that $V_A = V$, with pressures related by $P_A = P$. For the mirror system B we similarly have $U_B = U$, $V_B = -V$, $P_B = P$, and in addition gravity is reversed so that $g_A = -g$. The operation of this symmetry will be seen in the listing of MAC.

7.12 Polytropic gases

For many applications in fluid mechanics an equation is required to determine the variation of pressure, and this comes from the equation of state. In general, this needs an equation – that for energy balance – to supply the second thermodynamic variable required to specify the state of the fluid. However, inviscid flow is without dissipation (frictionless) and the entropy of a fluid element is therefore constant, and therefore adiabatic equations of state can be used. For a so-called polytropic fluid this is of the form

$$P = K\rho^\gamma, \tag{7.64}$$

which is the equation for an adiabatic change of state of a gas where γ is the ratio of the specific heat of the gas at constant pressure to that at constant

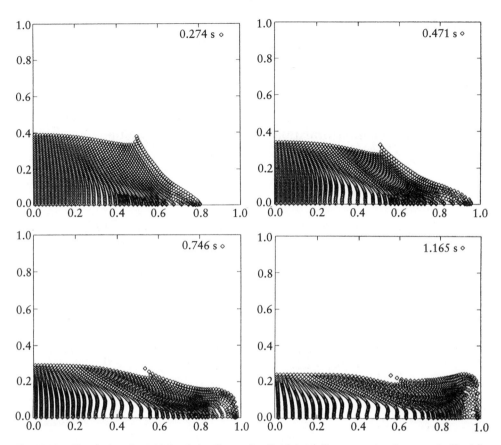

Fig. 7.19 Simulation by MAC of the flow of a fluid initially constrained to one half of the enclosure.

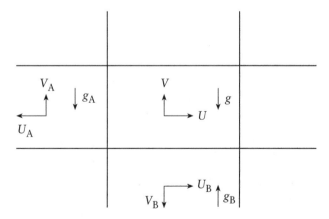

Fig. 7.20 The pattern of velocity components and gravity in mirror systems which give free movement of liquid parallel to boundaries.

volume. This condition is particularly easy to state in Lagrangian form, for the Lagrangian cell contains a fixed mass of gas for which

$$\frac{\mathrm{d}}{\mathrm{d}t}\left(\frac{P}{\rho^\gamma}\right)=0. \tag{7.65}$$

By now making the transformation to a Eulerian form, we find

$$\left\{\frac{\partial}{\partial t}+\mathbf{v}\cdot\nabla\right\}\left(\frac{P}{\rho^\gamma}\right)=0. \tag{7.66}$$

A more useful equation is found by combining (7.38b) and (7.66) in the form

$$\frac{P}{\rho^\gamma}\left\{\frac{\partial\rho}{\partial t}+\nabla\cdot(\rho\mathbf{v})\right\}+\rho\left(\frac{\partial}{\partial t}+\mathbf{v}\cdot\nabla\right)\left(\frac{P}{\rho^\gamma}\right)=0.$$

Regrouping the terms as

$$\left\{\frac{P}{\rho^\gamma}\frac{\partial\rho}{\partial t}+\rho\frac{\partial}{\partial t}\left(\frac{P}{\rho^\gamma}\right)\right\}+\left\{\frac{P}{\rho^\gamma}\nabla\cdot(\rho\mathbf{v})+\rho\mathbf{v}\cdot\nabla\left(\frac{P}{\rho^\gamma}\right)\right\}=0,$$

we find

$$\frac{\partial}{\partial t}\left(\rho\frac{P}{\rho^\gamma}\right)+\nabla\cdot\left(\rho\frac{P}{\rho^\gamma}\mathbf{v}\right)=0. \tag{7.67}$$

We now have three coupled partial differential equations involving density, velocity and pressure which, given initial boundary conditions, enable the behaviour of a fluid to be followed in time. Putting these together, in Eulerian form they are

$$\frac{\partial\rho}{\partial t}+\nabla\cdot(\rho\mathbf{v})=0, \tag{7.38b}$$

$$\frac{\partial(\rho\mathbf{v})}{\partial t}+(\rho\mathbf{v}\cdot\nabla)\mathbf{v}+(\nabla\cdot\rho\mathbf{v})\mathbf{v}+\nabla P=0 \tag{7.41b}$$

and

$$\frac{\partial}{\partial t}\left(\rho\frac{P}{\rho^\gamma}\right)+\nabla\cdot\left(\rho\frac{P}{\rho^\gamma}\mathbf{v}\right)=0. \tag{7.49}$$

7.13 The von Neumann–Richtmyer method for compressible fluids

The von Neumann–Richtmyer approach is a leapfrog finite-difference method which will be described here for systems which involve a single space coordinate, that is, for one dimension ($n=1$), two dimensions with cylindrical symmetry ($n=2$) or three dimensions with spherical symmetry ($n=3$). Cells are defined, as shown in Fig. 7.21 for one dimension, which cell edges at coordinates R_{i-2}, R_{i-1}, R_i, R_{i+1}, R_{i+2}, ... , along the x-axis, and a set of fluid particles are situated at the mid-points of the cells with coordinates $R_{i-3/2}$, $R_{i-1/2}$, $R_{i+1/2}$, $R_{i+3/2}$, ... The numerical algorithm follows the motions of these particles and finds the internal energy associated with them at every time step. The basic equations which are to be solved in a Lagrangian system for an inviscid compressible fluid are:

$$\frac{\partial \mathbf{R}}{\partial t} = \mathbf{u}, \tag{7.68}$$

$$\frac{\partial \mathbf{u}}{\partial t} = -\frac{1}{\rho}\nabla P \tag{7.45b}$$

and

$$\frac{d\varepsilon}{dt} = -P\frac{dV}{dt}, \tag{7.69}$$

where P, V and u are the pressure, specific volume ($=1/\rho$) and speed at the position, $\mathbf{R}$, of a fluid particle and ε is the specific internal energy, or internal energy per unit mass. Although (7.68) and (7.45b) have been written in vector form, for the systems we are considering there is only one non-zero component of the vectors concerned. Equation (7.69) is simply the first law of thermodynamics for an adiabatic change, which says that the change of energy $\delta\varepsilon$

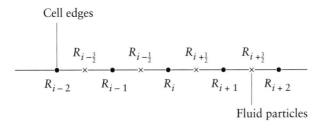

Fig. 7.21 The arrangement of cells and fluid particles for the von Neumann–Richtmyer algorithm.

equals the work done $(-P\delta V)$ on the gas. The equations are easily cast into a leapfrog finite-difference form by defining the spacial positions at time $j\Delta t$ and the velocity at intermediate time $(j-\frac{1}{2})\Delta t$ so that

$$R_{i+1/2}^{j+1} = R_{i+1/2}^{j} + u_{i+1/2}^{j+1/2}\Delta t, \tag{7.70}$$

where the superscripts indicate time, which is advanced in steps of Δt. We indicate as Δm_i the constant mass of material in a region bounded by $R_{i+1/2}$ and $R_{i-1/2}$ – if $n=1$, this is per unit area normal to the axis (planar geometry); if $n=2$, it is for the area defined by an angle of one radian perpendicular to the cylindrical axis and unit length along the axis (cylindrical geometry); and, if $n=3$, it is per steradian (spherical geometry). With n defining the appropriate geometry the following finite-difference expression is found for the specific volume:

$$V_i^{j+1} = \left\{ \left(R_{i+1/2}^{j+1} \right)^n - \left(R_{i-1/2}^{j+1} \right)^n \right\} \Big/ \Delta m_i. \tag{7.71}$$

The inverse of V_i^{j+1} gives ρ_i^{j+1} and from the equation of state, for a polytropic gas,

$$P = (\gamma - 1)\rho\varepsilon, \tag{7.72}$$

P_i^{j+1} can then be found. The specific internal energy at $(i, j+1)$ is found from a finite-difference form of (7.69) as

$$\varepsilon_i^{j+1} = \varepsilon_i^j - \tfrac{1}{2}(P_i^{j+1} + P_i^j)(V_i^{j+1} - V_i^j), \tag{7.73}$$

and finally, from (7.45b) with the appropriate form of Laplacian operator,

$$u_{i+1/2}^{j+3/2} = u_{i+1/2}^{j+1/2} - \frac{P_{i+1}^{j+1} - P_i^{j+1}}{\tfrac{1}{2}(\Delta m_i + \Delta m_{i+1})} \left(R_{i+1/2}^{j+1} \right)^{n-1} \Delta t. \tag{7.74}$$

This completes the leapfrog cycle and the value of $u_{i+1/2}^{j+3/2}$ goes into (7.70) to begin a new cycle.

The condition for stability of this leapfrog scheme is found to be

$$\frac{c_i^j \Delta t}{R_{i+1/2}^j - R_{i-1/2}^j} \leqslant 1 \tag{7.75}$$

for all (i, j), where

$$c_i^j = \sqrt{\gamma P_i^j V_i^j} \tag{7.76}$$

is the speed of sound in the fluid. This is the Courant–Friedrichs–Lewy condition for the stability of the von Neumann–Richtmyer method.

7.14 Artificial viscosity

In Section 7.4 the motion of a fluid was described in terms of a sum of wave motions of different wavelengths, and it is clear that for any mesh that is used the components of small wavelength will be less well defined. This is illustrated in Fig. 7.22. The wave represented in Fig. 7.22a has a wavelength covering four cells and the wave displacements on the mesh form the pattern 0, 1, 0, −1, 0, 1, ... Given that the energy per unit length associated with a point on the wave is proportional to the square of the displacement, then it is clear that the average energy per wavelength is 2 in our arbitrary units. If the wave is displaced on the grid as shown in Fig. 7.22b then the pattern of displacements is $2^{-1/2}, 2^{-1/2}, -2^{-1/2}, -2^{-1/2}, 2^{-1/2}, ...$ and the average energy per wavelength is the same. This component can be represented on our mesh without any energy dissipation. By contrast, we now consider a wave which covers two cells; in Fig. 7.22c the average energy per wavelength is 2 but if the wave is displaced (a phase shift) as in Fig. 7.22d then the energy per wavelength is zero. This illustrates that for systems where there are high gradients, the components of which are not well resolved by the grid, then

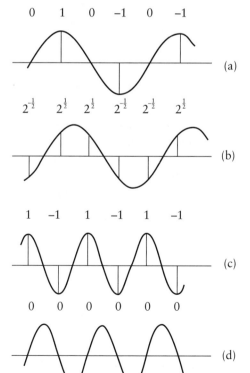

Fig. 7.22 When the wave in (a) is displaced as in (b) the mean intensity (displacement^2) at grid points remains constant. When the wave in (c) is displaced as in (d) the mean intensity at grid-points changes.

there will be energy dissipation. This manifests itself through the numerical algorithm being used, and with finite-difference schemes this depends on the number of terms present in the finite-difference equations from the Taylor expansions of the expressions being represented. The von Neumann–Richtmyer scheme has third-order accuracy, that is, it correctly represents the Taylor series (2.1) to four terms, and in general it is well behaved and gives little numerical energy dissipation.

A characteristic of many real fluid-dynamical systems, particulary where supersonic motions occur in compressible fluids, is the presence of shockfronts where density, pressure and temperature have such high gradients that they can be considered as *almost* discontinuous, although they do actually vary smoothly through the shocked region. In shock fronts entropy generation, or the transfer of energy of motion to thermal energy, is occurring. The processes that are causing this are on a molecular scale, both in space and time, and the macroscopic equations of fluid dynamics do not strictly apply on these scales. However, an accurate description of the discontinuity is obtained using fluid mechanics with viscosity and thermal conduction. In classical fluid dynamics entropy generation occurs due to the presence of viscosity or heat conduction. When viscosity is included in computational work, or if the algorithm contains numerical dissipation, then all transitions are smooth and continuous. However, the natural viscosity of a normal system is usually quite small and some algorithms, in particular that of von Neumann and Richtmyer, have little numerical dissipation, so if a shock is introduced into the calculation then large spurious oscillations occur on either side of the shock. To deal with this problem von Neumann and Richtmyer suggested the introduction of an artificial viscosity of such a form that the shock would be distributed over a few (typically three or four) grid intervals. By this device the numerical solution of the fluid dynamics equations could proceed normally and the shock, spread out over a few cells, would show the jump in conditions with about the correct magnitude and with the shockfront moving at about the correct speed.

A form of artificial dissipation suggested by von Neumann and Richtmyer is as an extra pressure term

$$q = \begin{cases} -\xi \rho (\Delta x)^2 \left(\dfrac{\mathrm{d}u}{\mathrm{d}x}\right)^2 & \dfrac{\mathrm{d}u}{\mathrm{d}x} < 0 \\[12pt] 0 & \dfrac{\mathrm{d}u}{\mathrm{d}x} \geq 0, \end{cases} \tag{7.77}$$

where, to obtain a suitable spread of the shockfront, ξ should be in the range 3.5–4, although trial and error may be required to find the best value. The form of (7.77) only gives entropy creation when the fluid is being compressed; in this form, where the viscosity is proportional to the square of the rate of change of strain (compression), the thickness of the shock is independent of the shock strength, which is an attractive feature.

The equations, including artificial viscosity, which must be solved where shocks are present are (7.68) and, in place of (7.45b) and (7.72),

$$\frac{d\mathbf{u}}{dt} = -\frac{1}{\rho}\nabla(P+q) \tag{7.78}$$

and

$$\frac{d\varepsilon}{dt} = -(P+q)\frac{dV}{dt}, \tag{7.79}$$

where q is given by (7.77). We shall now look at an application of the von Neumann and Richtmyer method with artificial viscosity included.

7.15 Blast-wave modelling

When atomic weapons were first introduced the efficiency of chain reactions was not well known and hence the energy yield of early tests could not be estimated. Actually a reasonable estimate of the energy can be made from the motion of the expanding front of the resultant fireball based on the hydro-dynamic theory of blast waves developed independently by Taylor in the UK and Sedov in Russia after the first atomic weapon tests in New Mexico in 1944. When unclassified photographs of the first test were available in 1947, Taylor applied his theory to give the first reasonably accurate estimate of the yield. While the analyses of Taylor and Sedov were quite complicated it is possible to derive the same information by matching the photographic infor-mation to the results of a numerical simulation.

The model looks at the hydrodynamic motion induced in a body of uniform density, ρ_0, by an instantaneous release of energy, of amount E_0, at a point, chosen as the origin, $r=0$. Gas near the origin is raised to a very high pressure and temperature which drives a shock wave into the undisturbed gas. The luminous front of the fireball, seen in the photographs, is identified with the shock wave. Behind the shock the gas expands and cools; such a flow is called a *blast wave*. The model is simplified by considering a polytropic gas with an equation of state given by (7.72) and with a constant value of $\gamma=1.4$ appropriate to air, which mainly consists of diatomic molecules. Actually, under the blast conditions the effective value of γ will change due to dissociation and ionization. The most serious deficiency of the model is the absence of radiation which, firstly, will remove energy from the system, and secondly, will also contribute in driving the shockfront.

A great deal may be learned about the system from dimensional analysis. The parameters which determine the radius r of the spherically expanding wave for a particular γ, which is dimensionless, are E_0, ρ_0 and t. The only dimensionless product which can be formed from these quantities is

$$\lambda = r \left(\frac{E_0}{\rho_0} \right)^{-1/5} t^{-2/5}. \tag{7.80}$$

The radius of the shock wave is thus given as a function of time by

$$r = \lambda_\gamma \left(\frac{E_0}{\rho_0} \right)^{1/5} t^{2/5}, \tag{7.81}$$

where λ must depend on γ, which controls the equation of state. Relationship (7.81) involves no arbitrary parameters and this system has the property of *self-similarity* which means that the same relationship will apply at all scales.

7.15.1 *A nuclear explosion program*

The program BLAST (see p. xv) applies the von Neumann–Richtmyer algorithm with artificial viscosity to this problem. A description of BLAST can be followed in a listing of the program. The flow is calculated in a polytropic gas of index GAMA and ambient density RHO. The energy, EIN, is deposited at $r = 0$ (J = 1) of a mesh of JM cells occupying a total width ROUT. The calculation can be performed in planar, cylindrical or spherical geometries (ID = 1, 2, 3, respectively). Also required as input data are the initial time step, DTIME, a total run time, TTIME, and an output interval, TOUT. The input data are provided by a file BLAST.DAT, and one particular set of input data is provided as an appendage to BLAST.FOR. The final output in a form suitable for printing is in BLAST.OUT, while up to ten other files, BLASTk.GRA (k = 0 to 9) give output information in a form suitable for a graphics package.

The program with the input data provided gives values of the radius of the shockfront, r, for various times, t. Figure 7.23 shows density as a function of distance for $t = 0$, 0.2, 0.4, 0.6 and 0.8 s for a run of BLAST with EIN = 1, RHO = 1, ROUT = 1.1, JM = 190 and GAMA = 1.4. The values of r estimated from the figure are 0.55, 0.72, 0.84 and 0.95, and the corresponding values of $r/t^{2/5}$ are 1.05, 1.04, 1.03 and 1.04 respectively, thus confirming the relationship

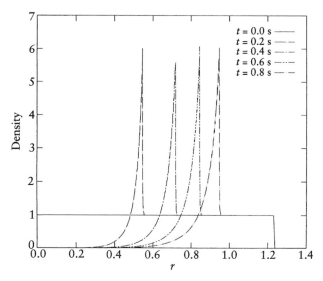

Fig. 7.23 Output from BLAST.

Table 7.1 Values of r and t from photographs of the New Mexico atomic bomb test.

t (ms)	r (m)	t (ms)	r (m)	t (ms)	r (m)
0.10	11.1	1.22	41.0	3.80	62.9
0.38	25.4	1.50	44.4	4.34	65.6
0.66	31.9	1.79	46.9	25.0	130.0
0.94	36.3	3.26	59.0	53.0	175.0

between r and t given by (7.81). Since E_0 and ρ_0 are both of unit value this is also the value of λ_γ. Table 7.1 gives a selection of values of r and t estimated from photographs of the New Mexico atomic bomb test. A plot of $\log r$ against $\log t$, with the exception of the first point, gives a good straight-line fit with a slope very close to 0.4, again confirming the relationship between r and t given in (7.81) for the actual explosion. From the self-similarity condition we may now express the energy in the real atomic bomb, E_b as

$$E_b = \frac{\rho_b}{\rho_0}\left(\frac{r_b^5}{t_b^2}\right)\left(\frac{t_0^2}{r_0^5}\right)E_0, \qquad (7.82)$$

where subscript b corresponds to atomic-test conditions and subscript 0 to computational modelling conditions. Using the values in the last entry in Table 7.1, $r_0/t_0^{2/5} = 1.04$ and the density of air $\rho_b = 1.25\,\text{kg m}^{-3}$, we find $E_b = 6.00 \times 10^{13}\,\text{J}$. It is customary to express the yields of atomic weapons in terms of the equivalent mass of the explosive TNT giving the same energy. From the conversion factor $1\,\text{kiloton} = 4.24 \times 10^{12}\,\text{J}$, the yield of the New Mexico test was somewhat over 14 kilotons.

In this particular case the theory of Taylor and Sedov enabled the yield to be obtained from analytical expressions but the analysis is very difficult. This atomic-test example is a good illustration of the way that computational methods can give the required answer in a simple way and, for other types of problem where no analysis was available, it may be the *only* way.

7.16   Multi-dimensional compressible flow

Most fluid dynamics simulation is concerned with the multi-dimensional flow of a compressible fluid – for example, in aerodynamics and plasma physics. The additional dimensions introduce severe complications to the simple von Neumann–Richtmyer algorithm discussed in Section 7.13. As a result, there are many different approaches appropriate for different problems. In this section we outline various classes of problems and sketch without detail the corresponding methods.

These methods split into two basic sets using either Eulerian or Lagrangian formulations of fluid mechanics. Eulerian techniques are much more widely used in multi-dimensional problems because of their general robustness and programming ease. They are usually based around some development of the Lax–Wendroff method with at least second-order accuracy to reduce numerical diffusion. Some form of artificial dissipation is used to control shock formation and to prevent the growth of high-order nonlinear instability. This can be achieved in one of two ways. Explicit artificial dissipation terms (as for the von Neumann–Richtmyer method) have been very successfully exploited by Jameson in programs designed for aeronautical simulation. Alternatively, the dissipation can be introduced implicitly by modifying the advection algorithm based on criteria required to ensure good physical behaviour. This has been successfully achieved in the schemes developed by van Leer and by Boris and Book. In such approaches the key is a sensitive application of strong dissipation controlled by the program itself, so that it is only applied when required and for most of the run a low-dissipation routine is used, thus ensuring little numerical diffusion. Phase errors can be reduced by introducing a measure of upstream differencing.

The very powerful and widely used Eulerian methods can handle both surface and open boundaries naturally. They may use a framework on which a large assembly of additional physics can be supported – for example, complex equations of state, chemical reactions under thermal equilibrium, thermal conduction, and heat release in explosions. This flexibility is enhanced by careful choice of the algorithm to maintain mass, momentum and energy conservation. They suffer from one major deficiency, an inability to treat contact surfaces, that is, material interfaces. Although methods to overcome this problem can be devised they are not entirely satisfactory. We note that this was the difficulty that led to the marker-in-cell adjunct to the pressure method.

Lagrangian methods, by following the fluid automatically, maintain contact surfaces. However, they suffer from major programming problems. The direct generalization of the von Neumann–Richtmyer method treats quadrilateral cells. Unfortunately these are subject to topological problems in shearing flow – for example, cells become pathological, resembling two triangles joined at a common apex instead of a rectangle in two dimensions, causing the program to fail. This can be prevented but makes the fluid 'stiff' by restricting shear. Instead of quadrilaterals we can use triangles which do not become pathological but may severely distort by becoming long and thin, so giving poor differencing. Triangles also give rise to mesh numbering problems for the programmer. The solution to these problems is to use free Lagrangian methods with no structure, only a set of Lagrangian points which can move freely. In this case the code starts to resemble a finite-element mesh and careful programming is essential to ensure efficient sorting routines in order to develop the necessary differencing relations. Despite the problems, multi-dimensional Lagrangian codes of all these types have been successfully constructed and used, although usually for specific tasks.

7.17 Smoothed particle hydrodynamics

Smoothed particle hydrodynamics (SPH) is a method developed by Lucy (1977) and Gingold and Monaghan (1977) which has been widely used for astrophysical problems. It is a free Lagrangian code where each particle represents one cell of the Lagrangian mesh but where the need to define the shapes of highly distorted cells does not arise. The ith particle has associated with it a mass m_i, velocity v_i, position r_i and a quantity of internal energy, u_i. At each point in the fluid being modelled the properties are a weighted average of properties contributed by neighbouring particles, with the weight function, called the *kernel* or *smoothing function*, monotonically decreasing with distance. The kernel is usually terminated at some distance and is a function of h, the *smoothing length*, which is a scale factor defining the range and standard deviation of the kernel. In an ideal situation it is desirable to have at least 20–30 particles contributing to the averaging process but the density of the fluid, and hence the number density of the particles, will be a function both of position and time so that the smoothing length is adjusted at each time step for each particle.

The kernel is a normalized function so that

$$\int W(\mathbf{r}, h)\, dV_r = 1, \tag{7.83}$$

where the integral is over the volume occupied by the kernel. As an example of its use, the density at point j in the fluid due to all the surrounding particles is given by

$$_s\rho_j = \sum_i m_i\, W(r_{i,j}, h) \tag{7.84}$$

where the pre-subscript s on the left-hand side indicates that it refers to a general point in space (which could be the position of a particle) and where $r_{i,j}$ is the distance from particle i to the point j. For the value of a general quantity, q, at point j we write

$$_sq_j = \sum_i \frac{m_i}{\rho_i} q_i\, W(r_{i,j}, h_i). \tag{7.85}$$

On the right-hand side ρ_i refers to the density at the point i and q_i the amount of property q associated with the point i. For example, the velocity of the material at point j is estimated as

$$\mathbf{v}_j = \sum_i \frac{m_i}{\rho_i} \mathbf{v}_i\, W(r_{i,j}, h_i). \tag{7.86}$$

Several analytical forms of kernel have been suggested, the necessary condition being that as $h \to 0$ the kernel should become a delta function and that it should also be differentiable. In their original work Gingold and Monaghan suggested a Gaussian form

$$W(r, h) = \left(\frac{1}{\pi h^2}\right)^{3/2} \exp\left(-\frac{r^2}{h^2}\right) \tag{7.87}$$

which was usually truncated when $r = 2h$, which slightly disturbed the normalization. In later work polynomial forms of kernel have been preferred.

The property of differentiability of the kernel is important when it comes to calculating quantities such as the divergence or gradient of some property at a point. As an example, if we want to find ∇q then we evaluate

$$\nabla q_j = \sum_i \frac{m_i}{\rho_i} q_i \nabla W(r_{i,j}, h_i). \tag{7.88}$$

On the other hand, if we wish to find $\nabla \cdot \mathbf{s}$, where $\mathbf{s}$ is a vector quantity, then we find

$$\nabla \cdot \mathbf{s} = \sum_i \frac{m_i}{\rho_i} \mathbf{s} \cdot \nabla W(r_{i,j}, h_i). \tag{7.89}$$

To deal with shocks, as previously explained, it is customary to introduce artificial viscosity which broadens the shocks to a width which is compatible with the distance between the particles and retains physically-plausible behaviour of the system. This is only necessary if the natural viscosity, as it appears in (7.47b), is too small to give the required effect.

Including contributions from gravitational forces, pressure gradients as given by (7.45b) and artificial viscosity, the equations of motion which have to be solved in the SPH process are

$$\frac{\mathrm{d}\mathbf{r}_j}{\mathrm{d}t} = \mathbf{v}_j \tag{7.90a}$$

and

$$\frac{\mathrm{d}\mathbf{v}_j}{\mathrm{d}t} = -\nabla \phi_j - \frac{1}{\rho_j} \nabla P_j + v_j^{\mathrm{a}}, \tag{7.90b}$$

where ϕ_j is the gravitational potential, P the pressure, ρ the density and v_j^{a} the artificial viscocity at the position of particle j.

If the contribution to the force on particle j due to particle i is not equal and opposite to the contribution of the force on particle i due to particle j there will be consequent non-conservation of linear and angular momentum. For this reason a symmetric form of the pressure-gradient term is used. Artificial viscosity is usually incorporated in the pressure term and a common form of pressure plus artificial viscosity, which preserves symmetry, is

$$\sum_i m_i \left(\frac{P_j}{\rho_j^2} + \frac{P_i}{\rho_i^2} + \Pi_{i,j} \right) \nabla W \left(r_{i,j}, \frac{h_i + h_j}{2} \right). \tag{7.91}$$

In (7.91)

$$\Pi_{i,j} = \begin{cases} \dfrac{-\alpha \bar{c}_{i,j} \mu_{i,j} + \beta \mu_{i,j}^2}{\bar{\rho}_{i,j}} & \mathbf{v}_{i,j} \cdot \mathbf{r}_{i,j} \leqslant 0 \\ 0 & \mathbf{v}_{i,j} \cdot \mathbf{r}_{i,j} > 0, \end{cases} \tag{7.92a}$$

where

$$\mu_{i,j} = \frac{\bar{h}_{i,j} \mathbf{v}_{i,j} \cdot r_{i,j}}{\mathbf{r}_{i,j}^2 + \eta^2}, \tag{7.92b}$$

$\bar{c}_{i,j}$, $\bar{\rho}_{i,j}$ and $\bar{h}_{i,j}$ are the means of the sound speeds, densities and smoothing lengths at the positions of the particles i and j, the numerical factors α and β are usually taken as 1 and 2 respectively, and $\eta^2 \sim 0.01\, \bar{h}_{i,j}^2$ is included to prevent numerical divergences.

The gravitational potential at the position of particle j due to the surrounding points cannot best be simulated by point-mass gravitational effects because each particle actually represents a distribution of matter. A common way of handling this has been by using a form such as

$$\phi_j = -\sum_i \frac{Gm_i}{(r^2 + \gamma^2)^{1/2}},\tag{7.93}$$

although more complex forms have also been used.

All the components are now in place to be inserted in (7.90b) and it only remains to consider the change in the internal energy associated with each particle. For a polytropic gas as defined in (7.46), the equation of state is given by (7.72)

$$P = (\gamma - 1)\rho\varepsilon,\tag{7.72}$$

where ε is the specific internal energy. The internal energy is changed by compression of the gas and by viscous dissipation. The rate of change in specific internal energy associated with particle j is given by

$$\frac{d\varepsilon_j}{dt} = \sum_i \frac{1}{2}m_i\left(\frac{P_j}{\rho_j^2} + \frac{P_i}{\rho_i^2} + \Pi_{i,j}\right)\mathbf{v}_{i,j} \cdot \nabla W\left(r_{i,j}, \frac{h_i + h_j}{2}\right).\tag{7.94}$$

From the density and internal energy the pressure can be found from (7.72) and then the temperature can be found from

$$P = \frac{\rho k\theta}{\mu},\tag{7.95}$$

where μ is the mean molecular mass of the material being modelled.

Jeans (1919) proposed a tidal theory for the origin of the solar system. In this theory a massive star pulled a filament of matter from the Sun and condensations in the filament gave rise to a family of planets. Jeans showed that a filament of density ρ would be gravitationally unstable and break up into a series of condensations. If the mass of gas in each condensation exceeds a certain critical mass related to the density and temperature of the material, then gravity would cause it to collapse to form a planet – otherwise it would dissipate. The instability of a filament under gravity was modelled by Coates (1980) using an SPH procedure. His result, shown in Fig. 7.24, illustrates the validity of the Jeans analysis which predicts break-up into five condensations.

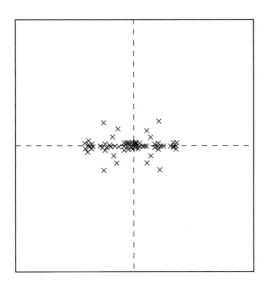

Fig. 7.24 Fragmentation of a filament modelled by SPH (Coates, 1980).

SPH is a good example of a free-zoning Lagrangian system which works very well in practice and does give very good simulations of the behaviour of astrophysical systems, although it does not have general application.

Problems

7.1 Modify the program ADVDIF to run in the mode using equation (7.8) for advection plus diffusion. With constant Courant number 0.5, diffusion coefficient $0.05 \, \mathrm{m^2 \, s^{-1}}$ and velocity $0.5 \, \mathrm{m \, s^{-1}}$ study the diffusion of a triangular distribution centred on $x = 8.0 \, \mathrm{m}$ with half-width $2.4 \, \mathrm{m}$ for a period of $12 \, \mathrm{s}$ with (i) $\Delta x = 0.8 \, \mathrm{m}$, (ii) $\Delta x = 0.4 \, \mathrm{m}$ and (iii) $\Delta x = 0.2 \, \mathrm{m}$. Compare plots of the distribution after $12 \, \mathrm{s}$ for the three conditions. Consider the stability of the computation in the light of the value of $C + 2r$.

7.2 Modify ADVDIF to run in the Lax–Wendroff mode for advection alone. Setting $v = 0.5 \, \mathrm{m \, s^{-1}}$ and $\Delta x = 1.0 \, \mathrm{m}$, plot the final configurations after $792 \, \mathrm{s}$ of a triangular distribution centred on $x = 4.0 \, \mathrm{m}$ with half-width $3.0 \, \mathrm{m}$ for (i) $C = 0.8$, (ii) $C = 0.9$ and (iii) $C = 1.0$.

7.3 Modify ADVDIF to run Problem 7.2 with ADVDIF in the QUICKEST mode. Confirm that, without diffusion, so that $r = 0$, the process is unstable for $C > 1.0$.

7.4 With ADVDIF in the QUICKEST mode, study the behaviour of a 'top-hat' distribution after $120 \, \mathrm{s}$ with $v = 0.5 \, \mathrm{m \, s^{-1}}$, $D = 0.15 \, \mathrm{m^2 \, s^{-1}}$ and

$\Delta x = 1.0\,\text{m}$. The distribution is defined by

$$q = \begin{cases} 1 & 10\,\text{m} \leqslant x \leqslant 16\,\text{m} \\ 0 & \text{otherwise.} \end{cases}$$

Run with values of C from 0.4 to 1.2 in steps of 0.2 and plot the final distribution. Calculate values of r corresponding to each value of C and confirm from Fig. 7.12 that the process should be stable in each case.

7.5 Modify the program MAC so that in the ranges $0 \leqslant x \leqslant 0.25\,\text{m}$ and $0.75 \leqslant x \leqslant 1.00\,\text{m}$ the fluid is initially at height $0.45\,\text{m}$ and elsewhere in the range is at a height of $0.15\,\text{m}$. Find the form of the fluid surface at various stages up to 64 iterations of the program.

7.6 By modifying the data file BLAST.DAT run the program BLAST with values of $\gamma = 1.1$, 1.2, 1.3, 1.4 and 1.5. The output file BLAST.OUT, which can be read in editing mode, gives the radius of the blast front at intervals of $0.1\,\text{s}$ up to $1.0\,\text{s}$. From this information estimate the values of λ_γ (7.81) for each value of γ and plot the results.

Appendices

Appendices

1 The elements of matrix algebra

We give here a very brief account of matrices, sufficient to explain the concepts of *eigenvalues* and *eigenvectors* which occur frequently in scientific theory. Fuller accounts will be found in standard mathematical texts.

A *matrix* is a rectangular array of quantities arranged in rows and columns with the convention that an $m \times n$ matrix has m rows and n columns. In practice the individual quantities, the *elements* of the matrix, with which we shall be concerned, are numbers although they can also be other kinds of quantity, such as partial derivatives. The 5×4 matrix $\mathbf{A}$ represents the array of elements

$$
\mathbf{A} = \begin{bmatrix}
a_{11} & a_{12} & a_{13} & a_{14} \\
a_{21} & a_{22} & a_{23} & a_{24} \\
a_{31} & a_{32} & a_{33} & a_{34} \\
a_{41} & a_{42} & a_{43} & a_{44} \\
a_{51} & a_{52} & a_{53} & a_{54}
\end{bmatrix}. \tag{A1.1}
$$

A special kind of matrix is a *vector*, which has either one row or one column. Thus we may have the *column vector*

$$
\mathbf{b} = \begin{bmatrix}
b_1 \\
b_2 \\
b_3 \\
b_4
\end{bmatrix} \tag{A1.2}
$$

and the *row vector*

$$
\mathbf{b}^{\mathrm{T}} = [b_1 \quad b_2 \quad b_3 \quad b_4]. \tag{A1.3}
$$

The relationship between $\mathbf{b}$ and $\mathbf{b}^{\mathrm{T}}$ is that each is the *transpose* of the other – that is, their rows and columns have been interchanged.

Matrices may be added or subtracted if they are of the same dimensions (have the same numbers of rows and columns); thus, if

$$
\mathbf{C} = \mathbf{A} \pm \mathbf{B}
$$

then

$$
c_{ij} = a_{ij} \pm b_{ij}. \tag{A1.4}
$$

It is also possible to take a product of matrices, written as

$$C = AB,$$

but the rule for the dimensions here is that the number of columns of A must equal the number of rows of B. The product of an $m \times n$ matrix with an $n \times p$ matrix is an $m \times p$ matrix. The individual elements of C are obtained from those of A and B by

$$c_{ij} = \sum_{k=1}^{n} a_{ik} b_{kj}. \tag{A1.5}$$

As an example,

$$\begin{bmatrix} 1 & -1 & 0 & 2 \\ 3 & -2 & 1 & 1 \\ 0 & 1 & 1 & -2 \end{bmatrix} \begin{bmatrix} 1 & 1 \\ -1 & 2 \\ 0 & 3 \\ 1 & -1 \end{bmatrix} = \begin{bmatrix} 4 & -3 \\ 6 & 1 \\ -3 & 7 \end{bmatrix}.$$

Square matrices, in which the number of rows equals the number of columns, play an important role in scientific theory. Valid products of such matrices can be taken in either order but, in general, they do not *commute*, which is to say that

$$AB \neq BA.$$

There are a number of special types of square matrix. Two such are the *diagonal* matrix, which has non-zero elements only along the principal diagonal, and the *unit* or *identity* matrix, usually indicated by I, which is a diagonal matrix in which each diagonal element equals unity. We show a general diagonal matrix and a unit matrix:

$$D = \begin{bmatrix} 1 & 0 & 0 & 0 \\ 0 & -1 & 0 & 0 \\ 0 & 0 & 3 & 0 \\ 0 & 0 & 0 & 2 \end{bmatrix}, \quad I = \begin{bmatrix} 1 & 0 & 0 & 0 \\ 0 & 1 & 0 & 0 \\ 0 & 0 & 1 & 0 \\ 0 & 0 & 0 & 1 \end{bmatrix}. \tag{A1.6}$$

The unit matrix has the property that it commutes with any other square matrix of the same dimension, so that

$$AI = IA. \tag{A1.7}$$

The unit matrix also gives a way of defining the *inverse* matrix of A, A^{-1}, by the relationship

$$AA^{-1} = A^{-1}A = I. \tag{A1.8}$$

It is possible to represent a set of linear equations in matrix form as

$$Ax = b. \tag{A1.9}$$

As an example,

$$\begin{bmatrix} 1 & -1 & 2 \\ 2 & -4 & 1 \\ 3 & 1 & 1 \end{bmatrix} \begin{bmatrix} x_1 \\ x_2 \\ x_3 \end{bmatrix} = \begin{bmatrix} 1 \\ 4 \\ -2 \end{bmatrix}$$

is equivalent to the set of equations

$$x_1 - x_2 + 2x_3 = 1$$

$$2x_1 - 4x_2 + x_3 = 4$$

$$3x_1 + x_2 + x_3 = -2.$$

Matrices may be treated algebraically, giving rise to the branch of mathematics called *matrix algebra* and, in the notation of that subject, (A1.9) may be manipulated to give

$$\mathbf{A}^{-1}\mathbf{A}\mathbf{x} = \mathbf{A}^{-1}\mathbf{b},$$

giving, from (A1.8),

$$\mathbf{I}\mathbf{x} = \mathbf{A}^{-1}\mathbf{b}.$$

Multiplying any matrix or vector by the unit vector leaves it unchanged, so the solution of the equations is

$$\mathbf{x} = \mathbf{A}^{-1}\mathbf{b}. \tag{A1.10}$$

Another important quantity is the *determinant* of a square matrix, written as

$$\det \mathbf{A} = |\mathbf{A}| = \begin{vmatrix} a_{11} & a_{12} & a_{13} \\ a_{21} & a_{22} & a_{23} \\ a_{31} & a_{32} & a_{33} \end{vmatrix}. \tag{A1.11}$$

The value of a determinant is a number which comes from a sum of terms involving products $a_{1j_1}a_{2j_2}a_{3j_3}$, where the first subscripts are in numerical order and j_1, j_2 and j_3 are the integers 1, 2 and 3 in all possible orders. In this case there are six possible combinations of j_1, j_2 and j_3 and, in general, for a determinant of dimension n, there would be $n!$ terms in the summation. The general form is given by

$$|\mathbf{A}| = \sum_{n!} \varepsilon_{j_1 j_2 \ldots j_n} a_{1j_1} a_{1j_2} \ldots a_{1j_n}. \tag{A1.12}$$

The values of ε are either $+1$ or -1 according to the following rule. If it takes an even number of interchanges of pairs of terms in $j_1 j_2 \ldots j_n$ to produce the natural order $1\,2 \ldots n$, then ε is $+1$. If it takes an odd number of interchanges then ε is -1. Thus, $3\,1\,2$ in one interchange gives $1\,3\,2$, and a second interchange gives $1\,2\,3$ – hence $\varepsilon_{312} = +1$. Similarly, $\varepsilon_{321} = -1$.

An important property of a determinant is that if the rows (or columns) of the matrix are linearly dependent, which means that any one row (or column) is equal to some linear combination of the others, then the value of the determinant is zero. A matrix, the determinant of which is zero, is referred to as a *singular* matrix.

Any square matrix, $\mathbf{A}$, will have associated with it a set of *eigenvalues*, λ_i, each with an associated *eigenvector*, $\mathbf{x}_i$, giving the relationship

$$\mathbf{A}\mathbf{x}_i = \lambda_i \mathbf{x}_i. \tag{A1.13}$$

However, since

$$\mathbf{I}\mathbf{x} = \begin{bmatrix} 1 & 0 & 0 & 0 & 0 & 0 & 0 \\ 0 & 1 & 0 & 0 & 0 & 0 & 0 \\ \cdot & \cdot & \cdot & \cdot & \cdot & \cdot & \cdot \\ \cdot & \cdot & \cdot & \cdot & \cdot & \cdot & \cdot \\ \cdot & \cdot & \cdot & \cdot & \cdot & \cdot & \cdot \\ \cdot & \cdot & \cdot & \cdot & \cdot & \cdot & \cdot \\ 0 & 0 & 0 & 0 & 0 & 0 & 1 \end{bmatrix} \begin{bmatrix} x_1 \\ x_2 \\ \cdot \\ \cdot \\ \cdot \\ \cdot \\ x_n \end{bmatrix} = \begin{bmatrix} x_1 \\ x_2 \\ \cdot \\ \cdot \\ \cdot \\ \cdot \\ x_n \end{bmatrix} = \mathbf{x}, \tag{A1.14}$$

then we may write a revised form of (A1.13), without suffixes, as

$$(\mathbf{A} - \lambda\mathbf{I})\mathbf{x} = 0, \tag{A1.15}$$

where 0 is the *null vector* which has all elements equal to zero. It should be noted that the bracketed quantity involves the difference of two matrices of the same dimensions and so is a valid matrix of form

$$\mathbf{A} - \lambda\mathbf{I} = \begin{bmatrix} a_{11} & a_{12} & \cdot & \cdot & \cdot & \cdot & a_{1n} \\ a_{21} & a_{22} & \cdot & \cdot & \cdot & \cdot & a_{2n} \\ \cdot & \cdot & \cdot & \cdot & \cdot & \cdot & \cdot \\ \cdot & \cdot & \cdot & \cdot & \cdot & \cdot & \cdot \\ \cdot & \cdot & \cdot & \cdot & \cdot & \cdot & \cdot \\ a_{n1} & a_{n2} & \cdot & \cdot & \cdot & \cdot & a_{nn} \end{bmatrix} - \begin{bmatrix} \lambda & 0 & \cdot & \cdot & \cdot & \cdot & 0 \\ 0 & \lambda & \cdot & \cdot & \cdot & \cdot & 0 \\ \cdot & \cdot & \cdot & \cdot & \cdot & \cdot & \cdot \\ \cdot & \cdot & \cdot & \cdot & \cdot & \cdot & \cdot \\ \cdot & \cdot & \cdot & \cdot & \cdot & \cdot & \cdot \\ 0 & 0 & \cdot & \cdot & \cdot & \cdot & \lambda \end{bmatrix}$$

$$= \begin{bmatrix} a_{11} - \lambda & a_{12} & \cdot & \cdot & \cdot & \cdot & a_{1n} \\ a_{21} & a_{22} - \lambda & \cdot & \cdot & \cdot & \cdot & a_{2n} \\ \cdot & \cdot & \cdot & \cdot & \cdot & \cdot & \cdot \\ \cdot & \cdot & \cdot & \cdot & \cdot & \cdot & \cdot \\ \cdot & \cdot & \cdot & \cdot & \cdot & \cdot & \cdot \\ a_{n1} & a_{n2} & \cdot & \cdot & \cdot & \cdot & a_{nn} - \lambda \end{bmatrix}. \tag{A1.16}$$

The relationship (A1.15) is equivalent to a set of *linear homogeneous* equations involving the elements of $\mathbf{x}$, meaning that they are linear equations for which the right-hand-side vector, $\mathbf{b}$, in (A1.9) has all elements zero. A trivial solution to all such equations is that $\mathbf{x}=0$ or that all the elements of the solution vector are zero. This solution is not usually of much interest if the problem is a scientific one but is the only solution in the general case. However, other solutions are possible if the matrix $\mathbf{A}$ is singular, which means that its determinant is zero and that its rows are linearly dependent. We shall illustrate this with the following numerical example:

$$3x_1 - 2x_2 - 4x_3 = 0$$

$$x_1 - x_2 - x_3 = 0 \qquad\qquad (A1.17)$$

$$4x_1 - 3x_2 - 5x_3 = 0.$$

Since the third equation is just the sum of the first two equations it may be discarded and the remaining two equations written as

$$3z_1 - 2z_2 = 4$$

$$z_1 - z_2 = 1,$$

where $z_1 = x_1/x_3$ and $z_2 = x_2/x_3$. The solution of these equations is $z_1 = 2$, $z_2 = 1$ or

$$x_1 = 2x_3, \qquad x_2 = x_3$$

but x_3 can have any value. Thus there are an infinite number of solutions of equations (A1.17), but the relative values of x_1, x_2 and x_3 are the same for all of them.

On this basis, for (A1.15) we can get non-null solutions for the eigenvectors under the condition

$$|\mathbf{A} - \lambda\mathbf{I}| = 0, \qquad\qquad (A1.18)$$

and the form of $\mathbf{A} - \lambda\mathbf{I}$ seen in (A1.16) shows that the left-hand side of (A1.18) is a polynomial of degree n in λ. This will have n different solutions for λ, each of which will be an eigenvalue, and each value of λ, substituted in (A1.15), will give a different eigenvector. As the solution of (A1.17) shows, an eigenvector is characterized by the ratios of its elements and an eigenvector multiplied by an arbitrary constant is still the same eigenvector. This property is evident from (A1.13), where the eigenvector was introduced.

There are various standard computer programs available for finding the eigenvalues and eigenvectors of a matrix. There is a simple way of finding the *principal* eigenvalue, the eigenvalue of greatest magnitude. This consists of

Table A1.1 The effect of repeatedly multiplying a vector, initially with unit elements, by the matrix **A** in (A1.19).

Cycle	Elements of vector		
0	1.000	1.000	1.000
1	3.000	1.000	1.000
2	5.000	5.000	3.000
3	11.000	5.000	7.000
⋮			
49	4.174×10^{15}	2.719×10^{15}	2.245×10^{15}
50	8.665×10^{15}	5.629×10^{15}	4.648×10^{15}
51	1.796×10^{16}	1.170×10^{16}	9.646×10^{15}

taking an arbitrary vector **r** (say, one with all unit elements), and repeatedly pre-multiplying it by the matrix. Eventually each new vector will just be some constant times the previous vector; at this stage the vector is the principal eigenvector and the constant is the principal eigenvalue. As an example of this process we take the matrix

$$\mathbf{A} = \begin{bmatrix} 1 & 0 & 2 \\ 2 & -1 & 0 \\ 1 & 1 & -1 \end{bmatrix} \tag{A1.19}$$

and an initial vector with all unit elements. The effect of multiplying this vector repeatedly by **A** is shown in Table A1.1 for the first few cycles and then for cycles 49, 50 and 51. For the final three cycles the ratio of the elements is almost, but not quite, constant and the eigenvalue is somewhere between 2.07 and 2.08. The elements of the eigenvectors could be renormalized to keep them as smaller numbers but, since we are interested in the ratios of elements from successive cycles, this has not been done.

This short treatment of matrices, eigenvalues and eigenvectors is by no means complete but may be helpful to those for whom the material is new and an aid to memory to those who have met it previously.

2 A simple conjugate-gradient method

The conjugate-gradient method is an efficient approach to the solution of a set of linear equations $\mathbf{Ax} = \mathbf{b}$ when the square matrix $\mathbf{A}$, of dimension N, is sparse – that is, has many fewer than N^2 non-zero elements. A straightforward solution is given by (A1.10) but the number of operations required to find $\mathbf{A}^{-1}$ is of order N^3, and that is true even for a sparse matrix since $\mathbf{A}^{-1}$ is dense.

In the conjugate-gradient method the problem of solving the set of linear equations is transformed into the minimization of the function

$$g(\mathbf{x}) = \frac{1}{2}|\mathbf{Ax} - \mathbf{b}|^2, \tag{A2.1}$$

which is clearly a minimum (zero) for the required solution vector. A straightforward mathematical procedure is illustrated in two dimensions in Fig. A2.1 which shows contours for a function of two variables $f(x_1, x_2)$. Starting at the point P, the goal is to reach the minimum of the function at point O. The first step is to move in the direction of the greatest rate of change of f, which is perpendicular to the contours – that is, in the direction of ∇f. The move is in the direction in which f decreases and up to the point Q, which corresponds to the minimum value of f along the line. At point Q this procedure is repeated to give point R, and so on until the minimum is reached or a point sufficiently close to the minimum for the purpose in hand. We shall now translate this *steepest-descent process* into a mathematical form by dealing with a specific 2×2 matrix from which we can derive the general formulation.

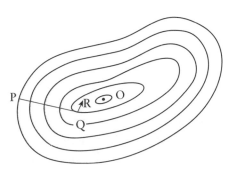

Fig. A2.1 A graphical illustration of the conjugate gradient method.

The equations we are considering are

$$\begin{bmatrix} a_{11} & a_{12} \\ a_{21} & a_{22} \end{bmatrix}\begin{bmatrix} x_1 \\ x_2 \end{bmatrix} = \begin{bmatrix} b_1 \\ b_2 \end{bmatrix}, \tag{A2.2}$$

so the function being minimized is

$$f(x_1, x_2) = \tfrac{1}{2}\{(a_{11}x_1 + a_{12}x_2 - b_1)^2 + (a_{21}x_1 + a_{22}x_2 - b_2)^2\}. \tag{A2.3}$$

The components of ∇f are $\partial f/\partial x_1$ and $\partial f/\partial x_2$, so that a vector in the direction of ∇f is

$$\mathbf{u} = \nabla f = \begin{bmatrix} a_{11}(a_{11}x_1 + a_{12}x_2 - b_1) + a_{21}(a_{21}x_1 + a_{22}x_2 - b_2) \\ a_{12}(a_{11}x_1 + a_{12}x_2 - b_1) + a_{22}(a_{21}x_1 + a_{22}x_2 - b_2) \end{bmatrix}$$

$$= \mathbf{A}^{\mathrm{T}}(\mathbf{A}\mathbf{x} - \mathbf{b}). \tag{A2.4}$$

We now seek a scalar quantity λ such that $f(\mathbf{x} + \lambda\mathbf{u})$ is a minimum, which will be so when

$$\frac{\mathrm{d}}{\mathrm{d}\lambda}\left(\frac{1}{2}\left[\{a_{11}(x_1 + \lambda u_1) + a_{12}(x_2 + \lambda u_2) - b_1\}^2 \right.\right.$$

$$\left.\left. + \{a_{21}(x_1 + \lambda u_1) + a_{22}(x_2 + \lambda u_2) - b_2\}^2\right]\right) = 0.$$

This gives

$$\lambda = \frac{(a_{11}u_1 + a_{12}u_2)(a_{11}x_1 + a_{12}x_2 - b_1) + (a_{21}u_1 + a_{22}u_2)(a_{21}x_1 + a_{22}x_2 - b_2)}{(a_{11}u_1 + a_{12}u_2)^2 + (a_{21}u_1 + a_{22}u_2)^2}$$

$$= -\frac{(\mathbf{A}\mathbf{u})^{\mathrm{T}} \cdot (\mathbf{A}\mathbf{x} - \mathbf{b})}{|\mathbf{A}\mathbf{u}|^2}. \tag{A2.5}$$

Moving to $\mathbf{x} + \lambda\mathbf{u}$ is equivalent to making one step, say from P to Q, in Fig. A2.1. The process converges at a rate which depends on how well conditioned the system is and may be stopped when successive iterations differ by less than some given tolerance.

Looking at the vector forms of (A2.4) and (A2.5), it is seen that one iteration requires three products of either $\mathbf{A}$ or $\mathbf{A}^{\mathrm{T}}$ with a vector and one scalar product of two vectors, and that no matrix inversion is required. If the matrices are sparse then by efficient programming only products with non-zero elements are computed so that the number of operations required for a complete solution is a few times the product of the number of non-zero elements with the number of iterations. For large N this will be considerably less than the $O(N^3)$ operations required for the direct one-step solution (A1.10).

The simple conjugate process described here is comparatively inefficient. If the multi-dimensional surfaces of constant g around the solution point give a long narrow valley configuration then successive steepest-gradient steps may be very short and very slowly move towards the required minimum. To overcome this, a number of pre-conditioning techniques can be applied. These use either an approximate solution to start the iteration or, more commonly, modify the matrix to a form which converges rapidly. One very effective way of increasing the efficiency involves finding an approximate inverse of the matrix $\mathbf{A}$, $\tilde{\mathbf{A}}^{-1}$, with a sparse form – typically that of the matrix $\mathbf{A}$. By pre-multiplying both sides of the original equation by $\tilde{\mathbf{A}}^{-1}$ the equations to be solved by the conjugate gradient method are $\tilde{\mathbf{A}}^{-1}\mathbf{A}\mathbf{x} = \tilde{\mathbf{A}}^{-1}\mathbf{b}$ which, since $\tilde{\mathbf{A}}^{-1}\mathbf{A}$ is nearly the identity matrix, converges very quickly. Other efficient approaches, with programs, that involve movements in the n-space in directions other than along ∇g, are given in Press *et al.* (1986). These approaches can be much faster than the one described here.

Even the simple approach involving (A2.4) and (A2.5) is significantly more efficient for a sparse-matrix problem than methods which use the equivalent of matrix inversion. In a test involving 1000 equations and 5000 non-zero matrix elements, the matrix inversion approach took 920 s to reach a solution on a Pentium 166 MHz PC. The simple conjugate-gradient approach, as described here, with a required precision of 0.001 in the determination of each element of the solution vector (elements of order unity) took about 2 s – nearly 500 times faster. However, if greater precision had been required the advantage factor would have been less. In another test, with 2000 equations and 10 000 non-zero matrix elements which could not be tackled on the PC because of limited RAM, the simple conjugate-gradient approach took 3.4 s while a pre-conditioning procedure which modified the matrix $\mathbf{A}$ led to a solution in 7.5 ms. This indicates the importance of using the best available procedures which can make a difference in timing of several orders of magnitude.

The program CONJUG (see p. xv) solves a set of up to 2000 linear equations where the left-hand-side sparse matrix has a particular five-banded structure which occurs in some kinds of finite-difference problems. Also available is CHOLESKY (see p. xv), which requires the supplied subroutine ICCG, which solves the same equations after they have been pre-conditioned. The much greater efficiency of the pre-conditioned algorithm may be confirmed by experiments with these programs.

3 *The virial theorem*

The virial theorem applies to any system of particles with pair conservative interactions for which the total volume of space occupied by the system is constant. This states that

$$2T+\Omega=0, \tag{A3.1}$$

where T is the translational kinetic energy and Ω is the potential energy. We shall demonstrate the validity of the theorem for a system of gravitationally-interacting bodies.

We consider a system of N bodies for which the ith has mass m_i, coordinates (x_i, y_i, z_i) and velocity components (u_i, v_i, w_i). We define the *geometrical moment of inertia* as

$$I=\sum_{i=1}^{N}m_i(x_i^2+y_i^2+z_i^2). \tag{A3.2}$$

Differentiating I twice with respect to time and dividing by 2, we obtain

$$\frac{1}{2}\ddot{I}=\sum_{i=1}^{N}m_i(\dot{x}_i^2+\dot{y}_i^2+\dot{z}_i^2)+\sum_{i=1}^{N}m_i(x_i\ddot{x}_i+y_i\ddot{y}_i+z_i\ddot{z}_i). \tag{A3.3}$$

The first term is $2T$; the second can be transformed by noting that $m_i\ddot{x}_i$ is the total force on body i in the x direction due to all the other particles, or

$$m_ix_i\ddot{x}_i=\sum_{\substack{j=1\\j\neq i}}^{N}Gm_im_j\frac{x_i(x_j-x_i)}{r_{i,j}^3}. \tag{A3.4}$$

Combining the contributions of the force on i due to j and the force on j due to i, we find, for the second term on the right-hand side of (A3.3),

$$\sum_{i=1}^{N}m_i(x_i\ddot{x}_i+y_i\ddot{y}_i+z_i\ddot{z}_i)=-\sum_{\text{pairs}}Gm_im_j\frac{(x_i-x_j)^2+(y_i-y_j)^2+(z_i-z_j)^2}{r_{i,j}^3}$$

$$=-\sum_{\text{pairs}}\frac{Gm_im_j}{r_{i,j}}=\Omega. \tag{A3.5}$$

Equation (A3.3) now appears as

$$\frac{1}{2}\ddot{I}=2T+\Omega, \tag{A3.6}$$

and if the system stays within the same volume and has the same distribution of particles, at least in a time-averaged sense, then $\langle\ddot{I}\rangle=0$ and the virial theorem is verified.

The virial theorem has a very wide range of uses, and can be applied to a cluster of stars or to the molecules in a star where the translational kinetic energy is just the thermal energy of the material. For a spherical cluster of N stars, each of mass m with a uniform distribution in a sphere of radius R, the potential energy will be

$$\Omega=-\frac{3G(mN)^2}{5R}. \tag{A3.7}$$

Equating $-\Omega$ to twice the translational kinetic energy of the stars gives

$$mN\langle v^2\rangle=\frac{3G(mN)^2}{5R} \tag{A3.8}$$

giving the rms speed of the stars,

$$\langle v^2\rangle^{1/2}=\left(\frac{3GmN}{5R}\right)^{1/2}.$$

4 The condition for collisionless PIC

In Fig. A4.1 we show an interaction between an electron and a singly-charged ion. The electron at C experiences an acceleration towards the ion at O equal to

$$a = \frac{e^2}{4\pi\varepsilon_0 m(D\sec\theta)^2},$$ (A4.1)

where D is the closest approach of the interaction. By symmetry, the net change of velocity of the electron due to the interaction will be in the direction AO and the component of the velocity change in that direction in time dt will be $dv_\perp = a\cos\theta\, dt$. If the velocity of the electron relative to the ion is v then $(ds/dt) = v$ and since $s = D\tan\theta$ then $(ds/d\theta) = D\sec^2\theta$. From these results we find that the change of velocity in the direction AO in going from C to C' is

$$dv_\perp = \frac{e^2}{4\pi\varepsilon_0 mDv}\cos\theta\, d\theta.$$ (A4.2)

The total change in velocity along AO due to the passage of the electron is

$$\Delta v_\perp = \frac{e^2}{4\pi\varepsilon_0 mDv}\int_{-\pi/2}^{\pi/2}\cos\theta\, d\theta = \frac{e^2}{2\pi\varepsilon_0 mDv}.$$ (A4.3)

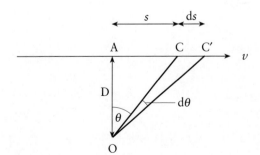

Fig. A4.1 An electron at C moving at speed v relative to a singly-charged ion at O.

This will cause a deviation in the path of the electron,

$$\Delta\phi = \frac{\Delta v_\perp}{v} = \frac{e^2}{2\pi\varepsilon_0 m D v^2}. \tag{A4.4}$$

The deviations due to close interactions will be in completely random directions and the root-mean-square deviation after N interactions at speed v will be

$$\langle\phi^2\rangle^{1/2} = N^{1/2}\frac{e^2}{2\pi\varepsilon_0 m v^2}\left\langle\frac{1}{D^2}\right\rangle^{1/2}. \tag{A4.5a}$$

The analysis is simplified by making the approximation $\langle 1/D^2\rangle^{1/2} = \langle 1/D\rangle$; the answer so obtained is changed by a factor of order unity but the conclusions drawn from it are still valid. We now have

$$\langle\phi^2\rangle^{1/2} = N^{1/2}\frac{e^2}{2\pi\varepsilon_0 m v^2}\left\langle\frac{1}{D}\right\rangle. \tag{A4.5b}$$

We assume a maximum value of D, D_{max}, for a close interaction. The total target area for a close interaction is thus πD_{max}^2 and for a closest approach between D and $D + \mathrm{d}D$ the target area is $2\pi D\mathrm{d}D$. From this the value of $\langle 1/D\rangle$ is found as

$$\left\langle\frac{1}{D}\right\rangle = \frac{1}{\pi D_{\mathrm{max}}^2}\int_0^{D_{\mathrm{max}}}\frac{1}{D}\times 2\pi D\mathrm{d}D = \frac{2}{D_{\mathrm{max}}}. \tag{A4.6}$$

The more precise analysis, without our simplification, involves finding $\langle 1/D^2\rangle$ and requires the introduction of a minimum distance for an interaction, D_{min}. This is taken as the *Landau length*, the distance of an interaction that will give a deviation of $\pi/2$.

From (A4.5) we can now find the expected number of close interactions required to give a root-mean-square deviation of $\pi/2$ which will happen in time t_c. This is

$$N_c = \frac{\pi^4\varepsilon_0^2 m^2 D_{\mathrm{max}}^2 v^4}{e^4}. \tag{A4.7}$$

As the electron travels through the plasma every ion within a distance D_{max} will give a close interaction. To give N_c close interactions requires a distance

$$L = \frac{\pi^3\varepsilon_0^2 m^2 v^4}{e^4 n}, \tag{A4.8}$$

requiring a time

$$t_c = \frac{L}{v} = \frac{\pi^3 \varepsilon_0^2 m^2 v^3}{e^4 n}, \tag{A4.9}$$

when n is the number density of ions. From (3.47), which gives an expression for the plasma period,

$$\frac{t_c}{t_p} = \frac{\pi^2 \varepsilon_0^{3/2} m^{3/2} v^3}{2 e^3 n^{1/2}}. \tag{A4.10}$$

Writing $mv^2 = 3kT$ and using (3.49b), the expression for the Debye length, we find

$$\frac{t_c}{t_p} = \frac{\pi^2 3^{3/2}}{2} n \lambda_D^3 \tag{A4.11}$$

which is about six times the number of particles in the Debye sphere.

   This result applies to the number of superparticles in the Debye sphere of the model since the root-N statistics we used will be relevant to the model and not to the plasma being modelled.

5   *The coefficients of a half-sine-wave Fourier series*

We consider a function, $f(i,j)$, defined on a two-dimensional grid forming $n \times n$ square cells and with $f(i,j)=0$ at all boundaries, represented by the half-sine-wave Fourier series

$$f(i,j) = \sum_{h=1}^{n-1} \sum_{k=1}^{n-1} D_{hk} \sin\left(\frac{\pi h i}{n}\right) \sin\left(\frac{\pi k j}{n}\right). \tag{A5.1}$$

Multiplying both sides by $\sin(\pi H i / n)\sin(\pi K j / n)$ and then summing over all i and j, we have

$$\sum_{h=1}^{n-1} \sum_{k=1}^{n-1} D_{hk} \sum_{i=1}^{n-1} \sin\left(\frac{\pi h i}{n}\right) \sin\left(\frac{\pi H i}{n}\right) \sum_{j=1}^{n-1} \sin\left(\frac{\pi k j}{n}\right) \sin\left(\frac{\pi K j}{n}\right)$$

$$= \sum_{i=1}^{n-1} \sum_{j=1}^{n-1} f(i,j) \sin\left(\frac{\pi H i}{n}\right) \sin\left(\frac{\pi K j}{n}\right). \tag{A5.2}$$

The half sine waves with different coefficients form an orthogonal series so that

$$\sum_{i=1}^{n-1} \sin\left(\frac{\pi h i}{n}\right) \sin\left(\frac{\pi H i}{n}\right) = \frac{n}{2} \delta_{h,H}, \tag{A5.3}$$

where $\delta_{h,H}$ is the Kronecker delta. Thus the only non-zero term on the left-hand side of (A5.2) is that for which $h=H$ and $k=K$. This gives the result

$$D_{HK} = \sum_{i=1}^{n-1} \sum_{j=1}^{n-1} f(i,j) \sin\left(\frac{\pi H i}{n}\right) \sin\left(\frac{\pi K j}{n}\right), \tag{A5.4}$$

which leads to (3.71) as required.

6 Numerical quadrature

Numerical quadrature, or 'finding the area under the curve', consists of evaluating definite integrals. Initially, we shall restrict our description to one dimension, to estimating

$$I = \int_a^b f(x)\,dx, \tag{A6.1}$$

but later these ideas will be extended to multi-dimensional integrals.

The simplest technique of numerical quadrature is the *trapezium method*, illustrated in Fig. A6.1. The range of x from b to a is divided into n equal segments (five in the figure), each of width h, and the area is simulated by the sum of the areas of the five trapezia shown. Since the area of a trapezium is the product of the base length and the average height the integral is estimated as

$$I \approx \frac{1}{2}(f_0+f_1)h + \frac{1}{2}(f_1+f_2)h + \frac{1}{2}(f_2+f_3)h + \frac{1}{2}(f_3+f_4)h + \frac{1}{2}(f_4+f_5)h.$$

For the general case of n equal segments this becomes

$$I = \frac{1}{2}h(f_0 + 2f_1 + 2f_2 + \cdots + 2f_{n-2} + 2f_{n-1} + f_n). \tag{A6.2}$$

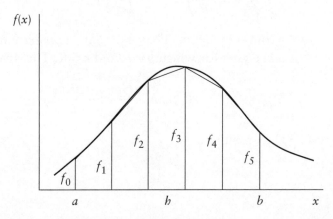

Fig. A6.1 The trapezium method gives the area under the curve as the sum of the areas of the trapezia shown.

Table A6.1 Values of the integral given in (A6.3) for various intervals h by the trapezium rule and Simpson's rule. The error of each estimate, in units of the least significant figure, is indicated in parentheses.

Segment (h)	Trapezium rule	Simpson's rule
$\pi/8$	0.987 12 (1288)	1.000 134 59 (13 459)
$\pi/16$	0.996 79 (321)	1.000 008 30 (830)
$\pi/32$	0.999 20 (80)	1.000 000 52 (52)

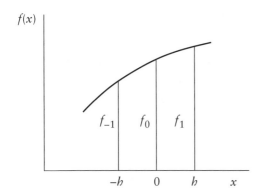

Fig. A6.2   Pairs of segments for Simpson's rule.

It is obvious from Fig. A6.1 that the smaller are the segments the better will be the estimate. Table A6.1 shows the estimate of

$$I = \int_0^{\pi/2} \sin x \, dx \tag{A6.3}$$

for the trapezium method for various values of h. It can be shown theoretically that the expected error in the trapezium-rule estimate is proportional to h^2, and the results in the table confirm this. Each reduction in h by a factor of 2 gives a reduction in the error by a factor of 4.

As an improvement on fitting a straight line to two neighbouring points to simulate part of the function $f(x)$, we now consider fitting a parabola to three equi-spaced points as shown in Fig. A6.2, where the x coordinates are arbitrarily taken as $-h$, 0 and h and the three ordinates of the curve as f_{-1}, f_0 and f_1. We fit the parabola $f(x) = ax^2 + bx + c$. From the centre point where $x = 0$ we find $c = f_0$ and from the flanking points

$$f_1 = ah^2 + bh + f_0$$
$$f_{-1} = ah^2 - bh + f_0. \tag{A6.4}$$

From these equations we find

$$a = \frac{f_1 + f_{-1} - 2f_0}{2h^2} \quad \text{and} \quad b = \frac{f_1 - f_{-1}}{2h}. \tag{A6.5}$$

The area under the parabola between $x = -h$ and $x = +h$ is

$$I^h_{-h} = \int_{-h}^{h} (ax^2 + bx + c)\,dx$$

$$= \frac{1}{3} h(2ah^2 + 6c) = \frac{h}{3} (f_{-1} + 4f_0 + f_1). \tag{A6.6}$$

The result (A6.6) leads to *Simpson's rule* for numerical quadrature. The interval from a to b must be divided into an *even* number of segments and then a parabola is fitted to the ordinates defining pairs of segments. The area under all these parabolas gives the estimate of the total area under the curve and is, for n segments,

$$I = \frac{h}{3} \{(f_0 + 4f_1 + f_2) + (f_2 + 4f_3 + f_4) + \cdots + (f_{n-4} + 4f_{n-3} + f_{n-2})$$

$$+ (f_{n-2} + 4f_{n-1} + f_n)\}.$$

This gives the Simpson's rule pattern of coefficients

$$I = \frac{h}{3} (f_0 + 4f_1 + 2f_2 + 4f_3 + 2f_4 + \cdots + 2f_{n-4} + 4f_{n-3} + 2f_{n-2} + 4f_{n-1} + f_n). \tag{A6.7}$$

Theoretically the estimates from Simpson's rule should have errors proportional to h^4; this is confirmed by examination of Table A6.1, which shows that halving the interval decreases the error by a factor close to 16.

It can be shown that Simpson's rule will give a precise solution for any function which is a polynomial of cubic power or less. If the function is of the form $f(x) = x^n$ within the range a to b then the true value of the definite integral is $(b^{n+1} - a^{n+1})/(n+1)$. Dividing the interval into two segments, so that $h = (\frac{1}{2})(b-a)$, the Simpson's rule estimate is

$$\frac{b-a}{6} \left\{ a^n + 4\left(\frac{a+b}{2}\right)^n + b^n \right\}.$$

It may be confirmed that the estimate is correct for $n = 0, 1, 2$ and 3, and this will also be true for a function $f(x)$ which is a linear combinations of such powers of x. A quadratic must give a correct result, since this is the form of the curve fitted to $f(x)$, but what we have shown here is that positive and negative errors due to fitting a quadratic function to a cubic $f(x)$ exactly cancel each other.

Returning to the results for the trapesium method in Table A6.1, we can write the errors for segments $h = \pi/8$ and $\pi/16$ (four and eight segments in the interval 0 to $\pi/2$) in the form

$$\varepsilon_4 = I - T_4 \quad (T_4 = 0.987\,115\,8)$$

and

$$\varepsilon_8 = I - T_8 \quad (T_8 = 0.996\,785\,2),$$

where I is the correct value for the integral. However, from theory $\varepsilon_4 = 4\varepsilon_8$ from which we find

$$I = \frac{4T_8 - T_4}{3} = 1.000\,008\,3. \tag{A6.8}$$

To get a result as good as this with the trapezium rule would require several hundred points, but we notice from Table A6.1 that it is also the answer for eight segments with Simpson's rule. In fact this is exactly what it is. If values of the function at equal intervals of x separated by h are f_0, f_1 and f_2 then

$$T_1 = \tfrac{1}{2} \times 2h \times (f_0 + f_2)$$

$$T_2 = h \times (\tfrac{1}{2}f_0 + f_1 + \tfrac{1}{2}f_2),$$

and

$$\frac{4T_2 - T_1}{3} = \frac{h}{3}(f_0 + 4f_1 + f_2),$$

which is the Simpson's rule result.

Since we also know the way that the error varies with h for Simpson's rule, a similar procedure can be carried out for these results. For the Simpson's rule method in Table A6.1 we can write the errors for $h = \pi/8$ and $\pi/16$ as

$$_S\varepsilon_4 = I - S_4 \quad (S_4 = 1.000\,134\,59)$$

$$_S\varepsilon_8 = I - S_8 \quad (S_8 = 1.000\,008\,30),$$

where I is the correct value for the integral. However, we know from theory that $_S\varepsilon_4 = 16_S\varepsilon_8$, from which we find

$$I = \frac{16S_8 - S_4}{15} = 0.999\,999\,88. \tag{A6.9}$$

Table A6.2   The generation of successively improved estimates of definite integrals by the Romberg method. The initial calculations are of T_n, the trapezium-method estimates with n segments. Others are calculated as: $S_n = (4T_n - T_{n/2})/3$; $R_n = (16S_n - S_{n/2})/15$; $Q_n = (64R_n - R_{n/2})/63$; $P_n = (256Q_n - Q_{n/2})/255$; $O_n = (1024P_n - P_{n/2})/1023$.

Number of segments						
1	T_1					
		S_2				
2	T_2		R_4			
		S_4		Q_8		
4	T_4		R_8		P_{16}	
		S_8		Q_{16}		Q_{32}
8	T_8		R_{16}		P_{32}	
		S_{16}		Q_{32}		
16	T_{16}		R_{32}			
		S_{32}				
32	T_{32}					

Table A6.3   A Romberg table with eight segments for the integral (A6.3).

$T_1 = 0.785\,398\,164$				
	$S_2 = 1.002\,279\,877$			
$T_2 = 0.948\,059\,449$		$R_4 = 0.999\,991\,567$		
	$S_4 = 1.000\,134\,586$		$Q_8 = 1.000\,000\,007$	
$T_4 = 0.987\,115\,802$		$R_8 = 0.999\,999\,875$		
	$S_8 = 1.000\,008\,295$			
$T_8 = 0.996\,785\,172$				

This result is one we could get by dividing the range into eight segments and fitting a quartic to each of two abutting ranges, each with five points. It would be possible, but complicated, to work out the coefficients of the five ordinates which would give the required estimate, but it is much easier to find it from (A6.9). The error in the estimate (A6.9) depends on h^6, so the principle by which the result (A6.9) was generated could be extended to give estimates depending on fitting an eighth-order polynomial to sets of nine points. This process is the basis of the *Romberg method* of quadrature which is illustrated in Table A6.2. The final result, O_{32}, is that which would be found by fitting a 32-order polynomial to all 33 ordinates. In practice, if a certain tolerance is acceptable, the Romberg method would terminate once all the results in a column agreed to within the tolerance limit. Table A6.3 shows the stages in estimating the integral (A6.3) starting with eight segments and four trapezium

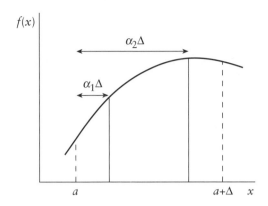

Fig. A6.3 The ordinates for Gauss two-point quadrature.

estimates. If only four decimal places of precision were required then one could accept the answer 1.0000 from R_4 and R_8.

The Romberg process involves repeated arithmetical operations affecting the least significant parts of the numbers being processed, so round-off errors can build up. However, with double-precision floating-point arithmetic this is rarely a problem.

A very effective alternative to methods which require division of the integration interval into equal segments is *Gauss quadrature*, which fixes the number of points at which the integrand must be evaluated but where these points are not equally spaced. We shall illustrate the principle of this method with two-point Gauss quadrature. The integral to be evaluated will be put in the form

$$\int_a^{a+\Delta} f(x)\mathrm{d}x, \tag{A6.10}$$

which is illustrated in Fig. A6.3. The problem we seek to solve is to find fractional numbers α_1 and α_2 with corresponding weights w_1 and w_2 such that

$$I \approx \Delta\{w_1 f(a+\alpha_1\Delta)+w_2 f(a+\alpha_2\Delta)\}. \tag{A6.11}$$

Since Δ is the integration interval then the bracketed expression in (A6.11) is an expression for the average value of the integrand in the range.

Clearly values of α_1, α_2, w_1 and w_2 cannot be chosen which will give a precise solution for every possible function $f(x)$ in (A6.10), but what *can* be done is to find values which will make the solution exact for $f(x)=1, f(x)=x$ and $f(x)=x^2$ and hence for linear combinations forming a quadratic expression.

These conditions give

$$\int_a^{a+\Delta} 1 \, dx = \Delta = \Delta(w_1 + w_2), \quad \text{or} \quad w_1 + w_2 = 1, \tag{A6.12}$$

$$\int_a^{a+\Delta} x \, dx = \frac{1}{2}\Delta(2a + \Delta) = \Delta\{w_1(a + \alpha_1\Delta) + w_2(a + \alpha_2\Delta)\},$$

which gives

$$a + \tfrac{1}{2}\Delta = a(w_1 + w_2) + \Delta(\alpha_1 w_1 + \alpha_2 w_2),$$

or, since $w_1 + w_2 = 1$,

$$2(\alpha_1 w_1 + \alpha_2 w_2) = 1. \tag{A6.13}$$

Finally,

$$\int_a^{a+\Delta} x^2 \, dx = \Delta\left(a^2 + a\Delta + \frac{1}{3}\Delta^2\right) = \Delta\{w_1(a + \alpha_1\Delta)^2 + w_2(a + \alpha_2\Delta)^2\}.$$

Using results (A6.12) and (A6.13), this gives

$$3(w_1\alpha_1^2 + w_2\alpha_2^2) = 1. \tag{A6.14}$$

To find an explicit solution to equations (A6.12), (A6.13) and (A6.14), we impose the condition that the points shown be placed symmetrically around the mid-point of the range so that

$$\alpha_1 + \alpha_2 = 1. \tag{A6.15}$$

From (A6.13), substituting from (A6.12) and (A6.15), we find

$$2\{w_1\alpha_1 + (1 - w_1)(1 - \alpha_1)\} = 1$$

or

$$(2w_1 - 1)(2\alpha_1 - 1) = 0. \tag{A6.16}$$

The solution of (A6.16), $\alpha_1 = \frac{1}{2}$, is not acceptable because this also makes $\alpha_2 = \frac{1}{2}$ which gives only one point and not two as required. The acceptable solution is to give equal weights $w_1 = w_2 = \frac{1}{2}$. From (A6.14), we now find

$$\tfrac{3}{2}\{\alpha_1^2 + (1-\alpha_1)^2\} = 1$$

or

$$2\alpha_1^2 - 2\alpha_1 + \tfrac{1}{3} = 0,$$

the two solutions of which give α_1 and α_2 as

$$\alpha_1 = \frac{1}{2} - \frac{1}{2\sqrt{3}} = 0.211\,324\,9$$

and

$$\alpha_2 = \frac{1}{2} + \frac{1}{2\sqrt{3}} = 0.788\,675\,1.$$

If we apply the two-point Gauss formula with these values to integral (A6.3), we find

$$I_G = \frac{\pi}{2}\left\{\frac{1}{2}\sin\left(0.211\,324\,9\frac{\pi}{2}\right) + \frac{1}{2}\sin\left(0.788\,675\,1\frac{\pi}{2}\right)\right\} = 0.998\,472\,6,$$

which is much better than the trapezium method estimate with two points, 0.7854, and is also slightly better than the three-point Simpson's rule estimate, 1.002\,279\,9.

It can be shown that the two-point Gauss formula gives a precise solution even for a cubic function. The reader should verify that

$$\int_a^{a+\Delta} x^3\,\mathrm{d}x = \frac{\Delta}{4}(4a^3 + 6a^2\Delta + 4a\Delta^2 + \Delta^3)$$

is equivalent to the Gauss two-point expression

$$\frac{1}{2}\Delta\left[\left\{a + \left(\frac{1}{2} - \frac{1}{2\sqrt{3}}\right)\Delta\right\}^3 + \left\{a + \left(\frac{1}{2} + \frac{1}{2\sqrt{3}}\right)\Delta\right\}^3\right].$$

In general a Gauss n-point formula gives a precise result for polynomials up to degree $2n-1$. Tables of weights and abscissae (values of α) can be found in mathematical tables (such as Abramowitz *et al.*, 1968). Some tables give the abscissae in the range $+1$ to -1, centred on zero with the sum of weights equal to 2, rather than 1 as given by our analysis. Conversion from one system

Table A6.4 Abscissae and weights for Gauss quadrature.

n	Abscissae	Weights
3	0.112 7017	0.277 7778
	0.5	0.444 4444
	0.887 2983	0.277 7778
4	0.069 4318	0.173 9274
	0.330 0095	0.326 0726
	0.669 9905	0.326 0726
	0.930 5682	0.173 9274
7	0.025 4460	0.064 7425
	0.129 2344	0.139 8527
	0.297 0774	0.190 9150
	0.5	0.208 9796
	0.702 9226	0.190 9150
	0.870 7656	0.139 8527
	0.974 5540	0.064 7425
10	0.013 0467	0.033 3357
	0.067 4683	0.074 7257
	0.160 2952	0.109 5432
	0.283 3023	0.134 6334
	0.425 5628	0.147 7621
	0.574 4372	0.147 7621
	0.716 6977	0.134 6334
	0.839 7048	0.109 5432
	0.932 5317	0.074 7257
	0.986 9533	0.033 3357

to the other is straightforward. Table A6.4 gives weights and abscissae for a few selected values of n.

The evaluation of multi-dimensional integrals will be illustrated by a two-dimensional integral; the principle can easily be extended to any number of dimensions. We consider the integral

$$I = \int_{y=c}^{d} \int_{x=a}^{b} f(x,y)\,\mathrm{d}x\,\mathrm{d}y. \tag{A6.17}$$

The x range is divided into n segments, each of width h, so that $nh = b - a$ and the y range into m segments, each of width k, so that $mk = d - c$. Both n and m must be even. For the application of Simpson's rule in each direction the estimate is given by

$$I \approx \sum_{j=1}^{m} \sum_{i=1}^{n} {}_n w_{i\,m} w_j f(a+ih, c+jk), \tag{A6.18}$$

where $_nw_i$ and $_mw_j$ follow the series $1, 4, 2, 4, ..., 4, 2, 4, 1$ with $n+1$ and $m+1$ members, respectively. For Gauss integration, n-point in the x direction and m-point in the y direction, the estimate is found from

$$I \approx \sum_{j=1}^{m} \sum_{i=1}^{n} {}_nw_i {}_mw_j f(a + {}_n\alpha_i \Delta x, c + {}_m\alpha_j \Delta y), \qquad (A6.19)$$

where $\Delta x = b - a$, $\Delta y = d - c$ and the ws and αs are abscissae and weights as given in Table A6.4.

Formulae such as (A6.18) and (A6.19) are simply coded in computer programs (as nested DO loops in FORTRAN, for example) up to the extent of nesting allowed by the software. For many dimensions, say more than four, Monte Carlo methods (Section 4.5) are more convenient and can give better precision for a given amount of computer effort.

7 Calculation of the four-element solution to (6.11)

In this appendix we follow in detail the steps in finding the four-linear-element solution to (6.11) by minimizing the functional

$$I(a_1, a_2, a_3) = T_1(a_1, a_2, a_3) - T_2(a_1, a_2, a_3) + T_3(a_1, a_2, a_3), \qquad (A7.1)$$

where

$$T_1(a_1, a_2, a_3) = \frac{1}{2} \int_0^{\pi/2} (y')^2 \, dx = \frac{1}{2} \int_0^{\pi/2} \left\{ \sum_{i=1}^{4} N_i'(x) \, a_i \right\}^2 dx, \qquad (A7.2a)$$

$$T_2(a_1, a_2, a_3) = \frac{1}{2} \int_0^{\pi/2} y^2 \, dx = \frac{1}{2} \int_0^{\pi/2} \left\{ \sum_{i=1}^{4} N_i(x) \, a_i \right\}^2 dx, \qquad (A7.2b)$$

$$T_3(a_1, a_2, a_3) = 2 \int_0^{\pi/2} y \cos x \, dx = 2 \int_0^{\pi/2} \cos x \left\{ \sum_{i=1}^{4} N_i(x) \, a_i \right\} dx. \qquad (A7.2c)$$

The variational parameters (ordinates) a_1, a_2 and a_3 correspond to $x = \pi/8$, $\pi/4$ and $3\pi/8$, so that $h = \pi/8$ and $1/h^2 = 64/\pi^2$. Since $a_0 = 0$ it is not included in the summations but the other boundary value $a_4 (= \pi/2)$ is included. The method of approach is to make $\partial I(a_1, a_2, a_3)/\partial a_i = 0$ for $i = 1, 2$ and 3, and then to solve the resulting linear equations for a_1, a_2 and a_3. This gives the approximate solution at the nodal values.

With a slight change of notation for the Ns, we begin by finding

$$\frac{\partial T_1}{\partial a_1} = \int_0^{\pi/2} N_1'(N_1' a_1 + N_2' a_2 + N_3' a_3 + N_4' a_4) \, dx, \qquad (A7.3)$$

where $a_4 = \pi/2$, the upper boundary condition. The last two terms give no contribution because of (6.24a), and the other products of N' values are given by (6.24b) and (6.24c). Hence

$$\frac{\partial T_1}{\partial a_1} = \frac{64}{\pi^2} \int_0^{\pi/4} a_1 \, dx - \frac{64}{\pi^2} \int_{\pi/8}^{\pi/4} a_2 \, dx = \frac{16}{\pi} a_1 - \frac{8}{\pi} a_2, \qquad (A7.4)$$

the limits of the integrals corresponding to the ranges within which $(N_1')^2$ and $N_1' N_2'$ are non-zero. Similarly

$$\frac{\partial T_1}{\partial a_2} = -\frac{8}{\pi} a_1 + \frac{16}{\pi} a_2 - \frac{8}{\pi} a_3,$$

(A7.5)

$$\frac{\partial T_1}{\partial a_3} = -\frac{8}{\pi} a_2 + \frac{16}{\pi} a_3 - 4.$$

We now turn our attention to terms involving T_2. From (6.25b), putting $a_4 = \pi/2$, we have

$$T_2 = \frac{1}{2} \int_0^{\pi/2} \left(N_1 a_1 + N_2 a_2 + N_3 a_3 + \frac{\pi}{2} N_4 \right)^2 dx.$$

(A7.6)

In the various ranges of x the values of N are as follows:

$$0 \leqslant x \leqslant \frac{\pi}{8} \qquad N_0 = \frac{8}{\pi}\left(\frac{\pi}{8} - x\right), \qquad N_1 = \frac{8}{\pi} x$$

$$\frac{\pi}{8} < x \leqslant \frac{\pi}{4} \qquad N_1 = \frac{8}{\pi}\left(\frac{\pi}{4} - x\right), \qquad N_2 = \frac{8}{\pi}\left(x - \frac{\pi}{8}\right)$$

(A7.7)

$$\frac{\pi}{4} < x \leqslant \frac{3\pi}{8} \qquad N_2 = \frac{8}{\pi}\left(\frac{3\pi}{8} - x\right), \qquad N_3 = \frac{8}{\pi}\left(x - \frac{\pi}{4}\right)$$

$$\frac{3\pi}{8} < x \leqslant \frac{\pi}{2} \qquad N_3 = \frac{8}{\pi}\left(\frac{\pi}{2} - x\right), \qquad N_4 = \frac{8}{\pi}\left(x - \frac{3\pi}{8}\right).$$

From (A7.6),

$$\frac{\partial T_2}{\partial a_1} = \int_0^{\pi/2} N_1\left(N_1 a_1 + N_2 a_2 + N_3 a_3 + \frac{\pi}{2} N_4 \right) dx,$$

but, because of (6.23), only the first two terms in the parentheses will give a finite result. Hence

$$\frac{\partial T_2}{\partial a_1} = \frac{64}{\pi^2} a_1 \left\{ \int_0^{\pi/8} x^2 \, dx + \int_{\pi/8}^{\pi/4} \left(\frac{\pi}{4} - x\right)^2 \right\} dx + \frac{64}{\pi^2} a_2 \int_{\pi/8}^{\pi/4} \left(\frac{\pi}{4} - x\right)\left(x - \frac{\pi}{8}\right) dx$$

$$= \frac{\pi}{12} a_1 + \frac{\pi}{48} a_2;$$

(A7.8a)

and similarly,

$$\frac{\partial T_2}{\partial a_2} = \frac{\pi}{48} a_1 + \frac{\pi}{12} a_2 + \frac{\pi}{48} a_3,$$

(A7.8b)

$$\frac{\partial T_2}{\partial a_3} = \frac{\pi}{48} a_2 + \frac{\pi}{12} a_3 + \frac{\pi^2}{96}.$$

Finally

$$T_3 = \int_0^{\pi/2} 2 \cos x \left(N_1 a_1 + N_2 a_2 + N_3 a_3 + N_4 \frac{\pi}{2} \right) dx,$$

which gives

$$\frac{\partial T_3}{\partial a_1} = \int_0^{\pi/2} 2 \cos x N_1 \, dx = \frac{16}{\pi} \int_0^{\pi/8} x \cos x \, dx + \frac{16}{\pi} \int_{\pi/8}^{\pi/4} \cos x \left(\frac{\pi}{4} - x \right) dx$$

$$= \frac{16}{\pi} \left(2 \cos \frac{\pi}{8} - \cos \frac{\pi}{4} - 1 \right);$$

(A7.9a)

similarly,

$$\frac{\partial T_3}{\partial a_2} = \frac{16}{\pi} \left(2 \cos \frac{\pi}{4} - \cos \frac{\pi}{8} - \cos \frac{3\pi}{8} \right)$$

$$\frac{\partial T_3}{\partial a_3} = \frac{16}{\pi} \left(2 \cos \frac{3\pi}{8} - \cos \frac{\pi}{4} \right).$$

(A7.9b)

Assembling terms,

$$\frac{\partial I}{\partial a_1} = \frac{\partial T_1}{\partial a_1} - \frac{\partial T_2}{\partial a_1} + \frac{\partial T_3}{\partial a_1} = a_1 \left(\frac{16}{\pi} - \frac{\pi}{12} \right) + a_2 \left(-\frac{8}{\pi} - \frac{\pi}{48} \right)$$

$$+ \frac{16}{\pi} \left(2 \cos \frac{\pi}{8} - \cos \frac{\pi}{4} - 1 \right) = 0,$$

or $4.83116a_1 - 2.61193a_2 = -0.71634$, which is equation (6.26a). Equations (6.26b) and (6.26c) are found similarly from $\partial I/\partial a_2 = 0$ and $\partial I/\partial a_3 = 0$.

Problems – solutions and comments

Chapter 1

1.1 The errors for the various steps should be found to be close to the following:

n	10	12	14	16	18	20
Error ($\times 10^5$ m)	1.0140	0.4803	0.2482	0.1345	0.0735	0.0385

This is approximately consistent with the error being proportional to h^5.

1.2 The $\log A$ against $\log f$ plotted points give a fairly good straight line between $f=1$ and $f=10^{-3}$. From this the relationship $A=1.58f^{-0.67}$, or something similar, should be found. For the smaller values of f the value of A tends to a constant corresponding to $f=0$.

1.3 The estimation of the range, R, of motion of the asteroids can only be found approximately from the graphical output, a typical example of which is in Fig. 1.6b. However, the results should give something close to

M_p ($M_\odot$)	2.5×10^{-4}	5×10^{-4}	10^{-3}	2×10^{-3}	4×10^{-3}
R (AU)	0.50	0.34	0.24	0.18	0.13

A plot of $\log R$ against $\log M_\mathrm{p}$ gives a straight line with a slope very close to -0.5, suggesting that $R \propto M_\mathrm{p}^{-1/2}$.

1.4 It is clear from Fig. 1.9 that the rate of change of e, indicated by the regions between the spikes, is not constant, so there is considerable uncertainty in estimating the mean slope. Some estimated results are now given, although different individuals will end up with different estimates:

e	0.4	0.5	0.6	0.7	0.8
de/dt (days^{-1})	5.3×10^{-4}	4.0×10^{-4}	3.4×10^{-4}	1.9×10^{-4}	1.3×10^{-4}

These points straddle a straight line and, in view of the uncertainty in each estimate, it is reasonable to postulate a straight-line relationship in this range.

1.5 The following results were found from the modified DRUNKARD program.

n	2	4	8	16	32	64	128	256	512	1024
d	1.65	2.67	4.07	5.95	8.44	11.91	17.49	24.18	31.81	46.65

A plot of $\log(d)$ against $\log(n)$ gives a distinct curvature, so no simple power–law relationship holds over the range. However, a simple polynomial fit may be possible.

1.6 The following results were found from the modified POLYWALK program.

n	2	4	8	16	32	64	128	256
d	1.63	2.84	4.85	8.66	16.14	31.05	61.21	119.19

For $n=256$ there were only four successful walks out of 1000 trials, so this result is not very reliable. It will be seen that the walks for each n are longer than those given in Table 1.4. This is reasonable as excluding motion in one direction stretches out the walk and also reduces the probability of path crossing – which is why longer walks were feasible in this case. A plot of $\log(d)$ against $\log(n)$ gives a distinct curvature so no simple power–law relationship holds over the range. However, as for the modified DRUNKARD results, a simple polynomial fit may be possible.

Chapter 2

2.1 The basic differential equation for this problem is

$$\frac{d\theta}{dx} = -\frac{40Q}{1+x},$$

and the statement function must be changed accordingly. Inserting the mean cross-sectional area, $0.00015\,\text{m}^2$, suggests an approximate heat flow of $3.75\,\text{W}$. A set of successive approximations leading to a solution is:

	Trial Q	Temperature (K) at $x=11.0\,\text{m}$
	3.75	396.03
	3.50	402.96
By linear interpolation	3.607	399.99
	3.606	400.02
By linear interpolation	3.6067	400.00

The temperatures at $x=0.25$, 0.50 and 0.75 m are 467.81, 441.50, 419.27 K.

2.2 The changes to the HEATRI program necessary for this application are

$$A(1,I)=1.0+(I-0.5/N)$$

$$2 \quad A(2, I) = -2.0 * (1.0 + \text{FLOAT}(I)/N)$$

$$A(3, I) = 1.0 + (I + 0.5/N)$$

$$C(1) = -(1.0 + 0.5/N) * T0$$

$$C(N-1) = -(2.0 - 0.5/N) * TN$$

The temperatures found are 467.80, 441.50, 419.26 K with heat flow 3.6068 W, slightly different from those found by the shooting method.

2.3 Each of the programs HEATEX, HEATCRNI and LEAPDF (Dufort–Frankel mode) was run with the parameters given in the problem and in each case with 100 s time steps, corresponding to $r = 0.3429$. The numerical solutions gave:

x (m) =	0.2	0.4	0.6	0.8	1.0	1.2	1.4	1.6	1.8
HEATEX	300.0	300.0	300.0	300.1	300.6	303.1	310.8	328.6	359.5
HEATCRNI	300.0	300.0	300.0	300.2	300.8	303.3	310.7	328.0	358.8
LEAPDF	300.0	300.0	300.0	300.0	300.0	300.4	303.0	314.4	346.3

There is reasonable agreement between the explicit and Crank–Nicholson methods, but the Dufort–Frankel result is significantly different from the other two. The leapfrog method is too unstable to be able to deal with this problem except for very short periods of time, much less than 2000 s.

2.4 Time $= 107.3$ s:

x	0.0	0.125	0.250	0.375	0.500	0.625	0.750	0.875	1.000
$\theta_{ext} = 300\,\text{K}$	375.7	450.3	488.2	498.8	500.0	500.0	500.0	500.0	500.0
$\theta_{ext} = 400\,\text{K}$	426.1	468.8	492.6	499.1	500.0	500.0	500.0	500.0	500.0

Time $= 214.7$ s:

x	0.0	0.125	0.250	0.375	0.500	0.625	0.750	0.875	1.000
$\theta_{ext} = 300\,\text{K}$	364.3	426.7	468.4	489.5	497.5	499.6	500.0	500.0	500.0
$\theta_{ext} = 400\,\text{K}$	419.6	455.8	480.6	493.5	498.4	499.7	500.0	500.0	500.0

Time $= 322$ s:

x	0.0	0.125	0.250	0.375	0.500	0.625	0.750	0.875	1.000
$\theta_{ext} = 300\,\text{K}$	357.5	412.5	453.6	479.1	492.1	497.6	499.4	499.9	500.0
$\theta_{ext} = 400\,\text{K}$	416.8	448.1	472.1	487.3	495.2	498.5	499.6	499.5	500.0

2.5 The solution is

x_1	x_2	x_3	x_4	x_5	x_6	x_7	x_8
2	-1	1	0	3	1	0	-2

The best over-relaxation factor is $w = 1.0$, which then requires 10 cycles starting from all zero estimates. For $w = 1.3$ a solution is not reached after 100 cycles and the system seems to be unstable for larger values of w.

2.6   The description of the plate as input into HOTPLATE is

```
400  I  I  I  I  I   600  X   X   X   X
400  U  U  U  U  U   U    600 X   X   X
400  U  U  U  U  U   U    U   600 X   X
400  U  U  U  U  U   U    U   U   600 X
400  U  U  U  U  U   U    U   U   U   600
400  U  U  U  U  800 U    U   U   U   E
400  U  U  U  I  X   800  U   U   U   E
400  U  U  I  X  X   X    800 U   U   E
400  U  I  X  X  X   X    X   800 U   E
400  I  X  X  X  X   X    X   X   800 E
400  X  X  X  X  X   X    X   X   X   800
```

The values of K and S for the five points marked E are 10 and 5×10^4, respectively. The relaxation factor chosen, 1.5, was not optimal but nevertheless gave the answer efficiently. The output solution, hand-contoured at $200\,K$ intervals, is shown in Fig. P.1.

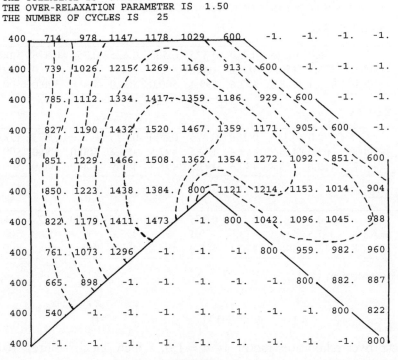

Fig. P.1

Chapter 3

3.1   The action of the lens can be seen with three electron trajectories, one from the origin leaving at some angle to the axis and two inclined to each other leaving from a point such as $(0, 0.001)$. The output in Fig. P.2 shows that the required value of D is close to 0.7.

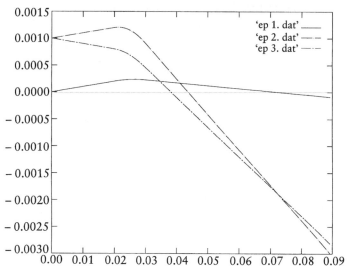

Fig. P.2

3.2   The values of R^2 and kinetic energy (KE) from the program are as follows:

Time (years)	R^2 (AU^2)	KE (solar system units)
0	7.1379	1.2163
10 000	7.2238	1.2145
20 000	7.3330	1.2107
30 000	7.4696	1.1854
40 000	7.6284	1.1772
50 000	7.8116	1.2614
60 000	8.0186	1.1506
70 000	8.2554	1.1228
80 000	8.5126	1.1013
90 000	8.7871	1.0978
100 000	9.0885	1.0688

The values of $d^2(R^2)/dt^2$ vary around 2.4 with quite large variations, while values of twice the kinetic energy vary between about 2.1 and 2.5 in solar system units. No better agreement can be expected in view of the lack of precision of the computation, which is evident from the jump in kinetic energy for 50 000 years.

From the virial theorem, (A3.1), $\frac{1}{2}\ddot{I} = 2T + \Omega$, and since, in this calculation, $T + \Omega = 0$ the relationship $d^2(R^2)/dt^2 = 2T$ follows.

3.3   The xenon results are shown in Fig. P.3 and are similar to those for argon. If the ratio of the temperature of the calculation to the temperature describing ε is the same for different Lennard-Jones liquids then the relationship between PV/NkT and V^* should be the same.

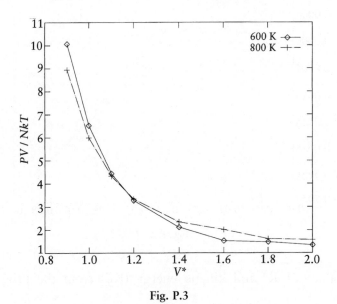

Fig. P.3

3.4   A graphical representation of the results is shown in Fig. P.4 for the times 5.105×10^{-14} s ((a) and (c)) and 1.0210×10^{-13} s ((b) and (d)). For the earlier time, reflection of the faster electrons can just be seen in the lower right-hand corner. At the later time, reflected particles have almost returned to $x = 0$ and sufficient time has elapsed for some slower electrons to be reflected back into the system. The field diagrams are similar to those in Fig. 3.13, and the explanation given in Section 3.7 applies here also.

Chapter 4

4.1   A program using the random number generator RAN1 (Press *et al.*, 1986) gave the results shown in Fig. P.5 and the plotted points are close to a line with slope -1. It can be shown theoretically that $\langle \delta_N^2 \rangle$ is proportional to N^{-1}.

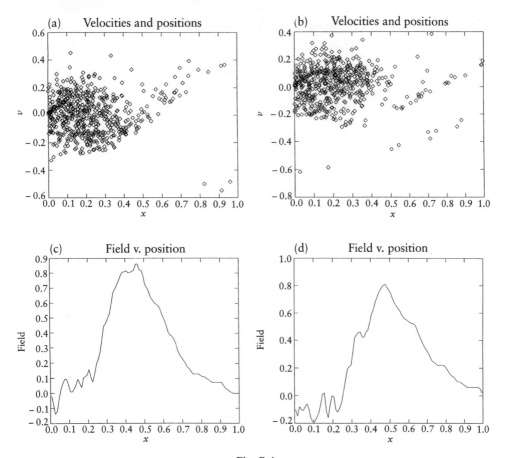

Fig. P.4

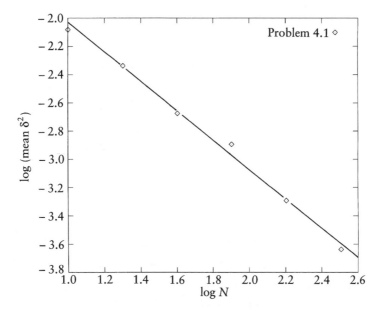

Fig. P.5

4.2   For three different seeds a program using the random number generator RAN1 gave the following results:

	σ	2σ	3σ
Run1	0.6818	0.9562	0.9977
Run2	0.6825	0.9536	0.9972
Run3	0.6822	0.9548	0.9977

These results agree well with the correct values, although for some purposes they might not be good enough. If, for example, the interest was in the tails of the distributions beyond 3σ then runs 1 and 3 indicate a proportion 0.0023 against the correct value 0.0027. By dividing all the sums by 3, a normal distribution with unit standard deviation would be obtained.

4.3   The normalizing constant C for $P(x)$ is found to be 1.904 76 and, by transformation, deviates from $Q(x)$ are found from uniform deviates (0–1), r, by

$$x = \frac{1 - \sqrt{1 - 0.9975r}}{0.95}.$$

The maximum ratio of $P(x)/Q(x)$ is unity for $x=0$ so no further scaling is necessary. The numbers from a program, compared with the analytical results, were:

Range	Program	Analytical
0.0–0.1	272 814	272 762
0.1–0.2	201 226	202 067
0.2–0.3	149 608	149 695
0.3–0.4	110 985	110 897
0.4–0.5	82 551	82 154
0.5–0.6	60 629	60 861
0.6–0.7	45 572	45 087
0.7–0.8	33 079	33 401
0.8–0.9	24 952	24 744
0.9–1.0	18 584	18 331

4.4   There is no unique solution to this problem but one possible stochastic matrix is:

$$\begin{bmatrix} \mathbf{0.2} & \mathbf{0.2} & \mathbf{0.3} & \mathbf{0.3} \\ 0.1 & \mathbf{0.2} & \mathbf{0.3} & 0.4 \\ 0.1 & 0.3 & \mathbf{0.2} & 0.4 \\ 0.075 & 0.2 & 0.3 & 0.425 \end{bmatrix}.$$

The elements in **bold** were those chosen arbitrarily. From a program using this matrix the number found for each of the variables was:

$$x_1\ (100\,319), \quad x_2\ (199\,805), \quad x_3\ (299\,707), \quad x_4\ (400\,169)$$

very close to $1:2:3:4$.

4.5 The results for METROPOL are shown in Fig. P.6. The results for 600 K and 800 K are related similarly to those from FLUIDYN but the values of *PV/NkT* are higher than for FLUIDYN, as is also seen in Fig. 3.6.

4.6 Some typical individual results for the integral, *I*, are:

N	10	100	1000	10 000	100 000
$I(\times 10^{-4})$	5.3686	5.4487	5.3556	5.3684	5.3728

A plot of $\log \sigma_N$ against $\log N$ is shown in Fig. P.7 and the slope close to $-\frac{1}{2}$ shows the required relationship.

4.7 The input for this problem is

X	X	X	450	X	X	X	X	X	X	X
X	X	400	U	500	X	X	X	X	X	X
X	400	U	U	U	500	X	X	X	X	X
350	U	U	U	U	U	450	400	400	400	350
300	U	U	U	U	U	U	U	U	U	300
300	U	U	U	U	U	U	U	U	U	300
300	U	U	500	500	500	500	450	U	U	300
300	U	U	500	X	X	X	X	400	U	300
300	U	U	500	X	X	X	X	X	400	300
300	U	U	500	X	X	X	X	X	X	350
350	400	400	450	X	X	X	X	X	X	X

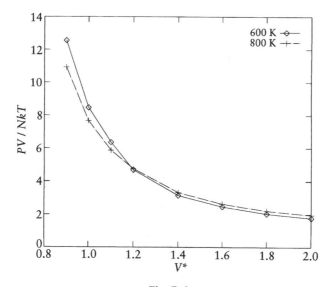

Fig. P.6

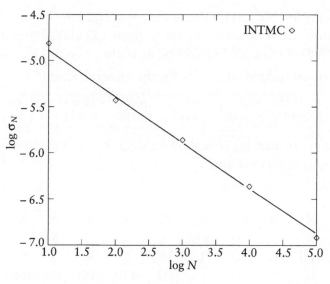

<figure>Fig. P.7</figure>

The output, contoured by hand, is shown in Fig. P.8a with the corresponding standard deviations in Fig. P.8b.

4.8　A run of REACTOR with the required data gave the following results:

Radius	1.0	2.0	3.0	4.0	5.0	6.0	7.0	8.0	9.0
Mult. const.	0.537	0.848	0.945	0.976	0.996	1.003	1.008	1.003	1.020

Allowing for the inevitable standard deviations in a Monte Carlo process, it is clear that the multiplication constant increases with radius but saturates at a value slightly greater than unity at a radius of about 6 m. For smaller radii many of the neutrons are absorbed by the walls of the reactor. However, the larger is the reactor the greater is the ratio of volume to surface area and so the less is the influence of wall absorption. It is clear that for given fuel–moderator conditions a minimum size of reactor is required but that increasing the size beyond that gives a diminishing return in terms of output per unit material.

Chapter 5

5.1　Graphical output using 50 intervals is shown in Fig. P.9. The six output profiles show the wave motion for slightly more than half a period.

5.2　Graphical output using 50 intervals is shown in Fig. P.10.

5.3　Figure P.11 shows the intensity patterns from a program written to carry out the processes required.

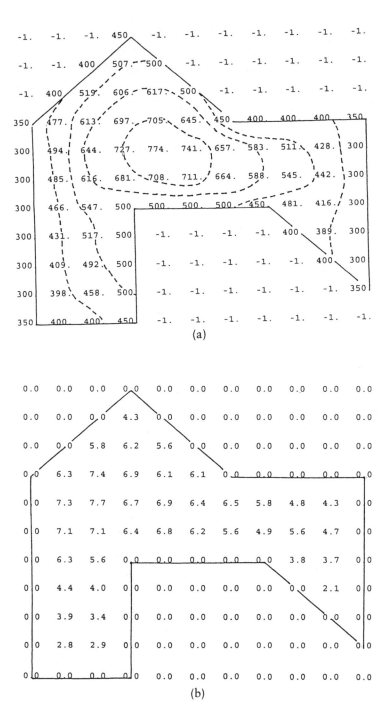

Fig. P.8

(i) The final row and column have been added to show the top and right-hand edges of the field. The arrow is exactly reproduced in Fig. P.11a.

(ii) The amplitude map shows two half-amplitude arrows, related by a centre of symmetry at $(\frac{1}{2}, \frac{1}{2})$, added together. The map in Fig. P.11b shows the shaft of the arrow with unit intensity and the heads with one-quarter intensity.

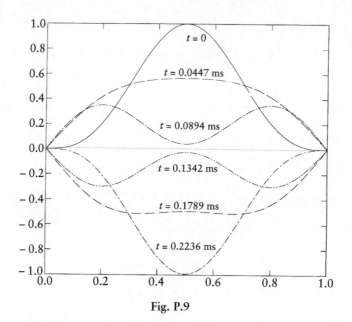

Fig. P.9

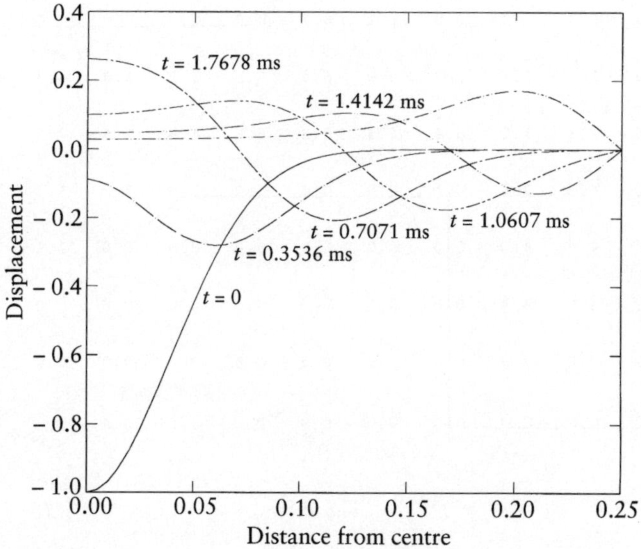

Fig. P.10

(iii) The amplitude map only shows non-zero results in the arrow head regions and these are the negative of each other. There are, in fact two half-amplitude arrows added together with phases differing by π so the two shafts cancel each other. The intensity map is shown in Fig. P.11c.

```
      0.00   0.00   0.00   0.00   1.00   0.00   0.00   0.00   0.00

      0.00   0.00   0.00   1.00   1.00   1.00   0.00   0.00   0.00

      0.00   0.00   1.00   0.00   1.00   0.00   1.00   0.00   0.00

      0.00   1.00   0.00   0.00   1.00   0.00   0.00   1.00   0.00

      0.00   0.00   0.00   0.00   1.00   0.00   0.00   0.00   0.00

      0.00   0.00   0.00   0.00   1.00   0.00   0.00   0.00   0.00

      0.00   0.00   0.00   0.00   1.00   0.00   0.00   0.00   0.00

      0.00   0.00   0.00   0.00   1.00   0.00   0.00   0.00   0.00

(a)   0.00   0.00   0.00   0.00   1.00   0.00   0.00   0.00   0.00
```

```
      0.00   0.00   0.00   0.00   1.00   0.00   0.00   0.00   0.00

      0.00   0.00   0.00   0.25   1.00   0.25   0.00   0.00   0.00

      0.00   0.00   0.25   0.00   1.00   0.00   0.25   0.00   0.00

      0.00   0.25   0.00   0.00   1.00   0.00   0.00   0.25   0.00

      0.00   0.00   0.00   0.00   1.00   0.00   0.00   0.00   0.00

      0.00   0.25   0.00   0.00   1.00   0.00   0.00   0.25   0.00

      0.00   0.00   0.25   0.00   1.00   0.00   0.25   0.00   0.00

      0.00   0.00   0.00   0.25   1.00   0.25   0.00   0.00   0.00

(b)   0.00   0.00   0.00   0.00   1.00   0.00   0.00   0.00   0.00
```

```
      0.00   0.00   0.00   0.00   0.00   0.00   0.00   0.00   0.00

      0.00   0.00   0.00   0.25   0.00   0.25   0.00   0.00   0.00

      0.00   0.00   0.25   0.00   0.00   0.00   0.25   0.00   0.00

      0.00   0.25   0.00   0.00   0.00   0.00   0.00   0.25   0.00

      0.00   0.00   0.00   0.00   0.00   0.00   0.00   0.00   0.00

      0.00   0.25   0.00   0.00   0.00   0.00   0.00   0.25   0.00

      0.00   0.00   0.25   0.00   0.00   0.00   0.25   0.00   0.00

      0.00   0.00   0.00   0.25   0.00   0.25   0.00   0.00   0.00

(c)   0.00   0.00   0.00   0.00   0.00   0.00   0.00   0.00   0.00
```

Fig. P.11

```
LENGTH OF ROD    2.00   CONDUCTIVITY    300.0
BOUNDARY CONDITION 1 IS I
BOUNDARY CONDITION 2 IS E800
POINT SOURCE STRENGTH   0.10E+05 AT NODE   10
     0   936.    1   936.    2   936.    3   936.    4   936.    5   936.
     6   936.    7   936.    8   936.    9   936.   10   936.   11   934.
    12   933.   13   931.   14   929.   15   928.   16   926.   17   924.
    18   923.   19   921.   20   919.   21   918.   22   916.   23   914.
    24   913.   25   911.   26   909.   27   908.   28   906.   29   904.
    30   903.   31   901.   32   899.   33   898.   34   896.   35   894.
(a) 36   893.   37   891.   38   889.   39   888.   40   886.
```

Fig. P.12a

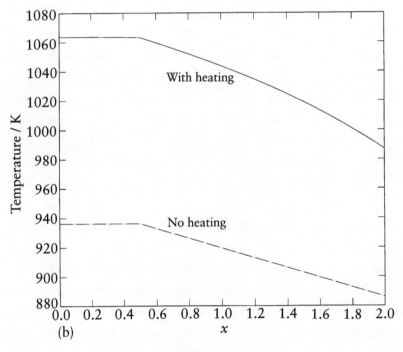

(b)

Fig. P.12b

Chapter 6

6.1   The variational function is found to be $y = 0.563\,85x + 2.154\,43x^2$. From the boundary conditions $b = e - a$ so there is only one variational parameter to be determined. The analytical solution of the differential equation is $y = xe^x$. The estimated values of y, together with the true values, are:

x	$\frac{1}{6}$	$\frac{1}{3}$	$\frac{1}{2}$	$\frac{2}{3}$	$\frac{5}{6}$
Estimated y	0.154	0.427	0.821	1.333	1.966
True y	0.197	0.465	0.824	1.298	1.917

6.2 The linear equations found which link the variational parameters are

$$6.2222a_1 - 2.9444a_2 = -0.93905,$$

$$-2.9444a_1 + 6.2222a_2 = 6.69314.$$

The solution of these equations gives a_1, the estimate of $y(\frac{1}{3}), = 0.461$ and a_2, the estimate of $y(\frac{2}{3}), = 1.294$. Fitting a parabola at $x = 0$, $\frac{1}{3}$ and $\frac{2}{3}$ gives an estimate of $y(\frac{1}{2}) = 0.831$. It is clear by comparison with the solution to Problem 6.1 that, overall, the straight-line variational function is superior in performance to the parabolic equation, although it requires two variational parameters to be determined.

6.3 Figure P.12a shows the printed output for the 'no extended heating' case and Fig. P.12b a graphical output showing the difference of the two cases. Despite the fact that the heating is more concentrated at the exposed end the general effect of heating is to increase the temperature by about 125 K at the insulated end and somewhat less at the exposed end.

6.4 The printed output and a graphical contoured representation of the temperature distribution are shown in Figs P.13 and P.14. The contours show the local influence of the point sources.

Chapter 7

7.1 The superimposed distributions for the three cases are shown in Fig. P.15. The larger values of Δx give additional numerical diffusion. The values of $C + 2r$ for the three cases are 0.625, 0.750 and 1.000, respectively.

7.2 The superimposed plots for the three values of C are shown in Fig. P.16. The lower the value of C, the greater the numerical diffusion. In addition, for these lower values, an asymmetry developes in the distribution and the peak is displaced from its true position.

7.3 The superimposed plots for the three values of C are shown in Fig. P.17. The improvement over the Lax–Wendroff results is evident. The distribution remains symmetrical and centred on the true value, although there is some numerical diffusion for the smaller values of C.

7.4 The superimposed plots for the five values of C, and associated values of r, are shown in Fig. P.18. They completely overlap and any differences do not show up on the plot. The lack of variation of results for the different combinations of C and r indicates the lack of numerical diffusion and accuracy of the results.

```
CONDUCTIVITY IS   400.0 W m**[-1] K**[-1]

NODE NUMBERS ASSOCIATED WITH EACH ELEMENT
         1    1    2    3      2    1    3    4      3    2    5    3
         4    3    6    4      5    2    7    8      6    2    8    5
         7    3    5    9      8    3    9    6      9    4    6   10
        10    4   10   11     11    5    8    9     12    6    9   10
        13    7   12    8     14    9   13   10     15   10   14   11
        16    7   15   12     17    8   12   16     18    9   17   13
        19   10   13   18     20   10   18   14     21   11   14   19
        22   12   15   16     23   13   17   18     24   14   18   19
        25   15   20   16     26   17   21   18     27   18   22   19
        28   15   23   20     29   16   20   24     30   17   25   21
        31   18   21   26     32   18   26   22     33   19   22   27
        34   20   23   24     35   21   25   26     36   22   26   27
        37   23   28   24     38   25   29   26     39   26   30   27
        40   23   31   28     41   24   28   32     42   25   33   29
        43   26   29   34     44   26   34   30     45   27   30   35
        46   28   31   32     47   29   33   34     48   30   34   35

COORDINATES OF NODES
         1 2.0000 5.0000      2 1.0000 4.0000      3 2.0000 4.0000
         4 3.0000 4.0000      5 1.5000 3.5000      6 2.5000 3.5000
         7 0.0000 3.0000      8 1.0000 3.0000      9 2.0000 3.0000
        10 3.0000 3.0000     11 4.0000 3.0000     12 0.5000 2.5000
        13 2.5000 2.5000     14 3.5000 2.5000     15 0.0000 2.0000
        16 1.0000 2.0000     17 2.0000 2.0000     18 3.0000 2.0000
        19 4.0000 2.0000     20 0.5000 1.5000     21 2.5000 1.5000
        22 3.5000 1.5000     23 0.0000 1.0000     24 1.0000 1.0000
        25 2.0000 1.0000     26 3.0000 1.0000     27 4.0000 1.0000
        28 0.5000 0.5000     29 2.5000 0.5000     30 3.5000 0.5000
        31 0.0000 0.0000     32 1.0000 0.0000     33 2.0000 0.0000
        34 3.0000 0.0000     35 4.0000 0.0000

NODES WITH FIXED TEMPERATURES
         1   500.0      4   500.0      7   400.0     11   500.0
        15   400.0     23   400.0     31   400.0     32   400.0
        33   500.0     34   500.0     35   500.0

POSITIONS AND STRENGTHS OF POINT SOURCES
         3    0.8000E+06
        20    0.2000E+06
        21    0.2000E+06
        22    0.2000E+06

DIFFERENTIAL BOUNDARY EDGES AND PARAMETERS
  NODE1 NODE2    M         S
      1     2  1.000  1000.000
      2     7  1.000  1000.000
     11    19  1.000  2000.000
     19    27  1.000  2000.000
     27    35  1.000  2000.000

  NODE    TEMP
      1    500.    2    989.    3   1268.    4    500.
      5    972.    6    853.    7    400.    8    730.
      9    899.   10    746.   11    500.   12    522.
     13    872.   14    756.   15    400.   16    558.
     17    937.   18    904.   19    874.   20    592.
     21   1001.   22    984.   23    400.   24    510.
     25    834.   26    829.   27    828.   28    428.
     29    666.   30    665.   31    400.   32    400.
     33    500.   34    500.   35    500.
```

Fig. P.13

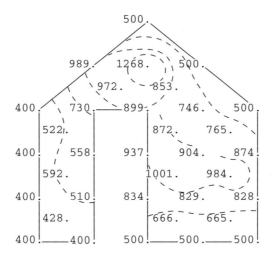

Fig. P.14

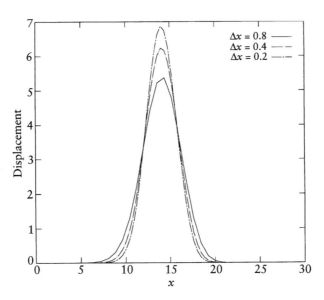

Fig. P.15

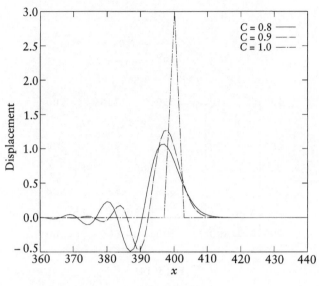

Fig. P.16

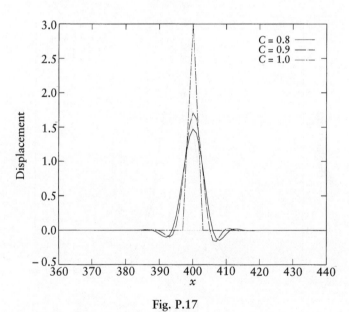

Fig. P.17

7.5   The graphical output in Fig. P.19 shows the liquid surface after 4, 16, 32 and 64 iterations. Some of the detail in the final view is probably due to the crudeness of the model; with a greater number of cells a smoother appearance would be evident.

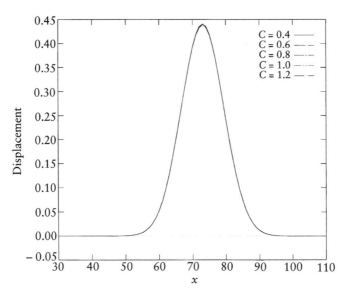

Fig. P.18

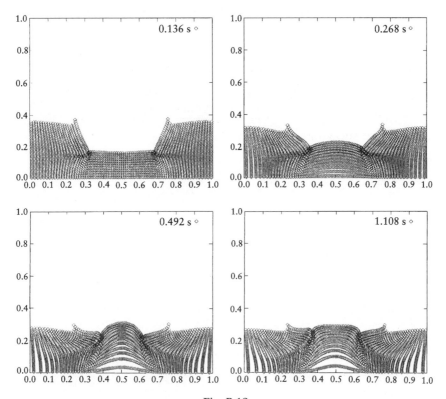

Fig. P.19

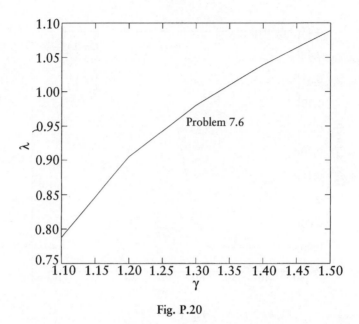

Fig. P.20

7.6   For each γ the values of $r/t^{2/5}$ at the different times give estimates of λ_γ. For example, the estimates at times from 0.1 s to 1.0 s at intervals of 0.1 s for $\gamma = 1.5$ are 1.090, 1.090, 1.090, 1.089, 1.089, 1.089, 1.088, 1.088, 1.087, 1.087 with a mean 1.089. For all values of γ the means are:

γ	1.1	1.2	1.3	1.4	1.5
λ_γ	0.788	0.905	0.980	1.039	1.089

These results are shown graphically in Fig. P.20.

References

Abramowitz, M., Milton, J. and Stegun, I. A. (1968). *Handbook of Mathematical Functions*. Dover: New York.

Amsden, A. A. and Harlow, F. H. (1970). The SMAC method – a numerical technique for calculating incompressible fluid flows. LA4370, Los Alamos.

Berman, R. H., Brownrigg, D. R. K. and Hockney, R. W. (1978). Numerical models of galaxies I. The variability of spiral structure. *Mon. Not. R. Astr. Soc.*, **185**, 861.

Coates, I. E. (1980). *On the origin of planets*. Ph.D. thesis, Council for National Academic Awards, Teesside Polytechnic (now Teesside University).

Cooley, J. W. and Tukey, J. W. (1965). An algorithm for the machine calculation of complex Fourier series. *Math. Comp.*, **19**, 297.

Courant, R., Friedrichs, K. and Lewy, H. (1928). Über die partiellen Differenzgleichungen der mathematischen Physik. *Math. Ann.*, **100**, 32–74. Translated as: On the partial differential equations of mathematical physics. *IBM J.*, **11**, 215–34.

Dormand, J. R. (1996). *Numerical Methods for Differential Equations: A Computational Approach*. CRC Press Inc.: Boca Raton, Florida.

Gingold, R. A. and Monaghan, J. J. (1977). Smoothed particle hydrodynamics: theory and application to non-spherical stars. *Mon. Not. R. Astr. Soc.*, **181**, 375.

Harlow, F. H., Shannon, J. P. and Welch, J. E. (1965). Liquid waves by computer. *Science*, **149**, 1092–3.

Hockney, R. W. and Eastwood, J. W. (1988). *Computer Simulation using Particles*. Adam Hilger: Bristol.

Jeans, J. (1919). *Problems of Cosmogony and Stellar Dynamics*. Cambridge University Press: Cambridge.

Langhaar, H. L. (1980). *Dimensional Analysis and Theory of Models*. Krieger: Huntingdon, NY.

Leonard, B. P. (1979). A stable and accurate convective modelling procedure based on quadratic upstream interpolation. *Comput. Meth. Appl. Mech. Engg.*, **19**, 59.

Lucy, L. B. (1977). A numerical approach to the testing of a fission hypothesis. *Astron. J.*, **82**, 1013.

Metropolis, N., Rosenbluth, A. W., Rosenbluth, M. N., Teller, A. H. and Teller, E. (1953). Equation of state calculations by fast computing machines. *J. Chem. Phys.*, **21**, 1087.

Press, W. H., Flannery, B. P., Teukolsky, S. A. and Vetterling, W. T. (1986). *Numerical Recipes*. Cambridge University Press: Cambridge.

Woolfson, M. M. (1997). *An Introduction to X-ray Crystallography*. Cambridge University Press: Cambridge.

Index

Box - Müller algorithm is for generating random nos. having a normal distribution